The Bible As Literature

Edited by

ALTON C. CAPPS

Instructor of English
Glenbard East High School
Lombard, Illinois

WEBSTER DIVISION
McGRAW-HILL BOOK COMPANY
New York   St. Louis
San Francisco
Dallas   Atlanta

Copyright © 1971 by McGraw-Hill, Inc. All Rights Reserved. Printed in the United States of America. No part of
this publication may be reproduced, stored in a retrieval system, or transmitted, in any form or by any means,
electronic, mechanical, photocopying, recording, or otherwise, without the prior written permission of the
publisher.

ISBN-07-009782-8   *Library of Congress Catalog Card Number:* 70-138989

Editorial Development, Jack R. Dyer: *Editing and Styling,* Barbara McDonough; *Design,* Ted Smith; *Production,*
Dick Shaw

KANSAS CENTER
for
PUBLIC EDUCATION RELIGION STUDIES
1300 Oread
Lawrance, Kansas 66045

Contents

iii

Introduction

Modern civilization is greatly indebted to the Bible. The foundations of modern Western culture evolved primarily from two sources: Athens and Jerusalem. Western culture, particularly the English-speaking world, is more indebted to the Hebrew influence than to the Greek. Such ancient Greeks as Homer, Hesiod, Sophocles, Aristophanes, Plato, and Aristotle molded the intellectual and moral attitudes of the English-speaking world, and their influence is generally acknowledged. But a more powerful influence has been exerted by Hebrews such as Moses, David, Solomon, Isaiah, Paul, and Jesus. This influence pervades every level of our lives. We can readily see it in the religious and moral attitudes of the Western world, but it does not stop there.

One has only to listen to the recorded speeches of Winston Churchill and the great labor leader John L. Lewis to hear the tone and cadence of the prophets. William Jennings Bryan was nominated for President of the United States in 1896 on the strength of one speech where he stated, "You shall not crucify man upon a cross of gold." Generals such as "Stonewall" Jackson in the Civil War and George S. Patton in World War II saw themselves as the reincarnations of Old Testament warriors. Orde Wingate, a famous British general and the father of the modern Israeli army, took his tactics directly from the Old Testament. Artists from unknown ikon painters to Salvador Dali have chosen Biblical scenes as their subjects. Even "Peanuts" is permeated with Biblical allusions.

It can be safely said that no facet of our lives remains untouched by the Hebraic vision, but its influence is most clearly seen in the great body of Western literature. The Bible has provided plots, themes, characters, and styles for writers from John Milton to John Steinbeck. Without some knowledge of this book, it is all but impossible to read and appreciate most of Western literature.

THE STRUCTURE OF THE BIBLE

The Bible is a collection or library of writings, called "books." The collection includes history, biography, essays, sermons, dramas, stories, songs, and poems. These writings cover the political and religious life of a nation for thousands of years and represent all social levels from simple fishermen to articulate physicians.

The collection is divided into two sections, each now called in English a "testament." The Hebrews first called their writings "The Book of the Covenant," for it contained a record of the solemn agreement between the Hebrews and God. The Latin translation of the word meaning "covenant" was *testamentum,* and from it developed the English word *testament.* The Old Testament (Covenant) is composed of writings before the birth of Christ; the New Testament (Covenant), writings after the birth of Christ. The Old Testament deals with the calling and history of the Jewish nation. The New Testament deals with the life of Jesus and the spread of His teachings. The New Testament represents a further development from the Hebrew tradition, the Christian religion.

The thirty-nine books of the Old Testament developed over centuries. First passed down orally from generation to generation, they were finally written down and then copied and recopied. It was not, however, until approximately 500 B.C. that the authoritative version of the first five books of the Old Testament was established. The twenty-seven books of the New Testament were written during the first seventy years following the death of Christ.

THE OLD TESTAMENT

Historical Books	Genesis Exodus Leviticus Numbers Deuteronomy Joshua	Judges Ruth 1 Samuel 2 Samuel 1 Kings 2 Kings	1 Chronicles 2 Chronicles Ezra Nehemiah Esther
Doctrinal Books	Job Psalms Proverbs	Ecclesiastes Song of Solomon	
Prophetical Books	Isaiah Jeremiah Lamentations Ezekiel Daniel Hosea	Joel Amos Obadiah Jonah Micah Nahum	Habakkuk Zephaniah Haggai Zechariah Malachi

THE NEW TESTAMENT

Historical Books	Matthew Mark Luke	John Acts of the Apostles	
Doctrinal Books	Romans 1 Corinthians 2 Corinthians Galatians Ephesians Philippians Colossians	1 Thessalonians 2 Thessalonians 1 Timothy 2 Timothy Titus Philemon Hebrews	James 1 Peter 2 Peter 1 John 2 John 3 John Jude
Prophetical Book	Revelation (Apocalypse)		

THE DEVELOPMENT AND SPREAD OF THE BIBLE

The Hebrews did not seek to discover God by processes of human reason. They assumed His existence and granted Him readily the worship that they felt was due Him. God revealed Himself to them in history by His appearances to Abraham and other great leaders.

Like all ancient peoples, the Hebrews did not always have a written language. The history was passed orally from one generation to another. Stories were recited, songs were sung, and laws were explained by religious leaders. As time passed and the art of writing developed, the Hebrews began to write their history in order to ensure a more accurate version than that of oral history.

The history was originally handwritten by priests and scholars. So beloved were these writings that they were kept in the most holy place and guarded zealously by the highest of priests. When copies were needed, priests and scholars transcribed them letter by letter, word by word. Unfortunately many errors crept in, for the priests often mistook one letter for another or lost their places and omitted lines. Thus, errors increased in a natural way. Little by little over the centuries, the original writings disappeared. The ancient writing materials, usually papyrus, wore out or were lost or destroyed. For these reasons there are now no correct originals to which the scholars can go. Although no original copies exist, the present copies have proved remarkably accurate as archaeologists have discovered and translated ancient copies of the Old Testament unearthed from diggings in Egypt, Syria, Assyria, and Babylonia, the ancient homes of the Hebrews.

The Old Testament basically recounts interaction between God and the Hebrew nation. When the Hebrews finally became a nation, God selected one family, the family of David, as a vehicle through which to present the Messiah, who was to live forever and establish a universal kingdom.

Jerusalem as a nation eventually became the symbol of a positive religious preparation for the coming of Christianity. The Hebrews, being monotheistic (believers in one God), were a striking contrast to the surrounding nations, who were atheistic, polytheistic, or paganistic. The Hebrews offered the world the hope of a coming Messiah. They offered the world a complete ethical system, including the Ten Commandments. They provided the world with a sacred book, the Old Testament. They provided the world with a religious institution, the synagogue. Also, Jerusalem had become a crossroads, linking Asia and Africa with Europe by land routes. These factors were to contribute greatly to the spread of Hebraic influence. However, without two other developments, the Hebraic influence would have been confined to a small region of Asia Minor.

First, the *Pax Romana* of the Roman Empire provided both a sense of unity and a universal legal code for all men. Also, the relative peace within the Empire, coupled with its excellent system of roads, allowed safe physical movement. The followers of Jesus could move from town to town spreading the teachings of the Bible. Second, Greek had become a universal language used by both the common man and the scholar. Since the New Testament was written in Greek rather than Hebraic, it was understandable to men throughout the Empire.

The Christian Church at first accepted the Old Testament as its sacred writings and used them in its assemblies. As the writings of the Apostles appeared, these works were added to the Hebrew scriptures and were held in the same high regard. Each church wanted not only the letters that had been addressed to them but also the copies addressed to other churches. The Old Testament books originated within the compass of one small nation; the New Testament books appeared in widely separated areas such as Palestine, Asia Minor, Greece, and Rome. There existed, however, various versions of the New Testament, and it was not until the Council of Carthage in A.D. 397 that the ratification of the twenty-seven books of the New Testament emerged.

THE LANGUAGE OF THE BIBLE

The essential quality of Old and New Testament language is its absolute sincerity. The Bible's authors were profoundly moved by their convictions and messages and tried to involve others in their religious view.

To understand the language of the Bible, one must first understand the nature and temperament of the Hebrews. The Oriental influence on the ancient Hebrews becomes evident in the concrete language and lofty imagery of the Old Testament. The Greek and Western influences on the later Hebrews become evident in the use of rationalization and abstract terminology in the New Testament. The common characteristics of ancient and later Hebrews are felt throughout the Bible.

The Hebrews freely exercised their feelings, whether they felt anger, sorrow, pleasure, or joy. They were eager to sympathize, and they rewarded sympathy generously and earnestly. They showed their suffering. They were not ashamed to show affection openly, and they loved devotedly. Throughout the Bible one can read such expressions as these: "He ran to meet him and embraced him, and kissed him"; "He wept aloud and the Egyptians and the house of Pharaoh heard"; or "Moreover he kissed all his brethren and wept." Every word and phrase was pictorial and richly colored. The vivid imagery and figurative language revealed the writers' deepest concerns. For example, one Hebrew writer describes his helpless despair:

"I sink in deep mire
   Whether there is no standing.
I am come into the deep waters
   Where the floods overflow me."

Modern readers do not judge the ancient Hebrews as weak, silly, or sentimental simply because they revealed their intense emotional nature. On the contrary, they are looked upon as a great people with strong character who were unafraid to reveal their deepest emotions.

Moreover, the Hebrews loved nature and were greatly influenced by their love for the sea, the sky, the mountains, and animal and bird life. They used nature constantly in their figurative and symbolic language. The following Hebrew writers express deep feelings and serious thoughts through nature:

"As a hart longs for flowing streams,
 so longs my soul for thee, O God."
               or
"Even the sparrow finds a home,
   and the swallow a nest for herself,
   where she may lay her young,
at thy altars, O Lord of hosts,
   my King and my God."

This imaginative quality of the Hebrews pervaded their language. For example, a typical American would probably say, "Several people gathered at the door," but the typical Hebrew would have said, "All the city gathered at the door." The Hebrews were not satisfied with simple or even single statements. They had to make every act impressive and meaningful. For example, they would say, "He arose and sent," or "They lifted up their eyes and looked," or "He opened his lips and spoke."

The Hebrews did not center their lives in commerce and industry. They centered their lives in religion. They were always worshippers. Even their menial tasks of everyday life were performed worshipfully. Consequently their language was highly religious. There was no distinction whether they were at work or at worship. The typical American might say when parting, "Take care of yourself." But the typical Hebrew would probably say, "Go, in the keeping and protection of God."

THE APPROACHES TO THE BIBLE

Apart from the purely religious motivations for reading the Bible, one may approach the Bible from two basic directions: (1) in order to build a substantial background of literary *allusions*; (2) in order to study the varied literary *forms*. Both approaches can improve the reading awareness and interpretative powers of the reader, and it is doubtful that one approach can be divorced from the other. However, one does not need either of these motives to read the Bible, for the uniqueness and the high quality of the Biblical writings offer their own rewards to the reader.

The particular advantage of the approach through *allusions* is that the reader may begin a systematic study of Bible stories and names of Bible characters and places. Many people read Greek and Roman mythology or the *Iliad* and the *Odyssey* primarily for the purpose of allusions. Since classical and modern literature make use of mythological allusions, such a study is considered vital to the understanding of literature. For example, it would be impossible to understand a modern classic such as James Joyce's *Ulysses* without a considerable background in Greek mythology and without having carefully read Homer's *Odyssey*. The Bible, however, ranks as an equally important source of allusions, particularly for American literature, and it is equally impossible to fully understand a writer such as Melville without some knowledge of the Bible.

Many people are unaware that the Bible has particular literary *forms*, such as epics, lyrics, dramas, essays, sonnets, philosophical works, histories, and the like. The peculiarities of Bible literature make a study of these forms interesting and even exciting. This comparative process provides excellent insight into the commonly used literary forms. One can clearly see the connections between present and earlier forms of literature, the progression of literature from primitive forms. In fact, the Bible supplies under one cover a text in the development of the two major literary forms, poetry and prose.

The Bible As Literature is arranged according to literary forms. However, because the forms themselves illustrate plots, characters, styles, and themes which are used over and over in literature and because it is impossible to completely separate the two basic approaches to Bible study, short commentaries are provided before many of the stories to suggest other instances in literature where a particular Biblical theme appears or is paralleled.

THE INFLUENCE OF THE BIBLE UPON THE GREAT WRITERS

For over one thousand years the Bible has influenced the greatest writers. In England, the first Anglo-Saxon singer/writer, Caedmon, sang the stories of the Bible in his verses. The total effect of the Bible upon the thousands of writers to follow Caedmon is simply incalculable. It was not merely that the phrases of the Bible became a part of the language of the common man, but that the very thoughts of the Bible became the thoughts of ordinary Englishmen to the extent that the cultural heritage of a whole nation was affected.

The effect of the Bible upon American literature, although not as pervasive, is equally as important. From the beginnings of our national literature, such writers as Michael Wigglesworth, Edward Taylor, and Jonathan Edwards drew upon the Bible not only for subject matter but for style as well. When one reads the giants of American literature, if he wishes to understand them, he must bring with him a deep fund of Biblical knowledge. *Moby Dick* opens with the sentence, "Call me Ishmael." For the unaware, a name is given. For those who have read the Bible, the theme of the novel is given. Hawthorne in the *Scarlet Letter* examines the historic Puritan view of life as contrasted with the spirit of the New Testament, a recurring theme in American literature. Steinbeck uses a parable form in his novel *Pearl*. Faulkner parallels the characters and events of 1 and 2 Samuel in *Absalom, Absalom!* Perhaps the most striking example of the need of a Biblical background for the understanding of literature is seen in Hemingway's novel *The Sun Also Rises*. When the novel was originally published, it was bitterly attacked for its seeming lack of values. The title of the book, however, is taken from Ecclesiastes:

> "One generation passeth away, and another generation cometh; but the earth abideth forever . . . The sun also ariseth, and the sun goeth down, and hasteth to the place where he arose . . . The wind goeth toward the south, and

turneth about unto the north; it whirleth about continually, and the wind returneth again according to his circuits ... All the rivers run into the sea; yet the sea is not full; unto the place from whence the rivers come, thither they return again."

Hemingway clearly meant to contrast the aimless wondering of "The Lost Generation" with those things which endure and whose value is timeless. The book read in the light of its Biblical title takes on an entirely different meaning.

The influence of the Bible is not limited to writers of serious fiction. The parables of Jesus and the speeches of Lincoln are similar in tone and intent. The sparse rhetoric of John F. Kennedy echoes the Old Testament. Even Huey P. Long derived his economic theories from the Bible. The list is endless and all inclusive. If one chose to deliberately ignore these Biblical influences, he still could not escape their subconscious implications which are a part of the fabric of American culture.

THE BIBLE IN TRANSLATION

Unfortunately, in spite of the unmatched popularity and influence of the Bible, the fate that befell it was generally escaped by all other ancient or modern literary masterpieces. In fact, without considerable training and much effort it is practically impossible to distinguish the original form. However, just as the beauty of language and the content of the Bible remain unsurpassed, the structure in the initial development was equally as impressive.

It is generally felt that the writers of the Old and New Testaments included men who, over and above their qualifications of a sacred nature, possessed unusual literary power. The years have eroded much of the literary beauty of the Bible. Rabbinical commentators divided the Bible into chapters, and medieval translators further divided the chapters into "verses," which not only did not agree with the original intent but often ran counter to it. Poetic couplets, triplets, quatrains, sextets, and octets were all grouped in similar verses without regard for the simplest characteristics of poetry. Prose and poetry were lumped together indistinctively. Stanzas that had generally balanced with varying longer and shorter lines and natural divisions to enhance easy access to the meaning were eliminated completely. The force of unliterary tradition proved too strong for the literary instincts of Bible translators. As a result, without knowing it, the reader often commences in the middle of a composition and concludes in the middle of another.

For more than two centuries the King James Version (Authorized Version) of the Bible was accepted as an accurate translation. In the nineteenth century, however, many old manuscripts were discovered, and scholars found that the Authorized Version was not entirely accurate. Minor translation problems and the advancement of the English language made new translations imminent. British and American scholars went to work. Fourteen years later, in 1885, they produced the Revised Standard Version. Although most writers in the area of Biblical literature used the Authorized Version because of its historical significance, for it did influence the English-speaking world for nearly five centuries, the modern reader has had increasing difficulties in understanding the translation. The outdated language and archaic terminology forced readers to turn to additional aids, such as Bible dictionaries. Since a reader's progress is made appreciably easier with improved comprehension in one of the modern versions, and since the Revised Standard Version although modernized comes closest to the language of the original English version (the Authorized Version), the Revised Standard Version is used in this book.

Epic
Literature

HERODOTUS, the Greek historian, is usually called the Father of History. When Greece was in her Golden Age, he wandered about the world with an immense curiosity to learn the thoughts of men. His tales were so interesting that the city of Athens awarded him a huge sum of money in the year 445 B.C. Yet, over four hundred years before Herodotus, a Hebrew had already set down an account of the world from its beginning. The Hebrew wrote the history of his nation from the first pioneers to his own day. Other writers followed and supplemented this primitive narrative until the fifth century before Christ, when the first continuous history of the world was written. The story develops from Genesis through Kings in the Old Testament.

CHANGING PURPOSES IN HEBREW HISTORY

The first historians were quite different from modern historians in both purposes and methods. These early historians were neither critical nor painstaking in the investigation of facts. They did not place high value on details. They proposed to charm the imagination by the artistic presentation of events. These early writings, thus, must not be judged by the ideals of the twentieth century. They should be judged by their own standards and times.

The Old Testament contains many history books, which are scattered throughout. As the Hebrew nation developed, the purposes of its historians changed. One can trace this change through the Old Testament.

The purpose of the early writers was to present a framework of history made up of genealogies, annals, and connected matter of

1

various kinds, such as incidents clearly introduced for some historic purpose—sometimes called epic incidents. These early histories were called by later historians *primitive history.* Genesis is largely Primitive History.

Following Genesis, the purpose of the histories was to describe the migration of the nation up to the arrival at the land of promise. These writers saw the chosen nation as governed directly by God, a theistic form of government, and its constitutional history was primarily the revelation of the Law by God. Thus, the natural divisions of Exodus, Leviticus, and part of Numbers cover the period of slavery in Egypt, deliverance, and the general constitution of the nation given at Mount Sinai. The rest of Numbers traces the march from Sinai and the thirty-eight years of wandering in the wilderness. This section of Old Testament history is commonly called *constitutional history.*

The next group of histories makes efforts to trace the formation of secular government through a series of judges, purely local governments, and then a monarchical rule. Joshua, Judges, and 1 Samuel consist mostly of epic incidents—separate stories or cycles of stories relating to Joshua, to Samson, and to Saul. This period is referred to as *incidental history.*

The narratives of 2 Samuel, 1 Kings, and 2 Kings are grouped under the heading of *regular history* by modern historians. The purpose of these books is to present a systematic account of successive reigns. First, the reigns of David and Solomon unite the people; then schism splits the nation into two parts, Judah and Israel, which continue side by side; and finally, after the fall of the northern kingdom, Israel, the history of Judah by itself is carried to its close.

The rest of the historical books, Chronicles, Ezra, and Nehemiah, carry the story along as far as the return of the exiles to Jerusalem. This series of histories is distinguished by the prominence of documents, genealogies, and statistics, and by many excerpts from other Old Testament books. These books deal with the formation of the Jewish church and are referred to as *ecclesiastical history.*

The New Testament histories are unique in that they are centered about the life of one individual, Christ; yet they are also the history of the early development of the Christian Church and detail the life of the Apostles and the direction of the Church. Therefore in this text the New Testament will be treated as *special history,* since it performs a dual function.

The following chart should help you keep these historical divisions in mind.

Primitive History	*Constitutional History*	*Incidental History*
Genesis	Exodus	Joshua
	Leviticus	Judges
	Numbers	1 Samuel

Regular History	*Ecclesiastical History*	*Special History*
2 Samuel	Chronicals	New Testament
1 and 2 Kings	Ezra	histories
	Nehemiah	

HISTORY AND THE EPIC

There is much speculation as to why the Hebrews first wrote histories of their civilization. The suggestion is made that the Hebrews were the first to develop a national concept, a concept still strong and vigorous as the modern nation of Israel attests. The uniqueness of their concept was that human affairs were developing under a divine purpose. The Hebrews interpreted God through man and his experiences rather than through nature and its processes. They wrote primarily to increase the nation's faith and to teach succeeding generations the ways of God.

Aside from the sacred nature of these writings, they give readers the clearest and most abundant knowledge available of how men lived and thought in those early civilizations.

As one reads continuously through the book of Genesis, he feels the different parts of the history affecting his literary sense in different ways. He finds himself traversing long genealogies or noting brief accounts of migrations; he moves through generations or centuries of time in a few verses. But suddenly he reaches other names and incidents and at once all is changed. For example, he is aware of a different direction and intent when he reaches the name of Joseph. In the first place, the section about Joseph is ten long chapters in length, about one-fifth of the whole book of Genesis. The story centers around this one man and his relations with his brothers. From the very beginning a striking personality begins to emerge. Even in childhood Joseph divides the household between envy and affection, a division which is felt later in captivity and in prison.

In the background the reader gets glimpses of varied life—scattered settlements of shepherds, merchant caravans, palace life in the empire of Egypt. A single chapter would have been sufficient to present the sons of Jacob as a link in the chain of history. Any additional data in the narrative must be credited to interest of story.

This portion is also history, but in its treatment it touches the imagination and emotions in the way of poetry. It is impossible to read the account without having one's literary sense awakened, impossible not to feel the difference of kind between the account of Joseph and his brothers and other portions of the book of Genesis.

The historical books are full of such incidents, called epic incidents. But they are merged in the histories of which they are a part, without anything to mark them off from the surrounding matter that is pure history.

DISTINCTIONS OF EPICS

The traditional definition of an epic varies from the Hebrew concept. Traditionally, an epic is a long serious poem, celebrating in a serious language the ideals underlying a society. Generally an epic deals with bravery in battle or resourcefulness in journey. It is strongly nationalistic. It concerns itself with a particular hero of a nation: his courage, his keen thought, and his goodness. Most of all it embodies, by history and example, by symbolic struggle and believable domestic scenes, the best that a nation could hope for in a man. To read an epic is to learn part of a culture; through the vehicle of plot and allegory, poets of the culture envisioned heroic goodness and greatness and demonstrated these traits in their writings.

That ancient Greek stories, like the *Iliad* and the *Odyssey,* fit into the epic framework is easily recognized, but there are no epics in the Bible resembling these two Greek epics. In fact, in the Bible there is no verse narrative. If the verse requirement were eliminated, Bible epics would closely resemble the commonly recognized characteristics of epics. Essentially, epic literature implies just two things: narrative, in contrast to dramatic presentation, and creative treatment, intending to touch the imagination and emotions in the regular way of creative poetry. The verse narrative of the Greeks was a Greek innovation to the Hebrew epics that had already existed for nearly five hundred years.

In both secular and Bible literature there are basically three forms of epic: (1) *Epic stories*—simple, isolated stories, usually called ballads; (2) *Epic cycles*—an aggregation of separate stories which form a family saga; and (3) *Epic history*—many incidents woven into an organic plot.

EPIC STORIES

Epic stories are simple, independent incidents sequentially related. There are many such incidents in Primitive History. Their earliest forms were combinations of music and imitative gesture. The rhythmical words were often chanted to a tune, with or without instrumental accompaniment. The early chapters of the book of Genesis contain several such important stories. Others are located in the books of Numbers and Judges.

THE BEGINNING

The story of life's beginnings has a strong emotional impact upon all of us. Writers have, of course, capitalized upon this reaction and have used the theme of creation again and again. James Weldon Johnson, a black poet, makes Genesis into a spiritual in his poem "The Creation." John Milton in *Paradise Lost* draws heavily on the Biblical account. William Blake's poetry and his famous engraving of God circumscribing the heavens owe a great deal to Genesis. Even the Broadway show *Green Pastures* by Marc Connelly uses this version of the creation. Although we may reject on scientific or religious grounds the following account, artistically it has seldom been equaled.

Genesis 1:1–31; 2:1–25

In the beginning God created the heavens and the earth. The earth was without form and void, and darkness was upon the face of the deep; and the Spirit of God was moving over the face of the waters. And God said, "Let there be light"; and there was light. And God saw that the light was good; and God separated the light from the darkness. God called the light Day, and the darkness he called Night. And there was evening and there was morning, one day.

And God said, "Let there be a firmament in the midst of the waters, and let it separate the waters from the waters." And God made the firmament and separated the waters which were under the firmament from the waters which were above the firmament. And it was so. And God called the firmament Heaven. And there was evening and there was morning, a second day.

And God said, "Let the waters under the heavens be gathered together in one place, and let the dry land appear." And it was so. God called the dry land Earth, and the waters that were gathered together he called Seas. And God saw that it was good. And God said, "Let the earth put forth vegetation, plants yielding seed, and fruit trees bearing fruit in which is their seed, each according to its kind, upon the earth." And it was so. The earth brought forth vegetation, plants yielding seed according to their own kinds, and trees bearing fruit in which is their seed, each according to its kind. And God saw that it was good. And there was evening and there was morning, a third day.

And God said, "Let there be lights in the firmament of the heavens to separate the day from the night; and let them be for signs and for seasons and for days and years, and let them be lights in the firmament of the heavens to give light upon the earth." And it was so. And God made the two great lights, the greater light to rule the day, and the lesser light to rule the night; he made the stars also. And God set them in the firmament of the heavens to give light upon the earth, to rule over the day and over the night, and to separate the light from the darkness. And God saw that it was good. And there was evening and there was morning, a fourth day.

And God said, "Let the waters bring forth swarms of living creatures, and let birds fly above the earth across the firmament of the heavens." So God created the great sea monsters, and every living creature that moves, with which the waters swarm, according to their kinds, and every winged bird according to its kind. And God saw that it was good. And God blessed them, saying, "Be fruitful and multiply and fill the waters of the seas, and let birds multiply upon the earth." And there was evening and there was morning, a fifth day.

And God said, "Let the earth bring forth living creatures according to their kinds: cattle and creeping things and beasts of the earth according to their kinds." And it was so. And God made the beasts of the earth according to their kinds and the cattle according to their kinds, and everything that creeps upon the ground according to its kind. And God saw that it was good.

Then God said, "Let us make man in our image, after our likeness; and let them have dominion over the fish of the sea, and over the birds of the air, and over the cattle, and over all the earth, and over every creeping thing that creeps upon the earth." So God created man in his own image, in the image of God he created them; male and female he created them. And God blessed them, and God said to them, "Be fruitful and multiply, and fill the earth and subdue it; and have dominion over the fish of the sea and over the birds of the air and over every living thing that moves upon the earth." And God said, "Behold, I have given you every plant yielding seed which is upon the face of all the earth, and every tree with seed in its fruit; you shall have them for food. And to every beast of the earth, and to every bird of the air, and to everything that creeps upon the earth, everything that has the breath of life,

I have given every green plant for food." And it was so. And God saw everything that he had made, and behold, it was very good. And there was evening and there was morning, a sixth day.

Thus the heavens and the earth were finished, and all the host of them. And on the seventh day God finished his work which he had done, and he rested on the seventh day from all his work which he had done. So God blessed the seventh day and hallowed it, because on it God rested from all his work which he had done in creation.

These are the generations of the heavens and the earth when they were created.

In the day that the Lord God made the earth and the heavens, when no plant of the field was yet in the earth and no herb of the field had yet sprung up—for the Lord God had not caused it to rain upon the earth, and there was no man to till the ground; but a mist went up from the earth and watered the whole face of the ground—then the Lord God formed man from the dust of the ground, and breathed into his nostrils the breath of life; and man became a living being. And the Lord God planted a garden in Eden, in the east; and there he put the man whom he had formed. And out of the ground the Lord God made to grow every tree that is pleasant to the sight and good for food, the tree of life also in the midst of the garden, and the tree of the knowledge of good and evil.

A river flowed out of Eden to water the garden, and there it divided and became four rivers. The name of the first is Pishon; it is the one which flows around the whole land of Havilah, where there is gold; and the gold of that land is good; bdellium and onyx stone are there. The name of the second river is Gihon; it is the one which flows around the whole land of Cush. The name of the third river is Tigris, which flows east of Assyria. And the fourth river is the Euphrates.

The Lord God took the man and put him in the garden of Eden to till it and keep it. And the Lord God commanded the man, saying, "You may freely eat of every tree of the garden; but of the tree of the knowledge of good and evil you shall not eat, for in the day that you eat of it you shall die."

Then the Lord God said, "It is not good that man should be alone; I will make him a helper fit for him." So out of the ground God formed every beast of the field and every bird of the air, and brought them to the man to see what he would call them; and whatever man called every living creature, that was its name. The man gave names to all cattle, and to the birds of the air, and to every beast of the field; but for the man there was not found a helper fit for him. So the Lord God caused a deep sleep to fall upon the man, and while he slept took one of his ribs and closed up its place with flesh; and the rib which the Lord God had taken from the man he made into a woman and brought her to the man. Then the man said,

"This at last is bone of my bones and flesh of my flesh;
she shall be called Woman, because she was taken out of Man."

Therefore a man leaves his father and his mother and cleaves to his wife, and they become one flesh. And the man and his wife were both naked, and were not ashamed.

TEMPTATION OF ADAM AND EVE

The loss of innocence as a theme has been used by serious writers many times. All of Ernest Hemingway's Nick Adams stories deal, as the last name suggests, with this topic. It is the central scene in *Paradise Lost.* Joseph Conrad uses it in *The Heart of Darkness,* and William Faulkner makes use of the same in *The Bear.* Hawthorne's *The Marble Faun* is a modern version of the Garden of Eden. The list is endless, for it represents a psychological passage from childhood and innocence to adulthood and wisdom, and it is a passage we must all make.

Genesis 3:1-24

Now the serpent was more subtle than any other wild creature that the Lord God had made. He said to the woman, "Did God say, 'You shall not eat of any tree of the garden'?" And the woman said to the serpent, "We may eat of the fruit of the trees of the garden, but God said, 'You shall not eat of the fruit of the tree which is in the midst of the garden, neither shall you touch it, lest you die.'" But the serpent said to the woman, "You will not die. For God knows that when you eat of it your eyes will be opened, and you will be like God, knowing good and evil." So when the woman saw that the tree was good for food, and that it was a delight to the eyes, and that the tree was to be desired to make one wise, she took of its fruit and ate; and she also gave some to her husband, and he ate. Then the eyes of both were opened, and they knew that they were naked; and they sewed fig leaves together and made themselves aprons.

And they heard the sound of the Lord God walking in the garden in the cool of the day, and the man and his wife hid themselves from the presence of the Lord God among the trees of the garden. But the Lord God called to the man, and said to him, "Where are you?" And he said, "I heard the sound of thee in the garden, and I was afraid, because I was naked; and I hid myself." He said, "Who told you that you were naked? Have you eaten of the tree of which I commanded you not to eat?" The man said, "The woman whom thou gavest to be with me, she gave me fruit of the tree, and I ate." Then the Lord God said to the woman, "What is this that you have done?" The woman said, "The serpent beguiled me, and I ate." The Lord God said to the serpent,

"Because you have done this,
    cursed are you above all cattle,
    and above all wild animals;
upon your belly you shall go,
    and dust you shall eat
    all the days of your life.
I will put enmity between you and the woman,
    and between your seed and her seed;
he shall bruise your head,
    and you shall bruise his heel."
To the woman he said,
"I will greatly multiply your pain in childbearing;
    in pain you shall bring forth children,
yet your desire shall be for your husband,
    and he shall rule over you."
And to Adam he said,
"Because you have listened to the voice of your wife,
    and have eaten of the tree
of which I have commanded you,
    'You shall not eat of it,'
cursed is the ground because of you;
    in toil you shall eat of it all the days of your life;
thorns and thistles it shall bring forth to you;
    and you shall eat the plants of the field.
In the sweat of your face
    you shall eat bread
till you return to the ground,
    for out of it you were taken;
you are dust,
    and to dust you shall return."

The man called his wife Eve, because she was the mother of all living. And the Lord God made for Adam and for his wife garments of skin, and clothed them.

Then the Lord God said, "Behold, the man has become like one of us, knowing good and evil; and now, lest he put forth his hand and take also of the tree of life, and eat, and live forever"—therefore the Lord God sent him forth from the garden of Eden, to till the ground from which he was taken. He drove out the man; and at the east of the garden of Eden he placed the cherubim, and a flaming sword which turned every way, to guard the way to the tree of life.

CAIN AND ABEL: THE FIRST MURDER

Murder has always fascinated us, and our literature reflects this perverse interest. Macbeth is a murderer, as is the hero of Dostoevski's *Crime and Punishment.* John Steinbeck in *East of Eden* takes the complete Cain and Abel theme and places it in rural, twentieth-century California. Detective stories such as those written by Dashiell Hammett and TV shows like the Perry Mason series reach a mass market. The actual killing of one's brother seems most abhorrent, but Freud scientifically explained by sibling rivalry what the story of Cain and Abel symbolically presents: There are times when some of us wish our brothers dead. Cain carries this wish to fulfillment.

Genesis 4:1–16

Now Adam knew Eve his wife, and she conceived and bore Cain, saying, "I have gotten a man with the help of the Lord." And again she bore his brother Abel. Now Abel was a keeper of sheep, and Cain a tiller of the ground. In the course of time Cain brought to the Lord an offering of the fruit of the ground, and Abel brought of the firstlings of his flock and of their fat portions. And the Lord had regard for Abel and his offering, but for Cain and his offering he had no regard. So Cain was very angry, and his countenance fell. The Lord said to Cain, "Why are you angry, and why has your countenance fallen? If you do well, will you not be accepted? And if you do not well, sin is couching at the door; its desire is for you, but you must master it."

Cain said to Abel his brother, "Let us go out to the field." And when they were in the field, Cain rose up against his brother Abel, and killed him. Then the Lord said to Cain, "Where is Abel your brother?" He said, "I do not know; am I my brother's keeper?" And the Lord said, "What have you done? The voice of your brother's blood is crying to me from the ground. And now you are cursed from the ground, which has opened its mouth to receive your brother's blood from your hand. When you till the ground, it shall no longer yield to you its strength; you shall be a fugitive and a wanderer on the earth." Cain said to the Lord, "My punishment is greater than I can bear. Behold, thou hast driven me this day away from the ground; and from thy face I shall be hidden; and I shall be a fugitive and a wanderer on the earth, and whoever finds me will slay me." Then the Lord said to him, "Not so! If anyone slays Cain, vengeance shall be taken on him sevenfold." And the Lord put a mark on Cain, lest any who came upon him should kill him. Then Cain went away from the presence of the Lord, and dwelt in the land of Nod, east of Eden.

THE FLOOD

All civilizations from recorded time have produced stories of the destruction of the human race, usually through a vast flood. The destruction of man is as powerful a theme as the creation. Science fiction writers continue to make wide use of the theme with notable variations. Robert Frost in his poem "Fire and Ice" suggests that the next time, rather than a flood, we may be destroyed in a new and novel manner. James Baldwin is more explicit in his group of essays *The Fire Next Time.* And artists from the unknown authors of the Wakefield Noah Play to Bill Cosby have found the theme interesting and at times even funny.

Genesis 6:1–22; 7:1–24; 8:1–22; 9:8–17

When men began to multiply on the face of the ground, and daughters were born to them, the sons of God saw that the daughters of men were fair; and they took to wife such of them as they chose. Then the Lord said, "My spirit shall not abide in man forever, for he is flesh, but his days shall be a hundred and twenty years." The Nephilim were on the earth in those days, and also afterward, when the sons of God came in to the daughters of men, and they bore children to them. These were the mighty men that were of old, the men of renown.

The Lord saw that the wickedness of man was great in the earth, and that every imagination of the thoughts of his heart was only evil continually. And the Lord was sorry that he had made man on the earth, and it grieved him to his heart. So the Lord said, "I will blot out man whom I have created from the face of the ground, man and beast and creeping things and birds of the air, for I am sorry that I have made them." But Noah found favor in the eyes of the Lord.

These are the generations of Noah. Noah was a righteous man, blameless in his generation; Noah walked with God. And Noah had three sons, Shem, Ham, and Japheth.

Now the earth was corrupt in God's sight, and the earth was filled with violence. And God saw the earth, and behold, it was corrupt; for all flesh had corrupted their way upon the earth. And God said to Noah, "I have determined to make an end of all flesh; for the earth is filled with violence through them; behold, I will destroy them with the earth. Make yourself an ark of gopher wood; make rooms in the ark, and cover it inside and out with pitch. This is how you are to make it: the length of the ark three hundred cubits, its breadth fifty cubits, and its height thirty cubits. Make a roof for the ark, and finish it to a cubit above; and set the door of the ark in its side; make it with lower, second, and third decks. For behold, I will bring a flood of waters upon the earth, to destroy all flesh in which is the breath of life from under heaven; everything that is on the earth shall die. But I will establish my covenant with you; and you shall come into the ark, you, your sons, your wife, and your sons' wives with you. And of every living thing of all flesh, you shall bring two of every sort into the ark, to keep them alive with you; they shall be male and female. Of the birds according to their kinds, and of the animals according to their kinds, of every creeping thing of the ground according to its kind, two of every sort shall come in to you, to keep them alive. Also take with you every sort of food that is eaten, and store it up; and it shall serve as food for you and for them." Noah did this; he did all that God commanded him.

Then the Lord said to Noah, "Go into the ark, you and all your household, for I have seen that you are righteous before me in this generation. Take with you seven pairs of all clean animals, the male and his mate; and a pair of the animals that are not clean, the male and his mate; and seven pairs of the birds of the air also, male and female, to keep their kind alive upon the face of the earth. For in seven days I will send rain upon the earth forty days and forty nights; and every living thing that I have made I will blot out from the face of the ground." And Noah did all that the Lord had commanded him.

Noah was six hundred years old when the flood of waters

came upon the earth. And Noah and his sons and his wife and his sons' wives with him went into the ark, to escape the waters of the flood. Of clean animals, and of animals that are not clean, and of birds, and of everything that creeps on the ground, two and two, male and female, went into the ark with Noah, as God had commanded Noah. And after seven days the waters of the flood came upon the earth.

In the six hundredth year of Noah's life, in the second month on the seventeenth day of the month, on that day all the fountains of the great deep burst forth, and the windows of the heavens were opened. And rain fell upon the earth forty days and forty nights. On the very same day Noah and his sons, Shem and Ham and Japheth, and Noah's wife and the three wives of his sons with them entered the ark, they and every beast according to its kind, and all the cattle according to their kinds, and every creeping thing that creeps upon the earth according to its kind, and every bird according to its kind, every bird of every sort. They went into the ark with Noah, two of two of all flesh in which there was the breath of life. And they that entered, male and female of all flesh, went in as God had commanded him; and the Lord shut him in.

The flood continued forty days upon the earth; and the waters increased, and bore up the ark, and it rose high above the earth. The waters prevailed and increased greatly upon the earth; and the ark floated on the face of the waters. And the waters prevailed so mightily upon the earth that all the high mountains under the whole heaven were covered. The waters prevailed above the mountains covering them fifteen cubits deep. And all flesh died that moved upon the earth, birds, cattle, beasts, all swarming creatures that swarm upon the earth, and every man; everything upon the dry land in whose nostrils was the breath of life died. He blotted out every living thing that was upon the face of the ground, man and animals and creeping things and birds of the air; they were blotted out from the earth. Only Noah was left, and those that were with him in the ark. And the waters prevailed upon the earth a hundred and fifty days.

But God remembered Noah and all the beasts and all the cattle that were with him in the ark. And God made a wind blow over the earth, and the waters subsided; the fountains of the deep and the windows of the heavens were closed, the rain from the heavens was restrained, and the waters receded from the earth continually. At the end of a hundred and fifty days the waters had abated; and in the seventh month, on the seventeenth day of the month, the ark came to rest upon the mountains of Ararat. And the waters continued to abate until the tenth month; in the tenth month, on the first day of the month, the tops of the mountains were seen.

At the end of forty days Noah opened the window of the ark which he had made, and sent forth a raven; and it went to and fro until the waters of the earth were dried up from the earth. Then he sent forth a dove from him, to see if the waters had subsided from the face of the ground; but the dove found no place to set her foot, and she returned to him to the ark, for the waters were still upon the face of the whole earth. So he put forth his hand and took her and brought her into the ark with him. He waited another seven days, and again he sent forth the dove out of the ark; and the dove came back to him in the evening, and lo, in her mouth a freshly plucked olive leaf; so Noah knew that the waters had subsided from the earth. Then he waited another seven days, and sent forth the dove; and she did not return to him anymore.

In the six hundred and first year, in the first month, the first day of the month, the waters were dried from off the earth; and Noah removed the covering of the ark, and looked, and behold, the face of the ground was dry. In the second month on the twenty-seventh day of the month, the earth was dry. Then God said to Noah, "Go forth from the ark, you and your wife, and your sons and your sons' wives with you. Bring forth with you every living thing that is with you of all flesh—birds and animals and every living thing that creeps upon the earth—that they may breed abundantly on the earth, and be fruitful and multiply upon the earth. So Noah went forth, and his sons and his wife and his sons' wives with him. And every beast, every creeping thing, and every bird, everything that moves upon the earth, went forth by families out of the ark.

Then Noah built an altar to the Lord, and took of every clean animal and of every clean bird, and offered burnt offerings on the altar. And when the Lord smelled the pleasing odor, the Lord said in his heart, "I will never again curse the ground because of man, for the imagination of man's heart is evil from his youth; neither will I ever again destroy every living creature as I have done. While the earth remains, seedtime and harvest, cold and heat, summer and winter, day and night, shall not cease."

Then God said to Noah and to his sons with him, "Behold, I establish my covenant with you and your descendants after you, and with every living creature that is with you, the birds, the cattle, and every living creature that is with you, as many as came out of the ark. I establish my covenant with you, that never again shall all flesh be cut off by the waters of a flood, and never again shall there be a flood to destroy the earth." And God said, "This is a sign of the covenant which I make between me and you and every living creature that is with you, for all future generations. I set my bow in the cloud, and it shall be a sign of the covenant between me and the earth. When I bring clouds over the earth and the bow is seen in the clouds, I will remember my covenant which is between me and you and every living creature of all flesh; and the waters shall never again become a flood to destroy all flesh. When the bow is in the clouds, I will look upon it and remember the everlasting covenant between God and every living creature of all flesh that is upon the earth." God said to Noah, "This is the sign of the covenant which I have established between me and all flesh that is upon the earth."

THE TOWER OF BABEL

Man's pride in his intellectual abilities has often played him false. Many a science fiction writer has used the Tower of Babel theme to illustrate the nightmarish results of man's false pride in his technology. Mary Shelly was probably aware of the theme when she wrote *Frankenstein.* Rudyard Kipling uses the idea in the *Jungle Book,* as does Joel Chandler Harris in the "Uncle Remus" tales. In many of his tales, the great American writer Nathaniel Hawthorne examines the various dire effects of "head" triumphing over "heart." T. S. Eliot, considered by many critics the single, most important poet in the twentieth century, projects this fault in "The Waste Land" into his examination of the decay of modern civilization.

Genesis 11:1–9

Now the whole earth had one language and few words. And as men migrated from the east, they found a plain in the land of Shinar and settled there. And they said to one another, "Come, let us make bricks, and burn them thoroughly." And they had brick for stone, and bitumen for mortar. Then they said, "Come, let us build ourselves a city, and a tower with its top in the heavens, and let us make a name for ourselves, lest we be scattered abroad upon the face of the whole earth." And the Lord came down to see the city and the tower, which the sons of men had built. And the Lord said, "Behold, they are one people, and they have all one language; and this is only the beginning of what they will do; and nothing that they propose to do will now be impossible for them. Come, let us go down, and there confuse their language, that they may not understand one another's speech." So the Lord scattered them abroad from there over the face of all the earth, and they left off building the city. Therefore its name was called Babel, because there the Lord confused the language of all the earth; and from there the Lord scattered them abroad over the face of all the earth.

GIDEON'S THREE HUNDRED

The idea of a small, chosen group of men overcoming a superior force in battle is not unique with Hebraic literature. The Spartans at Thermopylae, although they were finally defeated, exemplify the same idea. British history is filled with such incidents. American history is likewise dotted with such battles throughout the Revolutionary War, the Civil War, and the two World Wars. Some of the outstanding battles of this nature, such as the Alamo and Wake Island, were temporary defeats for American forces, but the concept holds. The feeling that the rightness of one's cause lends strength to him in battle is both historically and psychologically sound.

Judges 7:2–23

The Lord said to Gideon, "The people with you are too many for me to give the Midianites into their hands, lest Israel vaunt themselves against me, saying, 'My own hand has delivered me.' Now therefore proclaim in the ears of the people, saying, 'Whoever is fearful and trembling, let him return home.'" And Gideon tested them; twenty-two thousand returned, and ten thousand remained.

And the Lord said to Gideon, "The people are still too many; take them down to the water and I will test them for you there; and he of whom I say to you, 'This man shall go with you,' shall go with you; and any of whom I say to you, 'This man shall not go with you,' shall not go." So he brought the people down to the water; and the Lord said to Gideon, "Everyone that laps the water with his tongue, as a dog laps, you shall set by himself; likewise everyone that kneels down to drink." And the number of those that lapped, putting their hands to their mouths, was three hundred men; but all the rest of the people knelt down to drink water. And the Lord said to Gideon, "With the three hundred men that lapped I will deliver you, and give the Midianites into your hand; and let all the others go every man to his home." So he took the jars of the people from their hands, and their trumpets; and he sent all the rest of Israel every man to his tent, but retained the three hundred men; and the camp of Midian was below him in the valley.

That same night the Lord said to him, "Arise, go down against the camp; for I have given it into your hand. But if you fear to go down, go down to the camp with Purah your servant; and you shall hear what they say, and afterward your hand shall be strengthened to go down against the camp." Then he went down with Purah his servant to the outposts of the armed men that were in the camp. And the Midianites and the Amalekites and all the people of the East lay along the valley like locusts for multitude; and their camels were without number, as the sand which is upon the seashore for multitude. When Gideon came, behold, a man was telling a dream to his comrade; and he said, "Behold, I dreamed a dream; and lo, a cake of barley bread tumbled into the camp of Midian, and came to the tent, and struck it so that it fell, and turned it upside down, so that the tent lay flat." And his comrade answered, "This is no other than the sword of Gideon the son of Joash, a man of Israel; into his hand God has given Midian and all the host."

When Gideon had heard the telling of the dream and its interpretation, he worshipped; and he returned to the camp of Israel, and said, "Arise; for the Lord has given the host of Midian into your hand." And he divided the three hundred men into three companies, and put trumpets into the hands of all of them and empty jars, with torches inside the jars. And he said to them, "Look at me, and do likewise; when I come to the outskirts of the camp, do as I do. When I blow the trumpet, I and all who are with me, then blow the trumpets also on every side of all the camp, and shout, 'For the Lord and for Gideon.'"

So Gideon and the hundred men who were with him came to the outskirts of the camp at the beginning of the middle watch, when they had just set the watch; and they blew the trumpets and smashed the jars that were in their hands. And the three companies blew the trumpets and broke the jars, holding in their left hands the torches, and in the right hands the trumpets to blow; and they cried, "A sword for the Lord and for Gideon!" They stood every man in his place round about the camp, and all the army ran; they cried out and fled. When they blew the three hundred trumpets the Lord set every man's sword againt his fellow and against all the army; and the army fled as far as Beth-shittah toward Zererah, as far as the border of Abelmeholah, by Tabbath. And the men of

Israel were called out from Naphtali and from Asher and from all Manasseh, and they pursued after Midian.

THE BATTLE OF JERICHO

The fall of a great city has been a powerful literary theme from the fall of Homer's Troy to Margaret Mitchell's Atlanta. The more influential theme in this section, however, is that personified by Rahab. That good works often are performed by those least likely to do them is demonstrated again and again in literature. Mary Magdalen washes Christ's feet. Nancy, a prostitute, befriends and helps Oliver Twist. And the dance hall girl with the heart of gold once again saves John Wayne in *Stagecoach.*

Joshua 5:13–15; 6:1–27

When Joshua was by Jericho, he lifted up his eyes and looked, and behold, a man stood before him with a drawn sword in his hand; and Joshua went to him and said to him, "Are you for us, or for our adversaries?" And he said, "No; but as the commander of the army of the Lord I have now come." And Joshua fell on his face to the earth, and worshipped, and said, "What does my Lord bid his servant?" And the commander of the Lord's army said to Joshua, "Put off your shoes from your feet; for the place where you stand is holy." And Joshua did so.

Now Jericho was shut up from within and from without because of the people of Israel; none went out, and none came in. And the Lord said to Joshua, "See, I have given into your hand Jericho, with its king and mighty men of valor. You shall march around the city, all the men of war going around the city once. Thus shall you do for six days. And seven priests shall bear seven trumpets or rams' horns before the ark; and on the seventh day you shall march around the city seven times, the priests blowing the trumpets. And when they make a long blast with the ram's horn, as soon as you hear the sound of the trumpet, then all the people shall shout with a great shout; and the wall of the city will fall down flat, and the people shall go up every man straight before him." So Joshua the son of Nun called the priests and said to them, "Take up the ark of the covenant, and let seven priests bear seven trumpets of rams' horns before the ark of the Lord." And he said to the people, "Go forward; march around the city, and let the armed men pass on before the ark of the Lord."

And as Joshua had commanded the people, the seven priests bearing the seven trumpets of rams' horns before the Lord went forward, blowing the trumpets, with the ark of the covenant of the Lord following them. And the armed men went before the priests who blew the trumpets, and the rear guard came after the ark, while the trumpets blew continually. But Joshua commanded the people, "You shall not shout or let your voice be heard, neither shall any word go out of your mouth, until the day I bid you shout; then you shall shout." So he caused the ark of the Lord to compass the city, going about it once; and they came into the camp, and spent the night in the camp.

Joshua rose early in the morning, and the priests took up the ark of the Lord. And the seven priests bearing the seven trumpets of rams' horns before the ark of the Lord passed on, blowing the trumpets continually; and the armed men went before them, and the rear guard came after the ark of the Lord, while the trumpets blew continually. And the second day they marched around the city once, and returned into the camp. So they did for six days.

On the seventh day they rose early at the dawn of day, and marched around the city in the same manner seven times: it was only on that day that they marched around the city seven times. And on the seventh time, when the priests had blown the trumpets, Joshua said to the people, "Shout; for the Lord has given you the city. And the city and all that is within it shall be devoted to the Lord for destruction; only Rahab the harlot and all who are with her in her house shall live, because she hid the messengers that we sent. But you, keep yourselves from the things devoted to destruction, lest when you have devoted them you take any of the devoted things and make the camp of Israel a thing for destruction, and bring trouble upon it. But all silver and gold, and vessels of bronze and iron, are sacred to the Lord; they shall go into the treasury of the Lord." So the people shouted, and the trumpets were blown. As soon as the people heard the sound of the trumpets, the people raised a great shout, and the wall fell down flat, so that people went up into the city, every man straight before him, and they took the city. Then they utterly destroyed all in the city, both men and women, young and old, oxen, sheep, and asses, with the edge of the sword.

And Joshua said to the two men who had spied the land, "Go into the harlot's house, and bring out from it the woman, and all who belong to her, as you swore to her." So the young men who had been spies went in, and brought out Rahab, and her father and mother and brothers and all who belonged to her; and they brought all her kindred, and set them outside the camp of Israel. And they burned the city with fire, and all within it; only the silver and gold, and the vessels of bronze and iron, they put into the treasury of the house of the Lord. But Rahab the harlot, and her father's household, and all who belonged to her, Joshua saved alive; and she dwelt in Israel to this day, because she hid the messengers whom Joshua sent to spy out Jericho.

Joshua laid an oath upon them at that time, saying, "Cursed before the Lord be the man that rises up and rebuilds this city, Jericho.

At the cost of his first-born shall he lay its foundation,
and at the cost of his youngest son shall he set up its gates."
So the Lord was with Joshua; and his fame was in the land.

JOSHUA HALTS THE SUN

Divine intervention in battle is also not unique to Hebraic literature. The gods in the *Illiad* fight and help those whom they favor, and many a real life general has felt that he was divinely guided or protected. Today, however, the common opinion may be summarized in a statement made by the great German general and military strategist, Karl von Clausewitz: "God is on the side of the big battalions."

Joshua 10:6–14

And the men of Gibeon sent to Joshua at the camp in Gilgal, saying, "Do not relax your hand from your servants; come up to us quickly, and save us, and help us; for all the kings of the Amorites that dwell in the hill country are gathered against us." So Joshua went up from Gilgal, he and all the people of war with him, and all the mighty men of valor. And the Lord said to Joshua, "Do not fear them, for I have given them into your hands; there shall not a man of them stand before you." So Joshua came upon them suddenly, having marched all night from Gilgal. And the Lord threw them into a panic before Israel, who slew them with a great slaughter at Gibeon, and chased them by the way of the ascent of Bethhoron, and smote them as far as Azekah and Makkedah. And as they fled before Israel, while they were going down the ascent of Bethhoron, the Lord threw down great stones from heaven upon them as far as Azekah, and they died; there were more who died because of the hailstones than the men of Israel killed with the sword.

Then spoke Joshua to the Lord in the day when the Lord gave

the Amorites over to the men of Israel; and he said in the sight of Israel,

> "Sun, stand thou still at Gibeon,
>   and thou Moon in the valley of Aijalon."
> And the sun stood still, and the moon stayed,
>   until the nation took vengeance on their enemies.

Is this not written in the Book of Jashar? The sun stayed in the midst of heaven, and did not hasten to go down for about a whole day. There has been no day like it before or since, when the Lord harkened to the voice of a man; for the Lord fought for Israel.

EPIC CYCLES

Epic cycles in Bible literature are usually attached to the names of the great patriarchs and their descendants. The peculiar influence of family groups directed the formation of the entire nation of Israel. The successes of these family groups would be expected in any formal account of history. But, interestingly, the failures of these patriarchs are presented as well. The successes and failures of these men afford the opportunity to see the hand of God moving in these men's lives with a certain objectivity often missing in other ancient histories. The reader comes to know the true character of these patriarchs as they progressed personally and as their personality was projected in their descendants.

THE CYCLE OF ABRAHAM, ISAAC, AND JACOB

The family saga is a theme of perennial interest and has a widespread audience. At the lowest level it is seen in soap operas such as "As the World Turns" and in comic strips like "Gasoline Alley." At its highest level it is dramatized in a cycle of tragedies dealing with the house of Atreus. Recently, the success of a television series based upon John Galsworthy's *Forsyte Saga* attests to the continued popularity of this theme.

The pioneer spirit of Abraham to build for posterity is duplicated in many volumes, such as Willa Cather's *O Pioneer* or *My Antonio* and O.E. Rölvaag's *Giants in the Earth*. The twentieth-century astronauts know this spirit. There is an "Eldorado" for each of us. Of particular interest in the Abraham story is the circumstance of Sodom's destruction. The downfall of a culture as a punishment for its wickedness has fascinated such diverse writers as Edward Gibbon in his *History of the Decline and Fall of the Roman Empire* and Nathanael West in his *Day of the Locust.* The theme is reiterated daily by newscasters and editorial writers, so often, in fact, that we forget to read the powerful, original description.

The faith of Isaac is legendary. His submission to his father's sacrificial knife is an archtype of Christ's own sacrifice for humanity. Such strength of faith is overwhelming in the work of poets, such as Browning's "The Ring and the Book" and Whittier's "Our Master."

Jacob follows in a long line of brothers in conflict: Cain and Abel, Joseph and his brothers, the brothers Karamozov. The "falling out" of family members forms the plot of many modern serial dramas.

ABRAHAM: HIS CALL

Genesis 12:1-9

Now the Lord said to Abram, "Go from your country and your kindred and your father's house to the land that I will show you. And I will make of you a great nation, and I will bless you, and make your name great, so that you will be a blessing. I will bless those who bless you, and him who curses you I will curse; and by you all the families of the earth shall bless themselves."

So Abram went, as the Lord had told him; and Lot went with him. Abram was seventy-five years old when he departed from Haran. And Abram took Sarai his wife, and Lot his brother's son, and all their possessions which they had gathered, and the persons they had gotten in Haran; and they set forth to go to the land of Canaan. When they had come to the land of Canaan, Abram passed through the land to the place at Shechem, to the oak of Moreh. At that time the Canaanites were in the land. Then the Lord appeared to Abram, and said, "To your descendants I will give this land." So he built an altar to the Lord, who had appeared to him. Thence he removed to the mountain east of Bethel, and pitched his tent, with Bethel on the west and Ai on the east; and there he built an altar to the Lord and called on the name of the Lord. And Abram journeyed on, still going toward the Negeb.

ABRAHAM: HIS LIE TO PHARAOH

Genesis 12:10-20

Now there was a famine in the land. So Abram went down to Egypt to sojourn there, for the famine was severe in the land. When he was about to enter Egypt, he said to Sarai his wife, "I know that you are a woman beautiful to behold; and when the Egyptians see you, they will say, 'This is his wife'; then they will kill me, but they will let you live. Say you are my sister, that it will go well with me because of you, and that my life may be spared on your account." When Abram entered Egypt the Egyptians saw that the woman was very beautiful. And when the princes of Pharaoh saw her, they praised her to Pharaoh. And the woman was taken into Pharaoh's house. And for her sake he dealt well with Abram; and he had sheep, oxen, he-asses, menservants, maidservants, she-asses, and camels.

But the Lord afflicted Pharaoh and his house with great plagues because of Sarai, Abram's wife. So Pharaoh called Abram, and said, "What is this you have done to me! Why did you not tell me that she was your wife? Why did you say, 'She is my sister,' so that I took her for my wife? Now then, here is your wife, take her, and be gone." And Pharaoh gave men orders concerning him; and they sent him on the way, with his wife and all that he had.

ABRAHAM: THE PARTING WITH LOT

Genesis 13:1–18

So Abram went up from Egypt, he and his wife, and all that they had, and Lot with him, into the Negeb.

Now Abram was very rich in cattle, in silver, and in gold. And he journeyed on from the Negeb as far as Bethel, to the place where his tent had been at the beginning, between Bethel and Ai, to the place where he had made an altar at first; and there Abram called on the name of the Lord. And Lot, who went with Abram, also had flocks and herds and tents, so that the land could not support both of them dwelling together, and there was strife between the herdsmen of Abram's cattle and the herdsmen of Lot's cattle. At that time the Canaanites and the Perizzites dwelt in the land.

Then Abram said to Lot, "Let there be no strife between you and me, and between your herdsmen and my herdsmen; for we are kinsmen. Is not the whole land before you? Separate yourself from me. If you take the left hand, then I will go to the right; or if you take the right hand, then I will go to the left." And Lot lifted up his eyes, and saw that the Jordan valley was well watered everywhere like the garden of the Lord, like the land of Egypt, in the direction of Zoar; this was before the Lord destroyed Sodom and Gomorrah. So Lot chose for himself all the Jordan valley, and Lot journeyed east; thus they separated from each other. Abram dwelt in the land of Canaan, while Lot dwelt among the cities of the valley and moved his tent as far as Sodom. Now the men of Sodom were wicked, great sinners against the Lord.

The Lord said to Abram, after Lot had separated from him, "Lift up your eyes, and look from the place where you are, northward and southward and eastward and westward; for all the land which you see I will give to you and to your descendants forever. I will make your descendants as the dust of the earth; so that if one can count the dust of the earth, your descendants also can be counted. Arise, walk through the length and breadth of the land, for I will give it to you." So Abram moved his tent, and came and dwelt by the oaks of Mamre, which are at Hebron; and there he built an altar to the Lord.

ABRAHAM: GOD'S COVENANT
Genesis 17:1–8, 15–19

When Abram was ninety-nine years old the Lord appeared to Abram, and said to him, "I am God Almighty; walk before me, and be blameless. And I will make my covenant between me and you, and multiply you exceedingly." Then Abram fell on his face; and God said to him, "Behold, my covenant is with you, and you shall be the father of a multitude of nations. No longer shall your name be Abram, but your name shall be Abraham; for I have made you the father of a multitude of nations. I will make you exceedingly fruitful; and I will make nations of you, and kings shall come forth from you. And I will establish my covenant between me and you and your descendants after you. And I will give to you, and to your descendants, the land of your sojournings, all the land of Canaan, for an everlasting possession; and I will be your God."

And God said to Abraham, "As for Sarai your wife, you shall not call her name Sarai, but Sarah shall be her name. I will bless her, and moreover I will give you a son by her; I will bless her, and she shall be a mother of nations; kings of people shall come from her." Then Abraham fell on his face and laughed, and he said to himself, "Shall a child be born to a man who is a hundred years old? Shall Sarah, who is ninety years old, bear a child?" And Abraham said to God, "O that Ishmael might live in thy sight!" God said, "No, but Sarah your wife shall bear you a son, and you shall call his name Isaac. I will establish my covenant with him as an everlasting covenant for his descendants after him."

ABRAHAM: THE DESTRUCTION OF SODOM
Genesis 18:20–33; 19:1–29

The Lord said, "Because the outcry against Sodom and Gomorrah is great and their sin is very grave, I will go down to see whether they have done altogether according to the outcry which has come to me; and if not, I will know."

So the men turned from there, and went toward Sodom; but Abraham still stood before the Lord. Then Abraham drew near, and said, "Wilt thou indeed destroy the righteous with the wicked? Suppose there are fifty righteous within the city; wilt thou then destroy the place and not spare it for the fifty righteous who are in it? Far be it from thee to do such a thing, to slay the righteous with the wicked, so that the righteous fare as the wicked! Far be it from thee! Shall not the judge of all the earth do right?" And the Lord said, "If I find at Sodom fifty righteous in the city, I will spare the whole place for their sake." Abraham answered, "Behold, I have taken upon myself to speak to the Lord, I who am but dust and ashes. Suppose five of the fifty righteous are lacking? Wilt thou destroy the whole city for lack of five?" And he said, "I will not destroy it if I find forty-five there." Again he spoke to him, and said, "Suppose forty are found there." He answered, "For the sake of forty I will not do it." Then he said, "Oh let not the Lord be angry, and I will speak. Suppose thirty are found there?" He answered, "I will not do it if I find thirty there." He said, "Behold, I have taken upon myself to speak with the Lord. Suppose twenty are found there?" He answered, "For the sake of twenty, I will not destroy it." Then he said, "Oh let not the Lord be angry, and I will speak again but this once. Suppose ten are found there?" He answered, "For the sake of ten I will not destroy it." And the Lord went his way, when he finished speaking to Abraham; and Abraham returned to his place.

The two angels came to Sodom in the evening; and Lot was sitting in the gate of Sodom. When Lot saw them, he rose to meet them, and bowed himself with his face to the earth, and said, "My lords, turn aside, I pray you, to your servant's house and spend the night, and wash your feet; then you may rise up early and go on your way." They said, "No; we will spend the night in the street." But he urged them strongly; so they turned aside to him and entered his house; and he made them a feast, and baked them unleavened bread, and they ate. But before they lay down, the men of the city, the men of Sodom, both young and old, all the people to the last man, surrounded the house; and they called to Lot, "Where are the men who came to you tonight? Bring them out to us, that we may know them." Lot went out of the door to the men, shut the door after him, and said, "I beg you, my brothers, do not act so wickedly. Behold I have two daughters who have not known man; let me bring them out to you, and do to them as you please; only do nothing to these men, for they have come under the shelter of my roof." But they said, "Stand back!" And they said, "This fellow came to sojourn, and he will play the judge! Now we will deal worse with you than with them." Then they pressed hard against the man Lot, and drew near to break the door. But the men put forth their hands and brought Lot into the house to them, and shut the door. And they struck with blindness the men who were at the door of the house, both small and great, so that they wearied themselves groping for the door.

Then the men said to Lot, "Have you anyone else here? Sons-in-laws, sons, daughters, or anyone you have in this city, bring them out of the place; for we are about to destroy this place, because the outcry against its people has become great before the Lord, and the Lord has sent us to destroy it." So Lot went out and said to his sons-in-law, who were to marry his daughters, "Up, get out of this place; for the Lord is about to destroy the city." But he seemed to his sons-in-law to be jesting.

When morning dawned, the angels urged Lot, saying, "Arise, take your wife and your two daughters who are here, lest you be consumed in the punishment of the city." But he lingered; so the men seized him and his wife and his two daughters by the hand, the Lord being merciful to him, and they brought him forth and set him outside the city. And when they had brought him forth, they said, "Flee for your life; do not look back or stop anywhere in the valley; flee to the hills, lest you be consumed." And Lot said to them, "Oh no, my lords; behold, your servant has found favor in your sight, and you have shown me great kindness in saving my life; but I cannot flee to the hills, lest the disaster overtake me, and I die. Behold, yonder city is near enough to flee to, and it is a little one. Let me escape there—is it not a little one?—and my life will be saved!" He said to him, "Behold, I grant you this favor also, that I will not overthrow the city of which you have spoken. Make haste, escape there; for I can do nothing until you arrive there." Therefore the name of the city was called Zoar. The sun had risen on the earth when Lot came to Zoar.

Then the Lord rained on Sodom and Gomorrah brimstone and fire from the Lord out of heaven; and he overthrew these cities, and all the valley, and all the inhabitants of the cities, and what grew on the ground. But Lot's wife behind him looked back, and she became a pillar of salt. And Abraham went early in the morning to the place where he had stood before the Lord; and he looked down toward Sodom and Gomorrah and toward all the land of the valley, and beheld, and lo, the smoke of the land went up like the smoke of a furnace. So it was that, when God destroyed the cities of the valley, God remembered Abraham, and sent Lot out of the midst of the overthrow, when he overthrew the cities in which Lot dwelt.

ISAAC: HIS BIRTH

Genesis 21:1–4

And the Lord visited Sarah as he had said, and the Lord did to Sarah as he had promised. And Sarah conceived, and bore Abraham a son in his old age at the time of which God had spoken to him. Abraham called the name of his son who was born to him, whom Sarah bore him, Isaac. And Abraham circumcised his son Isaac when he was eight days old, as God had commanded him.

ISAAC: ABRAHAM OFFERS HIS SON

Genesis 22:1–18

God tested Abraham, and said to him, "Abraham!" And he said, "Here am I." He said, "Take your son, your only son Isaac, whom you love, and go to the land of Moriah, and offer him there as a burnt offering upon one of the mountains of which I shall tell you." So Abraham rose early in the morning, saddled his ass, and took two of his young men with him, and his son Isaac; and he cut the wood for the burnt offering, and arose and went to the place of which God had told him. On the third day Abraham lifted up his eyes and saw the place afar off. Then Abraham said to his young men, "Stay here with the ass; I and the lad will go yonder and worship, and come again to you." And Abraham took the wood of the burnt offering and laid it on Isaac his son; and he took in his hand the fire and the knife. So they went both of them together. And Isaac said to his father, Abraham, "My father!" And he said, "Here am I, my son." He said, "Behold, the fire and the wood, but where is the lamb for the burnt offering?" Abraham said, "God will provide himself the lamb for the burnt offering, my son." So they went both of them together.

When they came to the place of which God had told him, Abraham built an altar there, and laid the wood in order, and bound Isaac his son, and laid him upon the altar, upon the wood. Then Abraham put forth his hand, and took the knife to slay his son. But the angel of the Lord called to him from heaven, and said, "Abraham, Abraham!" And he said, "Here am I." He said, "Do not lay your hand on the lad or do anything to him; for now I know that you fear God, seeing that you have not withheld your son, your only son, from me." And Abraham lifted up his eyes and looked, and behold, behind him was a ram, caught in a thicket by his horns; and Abraham went and took the ram, and offered it up as a burnt offering instead of his son. So Abraham called the name of that place The Lord will provide; as it is said to this day, "On the mount of the Lord it shall be provided."

And the angel of the Lord called to Abraham a second time from heaven, and said, "By myself I have sworn, says the Lord, because you have done this, and have not withheld your son, your only son, I will indeed bless you, and I will multiply your descendants as the stars of heaven and as the sand on the seashore. And your descendants shall possess the gate of their enemies, and by your descendants shall all the nations of the earth bless themselves, because you have obeyed my voice."

ISAAC: WOOING OF REBEKAH

Genesis 24:1–67

Now Abraham was old, well advanced in years; and the Lord had blessed Abraham in all things. And Abraham said to his servant, the oldest of his house, who had charge of all that he had, "Put your hand under my thigh, and I will make you swear by the Lord, the God of heaven and of the earth, that you will not take a wife for my son from the daughters of the Canaanites, among whom I dwell, but will go to my country and to my kindred, and take a wife for my son Isaac." The servant said to him, "Perhaps the woman will not be willing to follow me to this land; must I then take your son back to the land from whence you came?" Abraham said to him, "See to it that you do not take my son back there. The Lord, the God of heaven, who took me from my father's house and from the land of my birth, and who spoke to me and swore to me, 'To your descendants I will give this land,' he will send his angel before you, and you shall take a wife for my son from there. But if the woman is not willing to follow you, then you will be free from this oath of mine; only you must not take my son back there." So the servant put his hand under the thigh of Abraham his master, and swore to him concerning this matter.

Then the servant took ten of his master's camels and departed, taking all sorts of choice gifts from his master; and he arose, and went to Mesopotamia, to the city of Nahor. And he made the camels kneel down outside the city by the well of water at the time of evening, the time when women go out to draw water. And he said, "O Lord, God of my master Abraham, grant me success today, I pray thee, and show steadfast love to my master Abraham. Behold, I am standing by the spring of water, and the daughters of the men of the city are coming out to draw water. Let the maiden to whom I shall say, 'Pray, let down your jar that I may drink,' and who shall say, 'Drink, and I will water your camels'—let her be the one whom thou has appointed for thy servant Isaac. By this I shall know that thou hast shown steadfast love to my master."

Before he had done speaking, behold, Rebekah, who was born to Bethuel the son of Milcah, the wife of Nahor, Abraham's brother, came out with her water jar upon her shoulder. The maiden was very fair to look upon, a virgin, whom no man had known. She went down to the spring, and filled her jar, and came up. Then the servant ran to meet her and said, "Pray give me a little water to drink from your jar." She said, "Drink, my lord"; and she quickly let down her jar upon her hand, and gave him a drink. When she had finished giving him a drink, she said, "I will draw for your camels also until they have finished drinking." So she quickly emptied her jar into the trough and ran again to the well to draw, and she drew for all his camels. The man gazed at her in silence to learn whether the Lord had prospered his journey or not.

When the camels had done drinking, the man took a gold ring weighing a half shekel, and two bracelets for her arms weighing ten gold shekels, and said, "Tell me whose daughter you are. Is there room in your father's house for us to lodge in?" She said to him, "I am the daughter of Bethuel the son of Milcah, whom she bore to Nahor." She added, "We have both straw and provender enough, and room to lodge in." The man bowed his head and worshipped the Lord, and said, "Blessed be the Lord, the God of my master Abraham, who has not forsaken his steadfast love and his faithfulness toward my master. As for me, the Lord has led me in the way to the house of my master's kinsmen."

Then the maiden ran and told her mother's household about these things. Rebekah had a brother whose name was Laban; and Laban ran out to the man, to the spring. When he saw the ring and the bracelets on his sister's arms, and when he heard the words of Rebekah, "Thus the man spoke to me," he went to the man; and behold, he was standing by the camels at the spring. He said, "Come in, O blessed of the Lord; why do you stand outside? For I have prepared the house and a place for the camels." So the man came into the house; and Laban ungirded the camels, and gave him straw and provender for the camels, and water to wash his feet and the feet of the men with him. The food was set before him to eat; but he said, "I will not eat until I have told my errand." He said, "Speak on."

So he said, "I am Abraham's servant. The Lord has greatly blessed my master, and he has become great; he has given him flocks and herds, silver and gold, menservants and maidservants, camels and asses. And Sarah my master's wife bore a son to my master when she was old; and to him he has given all that he has. My master made me swear, saying, 'You shall not take a wife for my son from the daughters of the Canaanites, in whose land I dwell; but you shall go to my father's house and to my kindred, and take a wife for my son.' I said to my master, 'Perhaps the woman will not follow me.' But he said to me, 'The Lord, before whom I walk, will send his angel before you and prosper your way; and you shall take a wife for my son from my kindred and from my father's house; then you will be free from my oath, when you come to my kindred; and if they will not give her to you, you will be free from my oath.'

"I came today to the spring, and said, 'O Lord, the God of my master Abraham, if now thou wilt prosper the way which I go, behold, I am standing by the spring of water; let the young woman who comes out to draw, to whom I shall say, 'Pray give me a little water from your jar to drink,' and who will say to me, 'Drink, and I will draw for your camels also,' let her be the woman whom the Lord has appointed for my master's son.'

"Before I had done speaking in my heart, behold, Rebekah came out with her water jar on her shoulder; and she went down to the spring and drew. I said to her, 'Pray let me drink.' She quickly let down her jar from her shoulder, and said, 'Drink, and I will give your camels drink also.' So I drank, and she gave the camels drink also. Then I asked her, 'Whose daughter are you?' She said, 'The daughter of Bethuel, Nahor's son, whom Milcah bore to him.' So I put the ring on her nose, and the bracelets on her arms. Then I bowed my head and worshipped the Lord, and blessed the Lord, the God of my master Abraham, who had led me by the right way to take the daughter of my master's kinsman for his son. Now then, if you will deal loyally and truly with my master, tell me; and if not, tell me; that I may turn to the right hand or to the left."

Then Laban and Bethuel answered, "The thing comes from the Lord; we cannot speak to you bad or good. Behold, Rebekah is before you, take her and go, and let her be the wife of your master's son, as the Lord has spoken."

When Abraham's servant heard their words, he bowed himself to the earth before the Lord. And the servant brought forth jewelry of silver and of gold, and raiment, and gave them to Rebekah; he also gave to her brother and to her mother costly ornaments. And he and the men who were with him ate and drank, and they spent the night there. When they arose in the morning, he said, "Send me back to my master." Her brother and mother said, "Let the maiden remain with us a while, at least ten days; after that she may go." But he said to them, "Do not delay me, since the Lord has prospered my way; let me go that I may go to my master." They said, "We will call the maiden and ask her." And they called Rebekah, and said to her, "Will you go with this man?" She said, "I will go." So they sent away Rebekah their sister and her nurse and Abraham's servant and his men. And they blessed Rebekah, and said to her, "Our sister, be the mother of thousands of ten thousands; and may your descendants possess the gate of those who hate them!" Then Rebekah and her maids arose, and rode upon the camels and followed the man; thus the servant took Rebekah, and went his way.

Now Isaac had come from Beerlahai-roi, and was swelling in the Negeb. And Isaac went out to meditate in the field in the evening; and he lifted up his eyes and looked, and behold, there were camels coming. And Rebekah lifted up her eyes, and when she saw Isaac, she alighted from the camel, and said to the servant, "Who is the man yonder, walking in the field to meet us?" The servant said, "It is my master." So she took her veil and covered herself. And the servant told Isaac all the things that he had done. Then Isaac brought her into the tent, and took Rebekah, and she became his wife; and he loved her. So Isaac was comforted after his mother's death.

JACOB: BIRTH OF ESAU AND JACOB

Genesis 25:19–26

These are the descendants of Isaac, Abraham's son: Abraham was the father of Isaac, and Isaac was forty years old when he took to wife Rebekah, the daughter of Bethuel the Aramean of Paddan-aram, the sister of Laban the Aramean. And Isaac prayed to the Lord for his wife, because she was barren; and the Lord granted his prayer, and Rebekah his wife conceived. The children struggled together within her; and she said, "If it is thus, why do I live?" So she went to inquire of the Lord. And the Lord said to her,

> "Two nations are in your womb,
>   and two peoples, born of you, shall be divided;
> the one shall be stronger than the other,
>   the elder shall serve the younger."

When her days to be delivered were fulfilled, behold, there were twins in her womb. The first came forth red, all his body like a hairy mantle; so they called his name Esau. Afterward his brother came forth, and his hand had taken hold of Esau's heel; so his name was called Jacob. Isaac was sixty years old when she bore them.

JACOB: ESAU SELLS HIS BIRTHRIGHT TO JACOB
Genesis 25:27–34

When the boys grew up, Esau was a skillful hunter, a man of the field, while Jacob was a quiet man, dwelling in tents. Isaac loved Esau, because he ate of his game; but Rebekah loved Jacob.
Once when Jacob was boiling pottage, Esau came in from the field, and he was famished. And Esau said to Jacob, "Let me eat some of your red pottage, for I am famished!" (Therefore his name was called Edom.) Jacob said, "First sell me your birthright." Esau said, "I am about to die; of what use is a birthright to me?" Jacob said, "Swear to me first." So he swore to him, and sold his birthright to Jacob. Then Jacob gave Esau bread and pottage of lentils, and he ate and drank, and rose and went his way. Thus Esau despised his birthright.

JACOB: THE STOLEN BLESSING
Genesis 27:1–46

When Isaac was old and his eyes were dim so that he could not see, he called Esau his older son, and said to him, "My son"; and he answered, "Here I am." He said, "Behold, I am old; I do not know the day of my death. Now then, take your weapons, your quiver and your bow, and go out into the field, and hunt game for me, and prepare for me savory food, such as I love, and bring it to me that I may eat; that I may bless you before I die."

Now Rebekah was listening when Isaac spoke to his son Esau. So when Esau went to field to hunt for game and bring it, Rebekah said to her son Jacob, "I heard your father speak to your brother Esau, 'Bring me game, and prepare for me savory food, that I may eat it, and bless you before the Lord before I die.' Now therefore, my son, obey my word as I command you. Go to the flock, and fetch me two good kids, that I may prepare from them savory food for your father, such as he loves; and you will bring it to your father to eat, so that he may bless you before he dies." But Jacob said to Rebekah his mother, "Behold, my brother Esau is a hairy man, and I am a smooth man. Perhaps my father will feel me, and I shall seem to be mocking him, and bring a curse upon myself and not a blessing." His mother said to him, "Upon me be your curse, my son, only obey my word, and go, fetch them to me." So he went and took and brought them to his mother; and his mother prepared savory food, such as his father loved. Then Rebekah took the best garments of Esau her older son, which were with her in the house, and put them on Jacob her younger son; and the skins of the kids she put upon his hands and upon the smooth part of his neck; and she gave the savory food and the bread, which she had prepared, into the hand of her son Jacob.

So he went in to his father, and said, "My father"; and he said, "Here I am; who are you, my son?" Jacob said to his father, "I am Esau your first-born. I have done as you told me; now sit up and eat of my game, that you may bless me." But Isaac said to his son, "How is it that you have found it so quickly, my son?" He answered, "Because the Lord your God granted me success." Then Isaac said to Jacob, "Come near, that I may feel you, my son, to know whether you are really my son Esau or not." So Jacob went near to Isaac his father, who felt him and said, "The voice is Jacob's voice, but the hands are the hands of Esau." And he did not recognize him, because his hands were hairy like his brother Esau's hands; so he blessed him. He said, "Are you really my son Esau?" He answered, "I am." Then he said, "Bring it to me, that I may eat of my son's game and bless you." So he brought it to him, and he ate; and he brought him wine, and he drank. Then his father Isaac said to him, "Come near and kiss me, my son." So he came near and kissed him, and he smelled the smell of his garments, and blessed him, and said,

"See, the smell of my son
   is as the smell of the field which the Lord has blessed!
May God give you of the dew of heaven,
   and of the fatness of the earth,
   and plenty of grain and wine.
Let peoples serve you,
   and nations bow down to you.
Be lord over your brothers,
   and may your mother's sons bow down to you.
Cursed be everyone who curses you,
   and blessed be everyone who blesses you!"

As soon as Isaac had finished blessing Jacob, when Jacob had scarcely gone out from the presence of Isaac his father, Esau his brother came in from his hunting. He also prepared savory food, and brought it to his father. And he said to his father, "Let my father arise, and eat of his son's game, that you may bless me." His father Isaac said to him, "Who are you?" He answered, "I am your son, your first-born, Esau." Then Isaac trembled violently, and said, "Who was it then that hunted game and brought it to me, and I ate it all before you came, and I have blessed him?—yes, and he shall be blessed." When Esau heard the words of his father, he cried out with an exceedingly great and bitter cry, and said to his father, "Bless me, even me also, O my father!" But he said, "Your brother came with guile, and he has taken away your blessing." Esau said, "Is he not rightly named Jacob? For he has supplanted me these two times. He took away my birthright; and, behold, now he has taken away my blessing." Then he said, "Have you not reserved a blessing for me?" Isaac answered Esau, "Behold, I have made him your lord, and all his brothers I have given to him for servants, and with grain and wine I have sustained him. What then can I do for you, my son?" Esau said to his father, "Have you but one blessing, my father? Bless me, even me also, O my father." And Esau lifted up his voice and wept.
   Then Isaac his father answered him:

   "Behold, away from the fatness of the earth shall your dwellings
         be,
      and away from the dew of heaven on high.
   By your sword shall you live,
      and you shall serve your brother;
   but when you break loose
      you shall break his yoke from your neck."

Now Esau hated Jacob because of the blessing with which his father had blessed him, and Esau said to himself, "The days of mourning for my father are approaching; then I will kill my brother Jacob." But the words of Esau her older son were told to Rebekah; so she sent and called Jacob her younger son, and said to him, "Behold, your brother Esau comforts himself by planning to kill you. Now, therefore, my son, obey my voice; arise, flee to Laban my brother in Haran, and stay with him a while, until your brother's fury turns away; until your brother's anger turns away, and he forgets what you have done to him; then I will send and fetch you from there. Why should I be bereft of you both in one day?"

Then Rebekah said to Isaac, "I am weary of my life because of the Hittite women. If Jacob marries one of the Hittite women such as these, one of the women of the land, what good will my life be to me?"

JACOB: THE PROMISE COMES TO JACOB

Genesis 28:10–22

Jacob left Beer-sheba, and went toward Haran. And he came to a certain place, and stayed there that night, because the sun had set. Taking one of the stones of the place, he put it under his head and lay down in that place to sleep. He dreamed that there was a ladder set up on the earth, and the top of it reached to heaven; and behold, the angels of God were ascending and descending on it! And behold, the Lord stood above it, and said, "I am the Lord, the God of Abraham your father and the God of Isaac; the land on which you lie I will give to you and to your descendants; and your descendants shall be like the dust of the earth, and you shall spread abroad to the west and to the east and to the north and to the south; and by you and your descendants shall all the families of the earth bless themselves.

Behold, I am with you and will keep you wherever you go, and will bring you back to this land; for I will not leave you until I have done that which I have spoken to you." Then Jacob awoke from his sleep and said, "Surely the Lord is in this place; and I did not know it." And he was afraid, and said, "How awesome is this place! This is none other than the house of God, and this is the gate of heaven."

So Jacob rose early in the morning, and he took the stone which he had put under his head and he set it up for a pillar and poured oil on the top of it. He called the name of that place Bethel; but the name of the city was Luz at the first. Then Jacob made a vow, saying, "If God will be with me, and will keep me in this way that I go, and will give me bread to eat and clothing to wear, so that I come again to my father's house in peace, then the Lord shall be my God, and this stone, which I have set up for a pillar, shall be God's house; and all that thou givest me I will give the tenth to thee."

JACOB: FOURTEEN-YEAR COURTSHIP OF RACHEL
Genesis 29:1–30

Then Jacob went on his journey, and came to the land of the people of the east. As he looked, he saw a well in the field, and lo, three flocks of sheep lying beside it; for out of that well the flocks were watered. The stone on the well's mouth was large, and when all the flocks were gathered there, the shepherds would roll the stone from the mouth of the well, and water the sheep, and put the stone back in its place upon the mouth of the well.

Jacob said to them, "My brothers, where do you come from?" They said, "We are from Haran." He said to them, "Do you know Laban the son of Nahor?" They said, "We know him." He said, to them, "Is it well with him?" They said, "It is well; and see, Rachel his daughter is coming with the sheep!" He said, "Behold, it is still high day, it is not time for the animals to be gathered together; water the sheep, and go, pasture them." But they said, "We cannot until all of the flocks are gathered together, and the stone is rolled from the mouth of the well; then we water the sheep."

While he was still speaking with them, Rachel came with her father's sheep; for she kept them. Now when Jacob saw Rachel the daughter of Laban his mother's brother, and the sheep of Laban his mother's brother, Jacob went up and rolled the stone from the well's mouth, and watered the flock of Laban his mother's brother. Then Jacob kissed Rachel, and wept aloud. And Jacob told Rachel that he was her father's kinsman, and that he was Rebekah's son; and she ran and told her father.

When Laban heard the tidings of Jacob his sister's son, he ran to meet him, and embraced him and kissed him, and brought him to his house. Jacob told Laban all these things. And Laban said to him, "Surely you are my bone and my flesh!" And he stayed with him a month.

Then Laban said to Jacob, "Because you are my kinsman, should you therefore serve me for nothing? Tell me, what shall your wages be?" Now Laban had two daughters; the name of the older was Leah, and the name of the younger was Rachel. Leah's eyes were weak, but Rachel was beautiful and lovely. Jacob loved Rachel; and he said, "I will serve you seven years for your younger daughter Rachel." Laban said, "It is better that I should give her to you than that I should give her to any other man; stay with me." So Jacob served seven years for Rachel, and they seemed to him but a few days because of the love he had for her.

Then Jacob said to Laban, "Give me my wife that I may go in to her, for my time is completed." So Laban gathered together all the men of the place, and made a feast. But in the evening he took his daughter Leah and brought her to Jacob; and he went to her. (Laban gave his maid Zilpah to his daughter Leah to be her maid.) And in the morning, behold, it was Leah; and Jacob said to Laban, "What is this you have done to me; Did I not serve with you for Rachel? Why then have you deceived me?" Laban said, "It is not so done in our country, to give the younger before the first-born. Complete the week of this one, and we will give you the other also in return for serving me another seven years." Jacob did so, and completed her week; then Laban gave him his daughter Rachel to wife. (Laban gave his maid Bilhah to his daughter Rachel to be her maid.) So Jacob went in to Rachel also, and he loved Rachel more than Leah, and served Laban for another seven years.

JACOB: WRESTLING THE ANGEL

Genesis 32:22–32

He arose and took his two wives, his two maids, and his eleven children, and crossed the ford of the Jabbok. He took them and sent them across the stream, and likewise everything that he had. And Jacob was left alone; and a man wrestled with him until the breaking of the day. When the man saw that he did not prevail against Jacob, he touched the hollow of his thigh; and Jacob's thigh was put out of joint as he wrestled with him. Then he said, "Let me go, for the day is breaking." But Jacob said, "I will not let you go, unless you bless me." And he said to him, "What is your name?" And he said, "Jacob." Then he said, "Your name shall be no more called Jacob, but Israel, for you have striven with God and with men, and have prevailed." Then Jacob asked him, "Tell me, I pray, your name." But he said, "Why is it that you ask my name?" And there he blessed him. So Jacob called the name of the place Peniel, saying, "For I have seen God face to face, and yet my life is preserved." And he passed Peniel, limping because of his thigh. To this day the Israelites do not eat the sinew of the hip which is upon the hollow of the thigh, because he touched the hollow of Jacob's thigh on the sinew of the hip.

JACOB: MEETING OF JACOB AND ESAU

Genesis 33:1–11

And Jacob lifted up his eyes and looked, and behold, Esau was coming, and four hundred men with him. So he divided the children among Leah and Rachel and the two maids. And he put the maids with their children in front, and then Leah with her children, and Rachel and Joseph last of all. He himself went on before them, bowing himself to the ground seven times, until he came near to his brother.

But Esau ran to meet him, and fell on his neck and kissed him, and they wept. And when Esau raised his eyes and saw the women and children, he said, "Who are these with you?" Jacob said, "The children whom God has graciously given your servant." Then the maids drew near, they and their children, and bowed down; Leah likewise and her children drew near and bowed down; and last Joseph and Rachel drew near, and they bowed down. Esau said, "What do you mean by this company which I met?" Jacob answered, "To find favor in the sight of my lord." But Esau said, "I have enough, my brother; keep what you have for yourself." Jacob said, "No, I pray you, if I have found favor in your sight, then accept my present from my hand; for truly to see your face is like seeing the face of God, with such favor have you received me. Accept, I pray you, my gift that is brought to you, because God has dealt graciously with me, and because I have enough." Thus he urged him, and he took it.

THE CYCLE OF SAMUEL, SAUL, DAVID, ABSALOM, AND SOLOMON

This type of cycle is based upon an agrarian, patriarchal society. The theme in this cycle is the tension between father and son and arises, like the conflict between Esau and Jacob, from the passage of rights and lands from the father to the oldest son. The plays of Shakespeare, especially such a tragedy as *Lear,* and many of the histories utilize this theme, and certainly such a novel as *The Brothers Karamazov* by Dostoevski illustrates it clearly. However, no writer has made better use of the theme or has come so close to the original Biblical mood as has William Faulkner in his series of novels and short stories about Yoknapatawpha County. In fact, one of his novels, *Absalom, Absalom!*, takes its name and plot directly from this section of the Bible. Alan Paton's *Cry, the Beloved*

Country closely duplicates the Absalom story, and John Dryden makes satire of the story in "Absalom and Achitophel."

SAMUEL: GIVEN TO ELI AT BIRTH

1 Samuel 1:19–28

Elkanah knew Hannah his wife, and the Lord remembered her; and in due time Hannah conceived and bore a son, and she called his name Samuel, for she said, "I have asked him of the Lord."

And the man Elkanah and all his house went up to offer to the Lord the yearly sacrifice, and to pay his vow. But Hannah did not go up, for she said to her husband, "As soon as the child is weaned, I will bring him, that he may appear in the presence of the Lord, and abide there forever." Elkanah her husband said to her, "Do what seems best to you, wait until you have weaned him: only, may the Lord establish his word." So the woman remained and nursed her son, until she weaned him. And when she had weaned him, she took him up with her, along with a three-year-old bull, an ephah of flour, and a skin of wine; and she brought him to the house of the Lord at Shiloh; and the child was young. Then they slew the bull, and they brought the child to Eli. And she said, "Oh, my lord! As you live, my lord, I am the woman who was standing here in your presence, praying to the Lord. For this child I prayed; and the Lord has granted me my petition which I made to him. Therefore I have lent him to the Lord; as long as he lives, he is lent to the Lord."

SAMUEL: MINISTERING IN THE TABERNACLE

1 Samuel 2:18–26

Samuel was ministering before the Lord, a boy girded with a linen ephod. And his mother used to make for him a little robe and take it to him each year, when she went up with her husband to offer the yearly sacrifice. Then Eli would bless Elkanah and his wife, and say, "The Lord give you children by this woman for the loan which she lent to the Lord"; so then they would return to their home.

And the Lord visited Hannah, and she conceived and bore three sons and two daughters. And the boy Samuel grew in the presence of the Lord.

Now Eli was very old, and he heard all that his sons were doing to all Israel, and how they lay with the women who served at the entrance to the tent of meeting. And he said to them, "Why do you do such things? For I hear of your evil dealings from all the people. No, my sons, it is no good report that I hear the people of the Lord spreading abroad. If a man sins against a man, God will mediate for him; but if a man sins against the Lord, who will intercede for him?" But they would not listen to the voice of their father; for it was the will of the Lord to slay them.

Now the boy Samuel continued to grow in stature and in favor with the Lord and with men.

SAMUEL: GOD'S CALL

1 Samuel 3:1–21; 4:1

Now the boy Samuel was ministering to the Lord under Eli. And the word of the Lord was rare in those days; there was no frequent vision.

At that time Eli, whose eyesight had begun to grow dim, so that he could not see, was lying down in his own place; the lamp of God had not yet gone out, and Samuel was lying down within the temple of the Lord, where the ark of God was. Then the Lord called, "Samuel! Samuel!" And he said, "Here I am!" and ran to Eli, and said, "Here I am, for you called me." But he said, "I did not call; lie down again." So he went and lay down. And the Lord called again, "Samuel!" And Samuel arose and went to Eli, and said, "Here I am, for you called me." But he said, "I did not call, my son; lie down again." Now Samuel did not yet know the Lord, and the word of the Lord had not yet been revealed to him. And the Lord called Samuel again the third time. And he arose and went to Eli and said, "Here I am, for you called me." And Eli perceived the Lord was calling the boy. Therefore he said to Samuel, "Go, lie down; and if he calls you, you shall say, 'Speak, Lord, for thy servant hears.'" So Samuel went and lay down in his place.

And the Lord came and stood forth, calling as at other times, "Samuel! Samuel!" And Samuel said, "Speak, for thy servant hears." Then the Lord said to Samuel, "Behold, I am about to do a thing in Israel, at which the two ears of everyone that hears it will tingle. On that day I will fulfill against Eli all that I have spoken concerning his house, from the beginning to end. I tell him that I am about to punish his house forever, for the iniquity which he knew, because his sons were blaspheming God, and he did not restrain them. Therefore I swear to the house of Eli that the iniquity of Eli's house shall not be expiated by sacrifice or offering forever."

Samuel lay until morning; then he opened the doors of the house of the Lord. And Samuel was afraid to tell the vision to Eli. But Eli called Samuel and said, "Samuel, my son." And he said, "Here I am." And Eli said, "What was it that he told you? Do not hide it from me. May God do so to you and more also, if you hide anything from me of all that he told you." So Samuel told him everything and hid nothing from him. And he said, "It is the Lord; let him do what seems good to him."

And Samuel grew, and the Lord was with him and let none of his words fall to the ground. And all Israel from Dan to Beer-sheba knew that Samuel was established as a prophet of the Lord. And the Lord appeared again at Shiloh, for the Lord revealed himself to Samuel at Shiloh by the word of the Lord. And the word of Samuel came to all Israel.

SAMUEL: ISRAEL DEMANDS A KING

1 Samuel 8:1–10

When Samuel became old, he made his sons judges over Israel. The name of his first-born son was Joel, and the name of his second, Abijah; they were judges in Beer-sheba. Yet his sons did not walk in his ways, but turned aside after gain; they took bribes and perverted justice.

Then all the elders of Israel gathered together and came to Samuel at Ramah, and said to him, "Behold, you are old and your sons do not walk in your ways; now appoint us a king to govern us like all the nations." But the thing displeased Samuel when they said, "Give us a king to govern us." And Samuel prayed to the Lord. And the Lord said to Samuel, "Hearken to the voice of the people in all that they say to you; for they have not rejected you, but they have rejected me from being king over them. According to all the deeds which they have done to me, from the day I brought them up out of Egypt even to this day, forsaking me and serving other gods, so they are also doing to you. Now then, hearken to their voice; only, you shall solemnly warn them, and show them the ways of the king who shall reign over them."

So Samuel told all the words of the Lord to the people who were asking a king from him.

SAUL: SELECTION AS KING

1 Samuel 9:1–2, 15–27; 10:1–9

There was a man of Benjamin whose name was Kish, the son of Abiel, son of Zeror, son of Becorath, son of Aphiah, a Benjaminite, a man of wealth; and he had a son whose name was Saul, a handsome young man. There was not a man among the people of Israel more handsome than he; from his shoulders upward he was taller than any of the people.

Now the day before Saul came, the Lord had revealed to Samuel: "Tomorrow about this time I will send to you a man from the land of Benjamin, and you shall anoint him to be prince over my people Israel. He shall save my people from the hand of the Philistines; for I have seen the affliction of my people, because their cry has come to me." When Samuel saw Saul, the Lord told him, "Here is the man of whom I spoke to you! He it is who shall rule over my people." Then Saul approached Samuel in the gate, and said, "Tell me, where is the house of the seer?" Samuel answered Saul, "I am the seer; go up before me to the high place, for today you shall eat with me, and in the morning I will let you go and will tell you all that is on your mind. As for your asses that were lost three days ago, do not set your mind on them, for they have been found. And for whom is all that is desirable in Israel? Is it not for you and for all your father's house?" Samuel answered, "Am I not a Benjaminite, from the least of the tribes of Israel? And is not my family the humblest of all the families of the tribe of Benjamin? Why then have you spoken to me in this way?"

Then Samuel took Saul and his servant and brought them into the hall and gave them a place at the head of those who had been invited, who were about thirty persons. And Samuel said to the cook, "Bring the portion that I gave you, of which I said to you, 'Put it aside.'" So the cook took up the leg and the upper portion and set them before Saul; and Samuel said, "See, what is kept is set before you. Eat, because it was kept for you until the hour appointed, that you might eat with the guests."

So Saul ate with Samuel that day. And when they came down from the high place into the city, a bed was spread for Saul upon the roof, and he lay down to sleep. Then at the break of dawn Samuel called to Saul upon the roof, "Up, that I may send you on your way." So Saul arose, and both he and Samuel went out into the street.

As they were going down to the outskirts of the city, Samuel said to Saul, "Tell the servant to pass on before us, and when he has passed on stop here yourself for a while, that I may make known to you the word of God."

Then Samuel took a vial of oil and poured it on his head, and kissed him and said, "Has not the Lord anointed you to be prince over his people Israel? And you shall reign over the people of the Lord and you will save them from the hand of their enemies round about. And this shall be the sign to you that the Lord has anointed you to be prince over his heritage. When you depart from me this day, you shall meet two men by Rachel's tomb in the territory of Benjamin at Zelzah, and they will say to you, 'The asses which you went to seek are found, and now your father has ceased to care about the asses and is anxious about you, saying, "What shall I do about my son?"' Then you shall go on from there further and come to the oak of Tabor; three men going up to God at Bethel will meet you there, one carrying three kids, another carrying three loaves of bread, and another carrying a skin of wine. And they will greet you and give you two loaves of bread, which you shall accept from their hand. After that you shall come to Gibeathelohim, where there is a garrison of the Philistines; and there, as you come to the city, you will meet a band of prophets coming down from the high place with harp, tambourine, flute, and lyre before them, prophesying. Then the spirit of the Lord will come mightily upon you, and you shall prophesy with them and be turned into another man. Now when these signs meet you, do whatever your hand finds to do, for God is with you. And you shall go down before me to Gilgal; and behold, I am coming to you to offer burnt offerings and to sacrifice peace offerings. Seven days you shall wait, until I come to you and show you what you shall do."

When he turned his back to leave Samuel, God gave him another heart; and all these signs came to pass that day.

SAUL: HIS MILITARY PROWESS

1 Samuel 11:1–6, 11–15

Nahash the Ammonite went up and besieged Jabesh-gilead; and all the men of Jabesh said to Nahash, "Make a treaty with us, and we will serve you." But Nahash the Ammonite said to them, "On this condition I will make a treaty with you, that I gouge out all your right eyes, and thus put disgrace upon all Israel." The elders of Jabesh said to him, "Give us seven days respite that we may send messengers through all the territory of Israel. Then, if there is no one to save us, we will give ourselves up to you." When the messengers came to Gibeah of Saul, they reported the matter in the ears of the people; and all the people wept aloud.

Now Saul was coming from the field behind the oxen; and Saul said, "What ails the people, that they are weeping?" So they told him the tidings of the men of Jabesh. And the spirit of God came mightily upon Saul when he heard these words, and his anger was greatly kindled.

And on the morrow Saul put the people into three companies; and they came into the midst of the camp in the morning watch, and cut down the Ammonites until the heat of the day; and those who survived were scattered, so that no two of them were left together.

Then the people said to Samuel, "Who is it that said, 'Shall Saul reign over us?' Bring the men, that we may put them to death." But Saul said, "Not a man shall be put to death this day, for today the Lord has wrought deliverance in Israel." Then Samuel said to the people, "Come, let us go to Gilgal and there renew the kingdom." So all the people went to Gilgal, and there they made Saul king before the Lord in Gilgal. There they sacrificed peace offerings before the Lord, and there Saul and all the men of Israel rejoiced greatly.

SAUL: BREACH WITH SAMUEL

1 Samuel 13:5–15

And the Philistines mustered to fight with Israel, thirty thousand chariots, and six thousand horsemen, and troops like the sand of the seashore in multitude; they came up and encamped in Michmash, to the east of Beth-aven. When the men of Israel saw that they were in straits (for the people were hard pressed), the people hid themselves in caves and in holes and in rocks and in tombs and in cisterns, or crossed the fords of the Jordan, to the land of Gad and Gilead. Saul was still at Gilgal, and all the people followed him trembling.

He waited seven days, the time appointed by Samuel; but Samuel did not come to Gilgal, and the people were scattered from him. So Saul said, "Bring the burnt offering here to me, and the peace offerings." And he offered the burnt offering. As soon as he had finished offering the burnt offering, behold, Samuel came; and Saul went out to meet him and salute him. Samuel said, "What have you done?" And Saul said, "When I saw that the people were scattering from me, and that you did not come within the days appointed, and that the Philistines had mustered at

Michmash, I said, 'Now the Philistines will come down upon me at Gilgal, and I have not entreated the favor of the Lord'; so I forced myself, and offered the burnt offering.'' And Samuel said to Saul, "You have done foolishly; you have not kept the commandment of the Lord your God, which he commanded you; for now the Lord would have established your kingdom over Israel for ever. But now your kingdom shall not continue; the Lord has sought out a man after his own heart; and the Lord has appointed him to be prince over his people, because you have not kept what the Lord commanded you.'' And Samuel arose, and went up from Gilgal to Gibeah of Benjamin.

SAUL: HIS FINAL REJECTION

1 Samuel 15:7–31

Saul defeated the Amalekites, from Havilah as far as Shur, which is east of Egypt. And he took Agag the king of the Amalekites alive, and utterly destroyed all the people with the edge of the sword. But Saul and the people spared Agag, and the best of the sheep and of the oxen and of the fatlings, and the lambs, and all that was good, and would not utterly destroy them; all that was despised and worthless they utterly destroyed.

The word of the Lord came to Samuel: "I repent that I have made Saul king; for he has turned back from following me, and has not performed my commandments.'' And Samuel was angry; and he cried to the Lord all night. And Samuel rose early to meet Saul in the morning; and it was told Samuel, "Saul came to Carmel, and behold, he set up a monument for himself and turned, and passed on, and went down to Gilgal.'' And Samuel came to Saul, and Saul said to him, "Blessed be you to the Lord; I have performed the commandment of the Lord.'' And Samuel said, "What then is the bleating of the sheep in my ears, and the lowing of the oxen which I hear?'' Saul said, "They have brought them from the Amalekites; for the people spared the best of the sheep and of the oxen, to sacrifice to the Lord your God; and the rest we have utterly destroyed.'' Then Samuel said to Saul, "Stop! I will tell you what the Lord said to me this night.'' And he said to him. "Say on.''

And Samuel said, "Though you are little in your own eyes, are you not the head of the tribes of Israel? The Lord anointed you king over Israel. And the Lord sent you on a mission, and said, 'Go, utterly destroy the sinners, the Amalekites, and fight against them until they are consumed.' Why then did you not obey the voice of the Lord? Why did you swoop on the spoil, and do what was evil in the sight of the Lord?" And Saul said to Samuel, "I have obeyed the voice of the Lord, I have gone on the mission which the Lord sent me, I have brought Agag the king of Amalek, and I have utterly destroyed the Amalekites. But the people took the spoil, sheep and oxen, the best of the things devoted to destruction, to sacrifice to the Lord your God in Gilgal." And Samuel said,

> "Has the Lord as great delight in burnt offerings and sacrifices,
>> as in obeying the voice of the Lord?
> Behold, to obey is better than sacrifice,
>> and to hearken than the fat of rams.
> For rebellion is as the sin of divination,
>> and stubbornness is as iniquity and idolatry.
> Because you have rejected the word of the Lord,
>> he has rejected you from being king."

And Saul said to Samuel, "I have sinned; for I have transgressed the commandment of the Lord and your words, because I feared the people and obeyed their voice. Now therefore, I pray, pardon my sin, and return with me, that I may worship the Lord." And Samuel said to Saul, "I will not return with you; for you have rejected the word of the Lord, and the Lord has rejected you from being king over Israel." As Samuel turned to go away, Saul laid hold upon the skirt of his robe, and it tore. And Samuel said to him, "The Lord has torn the kingdom of Israel from you this day, and has given it to a neighbor of yours, who is better than you. And also the Glory of Israel will not lie or repent; for he is not a man, that he should repent." Then he said, "I have sinned; yet honor me now before the elders of my people and before Israel, and return with me, that I may worship the Lord your God." So Samuel turned back after Saul; and Saul worshipped the Lord.

DAVID: SELECTED AS THE NEW KING

1 Samuel 16:1–23

The Lord said to Samuel, "How long will you grieve over Saul, seeing I have rejected him from being king over Israel? Fill your horn with oil, and go; I will send you to Jesse the Bethlehemite, for I have provided for myself a king from among his sons." And Samuel said, "How can I go? If Saul hears it, he will kill me." And the Lord said, "Take a heifer with you, and say, 'I have come to sacrifice to the Lord.' And invite Jesse to the sacrifice, and I will show you what you shall do; and you shall anoint for me him whom I name for you." Samuel did what the Lord commanded, and came to Bethlehem. The elders of the city came to meet him trembling, and said, "Do you come peaceably?" And he said, "Peaceably; I have come to sacrifice to the Lord; consecrate yourselves, and come with me to the sacrifice." And he consecrated Jesse and his sons, and invited them to the sacrifice.

When they came, he looked on Eliab and thought, "Surely the Lord's anointed is before him." But the Lord said to Samuel, "Do not look upon his appearance or on the height of his stature, because I have rejected him; for the Lord sees not as man sees; man looks on the outward appearance, but the Lord looks on the heart." Then Jesse called Abinadab, and made him pass before Samuel. And he said, "Neither has the Lord chosen this one." Then Jesse made Shammah pass by. And he said, "Neither has the Lord chosen this one." And Jesse made seven of his sons pass before Samuel. And Samuel said to Jesse, "The Lord has not chosen these." And Samuel said to Jesse, "Are all your sons here?" And he said, "There remains yet the youngest, but, behold, he is keeping the sheep." And Samuel said to Jesse, "Send and fetch him; for we will not sit down till he comes here." And he sent and brought him in. Now he was ruddy, and had beautiful eyes, and was handsome. And the Lord said, "Arise, anoint him; for this is he." Then Samuel took the horn of oil, and anointed him in the midst of his brothers; and the Spirit of the Lord came mightily upon David from that day forward. And Samuel rose up, and went to Ramah.

Now the spirit of the Lord departed from Saul, and an evil spirit from the Lord tormented him. And Saul's servants said to him, "Behold now, an evil spirit from God is tormenting you. Let our Lord now command your servants, who are now before you, to seek out a man who is skillful in playing the lyre; and when the evil spirit from God is upon you, he will play it, and you will be well." So Saul said to his servants, "Provide for me a man who can play well, and bring him to me." One of the young men answered, "Behold, I have seen a son of Jesse the Bethlehemite, who is skillful in playing, a man of valor, a man of war, prudent in speech, and a man of good presence; and the Lord is with him." Therefore Saul sent messengers to Jesse, and said, "Send me David your son, who is with the sheep." And Jesse took an ass laden with bread, and a skin of wine and a kid, and sent them by David his son to Saul. And David came to Saul, and entered his service. And Saul loved him greatly, and he became his armor-bearer. And Saul sent to

Jesse, saying, "Let David remain in my service, for he has found favor in my sight." And whenever the evil spirit from God was upon Saul, David took the lyre and played it with his hand; so Saul was refreshed, and was well, and the evil spirit departed from him.

DAVID AND GOLIATH

1 Samuel 17:1–54

Now the Philistines gathered their armies for battle; and they were gathered at Socoh, which belongs to Judah, and encamped between Socoh and Azekah, in Ephes-dammim. And Saul and the men were gathered, and encamped in the valley of Elah, and drew up in line of battle against the Philistines. And the Philistines stood on the mountain on the one side, and Israel stood on the mountain on the other side, with a valley between them. And there came out from the camp of the Philistines a champion named Goliath, of Gath, whose height was six cubits and a span. He had a helmet of bronze on his head, and he was armed with a coat of mail, and the weight of the coat was five thousand shekels of bronze. And he had greaves of bronze upon his leg, and a javelin of bronze slung between his shoulders. And the shaft of the spear was like a weaver's beam, and the spear's head weighed six hundred shekels of iron; and his shield-bearer went before him. He stood and shouted to the ranks of Israel, "Why have you come out to draw up for battle? Am I not a Philistine, and are you not servants of Saul? Choose a man for yourselves, and let him come down to me. If he is able to fight with me and kill me, then we will be your servants; but if I prevail against him and kill him, then you shall be our servants and serve us." And the Philistine said, "I defy the ranks of Israel this day; give me a man, that we may fight together." When Saul and all Israel hear these words of the Philistine, they were dismayed and greatly afraid.

Now David was the son of an Ephrathite of Bethlehem in Judah, named Jesse, who had eight sons. In the days of Saul the man was already old and advanced in years. The three eldest sons of Jesse had followed Saul to the battle; and the names of his three sons who went to the battle were Eliab the first-born, and next to him Abinadab, and the third Shammah. David was the youngest; the three eldest followed Saul, but David went back and forth from Saul to feed his father's sheep at Bethlehem. For forty days the Philistine came forward and took his stand, morning and evening.

And Jesse said to David, his son, "Take for your brothers an ephah of this parched grain, and these ten loaves, and carry them quickly to the camp to your brothers; and take these ten cheeses to the commander of their thousand. See how your brothers fare, and bring some token from them."

Now Saul, and they, and all the men of Israel, were in the valley of Elah, fighting with the Philistines. And David rose early in the morning, and left the sheep with a keeper, and took the provisions, and went, as Jesse had commanded him; and he came to the encampment as the host was going forth to the battle line, shouting the war cry. And Israel and the Philistines drew up for battle, army against army. And David left the things in charge of the keeper of the baggage, and ran to the ranks, and went and greeted his brothers. As he talked with them, behold, the champion, the Philistine of Gath, Goliath by name, came up out of the ranks of the Philistines, and spoke the same words as before. And David heard him.

All the men of Israel, when they saw the man, fled from him, and were much afraid. And the men of Israel said, "Have you seen this man who has come up? Surely he has come up to defy Israel; and the man who kills him, the king will enrich with great riches, and he will give him his daughter, and make his father's house free in Israel." And David said to the men who stood by him, "What shall be done to the man who kills this Philistine, and takes away the reproach from Israel? For who is this uncircumcised Philistine, that should defy the armies of the living God?" And the people answered him in the same way, "So shall it be done to the man who kills him."

Now Eliab his eldest brother heard when he spoke to the men; and Eliab's anger was kindled against David, and he said, "Why have you come down? With whom have you left those few sheep in the wilderness? I know your presumption, and the evil of your heart; for you have come down to see the battle." And David said, "What have I done now? Was it not but a word?" And he turned away from him toward another, and spoke in the same way; and the people answered him again as before.

When the words which David spoke were heard, they repeated them before Saul; and he sent for him. And David said to Saul, "Let no man's heart fail because of him; your servant will go and fight with this Philistine." And Saul said to David, "You are not able to go against this Philistine to fight with him; for you are but a youth, and he has been a man of war from his youth." But David said to Saul, "Your servant used to keep sheep for his father; and when there came a lion, or a bear, and took a lamb from the flock, I went after him and smote him and delivered it out of his mouth;

and if he rose against me, I caught him by his beard and smote him and killed him. Your servant has killed both lions and bears; and this uncircumcised Philistine shall be like one of them, seeing he has defied the armies of the living God." And David said, "The Lord who delivered me from the paw of the lion and from the paw of the bear, will deliver me from the hand of this Philistine." And Saul said to David, "Go, and the Lord be with you!" Then Saul clothed David with his armor; he put a helmet of bronze on his head, and clothed him with a coat of mail. And David girded his sword over his armor, and he tried in vain to go, for he was not used to them. Then David said to Saul, "I cannot go with these; for I am not used to them." And David put them off. Then he took his staff in his hand, and chose five smooth stones from the brook, and put them in his shepherd's bag or wallet; his sling was in his hand, and he drew near to the Philistine.

And the Philistine came on and drew near to David, with his shield-bearer in front of him. And when the Philistine looked, and saw David, he disdained him; for he was but a youth, ruddy and comely in appearance. And the Philistine said to David, "Am I a dog, that you come to me with sticks?" And the Philistine cursed David by his gods. The Philistine said to David, "Come to me, and I will give your flesh to the birds of the air and to the beasts of the field." Then David said to the Philstine, "You come to me with a sword and with a spear and with a javelin; but I come to you in the name of the Lord of hosts, the God of the armies of Israel, whom you have defied. This day the Lord will deliver you into my hand, and I will strike you down, and cut off your head; and I will give the dead bodies of the host of the Philistines this day to the birds of the air and to the wild beasts of the earth; and all the earth shall know that there is a God in Israel, and that all this assembly may know that the Lord saves not with the sword and spear; for the battle is the Lord's and he will give you into our hand."

When the Philistine arose and came and drew near to meet David, David ran quickly toward the battle line to meet the Philistine. And David put his hand in his bag and took out a stone, and slung it, and struck the Philistine on his forehead; the stone sank into his forehead, and he fell on his face to the ground.

So David prevailed over the Philistine with a sling and with a stone, and struck the Philistine and killed him; there was no sword in the hand of David. Then David ran and stood over the Philistine, and took his sword and drew it out of its sheath, and killed him, and cut off his head with it. When the Philistines saw that their champion was dead, they fled. And the men of Israel and Judah rose with a shout, and pursued the Philistines as far as Gath and the gates of Ekron, so that the wounded Philistines fell on the way from Sha-araim as far as Gath and Ekron. And the Israelites came back from chasing the Philistines, and they plundered their camp. And David took the head of the Philistine and brought it to Jerusalem; but he put his armor in his tent.

DAVID: SAUL ATTEMPTS TO KILL DAVID

1 Samuel 19:1–10

And Saul spoke to Jonathan his son and to all his servants, that they should kill David. But Jonathan, Saul's son, delighted much in David. And Jonathan told David, "Saul my father seeks to kill you; therefore take heed to yourself in the morning, stay in a secret place and hide yourself; and I will go out and stand beside my father in the field where you are, and I will speak to my father about you; and if I learn anything I will tell you." And Jonathan spoke well of David to Saul his father, and said to him, "Let not the king sin against his servant David; because he has not sinned against you, and because his deeds have been of good service to you; for he took his life in his hand and slew the Philistine, and the Lord wrought a great victory for all Israel. You saw it, and rejoiced; why then will you sin against innocent blood by killing David without cause?" And Saul hearkened to the voice of Jonathan; Saul swore, "As the Lord lives, he shall not be put to death." And Jonathan called David, and Jonathan showed him all these things. And Jonathan brought David to Saul, and he was in his presence as before.

And there was war again; and David went out and fought with the Philistines, and made a great slaughter among them, so that they fled before him. Then an evil spirit from the Lord came upon Saul, as he sat in his house with his spear in his hand; and David was playing the lyre. And Saul sought to pin David to the wall with the spear; but he eluded Saul, so that he struck the spear into the wall. And David fled, and escaped.

DAVID: SHOWS MERCY UPON SAUL

1 Samuel 24:1–22

When Saul returned from following the Philistines, he was told, "Behold, David is in the wilderness of Engedi." Then Saul took three thousand chosen men out of all Israel, and went to seek

David and his men in front of the Wildgoats' Rocks. And he came to the sheepfolds by the way, where there was a cave; and Saul went in to relieve himself. Now David and his men were sitting in the innermost parts of the cave. And the men of David said to him, "Here is the day of which the Lord said to you, 'Behold, I will give your enemy into your hand, and you shall do to him as it shall seem good to you.'" Then David arose and stealthily cut off the skirt of Saul's robe. And afterward David's heart smote him, because he had cut off Saul's skirt. He said to his men, "The Lord forbid that I should do this thing to my lord, the Lord's anointed, to put forth my hand against him, seeing he is the Lord's anointed." So David persuaded his men with these words, and did not permit them to attack Saul. And Saul rose up and left the cave, and went upon his way.

Afterward David also arose, and went out of the cave, and called after Saul, "My lord the king!" And when Saul looked behind him, David bowed with his face to the earth, and did obeisance. And David said to Saul, "Why do you listen to the words of men who say, 'Behold, David seeks your hurt'? Lo, this day your eyes have seen how the Lord gave you today into my hand in the cave, and some bade me kill you, but I spared you. I said, 'I will not put forth my hand against my lord; for he is the Lord's anointed.' See, my father, see the skirt of your robe in my hand; for by the fact that I cut off the skirt of your robe, and did not kill you, you may know and see that there is no wrong or treason in my hands. I have not sinned against you, though you hunt my life to take it. May the Lord judge between me and you, may the Lord avenge me upon you; but my hand shall not be against you. As the proverb of the ancients says, 'Out of the wicked comes forth wickedness'; but my hand shall not be against you. After whom has the king of Israel come out? After whom do you pursue? After a dead dog! After a flea! May the Lord therefore be judge, and give sentence between me and you, and see to it, and plead my cause, and deliver me from your hand."

When David had finished speaking these words to Saul, Saul said, "Is this your voice, my son David?" And Saul lifted up his voice and wept. He said to David, "You are more righteous than I; for you have repaid me good, whereas I have repaid you evil. And you have declared this day how you have dealt well with me, in that you did not kill me when the Lord put me into your hands. For if a man finds his enemy, will he let him go away safe? So may the Lord reward you with good for what you have done for me this day. And now, behold, I know that you shall surely be king, and that the kingdom of Israel shall be established in your hand. Swear to me therefore by the Lord that you will not cut off my descendants after me, and that you will not destroy my name out of my father's house." And David swore this to Saul. Then Saul went home; but David and his men went up to the stronghold.

DAVID: SAUL ACKNOWLEDGES DAVID'S INNOCENCE

1 Samuel 26:1–25

Then the Ziphites came to Saul at Gibeah, saying, "Is not David in the wilderness of Ziph. And Saul encamped on the east of Jeshimon?" So Saul arose and went down to the wilderness of Ziph, with three thousand chosen men of Israel, to seek David in the wilderness of Ziph. And Saul encamped on the hill of Hachilah, which is beside the road on the east of Jeshimon. But David remained in the wilderness; and when he saw that Saul came after him into the wilderness, David sent out spies, and learned of a certainty that Saul had come. Then David arose and came to the place where Saul had encamped; and David saw the place where Saul lay, with Abner the son of Ner, the commander of his army; Saul was lying within the encampment, while the army was encamped around him.

Then David said to Ahimelech the Hittite, and to Joab's brother Abishai the son of Zeruiah, "Who will go down with me into the camp of Saul?" And Abishai said, "I will go down with you." So David and Abishai went to the army by night; and there lay Saul sleeping within the encampment, with his spear stuck in the ground at his head; and Abner and the army lay around him. Then said Abishai to David, "God has given your enemy into your hand this day; now therefore let me pin him to the earth with one stroke of the spear, and I will not strike him twice." But David said to Abishai, "Do not destroy him; for who can put forth his hand against the Lord's anointed, and be guiltless?" And David said, "As the Lord lives, the Lord will smite him; or his day shall come to die; or he shall go down into battle and perish. The Lord forbid that I should put forth my hand against the Lord's anointed; but take now the spear that is at his head, and the jar of water, and let us go." So David took the spear and the jar of water from Saul's head; and they went away. No man saw it, or knew it, nor did any awake; for they were all asleep, because a deep sleep from the Lord had fallen upon them.

Then David went over to the other side, and stood afar off

on the top of the mountain, with a great space between them; and David called to the army, and to Abner the son of Ner, saying, "Will you not answer, Abner?" Then Abner answered, "Who are you who calls to the king?" And David said to Abner, "Are you not a man? Who is like you in Israel? Why then have you not kept watch over the lord your king? For one of the people came in to destroy the king your lord. This thing that you have done is not good. As the Lord lives, you deserve to die, because you have not kept watch over your lord, the Lord's anointed. And now see where the king's spear is, and the jar of water that was at his head."

Saul recognized David's voice, and said, "Is this your voice, my son David?" And David said, "It is my voice, my lord, O king." And he said, "Why does my lord pursue his servant? For what have I done? What guilt is on my hands? Now therefore let my lord the king hear the words of his servant. If it is the Lord who has stirred you up against me, may he accept an offering; but if it is men, may they be cursed before the Lord, for they have driven me out this day that I should have no share in the heritage of the Lord, saying, 'Go, serve other gods.' Now therefore, let not my blood fall to the earth away from the presence of the Lord; for the king of Israel has come out to seek my life, like one who hunts a partridge in the mountains."

Then Saul said, "I have done wrong; return, my son David, for I will no more do you harm, because my life was precious in your eyes this day; behold, I have played the fool and have erred exceedingly." And David made answer, "Here is the spear, O king! Let one of the young men come over and fetch it. The Lord rewards every man for his righteousness and his faithfulness; for the Lord gave you into my hand today, and I would not put forth my hand against the Lord's anointed. Behold, as your life was precious this day in my sight, so may my life be precious in the sight of the Lord, and may he deliver me out of all tribulation." Then Saul said to David, "Blessed be you, my son David! You will do many things and you will succeed in them." So David went his way, and Saul returned to his place.

DAVID: DEATH OF SAUL

1 Samuel 31:1–5

Now the Philistines fought against Israel; and the men of Israel fled before the Philistines, and fell slain on Mount Gilboa. And the Philistines overtook Saul and his sons; and the Philistines slew Jonathan and Abinadab and Malchishua, the sons of Saul. The battle pressed hard upon Saul, and the archers found him; and he was badly wounded by the archers. Then Saul said to his armor-bearer, "Draw your sword, and thrust me through with it, lest these uncircumcised come and thrust me through, and make sport of me." But his armor-bearer would not; for he feared greatly. Therefore Saul took his own sword, and fell upon it. And when his armor-bearer saw that Saul was dead, he also fell on his own sword, and died with him.

DAVID: LAMENT OVER SAUL

2 Samuel 1:17–27

And David lamented with this lamentation over Saul and Jonathan his son, and he said it should be taught to the people of Judah; behold, it is written in the Book of Jashar. He said:

> "Thy glory, O Israel, is slain upon thy high places!
> How are the mighty fallen!
> Tell it not in Gath,
> publish it not in the streets of Ashkelon;
> lest the daughters of the Philistines rejoice,
> lest the daughters of the uncircumcised exult.

> "Ye mountains of Gilboa,
> let there be no dew or rain upon you,
> nor upsurging of the deep!
> For there the shield of the mighty was defiled,
> the shield of Saul, not anointed with oil.

> "From the blood of the slain,
> from the fat of the mighty,
> the bow of Jonathan turned not back,
> and the sword of Saul returned not empty.

> "Saul and Jonathan, beloved and lovely!
> In life and in death they were not divided;
> they were swifter than eagles,
> they were stronger than lions.

> "Ye daughters of Israel, weep over Saul,
> who clothed you daintily in scarlet,
> who put ornaments of gold upon your apparel.

"How are the mighty fallen
in the midst of the battle!

"Jonathan lies slain upon thy high places.
I am distressed for you, my brother Jonathan;
very pleasant have you been to me;
your love to me was wonderful,
passing the love of women.

"How are the mighty fallen,
and the weapons of war perished!"

DAVID: THE GREAT SIN

2 Samuel 11:1–27; 12:1–15

In the spring of the year, the time when kings go forth to battle, David sent Joab, and his servants with him, and all Israel; and they ravaged the Ammonites, and besieged Rabbah. But David remained at Jerusalem.

It happened, late one afternoon, when David arose from his couch and was walking upon the roof of the king's house, that he saw from the roof a woman bathing; and the woman was very beautiful. And David sent and inquired about the woman. And one said, "Is not this Bathsheba, the daughter of Eliam, the wife of Uriah the Hittite?" So David sent messengers and took her, and she came to him, and he lay with her. (Now she was purifying herself from her uncleanness.) Then she returned to her house. And the woman conceived; and she sent and told David, "I am with child."

So David sent word to Joab, "Send me Uriah the Hittite." And Joab sent Uriah to David. When Uriah came to him, David asked how Joab was doing, and how the people fared, and how the war prospered. Then David said to Uriah, "Go down to your house, and wash your feet." And Uriah went out of the king's house, and there followed him a present from the king. But Uriah slept at the door of the king's house with all the servants of his lord, and did not go down to his house. When they told David, "Uriah did not go down to his house," David said to Uriah, "Have you not come from a journey? Why did you not go down to your house?" Uriah said to David, "The ark and Israel and Judah dwell in booths; and my lord Joab and the servants of my lord are camping in the open field; shall I then go to my house, to eat and to drink, and to lie with my wife?

As you live, and as your soul lives, I will not do this thing." Then David said to Uriah, "Remain here today also, and tomorrow I will let you depart." So Uriah remained in Jerusalem that day, and the next. And David invited him, and he ate in his presence and drank, so that he made him drunk; and in the evening he went out to lie on his couch with the servants of his lord, but he did not go down to his house.

In the morning David wrote a letter to Joab, and sent it by the hand of Uriah. In the letter he wrote, "Set Uriah in the forefront of the hardest fighting, and then draw back from him, that he might be struck down, and die." And as Joab was besieging the city, he assigned Uriah to the place where he knew there were valiant men. And the men of the city came out and fought with Joab; and some of the servants of David among the people fell. Uriah the Hittite was slain also. Then Joab sent and told David all the news about the fighting; and he instructed the messenger, "When you have finished telling all the news about the fighting to the king, then, if the king's anger rises, and if he says to you, 'Why did you go so near the city to fight? Did you not know that they would shoot from the wall? Who killed Abimelech the son of Jerubbesheth? Did not a woman cast an upper millstone upon him from the wall, so that he died at Thebez? Why did you go so near the wall?' then you shall say, 'Your servant Uriah the Hittite is dead also.' "

So the messenger went, and came and told David all that Joab had sent him to tell. The messenger said to David, "The men gained an advantage over us, and came out against us in the field; but we drove them back to the entrance of the gate. Then archers shot at your servants from the wall; some of the king's servants are dead; and your servant Uriah the Hittite is dead also." David said to the messenger, "Thus shall you say to Joab, 'Do not let this matter trouble you, for the sword devours now one and now another; strengthen your attack upon the city, and overthrow it.' And encourage him."

When the wife of Uriah heard that Uriah her husband was dead, she made lamentation for her husband. And when the morning was over, David sent and brought her to his house, and she became his wife, and bore him a son. But the thing that David had done displeased the Lord.

And the Lord sent Nathan to David. He came to him, and said to him, "There were two men in a certain city, the one rich and the other poor. The rich man had many flocks and herds; but the poor man had nothing but one little ewe lamb, which he had bought. And he brought it up, and it grew up with him and his children; it used to eat of his morsel, and drink from his cup, and lie in his bosom, and it was like a daughter to him. Now there came a traveler to the rich man, and he was unwilling to take one of his own flock or herd to prepare for the wayfarer who had come to him, but he took the poor man's lamb, and prepared it for the man who had come to him." Then David's anger was greatly kindled against the man; and he said to Nathan, "As the Lord lives, the man who has done this deserves to die; and he shall restore the lamb fourfold, because he did this thing, and because he had no pity."

Nathan said to David, "You are the man. Thus says the Lord, the God of Israel, 'I anointed you king over Israel, and I delivered you out of the hand of Saul; and I gave you your master's house, and your master's wives into your bosom, and gave you the house of Israel and of Judah; and if this were too little, I would add to you as much more. Why have you despised the word of the Lord, to do what is evil in his sight? You have smitten Uriah the Hittite with the sword, and have taken his wife to be your wife, and have slain him with the sword of the Ammorites. Now therefore the sword shall never depart from your house, because you have despised me, and have taken the wife of Uriah the Hittite to be your wife.' Thus says the Lord, 'Behold, I will raise up evil against you out of your own house; and I will take your wives before your eyes, and give them to your neighbor, and he shall lie with your wives in the sight of this sun. For you did it secretly; but I will do this thing before all Israel, and before the sun.'" David said to Nathan, "I have sinned against the Lord." And Nathan said to David, "The Lord also has put away your sin; you shall not die. Nevertheless, because by this deed you have utterly scorned the Lord, the child that is born to you shall die." Then Nathan went to his house.

ABSALOM AVENGES HIS FATHER'S HONOR

2 Samuel 13:1–17, 19–39

Now Absalom, David's son, had a beautiful sister, whose name was Tamar; and after a time Amnon, David's son loved her. And Amnon was so tormented that he made himself ill because of his sister Tamar; for she was a virgin, and it seemed impossible to Amnon to do anything to her. But Amnon had a friend, whose name was Jonadab, the son of Shime-ah, David's brother; and Jonadab was a very crafty man. And he said to him, "O son of the king, why are you so haggard morning after morning? Will you not tell me?" Amnon said to him, "I love Tamar, my brother Absalom's sister." Jonadab said to him, "Lie down on your bed, and pretend to be ill; and when your father comes to see you, say to him, 'Let my sister Tamar come and give me bread to eat, and prepare the food in my sight, that I may see it, and eat it from her hand.' " So Amnon lay down, and pretended to be ill; and when the king came to see him, Amnon said to the king, "Pray let my sister Tamar come and make a couple of cakes in my sight, that I may eat from her hand."

Then David sent home to Tamar, saying, "Go to your brother Amnon's house, and prepare food for him." So Tamar went to her brother Amnon's house, where he was lying down. And she took dough, and kneaded it, and made cakes in his sight, and baked the cakes. And she took the pan and emptied it out before him, but he refused to eat. And Amnon said, "Send out everyone from me." So everyone went out from him. Then Amnon said to Tamar, "Bring the food into the chamber, that I may eat from your hand." And Tamar took the cakes she had made, and brought them into the chamber to Amnon her brother. But when she brought them near him to eat, he took hold of her, and said to her, "Come, lie with me, my sister." She answered him, "No, my brother, do not force me; for such a thing is not done in Israel; do not do this wanton folly. As for me, where could I carry my shame? And as for you, you would be as one of the wanton fools in Israel. Now therefore, I pray you, speak to the king; for he will not withhold me from you." But he would not listen to her; and being stronger than she, he forced her, and lay with her.

Then Amnon hated her with very great hatred; so that the hatred with which he hated her was greater than the love with which he loved her. And Amnon said to her, "Arise, be gone." But she said to him, "No, my brother; for this wrong in sending me away is greater than the other that you did to me." But he would not listen to her. He called the young man who served him and said, "Put this woman out of my presence, and bolt the door after her." And Tamar put ashes on her head, and rent the long robe which she wore; and she laid her hand on her head, and went away, crying aloud as she went.

And her brother Absalom said to her, "Has Amnon your brother been with you? Now hold your peace, my sister; he is your brother; do not take this to heart." So Tamar dwelt, a desolate woman, in her brother Absalom's house. When king David heard of all these things, he was very angry. But Absalom spoke to Amnon neither good or bad; for Absalom hated Amnon, because he had forced his sister Tamar.

After two full years, Absalom had sheepshearers at Baal-hazor, which is near Ephraim, and Absalom invited all the king's sons. And Absalom came to the king, and said, "Behold, your servant has sheepshearers; pray let the king and his servants go with your servant." But the king said to Absalom, "No, my son, let us not all go, lest we be burdensome to you." He pressed him, but he would not go but gave him his blessing. Then Absalom said, "If not, pray let my brother Amnon go with us." And the king said to him, "Why should he go with you?" But Absalom pressed him until he let Amnon and all the king's sons go with him. Then Absalom commanded his servants, "Mark when Amnon's heart is merry with wine, and when I say to you, 'Strike Amnon,' then kill him. Fear not; have I not commanded you? Be courageous and be valiant." So the servants of Absalom did to Amnon as Absalom had commanded. Then all the king's sons arose, and each mounted his mule and fled.

While they were on the way, tidings came to David, "Absalom has slain all the king's sons, and not one of them is left." Then the king arose, and rent his garments and lay on the earth; and all his servants who were standing by rent their garments. But Jonadab the son of Shime-ah, David's brother, said, "Let not my lord suppose that they have killed all the young men the king's sons, for Amnon alone is dead, for by the command of Absalom this has been determined from the day he forced his sister Tamar. Now therefore let not my lord the king so take it to heart as to suppose that all the king's sons are dead; for Amnon alone is dead."

But Absalom fled. And the young man who kept the watch lifted up his eyes, and looked, and behold, many people were coming from the Horonaim road by the side of the mountain. And Jonadab said to the king, "Behold, the king's sons have come; as your servant said, it has come about." And as soon as he had finished speaking, behold, the king's sons came, and lifted up their voice and wept; and the king also and all his servants wept very bitterly.

But Absalom fled, and went to Talmai the son of Ammihud, king of Geshur. And David mourned for his son day after day. So Absalom fled, and went to Geshur, and was there three years. And the spirit of the king longed to go forth to Absalom; for he was comforted about Amnon, seeing he was dead.

ABSALOM: DAVID AND ABSALOM REUNITED

2 Samuel 14:28–33

So Absalom dwelt two full years in Jerusalem, without coming into the king's presence. Then Absalom sent for Joab, to send him to the king; but Joab would not come to him. And he sent a second time, but Joab would not come. Then he said to his servants, "See, Joab's field is next to mine, and he has barley there; go and set it on fire." So Absalom's servants set the field on fire. Then Joab arose and went to Absalom at his house and said to him, "Why have your servants set my field on fire?" Absalom answered Joab, "Behold, I sent word to you, 'Come here, that I may send you to the king to ask, "Why have I come from Geshur? It would be better for me to be there still." Now therefore let me go into the presence of the king; and if there is guilt in me, let him kill me.' " Then Joab went to the king, and told him; and he summoned Absalom. So he came to the king, and bowed himself on his face to the ground before the king; and the king kissed Absalom.

ABSALOM REBELS

2 Samuel 15:7–18; 16:15–22

At the end of four years Absalom said to the king, "Pray let me go and pay my vow, which I have vowed to the Lord, in Hebron. For your servant vowed a vow while he dwelt at Geshur in Aram, saying, 'If the Lord will indeed bring me back to Jerusalem, then I will offer worship to the Lord.' " The king said to him, "Go in peace." So he arose, and went to Hebron. But Absalom sent secret messengers throughout all the tribes of Israel, saying, "As soon as you hear the sound of the trumpet, then say, "Absalom is king at Hebron!" With Absalom went two hundred men from Jerusalem who were invited guests, and they went in their simplicity, and knew nothing. And while Absalom was offering the sacrifices, he sent for Ahithophel the Gilonite, David's counselor, from his city Giloh. And the conspiracy grew strong, and the people with Absalom kept increasing.

And a messenger came to David, saying, "The hearts of the men of Israel have gone after Absalom." Then David said to all his servants who were with him at Jerusalem, "Arise, and let us flee; or else there will be no escape for us from Absalom; go in haste, lest he overtake us quickly, and bring down evil upon us, and smite the city with the edge of the sword." And the king's servants said to the king, "Behold, your servants are ready to do whatever my lord the king decides." So the king went forth, and all his household after him. And the king left ten concubines to keep the house. And the king went forth, and all the people after him; and they halted at the last house. And all his servants passed by him; and all the Cherethites, and all the Pelethites, and all the six hundred Gittites who had followed him from Gath, passed on before the king.

Now Absalom and all the people, the men of Israel, came to Jerusalem, and Ahithophel with him. And when Hushai the Archite, David's friend, came to Absalom, Hushai said to Absalom, "Long live the king! Long live the king!" And Absalom said to Hushai, "Is this your loyalty to your friend? Why did you not go with your friend?" And Hushai said to Absalom, "No; for whom the Lord and this people and all the men of Israel have chosen, his I will be, and with him I will remain. And again, whom shall I serve? Should it not be his son? As I have served your father, so I will serve you."

Then Absalom said to Ahithophel, "Give your counsel; what shall we do?" Ahithophel said to Absalom, "Go in to your father's concubines, whom he has left to keep the house; and all Israel will hear that you have made yourself odious to your father, and the hands of all who are with you will be strengthened." So they pitched a tent for Absalom upon the roof; and Absalom went in to his father's concubines in the sight of all Israel.

ABSALOM: DAVID AND ABSALOM MEET IN BATTLE

2 Samuel 18:1–17, 24–33

Then David mustered the men who were with him, and set over them commanders of thousands and commanders of hundreds. And David sent forth the army, one third under the command of Joab, one third under the command of Abishai the son of Zeruiah, Joab's brother, and one third under the command of Ittai the Gittite. And the king said to the men, "I myself will also go out with you." But the men said, "You shall not go out. For if we flee, they will not care about us. If half of us die, they will not care about us. But you are worth ten thousand of us; therefore, it is better that you send us help from the city." The king said to them, "Whatever seems best to you I will do." So the king stood at the side of the gate, while all the army marched out by hundreds and by thousands. And the king ordered Joab and Abishai and Ittai, "Deal gently for my sake with the young man Absalom." And all the people heard when the king gave orders to the commanders about Absalom.

So the army went out into the field against Israel; and the battle was fought in the forest of Ephraim. And the men of Israel were defeated there by the servants of David, and the slaughter there was great on that day, twenty thousand men. The battle spread over the face of all the country; and the forest devoured more people that day than the sword.

And Absalom chanced to meet the servants of David. Absalom was riding upon his mule, and the mule went under the thick branches of a great oak, and his head caught fast in the oak, and he was left hanging between heaven and earth, while the mule that was under him went on. And a certain man saw it, and told Joab, "Behold, I saw Absalom hanging in an oak." Joab said to the man who told him, "What, you saw him! Why then did you not strike him there to the ground? I would have been glad to give you ten pieces of silver and a girdle." But the man said to Joab, "Even if I felt in my hand the weight of a thousand pieces of silver, I would not put forth my hand against the king's son; for in all our hearing the king commanded you and Abishai and Ittai, 'For my sake protect the young man Absalom." On the other hand, if I had dealt treacherously against his life (and there is nothing hidden from the king), then you yourself would have stood aloof." Joab said, "I will not waste time like this with you." And he took three darts in his hand, and thrust them into the heart of Absalom, while he was still alive in the oak. And ten young men, Joab's armor-bearers, surrounded Absalom and struck him, and killed him.

Then Joab blew the trumpet, and the troops came back from pursuing Israel; for Joab restrained them. And they took Absalom, and threw him into a great pit in the forest, and raised over him a great heap of stones; and all Israel fled every one to his own home.

Now David was sitting between the two gates; and the watchman went up to the roof of the gate by the wall, and when he lifted up his eyes and looked, he saw a man running alone. And the watchman called out and told the king. And the king said, "If he is alone, there are tidings in his mouth." And he came apace, and drew near. And the watchman saw another man running; and the watchman called to the gate and said, "See, another man running alone!" The king said, "He also brings tidings." And the watchman said, "I think the running of the foremost is like the running of Ahima-az the son of Zadok."

And the king said, "He is a good man, and comes with good tidings."

Then Ahima-az cried out to the king, "All is well." And he bowed before the king with his face to the earth, and said, "Blessed be the Lord your God, who has delivered up the men who raised their hand against the lord the king." And the king said, "Is it well with the young man Absalom?" Ahima-az answered, "When Joab sent your servant, I saw a great tumult, but I do not know what it was." And the king said, "Turn aside, and stand here." So he turned aside, and stood still.

And behold, the Cushite came; and the Cushite said, "Good tidings for my lord the king! For the Lord has delivered you this day from the power of all who rose up against you." The king said to the Cushite, "Is it well with the young man Absalom?" And the Cushite answered, "May the enemies of my lord the king, and all who rise up against you for evil, be like that young man." And the king was deeply moved, and went up to the chamber over the gate, and wept; and as he went, he said, "O my son Absalom, my son, my son Absalom! Would I had died instead of you, O Absalom, my son, my son!"

ABSALOM: DAVID'S PSALM OF THANKSGIVING

2 Samuel 22:1–31

And David spoke to the Lord the words of this song on the day when the Lord delivered him from the hand of all his enemies, and from the hand of Saul. He said:

> "The Lord is my rock, and my fortress, and my deliverer,
>   my God, my rock, in whom I take refuge,
> my shield and the horn of my salvation,
>   my stronghold and my refuge,
>   my savior; thou savest me from violence.
> I call upon the Lord, who is worthy to be praised,
>   and I am saved from my enemies.
>
> "For the waves of death encompassed me,
>   the torrents of perdition assailed me;
> The cords of Sheol entangled me,
>   the snares of death confronted me.
>
> "In my distress I called upon the Lord;
>   to my God I called.

From his temple he heard my voice,
    and my cry came to his ears.

"Then the earth reeled and rocked;
    the foundations of the heavens trembled
    and quaked, because he was angry.
Smoke went up from his nostrils,
    and devouring fire from his mouth;
    glowing coals flamed forth from him.
He bowed the heavens, and came down;
    thick darkness was under his feet.
He rode on a cherub, and flew;
    he was seen upon the wings of the wind.
He made darkness around him
    his canopy, thick clouds, a gathering of water.
Out of the brightness before him
    coals of fire flamed forth.
The Lord thundered from heaven
    and the Most High uttered his voice.
And he sent out arrows, and scattered them;
    lightning, and routed them.
Then the channels of the sea were seen,
    the foundations of the world were laid bare,
at the rebuke of the Lord,
    at the blast of the breath of his nostrils.

"He reached from on high, he took me,
    he drew me out of many waters.
He delivered me from my strong enemy,
    from those who hated me;
    for they were too mighty for me.
They came upon me in the day of my calamity;
    but the Lord was my stay.
He brought me forth into a broad place;
    he delivered me, because he delighted in me.

"The Lord rewarded me according to my righteousness;
    according to the cleanness of my hands he recompensed me.
For I have kept the ways of the Lord,
    and have not wickedly departed from my God.
For all his ordinances were before me,
    and from his statutes I did not turn aside.
I was blameless before him,
    and I kept myself from guilt.

Therefore the Lord has recompensed me according to my
    righteousness,
according to my cleanness in his sight.

"With the loyal thou dost show thyself loyal;
    with the blameless man thou dost show thyself blameless;
with the pure thou dost show thyself pure,
    and with the crooked thou dost show thyself perverse.
Thou dost deliver a humble people,
    but thy eyes are upon the haughty to bring them down.
Yea, thou art my lamp, O Lord,
    and my God lightens my darkness.
Yea, by thee I can crush a troop,
    and by my God I can leap over a wall.
This God—his way is perfect;
    the promise of the Lord proves true;
he is a shield for all those who take refuge in him."

SOLOMON: HIS BIRTH

2 Samuel 12:24–25

Then David comforted his wife, Bathsheba, and went in to her,
and lay with her; and she bore a son, and he called his name
Solomon. And the Lord loved him, and sent a messenger by
Nathan the prophet; so he called his name Jedidiah, because
of the Lord.

SOLOMON: DAVID'S CHARGE TO SOLOMON

1 Kings 2:1–12

When David's time to die drew near, he charged Solomon
his son, saying, "I am about to go the way of all the earth. Be
strong, and show yourself a man, and keep the charge of the
Lord your God, walking in his ways and keeping his statutes, his
commandments, his ordinances, and his testimonies, as it is
written in the law of Moses, that you may prosper in all that
you do and wherever you turn; that the Lord may establish
his word which he spoke concerning me, saying, 'If your sons take
heed to their way, to walk before me in faithfulness with all their
heart and with all their soul, there shall not fail you a man on the
throne of Israel.'

"Moreover you know also what Joab the son of Zeruiah did to
me, how he dealt with the two commanders of the armies of

Israel, Abner the son of Ner, and Amasa the son of Jether, whom he murdered, avenging in time of peace blood which had been shed in war, and putting innocent blood upon the girdle about my loins, and upon the sandals of my feet. Act therefore according to your wisdom, but do not let his gray head go down to Sheol in peace. But deal loyally with the sons of Barzillai the Gileadite, and let them be among those who eat at your table; for with such loyalty they met me when I fled from Absalom your brother. And there is also with you Shime-i the son of Gera, the Benjaminite from Bahurim, who cursed me with a grievous curse on the day when I went to Mahanaim; but when he came down to meet me at the Jordan, I swore to him by the Lord, saying, 'I will not put you to death with the sword.' Now therefore hold him not guiltless, for you are a wise man; you will know what you ought to do to him, and you shall bring his gray head down with blood to Sheol."

Then David slept with his fathers, and was buried in the city of David. And the time that David reigned over Israel was forty years; he reigned seven years in Hebron, and thirty-three years in Jerusalem. So Solomon sat upon the throne of David his father; and his kingdom was firmly established.

SOLOMON ASKS GOD FOR WISDOM

1 Kings 3:5–15

At Gibeon the Lord appeared to Solomon in a dream by night; and God said, "Ask what I shall give you." And Solomon said, "Thou hast shown great and steadfast love to thy servant David my father, because he walked before thee in faithfulness, in righteousness, and in uprightness of heart toward thee; and thou hast kept for him this great and steadfast love, and hast given him a son to sit on his throne this day. And now, O Lord my God, thou hast made thy servant king in place of David my father, although I am but a little child; I do not know how to go out or come in. And thy servant is in the midst of thy people whom thou hast chosen, a great people, that cannot be numbered or counted for multitude. Give thy servant therefore an understanding mind to govern thy people, that I may discern between good and evil; for who is able to govern this thy great people?"

It pleased the Lord that Solomon had asked this. And God said to him, "Because you have asked this, and have not asked for yourself long life or riches or the life of your enemies, but have asked for yourself understanding to discern what is right, behold, I now do according to your word. Behold, I give you a wise and discerning mind, so that none like you has been before you and none like you shall rise after you. I give you also what you have not asked, both riches and honor, so that no other king shall compare with you, all your days. And if you will walk in my ways, keeping my statutes and my commandments, as your father David walked, then I will lengthen your days.

And Solomon awoke, and behold, it was a dream. Then he came to Jerusalem, and stood before the ark of the covenant of the Lord, and offered up burnt offerings and peace offerings, and made a feast for all his servants.

SOLOMON: HIS WISDOM DISPLAYED—JUDGMENT OF TWO HARLOTS

1 Kings 3:16–28

Then two harlots came to the king, and stood before him. The one woman said, "Oh, my lord, this woman and I dwell in the same house; and I gave birth to a child while she was in the house. Then on the third day after I was delivered, this woman also gave birth; and we were alone; there was no one else with us in the house, only we two were in the house. And this woman's son died in the night, because she lay on it. And she arose at midnight and took my son from beside me, while your maid-servant slept, and laid it in her bosom, and laid her dead son in my bosom. When I rose in the morning to nurse my child, behold, it was dead; but when I looked at it closely in the morning, behold, it was not the child that I had borne." But the other woman said, "No, the living child is mine, and the dead child is yours." Thus they spoke before the king.

Then the king said, "The one says, 'This is my son that is alive, and your son is dead'; and the other says, 'No, but your son is dead, and my son is the living one.'" And the king said, "Bring me a sword." So a sword was brought before the king. And the king said, "Divide the living child in two, and give half to the one, and half to the other." Then the woman whose son was alive said to the king, because her heart yearned for her son, "Oh, my lord, give her the living child, and by no means slay it." But the other said, "It shall be neither mine nor yours; divide it." Then the king answered and said, "Give the living child to the first woman, and by no means slay it; she is its mother." And all Israel heard of the judgment which the king had rendered; and they stood in awe of the king, because they perceived that the wisdom of God was in him, to render justice.

SOLOMON: HIS GREAT WISDOM ACCLAIMED

1 Kings 4:29–34

And God gave Solomon wisdom and understanding beyond measure, and largeness of mind like the sand of the seashore, so that Solomon's wisdom surpassed the wisdom of all the people of the east, and all the wisdom of Egypt. For he was wiser than all other men, wiser than Ethan the Ezrahite, and Heman, Calcol, and Darda, the sons of Mahol; and his fame was in all the nations round about. He also uttered three thousand proverbs; and his songs were a thousand and five. He spoke of trees, from the cedar that is in Lebanon to the hyssop that grows out of the wall; he spoke also of beasts, and of birds, and of reptiles, and of fish. The men came from all peoples to hear the wisdom of Solomon, and from all the kings of the earth, who had heard of his wisdom.

SOLOMON COMPLETES THE TEMPLE

1 Kings 8:1–27

Then Solomon assembled the elders of Israel and all the heads of the tribes, the leaders of the fathers' houses of the people of Israel, before King Solomon in Jerusalem, to bring up the ark of the covenant of the Lord out of the city of David, which is Zion. And all the men of Israel assembled to King Solomon at the feast in the month Ethanim, which is the seventh month. And all the elders of Israel came, and the priests took up the ark. And they brought up the ark of the Lord, the tent of meeting, and all the holy vessels that were in the tent; the priests and the Levites brought them up. And King Solomon and all the congregation of Israel, who had assembled before him, were with him before the ark, sacrificing so many sheep and oxen that they could not be counted or numbered. Then the priests brought the ark of the covenant to its place, in the inner sanctuary of the house, in the most holy place, underneath the wings of the cherubim. For the cherubim spread out their wings over the place of the ark, so that the cherubim made a covering above the ark and its poles. And the poles were so long that the ends of the poles were seen from the holy place before the inner sanctuary; but they could not be seen from outside; and they are there to this day. There was nothing in the ark except the two tables of stone which Moses put there at Horeb, where the Lord made a covenant with the people of Israel, when they came out of the land of Egypt. And when the priests came out of the holy place, a cloud filled the house of the

Lord, so that the priests could not stand to minister because of the cloud; for the glory of the Lord filled the house of the Lord.

Then Solomon said,

"The Lord has set the sun in the heavens.
    but has said he would dwell in thick darkness.
I have built thee an exalted house,
    a place for thee to dwell in forever."

Then the king faced about, and blessed all the assembly of Israel, while all the assembly of Israel stood. And he said, "Blessed be the Lord, the God of Israel, who with his hand has fulfilled what he promised with his mouth to David my father, saying, 'Since the day that I brought my people out of Egypt, I chose no city in all the tribes of Israel in which to build a house, that my name might be there; but I chose David to be over my people Israel.' Now it was in the heart of David my father to build a house for the name of the Lord, the God of Israel. But the Lord said to David my father, 'Whereas it was in your heart to build a house for my name, you did well that it was in your heart; nevertheless you shall not build the house, but your son who shall be born to you shall build the house for my name.' Now the Lord has fulfilled his promise which he made; for I have risen in the place of David my father, and sit on the throne of Israel, as the Lord promised, and I have built the house for the name of the Lord, the God of Israel. And there I have provided a place for the ark, in which is the covenant of the Lord which he made with our fathers, when he brought them out of the land of Egypt."

Then Solomon stood before the altar of the Lord in the presence of all the assembly of Israel, and spread forth his hands toward heaven; and said, "O Lord, God of Israel, there is no God like thee, in heaven above or on earth beneath, keeping covenant and showing steadfast love to thy servants who walk before thee with all their heart; who hast kept with thy servant David my father what thou didst declare to him; yea, thou didst speak with thy mouth, and with thy hand hast fulfilled it this day.

"Now therefore, O Lord, God of Israel, keep with thy servant David my father what thou hast promised him, saying, 'There shall never fail you a man before me to sit upon the throne of Israel, if only your sons take heed to their way, to walk before me as you have walked before me.' Now therefore, O God of Israel, let thy word be confirmed, which thou hast spoken to thy servant David my father.

"But will God indeed dwell on the earth? Behold, heaven and the highest heaven cannot contain thee; how much less this house which I have built."

SOLOMON: GOD'S COVENANT WITH SOLOMON

1 Kings 9:1–9

When Solomon had finished building the house of the Lord and the king's house and all that Solomon desired to build, the Lord appeared to Solomon a second time, as he had appeared to him at Gibeon. And the Lord said to him, "I have heard your prayer and your supplications, which you have made before me; I have consecrated this house which you have built, and put my name there forever; my eyes and my heart will be there for all time. And as for you, if you will walk before me, as David your father walked, with integrity of heart and uprightness, doing according to all that I have commanded you, and keeping my statutes and my ordinances, then I will establish your royal throne over Israel forever, as I promised David your father, saying, 'There shall not fail you a man upon the throne of Israel.' But if you turn aside from following me, you and your children, and do not keep my commandments and my statutes which I have set before you, but go and serve other gods and worship them, then I will cut off Israel from the land which I have given them; and the house which I have consecrated for my name I will cast out of my sight; and Israel will become a proverb and a byword among all peoples. And this house will become a heap of ruins; everyone passing by it will be astonished, and will hiss; and they will say, 'Why has the Lord done thus to this land, and to this house?' Then they will say, 'Because they forsook the Lord their God who brought their fathers out of the land of Egypt, and laid hold on other gods, and worshipped them and served them; therefore the Lord has brought all this evil upon them.' "

SOLOMON: THE QUEEN OF SHEBA VISITS SOLOMON

1 Kings 10:1–13

Now when the queen of Sheba heard of the fame of Solomon concerning the name of the Lord, she came to test him with hard questions. She came to Jerusalem with a great retinue, with camels bearing spices, and very much gold, and precious stones; and when she came to Solomon she told him all that was on her mind. And Solomon answered all her questions; there was nothing hidden from the king which he could not explain to her. And when the queen of Sheba had seen all the wisdom, the house that he had built, the food of his table, the seating of his officials, and the attendance of his servants, their clothing, his cup-bearers, and his burnt offerings which he offered at the house of the Lord, there was no more spirit in her.

And she said to the king, "The report was true which I heard in my own land of your affairs and your wisdom, but I did not believe the reports until I came and my own eyes had seen it; and, behold, the half was not told to me; your wisdom and prosperity surpass the report which I heard. Happy are your wives! Happy are these your servants, who continually stand before you and hear your wisdom. Blessed be the Lord your God, who has delighted in you and set you on the throne of Israel! Because the Lord loved Israel forever, he has made you king, that you may execute justice and righteousness." Then she gave the king a hundred and twenty talents of gold, and a very great quantity of spices, and precious stones; never again came such an abundance of spices as these which the queen of Sheba gave to King Solomon.

Moreover the fleet of Hiram, which brought gold from Ophir, brought from Ophir a very great amount of almug wood and precious stones. And the king made of the almug wood supports for the house of the Lord, and for the king's houses, lyres also and harps for the singers; no such almug wood has come or been seen, to this day.

And King Solomon gave to the queen of Sheba all that she desired, whatever she asked besides what was given her by the bounty of King Solomon. So she turned and went back to her own land, with her servants.

THE CYCLE OF ELIJAH AND ELISHA

The emphasis shifts in the Elijah and Elisha cycle from the physical leader of a family or nation to the spiritual spokesman of God. Elijah does not found a great nation, for he is the mouthpiece of God, a prophet. Like all prophets, he is ridiculed until his prophecy is fulfilled. The mocked prophet figure is seen in Greek literature in *Oedipus Rex* where Tiresias, the blind seer, is the only character who really sees and in *Lear* where the Fool is the only wise man.

Elijah's rugged individualism equals the modern western heroes Shane, the Virginian, and Dillon. The lone individual standing against totally unfair odds and yet succeeding through his own personal ingenuity interests audiences of all ages. Elijah's confrontation with King Ahab has made its way into literature. King Ahab, who had done "evil in the sight of the Lord," was led by a "lying spirit" to a bad but somewhat accidental end and is reflected by Melville's Ahab in *Moby Dick*.

ELIJAH: BEGINNINGS OF HIS MINISTRY—JUDGMENT PREDICTED

1 Kings 17:1–24

Now Elijah the Tishbite, of Tishbe in Gilead, said to Ahab, "As the Lord the God of Israel lives, before whom I stand, there shall be neither dew nor rain these years, except by my word." And the word of the Lord came to him, "Depart from here and turn eastward, and hide yourself by the brook Cherith, that is east of the Jordan. You shall drink from the brook; I have commanded the ravens to feed you there." So he went and did according to the word of the Lord; he went and dwelt by the brook Cherith that is east of the Jordan. And the ravens brought him bread and meat in the morning, and bread and meat in the evening; and he drank from the brook. And after a while the brook dried up, because there was no rain in the land.

Then the word of the Lord came to him, "Arise, go to Zarephath, which belongs to Sidon, and dwell there. Behold, I have commanded a widow there to feed you." So he arose and went to Zarephath; and when he came to the gate of the city, behold, a widow was there gathering sticks; and he called to her and said, "Bring me a little water in a vessel, that I may drink." As she was going to bring it, he called to her and said, "Bring me a morsel of bread in your hand." And she said, "As the Lord God lives, I have nothing baked, only a handful of meal in a jar, and a little oil in a cruse; and now, I am gathering a couple of sticks, that I may go in and prepare it for myself and my son, that we may eat it, and die." And Elijah said to her, "Fear not, go and do as you have said; but first make me a little cake of it and bring it to me, and afterward make for yourself and your son. For thus says the Lord God of Israel, 'The jar of meal shall not be spent, and the cruse of oil shall not fail, until the day that the Lord sends rain upon the earth.'" And she went and did as Elijah said; and she, and he, and her household ate for many days. The jar of meal was not spent, neither did the cruse of oil fail, according to the word of the Lord which he spoke by Elijah.

After this the son of the woman, the mistress of the house, became ill; and his illness was so severe that there was no breath left in him. And she said to Elijah, "What have you against me, O man of God? You have come to me to bring my sin to remembrance, and to cause the death of my son!" And he said to her, "Give me your son." And he took him from her bosom, and carried him up into the upper chamber where he lodged, and laid him upon his own bed. And he cried to the Lord, "O Lord my God, hast thou brought calamity even upon the widow with whom I sojourn, by slaying her son?" Then he stretched himself upon the child three times, and cried to the Lord, "O Lord my God, let this child's soul come into him again." And the Lord hearkened to the voice of Elijah; and the soul of the child came into him again, and he revived. And Elijah took the child, and brought him down from the upper chamber into the house, and delivered him to his mother; and Elijah said, "See, your son lives." And the woman said to Elijah, "Now I know that you are a man of God, and that the word of the Lord in your mouth is truth."

ELIJAH VERSUS BAAL

1 Kings 18:17–41

When Ahab saw Elijah, Ahab said to him, "Is it you, you troubler of Israel?" And he answered, "I have not troubled Israel, but you have, and your father's house, because you have forsaken the commandments of the Lord and followed the Baals. Now therefore send and gather all Israel to me at Mount Carmel, and the four hundred and fifty prophets of Baal and the four hundred prophets of Asherah, who ate at Jezebel's table."

So Ahab sent to all the people of Israel, and gathered the prophets together at Mount Carmel. And Elijah came near to all the people, and said, "How long will you go limping with two different opinions; if the Lord is God, follow him; but if Baal, then follow him." And the people did not answer him a word. Then Elijah said to the people, "I, even I only, am left a prophet of the Lord; but Baal's prophets are four hundred and fifty men. Let two bulls be given to us; and let them choose one bull for themselves, and cut it in pieces and lay it on the wood, but put no fire to it; and I will prepare the other bull and lay it on the wood, and put no fire to it. And you call on the name of your god and I I will call on the name of the Lord; and the God who answers by fire, he is God." And all the people answered, "It is well spoken." Then Elijah said to the prophets of Baal, "Choose for yourselves one bull and prepare it first, for you are many; and call on the name of your god; but put no fire to it." And they took the bull which was given them, and they prepared it, and called on the name of Baal from morning until noon, saying, "O Baal, answer us!" But there was no voice, and no one answered. And they limped about the altar which they had made. And at noon Elijah mocked them, saying, "Cry aloud, for he is a god; either he is musing, or he has gone aside, or he is on a journey, or perhaps he is asleep and must be awakened." And they cried aloud and cut themselves after their custom with swords and lances, until the blood gushed out upon them. And as midday passed, they raved on until the time of the offering of the oblation, but there was no voice; no one answered, no one heeded.

Then Elijah said to all the people, "Come near to me"; and all the people came near to him. And he repaired the altar of the Lord that had been thrown down; and Elijah took twelve stones, according to the number of tribes of the sons of Jacob, to whom the word of the Lord came, saying, "Israel shall be your name"; and with the stones he built an altar in the name of the Lord. And he made a trench about the altar, as great as would contain two measures of seed. And he put the wood in order, and cut the bull in pieces and laid it on the wood. And he said, "Fill four jars with water, and pour it on the burnt offering, and on the wood." And he said, "Do it a second time"; and they did it a second time. And he said, "Do it a third time"; and they did it a third time. And the water ran about the altar, and filled the trench also with water.

And at the time of the offering of the oblation, Elijah the prophet came near and said, "O Lord, God of Abraham, Isaac, and Israel, let it be known this day that thou art God in Israel, and that I am thy servant, and that I have done all these things at thy word. Answer me, O Lord, answer me, that this people may know that thou, O Lord, art God, and that thou hast turned their hearts back." Then the fire of the Lord fell, and consumed the burnt offering, and the wood, and the stones, and the dust, and licked up the water that was in the trench. And when all the people saw it, they fell on their faces; and they said, "The Lord, he is God; the Lord, he is God." And Elijah said to them, "Seize the prophets of Baal; let not one of them escape." And they seized them; and Elijah brought them down to the brook Kishon, and killed them there.

And Elijah said to Ahab, "Go up, eat and drink; for there is a sound of the rushing of rain."

ELIJAH: THE ANGER AND DEATH OF JEZEBEL

1 Kings 19:1–8; 2 Kings 9:29–37

Ahab told Jezebel all that Elijah had done, and how he had slain all the prophets with the sword. Then Jezebel sent a messenger to Elijah, saying, "So may the gods do to me, and more also, if I do not make your life as the life of one of them by this time tomorrow." Then he was afraid, and he arose and went for his life, and came to Beer-sheba, which belongs to Judah, and left his servant there.

But he himself went a day's journey into the wilderness, and came and sat down under a broom tree; and he asked that he might die, saying, "It is enough; now, O Lord, take away my life; for I am no better than my fathers." And he lay down and slept under a broom tree; and behold, an angel touched him, and said to him, "Arise and eat." And he looked, and behold, there was at his head a cake baked on hot stones and a jar of water. And he ate and drank, and lay down again. And the angel of the Lord came again a second time, and touched him, and said, "Arise and eat, else the journey will be too great for you." And he arose, and ate and drank, and went in the strength of that food forty days and forty nights to Horeb the mount of God. In the eleventh year of Joram the son of Ahab, Ahaziah began to reign over Judah.

When Jehu came to Jezreel, Jezebel heard of it; and she painted her eyes, and adorned her head, and looked out of the window. And as Jehu entered the gate, she said, "Is it peace, you Zimri, murderer of your master?" And he lifted up his face to the window, and said, "Who is on my side? Who?" Two or three eunuchs looked out at him. He said, "Throw her down." So they threw her down, and some of her blood splattered on the wall and on the horses, and they trampled on her. And he went in and ate and drank; and he said, "See now to this cursed woman, and bury her; for she is a king's daughter." But when they went to bury her, they found no more of her than the skull and the feet and the palms of her hands. When they came back and told him, he said, "This is the word of the Lord, which he spoke to his servant Elijah the Tishbite, 'In the territory of Jezreel the dogs shall eat the flesh of Jezebel; and the corpse of Jezebel shall be as dung upon the face of the field in the territory of Jezreel, so that no one can say, This is Jezebel.'"

ELISHA: ELIJAH'S TRANSLATION

2 Kings 2:1–12

Now when the Lord was about to take Elijah up to heaven by a whirlwind, Elijah and Elisha were on their way from Gilgal. And Elijah said to Elisha, "Tarry here, I pray you; for the Lord has sent me as far as Bethel." But Elisha said, "As the Lord lives, and as you yourself live, I will not leave you." So they went down to Bethel. And the sons of the prophets who were in Bethel came out to Elisha, and said to him, "Do you know that today the Lord will take away your master from over you?" And he said, "Yes, I know it; hold your peace."

Elijah said to him, "Elisha, tarry here, I pray you; for the Lord has sent me to Jericho." But he said, "As the Lord lives, and as you yourself live, I will not leave you." So they came to Jericho. The sons of the prophets who were at Jericho drew near to Elisha, and said to him, "Do you know that today the Lord will take away your master from over you?" And he answered, "Yes, I know it; hold your peace."

Then Elijah said to him, "Tarry here, I pray you; for the Lord has sent me to the Jordon." But he said, "As the Lord lives, and as you yourself live, I will not leave you." So the two of them went on. Fifty men of the sons of the prophets also went, and stood at some distance from them, as they both were standing by the Jordan. Then Elijah took his mantle, and rolled it up, and struck the water, and the water was parted to the one side and to the other, till the two of them could go over on dry ground.

When they had crossed, Elijah said to Elisha, "Ask what I shall do for you, before I am taken from you." And Elisha said, "I pray you, let me inherit a double share of your spirit." And he said, "You have asked a hard thing; yet, if you see me as I am being taken from you, it shall be so for you; but if you do not see me, it shall not be so." And as they still went on and talked, behold, a chariot of fire and horses of fire separated the two of them. And Elijah went up by a whirlwind into heaven. And Elisha saw it and he cried, "My father, my father! the chariots of Israel and its horsemen!" And he saw him no more.

ELISHA: CAUSING THE WATERS TO DIVIDE

2 Kings 2:14–15

Then he took the mantle of Elijah that had fallen from him, and struck the water, saying, "Where is the Lord, the God of

Elijah?" And when he had struck the water, the water was parted to one side and to the other; and Elisha went over.

Now when the sons of the prophets who were at Jericho saw him over against them, they said, "The spirit of Elijah rests on Elisha."

ELISHA: THE HEALING OF NAAMAN, THE LEPER

2 Kings 5:1–19

Naaman, commander of the army of the king of Syria, was a great man with his master and in high favor, because by him the Lord had given victory to Syria. He was a mighty man of valor, but he was a leper. Now the Syrians on one of their raids had carried off a little maid from the land of Israel, and she waited on Naaman's wife. She said to her mistress, "Would that my lord were with the prophet who is in Samaria! He would cure him of his leprosy." So Naaman went in and told his lord, "Thus and so spoke the maiden from the land of Israel." And the king of Syria said, "Go now, and I will send a letter to the king of Israel."

So he went, taking with him ten talents of silver, six thousand shekels of gold, and ten festal garments. And he brought the letter to the king of Israel, which read, "When this letter reaches you, know that I have sent to you Naaman my servant, and that you may cure him of his leprosy." And when the king of Israel read the letter, he rent his clothes and said, "Am I God, to kill and to make alive, that this man sends word to me to cure a man of his leprosy? Only consider, and see how he is seeking a quarrel with me."

But when Elisha the man of God heard that the king of Israel had rent his clothes, he sent to the king, saying, "Why have you rent your clothes? Let him come now to me, that he may know that there is a prophet in Israel." So Naaman came with his horses and chariots, and halted at the door of Elisha's house. And Elisha sent a messenger to him, saying, "Go and wash in the Jordan seven times, and your flesh shall be restored, and you shall be clean." But Naaman was angry, and he went away, saying, "Behold, I thought that he would surely come out to me, and stand, and call on the name of the Lord his God, and wave his hand over the place, and cure the leper. Are not Abana and Pharpar, the rivers of Damascus, better than all the waters of Israel? Could I not wash in them, and be clean?" So he turned and went away in a rage. But his servants came near to him and said, "If the prophet had commanded you to do some great thing, would you not have done it? How much rather, then, when he says to you, 'Wash, and be clean'?" So he went down and dipped himself seven times in the Jordan, according to the word of the man of God; and his flesh was restored like the flesh of a little child, and he was clean.

Then he returned to the man of God, he and all his company, and he came and stood before him; and he said, "Behold, I know that there is no God in all the earth but in Israel; so accept now a present from your servant." But he said, "As the Lord lives, whom I serve, I will receive none." And he urged him to take it, but he refused. Then Naaman said, "If not, I pray to you, let there be given your servant two mules' burden of earth; for henceforth your servant will not offer burnt offering or sacrifice to any god but the Lord. In this matter may the Lord pardon your servant; when my master goes into the house of Rimmon to worship there, when I bow myself in the house of Rimmon, the Lord pardon your servant in this matter." He said to him, "Go in peace."

ELISHA: THE AXE HEAD SWIMS

2 Kings 6:1–7

Now the sons of the prophets said to Elisha, "See, the place where we dwell under your charge is too small for us. Let us go to the Jordan and each of us get there a log, and let us make a place for us to dwell there." And he answered, "Go." Then one of them said, "Be pleased to go with your servants." And he answered, "I will go." So he went with them. And when they came to the Jordan, they cut down trees. But as one was felling a log, the axe head fell into the water; and he cried out, "Alas, my master! It was borrowed." Then the man of God said, "Where did it fall?" When he showed him the place, he cut off a stick, and threw it in there, and made the iron float. And he said, "Take it up." So he reached out his hand and took it.

EPIC HISTORY

Epic history binds a wide range of incidents into an organic whole, not only tracing the adventures of the great leaders of the Hebrew nation, but revealing the character of the nation itself: the interests, the philosophy, the daily routine, and the religious concerns of an entire people. As such, this form comes closest to resembling well-known epics such as *The Odyssey*. But it also contains all the common elements of the short story and novel.

Epic history includes large portions of Scripture, encompassing such stories as Joseph, Moses, and Ruth. In these we see the hand of God move directly into human affairs to preserve a testimony among the peoples of the world. and we can view rebellion, punishment, and mercy in action.

JOSEPH

The betrayal of a brother by his siblings and his later forgiveness of them is a universal theme found in folklore and serious writing. Certainly the Cinderella story parallels the plight of the Biblical Joseph, and on the more serious side, Thomas Mann takes from this section of the Bible title, plot, and characters for his novel *Joseph and His Brothers.* Of particular interest is the temptation of Joseph by an older woman, Potiphar's wife, a recurring theme in literature. In fact, those who have seen *The Graduate* will recognize the situation, although Joseph responds with more wisdom than does Benjamin, the hero of the film.

However, most importantly, in the story of Joseph we begin to see the Jewish people becoming aware of their religious and national identity. Joseph is the focal point of this awareness, and it is through him and his family that God's design is demonstrated.

JOSEPH: BELOVED OF HIS FATHER
Genesis 37:1–4

Jacob dwelt in the land of his father's sojournings, in the land of Canaan. This is the history of the family of Jacob.

Joseph, being seventeen years old, was shepherding the flock with his brothers; he was a lad with the sons of Bilhah and Zilpah, his father's wives; and Joseph brought an ill report of them to their father. Now Israel loved Joseph more than the other of his children, because he was the son of his old age; and he made him a long robe with sleeves. But when his brothers saw that their father loved him more than all his brothers, they hated him, and could not speak peaceably to him.

JOSEPH: HIS DREAM
Genesis 37:5–11

Now Joseph had a dream, and when he told it to his brothers they only hated him the more. He said to them, "Hear this dream which I have dreamed: behold, we were binding sheaves in the field, and lo, my sheaf arose and stood upright; and behold, your sheaves gathered round it, and bowed down to my sheaf." His brothers said to him, "Are you indeed to reign over us? Or are you indeed to have dominion over us?" So they hated him yet more for his dreams and for his words. Then he dreamed another dream, and told it to his brothers, and said, "Behold, I have dreamed another dream; and behold, the sun, the moon, and eleven stars were bowing down to me." But when he told it to his father and to his brothers, his father rebuked him, and said to him, "What is this dream that you have dreamed? Shall I and your mother and your brothers indeed come to bow ourselves to the ground before you?" And his brothers were jealous of him, but his father kept the saying in mind.

JOSEPH SOLD INTO SLAVERY BY HIS BROTHERS

Genesis 37:12–36

Now his brothers went to pasture their father's flock near Shechem. And Israel said to Joseph, "Are not your brothers pasturing the flock at Shechem? Come, I will send you to them." And he said to him, "Here I am." So he said to him, "Go now, see if it is well with your brothers and the flock; and bring me word again." So he sent him from the valley of Hebron, and he came to Shechem. And a man found him wandering in the fields; and the man asked him, "What are you seeking?" "I am seeking my brothers," he said, "tell me, I pray you, where they are pasturing the flock." And the man said, "They have gone away, for I heard them say, 'Let us go to Dothan.'" So Joseph went after his brothers, and found them at Dothan. They saw him afar off, and before he came near to them they conspired against him to kill him. They said to one another, "Here comes the dreamer. Come now, let us kill him and throw him into one of the pits; then we shall say that a wild beast has devoured him, and we shall see what will become of his dreams." But when Reuben heard it, he delivered him out of their hands, saying, "Let us not take his life." And Reuben said to them, "Shed no blood; cast him into this pit here in the wilderness, but lay no hand upon him"—that he might rescue him out of their hand, to restore him to his father. So when Joseph came to his brothers, they stripped him of his robe, the long robe with the sleeves that he wore; and they took him and cast him into a pit. The pit was empty, there was no water in it.

Then they sat down to eat; and looking up they saw a caravan of Ishmaelites coming from Gilead, with their camels bearing gum, balm, and myrrh, on their way to carry it down to Egypt. Then

Judah said to his brothers, "What profit is it if we slay our brother and conceal his blood? Come, let us sell him to the Ishmaelites, and let not our hand be upon him, for he is our brother, our own flesh." And his brothers heeded him. Then Midianite traders passed by, and they drew Joseph up and lifted him out of the pit, and sold him to the Ishmaelites for twenty shekels of silver, and they took Joseph to Egypt.

When Reuben returned to the pit and saw that Joseph was not in the pit, he rent his clothes and returned to his brothers, and said, "The lad is gone; and I, where shall I go?" Then they took Joseph's robe, and killed a goat, and dipped the robe in blood; and they sent the long robe with sleeves, and brought it to their father, and said, "This we have found; see now whether it is your son's robe or not." And he recognized it, and said, "It is my son's robe; a wild beast has devoured him; Joseph without doubt is torn to pieces." Then Jacob rent his garments, and put sackcloth upon his loins, and mourned for his son many days. All his sons and his daughters rose up to comfort him; but he refused to be comforted, and said, "No, I shall go down to Sheol to my son, mourning." Thus his father wept for him. Meanwhile the Midianites had sold him in Egypt to Potiphar, an officer of Pharaoh, the captain of the guard.

JOSEPH: HIS TEST

Genesis 39:1–20

Now Joseph was taken down to Egypt, and Potiphar, an officer of Pharaoh, the captain of the guard, an Egyptian, bought him from the Ishmaelites who had brought him down there. The Lord was with Joseph, and he became a successful man; and he was in the house of his master the Egyptian, and his master saw that the Lord was with him, and that the Lord caused all that he did to prosper in his hands. So Joseph found favor in his sight, and attended him, and he made him overseer of his house and put him in charge of all that he had. From the time that he had made him overseer in his house and over all that he had the Lord blessed the Egyptian's house for Joseph's sake; the blessing of the Lord was upon all that he had, in house and field. So he left all that he had in Joseph's charge; and having him he had no concern for anything but the food which he ate.

Now Joseph was handsome and good-looking. And after a time his master's wife cast her eyes upon Joseph and said, "Lie with me." But he refused and said to his master's wife, "Lo, having me my master has no concern about anything in the house, and he has put everything that he has in my hand; he is not greater in this house than I am; nor has he kept back anything from me except yourself, because you are his wife; how then can I do this great wickedness, and sin against God?" And although she spoke to Joseph day after day, he would not listen to her, to lie with her or to be with her. But one day, when he went into the house to do his work and none of the men of the house was there in the house, she caught him by his garment, saying, "Lie with me." But he left his garment in her hand, and fled and got out of the house. And when she saw that he had left his garment in her hand, and fled out of the house, she called to the men of the household and said to them, "See, he has brought among us a Hebrew to insult us; he came in to me to lie with me, and I cried out with a loud voice; and when he heard that I lifted up my voice and cried, he left his garment with me, and fled and got out of the house." Then she laid up his garment by her until his master came home, and she told him the same story, saying, "The Hebrew servant, whom you have brought among us, came in to me to insult me; but as soon as I lifted up my voice and cried, he left his garment with me, and fled out of the house."

When his master heard the words which his wife spoke to him, "This is the way your servant treated me," his anger was kindled. And Joseph's master took him and put him into the prison, the place where the king's prisoners were confined, and he was there in prison.

JOSEPH IN PRISON

Genesis 39:21–23; 40:1–23

But the Lord was with Joseph and showed him steadfast love, and gave him favor in the sight of the keeper of the prison. And the keeper of the prison committed to Joseph's care all the prisoners who were in the prison; and whatever was done there, he was the doer of it; the keeper of the prison paid no heed to anything that was in Joseph's care, because the Lord was with him; and whatever he did, the Lord made it prosper.

Some time after this, the butler of the king of Egypt and his baker offended their lord the king of Egypt. And Pharaoh was angry with his two officers, the chief butler and the chief baker, and he put them in custody in the house of the captain of the guard, in the prison where Joseph was confined. The captain of the guard charged Joseph with them, and he waited on them; and they continued for some time in custody. And one night they both dreamed—the butler and the baker of the king of Egypt, who were confined in the prison—each his own dream, and each dream with its own meaning. When Joseph came to them in the morning and saw them, they were troubled. So he asked Pharaoh's officers who were with him in custody in his master's house, "Why are your faces downcast today?" They said to him, "We have had dreams, and there is no one to interpret them." And Joseph said to them, "Do not interpretations belong to God? Tell them to me, I pray you."

So the chief butler told his dream to Joseph, and said to him, "In my dream there was a vine before me, and on the vine there were three branches; as soon as it budded, its blossoms shot forth, and the clusters ripened into grapes. Pharaoh's cup was in my hand; and I took the grapes and pressed them into Pharaoh's cup, and placed the cup in Pharaoh's hand." Then Joseph said to him, "This is its interpretation: the three branches are three days; within three days Pharaoh will lift up your head and restore you to your office; and you shall place Pharaoh's cup in his hand as formerly, when you were his butler. But remember me, when it is well with you, and do me the kindness, I pray you, to make mention of me to Pharaoh, and so get me out of this house. For I was indeed stolen out of the land of the Hebrews; and here also I have done nothing that they should put me into the dungeon."

When the chief baker saw that the interpretation was favorable, he said to Joseph, "I also had a dream: there were three cake baskets on my head, and in the uppermost basket there were all sorts of baked food for Pharaoh, but the birds were eating it out of the basket on my head." And Joseph answered, "This is its interpretation: within three days Pharaoh will lift up your head— from you!—and hang you on a tree; and the birds will eat the flesh from you."

On the third day, which was Pharaoh's birthday, he made a feast for all his servants, and lifted up the head of the chief butler and the head of the chief baker among his servants. He restored the chief butler to his butlership, and he placed the cup in Pharaoh's hand; but he hanged the chief baker, as Joseph had interpreted to them. Yet the chief butler did not remember Joseph, but forgot him.

JOSEPH: PHARAOH'S DREAMS

Genesis 41:1–57

After two whole years, Pharaoh dreamed that he was standing by the Nile, and behold, there came up out of the Nile seven cows sleek and fat, and they fed in the reed grass. And behold, seven other cows, gaunt and thin, came up out of the Nile after them, and stood by the other cows on the bank of the Nile. And the gaunt and thin cows ate up the seven sleek and fat cows. And Pharaoh awoke. And he fell asleep, and dreamed a second time; and behold, seven ears of grain, plump and good, were growing on one stalk. And behold, after them sprouted seven ears, thin and blighted by the east wind. And the seven thin ears swallowed up the seven plump and full ears. And Pharaoh awoke, and behold, it was a dream. So in the morning his spirit was troubled; and he sent and called for all the magicians in Egypt and all its wise men; and Pharaoh told them his dream, but there was none who could interpret it to Pharaoh.

Then the chief butler said to Pharaoh, "I remember my faults today. When Pharaoh was angry with his servants, and put me and the chief baker in custody in the house of the captain of the guard, we dreamed on the same night, he and I, each having a dream with its own meaning. A young Hebrew was there with us, a servant of the captain of the guard, and when we told him, he interpreted our dreams to us, giving an interpretation to each man according to his dream. And as he interpreted to us, so it came to pass; I was restored to my office, and the baker was hanged."

Then Pharaoh sent and called Joseph, and they brought him hastily out of the dungeon; and when they had shaved him and changed his clothes, he came in before Pharaoh. The Pharaoh said to Joseph, "I have had a dream, and there is no one who can interpret it; and I have heard it said of you that when you hear a dream you can interpret it." Joseph answered Pharaoh, "It is not in me; God will give Pharaoh a favorable answer." Then Pharaoh said to Joseph, "Behold, in my dream I was standing on the banks of the Nile, and seven cows, fat and sleek, came up out of the Nile and fed in the reed grass; and seven other cows came up after them, poor and very gaunt and thin, such as I have never seen in all the land of Egypt. And the thin and gaunt cows ate up the first seven fat cows, but when they had eaten them, no one would have known that they had eaten them, for they were still as gaunt as at the beginning. Then I awoke. I also saw in my dream seven ears growing on one stalk, full and good; and seven ears, withered, thin, and blighted by the east wind, sprouted after them, and the thin ears swallowed up the seven good ears. And I told it to the magicians, but there was no one who could explain it to me."

Then Joseph said to Pharaoh, "The dream of Pharaoh is one; God has revealed to Pharaoh what he is about to do. The seven good cows are seven years, and the seven good ears are seven years; the dream is one. The seven lean and gaunt cows that came up after them are seven years, and the seven empty ears blighted by the east wind are also seven years of famine. It is as I told Pharaoh, God has shown to Pharaoh what he is about to do. There will come seven years of great plenty throughout all the land of Egypt, but after them there will arise seven years of famine, and all the plenty will be forgotten in the land of Egypt; the famine will consume the land, and the plenty will be unknown in the land by reason of the famine which will follow, for it will be very grievous. And the doubling of Pharaoh's dream means that the thing is fixed by God, and God will shortly bring it to pass. Now therefore, let Pharaoh select a man discreet and wise, and set him over the land of Egypt. Let Pharaoh proceed to appoint overseers over the land, and take the fifth part of the produce of the land of Egypt during the seven plenteous years. And let them gather all the food of these good years that are coming, and lay up grain under the authority of Pharaoh for food in the cities, and let them keep it. That food shall be reserved for the land against the seven years of famine which are to befall the land of Egypt, so that the land may not perish through the famine."

This proposal seemed good to Pharaoh and to all his servants. And Pharaoh said to his servants, "Can we find such a man as this, in whom is the spirit of God?" So Pharaoh said to Joseph, "Since God has shown you all this, there is none so discreet and wise as you are; you shall be over my house, and all my people shall order themselves as you command; only as regards the throne will I be greater than you." And Pharaoh said to Joseph, "Behold, I have set you over all the land of Egypt." Then Pharaoh took his signet ring from his hand and put it on Joseph's hand, and arrayed him in garments of fine linen, and put a gold chain about his neck; and he made him to ride in the second chariot; and they cried after him, "Bow the knee!" Thus he set him over all the land of Egypt. Moreover Pharaoh said to Joseph, "I am Pharaoh, and without your consent no man shall lift up hand or foot in all the land of Egypt." And Pharaoh called Joseph's name Zaphenath-paneah; and he gave him in marriage Asenath, the daughter of Potiphera priest of On. So Joseph went out over the land of Egypt.

Joseph was thirty-seven years old when he entered the service of Pharaoh king of Egypt. And Joseph went out from the presence of Pharaoh, and went through all the land of Egypt. During the seven plenteous years the earth brought forth abundantly, and he gathered up all the food of the seven years when there was plenty in the land of Egypt, and stored up food in the cities; he stored up in every city the food from the fields around it. And Joseph stored up grain in great abundance, like the sand of the sea, until he ceased to measure it, for it could not be measured.

Before the year of famine came, Joseph had two sons, whom Asenath, the daughter of Potiphera priest of On, bore to him. Joseph called the name of the first-born Manasseh, "For," he said, "God has made me forget all my hardship and all my father's house." The name of the second he called Ephraim, "For God has made me fruitful in the land of my affliction."

The seven years of plenty that prevailed in the land of Egypt came to an end; and the seven years of famine began to come, as Joseph had said. There was famine in all lands; but in all the land of Egypt there was bread. When all the land of Egypt was famished, the people cried to Pharaoh for bread; and Pharaoh said to all the Egyptians, "Go to Joseph; what he says to you, do." So when the famine had spread over all the land, Joseph opened all the storehouses, and sold to the Egyptians, for the famine was severe in the land of Egypt. Moreover, all the earth came to Egypt to Joseph to buy grain, because the famine was severe over all the earth.

JOSEPH: HIS BROTHERS ARRIVE IN EGYPT

Genesis 42:1–29

When Jacob learned that there was grain in Egypt, he said to his sons, "Why do you look at one another?" And he said, "Behold, I have heard that there is grain in Egypt; go down, and buy grain for us there, that we may live, and not die." So ten of Joseph's brothers went down to buy grain in Egypt. But Jacob did not send Benjamin, Joseph's brother, with his brothers, for he feared that harm might befall him. Thus the sons of Israel came to buy among the others who came, for the famine was in the land of Canaan.

Now Joseph was governor over all the land; he it was who sold to all the people of the land. And Joseph's brothers came, and bowed themselves before him with their faces to the ground. Joseph saw his brothers, and knew them, but he treated them like strangers and spoke roughly to them. "Where do you come from?" he said. They said, "From the land of Canaan, to buy food." Thus Joseph knew his brothers, but they did not know him. And Joseph remembered the dreams which he had dreamed of them; and he said to them, "You are spies, you have come to see the weakness of the land." They said to him, "No, my lord, but to buy food have your servants come. We are all sons of one man, we are honest men, your servants are not spies." He said to them, "No, it is the weakness of the land that you have come to see." And they said, "We, your servants, are twelve brothers, the sons of one man in the land of Canaan; and behold, the youngest is this day with our father, and one is no more." But Joseph said to them, "It is as I have said, you are spies. By this you shall be tested: by the life of Pharaoh, you shall not go from this place unless your youngest brother comes here. Send one of you, and let him bring your brother, while you remain in prison, that your words may be tested, whether there is truth in you; or else, by the life of Pharaoh, surely you are spies." And he put them all together in prison for three days.

On the third day Joseph said to them, "Do this and you will live, for I fear God; if you are honest men, let one of your brothers remain confined in your prison, and let the rest go and carry grain for the famine of your households, and bring your youngest brother to me; so your words will be verified, and you shall not die." And they did so. Then they said to one another, "In truth we are guilty concerning our brother, in that we saw the distress of his soul, when he besought us and we would not listen; therefore is this distress come upon us." And Reuben answered them, "Did I not tell you not to sin against the lad? But you would not listen. So now there comes a reckoning for his blood." They did not know that Joseph understood them, for there was an interpreter between them. Then he turned away from them and wept; and he returned to them and spoke to them. And he took Simeon from them and bound him before their eyes. And Joseph gave orders to fill their bags with grain, and replace every man's money in his sack, and to give them provisions for the journey. This was done for them.

Then they loaded their asses with their grain, and departed. And as one of them opened his sack to give his ass provender at the lodging place, he saw his money in the mouth of his sack; and he said to his brothers, "My money has been put back; here it is in the mouth of my sack!" At this their hearts failed them, and they turned trembling to one another, saying, "What is this that God has done to us?"

When they came to Jacob their father in the land of Canaan, they told him all that had befallen them.

JOSEPH: THE PLAN TO MEET HIS AGED FATHER

Genesis 43:1–14, 26–34; 44:1–34; 45:1–28; 46:1–7, 29–34;
47:1–12

Now the famine was severe in the land. And when they had eaten the grain which they had brought from Egypt, their father said to them, "Go again, buy us a little food." But Judah said to him, "The man solemnly warned us, saying, 'You shall not see my face, unless your brother is with you.' If you will send our brother with us, we will go down and buy you food; but if you will not send him, we will not go down, for the man said to us, 'You shall not see my face unless your brother is with you.'" Israel said, "Why did you treat me so ill as to tell the man that you had another brother?" They replied, "The man questioned us carefully about ourselves and our kindred, saying, 'Is your father alive? Have you another brother?' What we told him was in answer to these questions; could we in any way know that he would say, 'Bring your brother down'?" And Judah said to Israel his father, "Send the lad with me, and we will arise and go, that we might live and not die, both we and you and also our little ones. I will be surety for him; of my hand you shall require him. If I do not bring him back to you and set him before you, then let me bear the blame forever; for if we had not delayed, we would now have returned twice."

Then their father Israel said to them, "If it must be so, then do this: take some of the choice fruits of the land in your bags, and carry down to the man a present, a little balm and a little honey, gum, myrrh, pistachio nuts, and almonds. Take double the money with you; carry back with you the money that was returned in the mouth of your sacks; perhaps it was an oversight. Take also your brother, and arise, go again to the man; may God Almighty grant you mercy before the man, that he may send back your other brother and Benjamin.

When Joseph came home, they brought into the house to him the present which they had with them, and bowed down to the ground. And he inquired about their welfare, and said, "Is your father well, the old man of whom you spoke? Is he still alive?" They said, "Your servant our father is well, he is still alive."

And they bowed their heads and made obeisance. And he lifted up his eyes, and he saw his brother Benjamin, his mother's son, and said, "Is this your youngest brother, of whom you spoke to me? God be gracious to you, my son!" Then Joseph made haste, for his heart yearned for his brother, and he sought a place to weep. And he entered his chamber and wept there. Then he washed his face and came out; and controlling himself he said, "Let food be served." They served him by himself, and them by themselves, and the Egyptians who ate with him by themselves, because the Egyptians might not eat bread with the Hebrews, for that is an abomination to the Egyptians. And they set before him, the first-born according to his birthright, and the youngest according to his youth; and the men looked at one another in amazement. Portions were taken to them for Joseph's table, but Benjamin's portion was five times as much as any of theirs. So they drank and were merry with him.

Then he commanded the steward of his house, "Fill the men's sacks with food, as much as they can carry, and put each man's money in the mouth of his sack, and put my cup, the silver cup, in the mouth of the sack of the youngest, with his money for the grain." And he did as Joseph told him. As soon as the morning was light, the men were sent away with their asses. When they had gone but a short distance from the city, Joseph said to his steward, "Up, follow after the men; and when you overtake them, say to them, 'Why have you returned evil for good? Why have you stolen my silver cup? Is it not from this that my lord drinks, and by this he divines? You have done wrong in so doing.'"

When he overtook them, he spoke to them these words. They said to him, "Why does my lord speak such words as these? Far be it from your servants that they should do such a thing! Behold, the money which we found in the mouth of our sacks, we brought back to you from the land of Canaan; how then shall we steal silver or gold from your lord's house? With whomever of your servants it be found, let him die, and we also will be my lord's slaves." He said, "Let it be as you say: he with whom it is found shall be my slave, and the rest of you shall be blameless." Then every man quickly lowered his sack to the ground, and every man opened his sack. And he searched, beginning with the eldest and ending with the youngest; and the cup was found in Benjamin's sack. Then they rent their clothes, and every man loaded his ass, and they returned to the city.

When Judah and his brothers came to Joseph's house, he was still there; and they fell before him to the ground. Joseph said to them, "What deed is this that you have done? Do you not know that such a man as I can indeed divine?" And Judah said, "What shall we say to my lord? What shall we speak? Or how can we clear ourselves? God has found out the guilt of your servants; behold, we are my lord's slaves, both we and he also in whose hand the cup has been found." But he said, "Far be it from me that I should do so! Only the man in whose hand the cup was found shall be my slave; but as for you, go up in peace to your father."

Then Judah went up to him and said, "O my lord, let your servant, I pray you, speak a word in my lord's ears, and let not your anger burn against your servant; for you are like Pharaoh himself. My lord asked his servants, saying, 'Have you a father, or a brother?' And we said to my lord, 'We have a father, an old man, and a young brother, the child of his old age; and his brother is dead, and he alone is left of his mother's children; and his father loves him.' Then you said to your servants, 'Bring him down to me, that I may set my eyes upon him.' We said to my lord, 'The lad cannot leave his father, for if he should leave his father, the father would die.' Then you said to your servants, 'Unless your youngest brother comes down with you, you shall see my face no more.' When we went back to your servant my father we told him the words of my lord. And when our father said, 'Go again, buy us a little food,' we said, 'We cannot go down. If our youngest brother goes with us, then we will go down; for we cannot see the man's face unless our youngest brother is with us.' Then your servant our father said to us, 'You know that my wife bore me two sons; one left me, and I said, Surely he has been torn to pieces; and I have never seen him since. If you take this one also from me, and harm befalls him, you will bring down my gray hairs in sorrow to Sheol.'

"Now therefore, when I come to your servant my father, and the lad is not with us, then, as his life is bound up in the lad's life, when he sees that the lad is not with us, he will die; and your servants will bring down the gray hairs of your servant our father with sorrow to Sheol. For your servant became surety for the lad to my father, saying, 'If I do not bring him back to you, then I shall bear the blame in the sight of my father all my life.' Now therefore, let your servant, I pray you, remain instead of the lad as a slave to my lord; and let the lad go back with his brothers. For how can I go back to my father if the lad is not with me? I fear to see the evil that would come upon my father."

Then Joseph could not control himself before all those who stood by him; and he cried, "Make everyone go out from me." So no one stayed with him when Joseph made himself known to his brothers. And he wept aloud, so that the Egyptians heard it, and the household of Pharaoh heard it. And Joseph said to his brothers, "I am Joseph; is my father still alive?" But his brothers could not answer him, for they were dismayed at his presence.

So Joseph said to his brothers, "Come near to me, I pray you." And they came near. And he said, "I am your brother, Joseph, whom you sold into Egypt. And now do not be distressed, or angry with yourselves, because you sold me here; for God sent me before you to preserve life. For the famine has been in the land these two years; and there are yet five years in which there will be neither plowing nor harvest. And God sent me before you to preserve for you a remnant on earth, and to keep alive for you many survivors. So it was not you who sent me here, but God; and he has made me a father to Pharaoh, and lord of all his house and ruler over all the land of Egypt. Make haste and go up to my father and say to him, 'Thus says your son Joseph, God has made me lord of all Egypt; come down to me, do not tarry; you shall dwell in the land of Goshen, and you shall be near me, you and your children and your children's children, and your flocks, your herds, and all that you have; and there I will provide for you, for there are yet five years of famine to come; lest you and your household, and all that you have, come to poverty.' And now your eyes see, and the eyes of my brother Benjamin see, that it is my mouth that speaks to you. You must tell my father of all my splendor in Egypt, and of all that you have seen. Make haste and bring my father down here." Then he fell upon his brother Benjamin's neck and wept; and Benjamin wept upon his neck. And he kissed all his brothers and wept upon them; and after that his brothers talked with him.

When the report was heard in Pharaoh's house, "Joseph's brothers have come," it pleased Pharaoh and his servants well. And Pharaoh said to Joseph, "Say to your brothers, 'Do this: load your beasts and go back to the land of Canaan; and take your father and your households, and come to me, and I will give you the best of the land of Egypt, and you shall eat the fat of the land.' Command them also, 'Do this: take wagons from the land of Egypt for your little ones and for your wives, and bring your father, and come. Give no thought to your goods, for the best of all the land of Egypt is yours.'"

The sons of Israel did so; and Joseph gave them wagons, according to the command of Pharaoh, and gave them the provisions for the journey. To each and all of them he gave festal garments; but to Benjamin he gave three hundred shekels of silver and five festal garments. To his father he sent as follows: ten asses loaded with the good things of Egypt, and ten she-asses loaded with grain, bread, and provision for his father on the journey. Then he sent his brothers away, and as they departed, he said to them, "Do not quarrel on the way." So they went up out of Egypt, and came to the land of Canaan to their father Jacob. And they told him, "Joseph is still alive, and he is ruler over all the land of Egypt." And his heart fainted, for he did not believe them. But when they told him all the words of Joseph, which he had said to them, and he saw the wagons which Joseph had sent to carry him, the spirit of their father Jacob revived; and Israel said, "It is enough; Joseph my son is still alive; I will go and see him before I die."

So Israel took his journey with all that he had, and came to Beer-sheba, and offered sacrifices to the God of his father Isaac. And God spoke to Israel in visions of the night, and said, "Jacob, Jacob." And he said, "Here am I." Then he said, "I am God, the God of your father; do not be afraid to go down to Egypt; for I will there make you a great nation; I will go down with you to Egypt, and I will also bring you up again; and Joseph's hands shall close your eyes." Then Jacob set out from Beer-sheba; and the sons of Israel carried Jacob their father, their little ones, and their wives, in the wagons which Pharaoh had sent to carry him. They also took their cattle and their goods, which they had gained in the land of Canaan, and came into Egypt, Jacob and all his offspring with him, his sons, and his sons' sons with him, his daughters, and his sons' daughters; all his offspring he brought with him into Egypt.

Then Joseph made ready his chariot and went up to meet his father in Goshen; and they came into the land of Goshen; and he presented himself to him, and fell on his neck, and wept on his neck a good while. Israel said to Joseph, "Now let me die, since I have seen your face and know that you are still alive." Joseph said to his brothers and to his father's household, "I will go up and tell Pharaoh, and will say to him, 'My brothers and my father's household, who were in the land of Canaan, have come to me; and the men are shepherds, for they have been keepers of cattle; and they have brought their flocks, and their herds, and all that they have.' When Pharaoh calls you and says, 'What is your occupation?' you shall say, 'Your servants have been keepers of cattle from our youth even until now, both we and our fathers.' in order that you may dwell in the land of Goshen; for every shepherd is an abomination to the Egyptians."

So Joseph went in and told Pharaoh, "My father and my

brothers, with their flocks and herds and all that they possess, have come from the land of Canaan; they are now in the land of Goshen." And from among his brothers he took five men and presented them to Pharaoh. Pharaoh said to his brothers, "What is your occupation?" And they said to Pharaoh, "Your servants are shepherds, as our fathers were." They said to Pharaoh, "We have come to sojourn in the land; for there is no pasture for your servants' flocks, for the famine is severe in the land of Canaan; and now, we pray you, let your servants dwell in the land of Goshen." Then Pharoah said to Joseph, "Your father and your brothers have come to you. The land of Egypt is before you; settle your father and brothers in the best of the land; let them dwell in the land of Goshen; and if you know any able men among them, put them in charge of my cattle."

Then Joseph brought in Jacob his father, and set him before Pharaoh, and Jacob blessed Pharaoh. And Pharaoh said to Jacob, "How many are the days of the years of your life?" And Jacob said to Pharaoh, "The days of the years of my sojourning are a hundred and thirty years; few and evil have been the days of the years of my life, and they have not attained to the days of the years of the life of my fathers in the days of their sojourning." And Jacob blessed Pharaoh and went out from the presence of Pharaoh. Then Joseph settled his father and his brothers, and gave them a possession in the land of Egypt, in the best of the land, in the land of Rameses, as Pharaoh had commanded. And Joseph provided his father, his brothers, and all his father's household with food, according to the number of their dependents.

JOSEPH: HIS FATHER'S DEATH AND BURIAL
Genesis 48:21–22; 49:1, 33; 50:8, 15–22

Israel said to Joseph, "Behold, I am about to die, but God will be with you, and will bring you again to the land of your fathers. Moreover I have given to you rather than to your brothers one mountain slope which I took from the hand of the Amorites with my sword and with my bow."

Then Jacob called his sons, and said, "Gather yourselves together. . . ."

When Jacob finished charging his sons, he drew up his feet into the bed, and breathed his last, and was gathered to his people.

Then Joseph fell on his father's face, and wept over him, and kissed him. And Joseph commanded his servants the physicians to embalm his father. So the physicians embalmed Israel; forty days were required for it, for so many are required for embalming.

And the Egyptians wept for him seventy days. And when the days of weeping for him were past, Joseph spoke to the household of Pharaoh, saying, "If now I have found favor in your eyes, speak, I pray you, in the ears of Pharaoh, saying, My father made me swear, saying, 'I am about to die: in my tomb which I hewed out for myself in the land of Canaan, there shall you bury me.' Now therefore let me go up, I pray you, and bury my father; then I will return." And Pharaoh answered, "Go up, and bury your father, as he made you swear." So Joseph went up to bury his father; and with him all the servants of Pharaoh, the elders of the household, and all the elders of the land of Egypt, as well as all the household of Joseph, his brothers, and his father's household.

When Joseph's brothers saw that their father was dead, they said, "It may be that Joseph will hate us and pay us back for all the evil which we did to him." So they sent a message to Joseph, saying, "Your father gave this command before he died, 'Say to Joseph, Forgive, I pray you, the transgressions of your brothers and their sin, because they did evil to you.' And now, we pray you, forgive the transgression of the servants of the God of your father." Joseph wept when he spoke to him. His brothers also came and fell down before him, and said, "Behold, we are your servants." But Joseph said to them, "Fear not, for am I in the place of God? As for you, you meant evil against me; but God meant it for good, to bring it about that many people should be kept alive, as they are today. So do not fear; I will provide for you and your little ones." Thus he assured them and comforted them.

So Joseph dwelt in Egypt, he and his father's house; and Joseph lived a hundred and ten years.

MOSES

Every nation must have a Moses, the leader who takes them out of captivity, gives them their basic laws, forms their national identity. Moses is a prototype for the father of every country, whether his name is George Washington or Kemal Ataturk.

A Ulysses or Beowulf parallels Moses in literature, but for figures truly comparable to this giant, one must turn to the pages of history.

MOSES: PREPARATION FOR SERVICE—HIS BIRTH

Exodus 1:6–22; 2:1–2

Then Joseph died, and all his brothers, and all that generation. But the descendants of Israel were fruitful and increased greatly;

they multiplied and grew exceedingly strong; so that the land was filled with them.

Now there arose a new king over Egypt, who did not know Joseph. And he said to his people, "Behold, the people of Israel are too many and too mighty for us. Come, let us deal shrewdly with them, lest they multiply, and, if war befall us, they join our enemies and fight against us and escape from the land." Therefore they set taskmasters over them to afflict them with heavy burdens; and they built for Pharaoh store-cities, Pithom and Raamses. But the more they were oppressed, the more they multiplied and the more they spread abroad. And the Egyptians were in dread of the people of Israel. So they made the people of Israel serve with rigor, and made their lives bitter with hard service, in mortar and brick, and all kinds of work in the field; in all their work they made them serve with rigor.

Then the king of Egypt said to the Hebrew midwives, one of whom was named Shiphrah and the other Puah, "When you serve as midwife to the Hebrew women, and see them upon the birthstool, if it is a son, you shall kill him; but if it is a daughter, she shall live." But the midwives feared God, and did not do as the king of Egypt commanded them, but let the male children live. So the king of Egypt called the midwives, and said to them, "Why have you done this, and let the male children live?" The midwives said to Pharaoh, "Because the Hebrew women are not like the Egyptian women; for they are vigorous and are delivered before the midwife comes to them." So God dealt well with the midwives, and the people multiplied and grew very strong. And because the midwives feared God he gave them families. Then Pharaoh commanded all his people, "Every son that is born to the Hebrews, you shall cast into the Nile, but you shall let every daughter live."

Now a man from the house of Levi went and took to wife a daughter of Levi. The woman conceived and bore a son; and when she saw that he was a goodly child, she hid him three months.

MOSES: PREPARATION FOR SERVICE— BROUGHT TO PHARAOH'S PALACE

Exodus 2:3–10

And when she could hide him no longer she took for him a basket made of bulrushes, and daubed it with bitumen and pitch; and she put the child in it and placed it among the reeds at the river's brink. And his sister stood at a distance, to know what would be done to him. Now the daughter of Pharaoh came down to bathe at the river, and her maidens walked beside the river; she saw the basket among the reeds and sent her maid to fetch it. When she opened it, she saw the child; and lo, the babe was crying. She took pity on him and said, "This is one of the Hebrews' children." Then his sister said to Pharaoh's daughter, "Shall I go and call you a nurse from the Hebrew women to nurse the child for you?" And Pharaoh's daughter said to her, "Go." So the girl went and called the child's mother. And Pharaoh's daughter said to her, "Take this child away, and nurse him for me, and I will give you your wages." So the woman took the child and nursed him. And the child grew, and she brought him to Pharaoh's daughter, and he became her son; and she named him Moses, for she said, "Because I drew him out of the water."

MOSES: PREPARATION FOR SERVICE— SIDES WITH ISRAEL

Exodus 2:11–25

One day, when Moses had grown up, he went out to his people and looked on their burdens; and he saw an Egyptian beating a Hebrew, one of his people. He looked this way and that, and seeing no one he killed the Egyptian and hid him in the sand. When he went out the next day, behold, two Hebrews were struggling together; and he said to the man that did the wrong, "Why do you strike your fellow?" He answered, "Who made you a prince and a judge over us? Do you mean to kill me as you killed the Egyptian?" Then Moses was afraid, and thought, "Surely this thing is known." When Pharaoh heard of it, he sought to kill Moses.

But Moses fled from Pharaoh, and stayed in the land of Midian; and he sat down by a well. Now the priest of Midian had seven daughters; and they came and drew water, and filled the troughs to water their father's flocks. The shepherds came and drove them away; but Moses stood up and helped them, and watered their flock. When they came to their father Reuel, he said, "How is it that you have come so soon today?" They said, "An Egyptian delivered us out of the hand of the shepherds, and even drew water for us and watered the flock." He said to his daughters, "And where is he: Why have you left the man? Call him, that he may eat bread." And Moses was content to dwell with the man, and he gave Moses his daughter Zipporah. She bore a son, and he called his name Gershom; for he said, "I have been a sojourner in a foreign land."

In the course of those many days, the king of Egypt died. And the people of Israel groaned under their bondage, and cried out for help, and their cry under bondage came up to God. And God heard their groaning, and God remembered his covenant with Abraham, with Isaac, and with Jacob. And God saw the people of Israel, and God knew their condition.

MOSES: CALL TO SERVICE— THE BURNING BUSH EXPERIENCE

Exodus 3:1–15

Now Moses was keeping the flock of his father-in-law, Jethro, the priest of Midian; and he led his flock to the west side of the wilderness, and came to Horeb, the mountain of God. And the angel of God appeared to him in a flame of fire out of the midst of a bush; and he looked, and lo, the bush was burning, yet it was not consumed. And Moses said, "I will turn aside and see this great sight, why the bush is not burnt." When the Lord saw that he turned aside to see, God called to him out of the bush, "Moses, Moses!" And he said, "Here am I." Then he said, "Do not come near; put off your shoes from your feet, for the place on which you are standing is holy ground." And he said, "I am the God of your father, the God of Abraham, the God of Isaac, and the God of Jacob." And Moses hid his face, for he was afraid to look at God.

Then the Lord said, "I have seen the affliction of my people who are in Egypt, and have heard their cry because of their taskmasters; and I know their sufferings, and I have come down to deliver them out of the hand of the Egyptians, and to bring them up out of that land to a good and broad land, a land flowing with milk and honey, to the place of the Canaanites, the Hittites, the Amorites, the Perizzites, the Hivites, and the Jebusites. And now, behold, the cry of the people of Israel has come to me, and I have seen the oppression with which the Egyptians oppress them. Come, I will send you to Pharaoh, that you may bring forth my people, the sons of Israel, out of Egypt." But Moses said to God, "Who am I that I should go to Pharaoh, and bring the sons of Israel out of Egypt?" He said, "But I will be with you; and this shall be a sign for you, that I have sent you; when you have brought forth the people out of Egypt, you shall serve God upon this mountain."

Then Moses said to God, "If I come to the people of Israel and say to them, 'The God of your fathers has sent me to you,' and they ask me, 'What is his name?' what shall I say to them?'' God said to Moses, ''I AM WHO I AM.'' And he said, ''Say to the people of Israel, 'I AM has sent me to you.''' God also said to Moses, ''Say this to the people of Israel, 'The Lord, the God of your fathers, the God of Abraham, the God of Isaac, and the God of Jacob, has sent me to you': this is my name forever, and thus I am to be remembered throughout all generations.''

MOSES: CALL TO SERVICE—HIS OBJECTIONS TO GOD'S COMMISSION

Exodus 4:1–17

Then Moses answered, ''But behold, they will not believe me or listen to my voice, for they will say, 'The Lord did not appear to you.' '' The Lord said to him, ''What is that in your hand?'' He said, ''A rod.'' And he said, ''Cast it on the ground.'' So he cast it on the ground, and it became a serpent; and Moses fled from it. But the Lord said to Moses, ''Put out your hand, and take it by the tail''—so he put out his hand and caught it, and it became a rod in his hand—''That they may believe that the Lord, the God of their fathers, the God of Abraham, the God of Isaac, and the God of Jacob, has appeared to you.'' Again the Lord said to him, ''Put your hand into your bosom.'' And he put his hand into his bosom; and when he took it out, behold, his hand was leprous, as white as snow. Then God said, ''Put your hand back into your bosom.'' So he put his hand back into his bosom; and when he took it out, behold, it was restored like the rest of his flesh. ''If they will not believe you,'' God said, ''or heed the first sign, they may believe the latter sign. If they will not believe even these two signs or heed your voice, you shall take some water from the Nile and pour it upon the dry ground; and the water which you shall take from the Nile will become blood upon the dry ground.''

But Moses said to the Lord, ''Oh, my Lord, I am not eloquent, either heretofore or since thou hast spoken to thy servant; but I am slow of speech and of tongue.'' Then the Lord said to him, ''Who has made man's mouth? Who makes him dumb, or deaf, or seeing, or blind? Is it not I, the Lord? Now therefore go and I will be with thy mouth and teach you what you shall speak.'' But he said, ''Oh, my Lord, send, I pray, some other person.'' Then the anger of the Lord was kindled against Moses and he said, ''Is there not Aaron, your brother, the Levite? I know that he can speak well; and behold he is coming out to meet you, and when he sees you he will be glad in his heart. And you shall speak to him and put the words in his mouth; and I will be with your mouth and with his mouth, and will teach you what you shall do. He will speak for you to the people; and he shall be a mouth for you, and you shall be to him as God. And you shall take in your hand this rod, with which you shall do the signs."

MOSES: CALL TO SERVICE—RETURN TO AID THE ISRAELITES

Exodus 4:29–31; 5:1–9

Then Moses and Aaron went and gathered together all the elders of the people of Israel. And Aaron spoke all the words which the Lord had spoken to Moses, and did the signs in the sight of the people. And the people believed; and when they heard that the Lord had visited the people of Israel and that he had seen their affliction, they bowed their heads and worshipped.

Afterward Moses and Aaron went to Pharaoh and said, "Thus says the Lord, the God of Israel, 'Let my people go, that they may hold a feast to me in the wilderness.'" But Pharaoh said, "Who is the Lord, that I should heed his voice and let Israel go? I do not know the Lord, and moreover I will not let Israel go." Then they said, "The God of the Hebrews has met with us; let us go, we pray, a three days' journey into the wilderness, and sacrifice to the Lord our God, lest he fall upon us with pestilence or with the sword." But the king of Egypt said to them, "Moses and Aaron, why do you take the people away from their work? Get to your burdens." And Pharaoh said, "Behold, the people of the land are now many and you make them rest from their burdens!" The same day Pharaoh commanded the taskmasters of the people and their foremen, "You shall no longer give the people straw to make bricks, as heretofore; let them go and gather straw for themselves. But the number of bricks which they made heretofore you shall lay upon them, and you shall by no means lessen it; for they are idle; therefore they cry, 'Let us go and offer sacrifice to our God.' Let heavier work be laid upon the men that they may labor at it and pay no regard to lying words."

MOSES: RETURN VISIT TO PHARAOH

Exodus 7:10–13

So Moses and Aaron went to Pharaoh and did as the Lord commanded; Aaron cast down his rod before Pharaoh and his servants, and it became a serpent. Then Pharaoh summoned the wise men and the sorcerers; and they also, the magicians of Egypt, did the same by their secret arts. For every man cast down his rod, and they became serpents. But Aaron's rod swallowed up their rods. Still Pharaoh's heart was hardened, and he would not listen to them; as the Lord had said.

MOSES: JUDGMENTS OF GOD—RIVERS TURNED TO BLOOD

Exodus 7:14–22

Then the Lord said to Moses, "Pharaoh's heart is hardened, he refuses to let the people go. Go to Pharaoh in the morning, as he is going to the water; wait for him by the river's brink, and take in your hand the rod which was turned into a serpent. And you shall say to him, 'The Lord, the God of the Hebrews, sent me to you, saying, "Let the people go that they may serve me in the wilderness; and behold, you have not yet obeyed." Thus says the Lord, "By this you shall know that I am the Lord; behold, I will strike the water that is in the Nile with the rod that is in my hands, and it shall be turned to blood, and the fish in the Nile shall die, and the Nile shall become foul, and the Egyptians will loathe to drink water from the Nile."'" And the Lord said to Moses, "Say to Aaron, 'Take your rod and stretch out your hand over the waters of Egypt, over their rivers, their canals, their ponds, and all their pools of water, that they may become blood; and there shall be blood throughout all the land of Egypt, both in vessels of wood and in vessels of stone.'"

So Moses and Aaron did as the Lord commanded; in the sight of Pharaoh and in the sight of his servants, he lifted up the rod and struck the water that was in the Nile, and all the water that was in the Nile turned to blood. And the fish in the Nile died; and the Nile became foul, so that the Egyptians could not drink water from the Nile; and there was blood throughout all the land of Egypt. But the magicians of Egypt did the same by their secret arts; so Pharaoh's heart remained hardened, and he would not listen to them; as the Lord had said.

MOSES: JUDGMENTS OF GOD—FROGS

Exodus 8:5–8, 12–15

And the Lord said to Moses, "Say to Aaron, 'Stretch out your hand with your rod over the rivers, over the canals, and over the pools, and cause frogs to come upon the land of Egypt!'" So

Aaron stretched out his hand over the waters of Egypt; and the frogs came up and covered the land of Egypt. But the magicians did the same with their secret arts, and brought frogs upon the land of Egypt.

Then Pharaoh called Moses and Aaron, and said, "Entreat the Lord to take away the frogs from me and from my people; and I will let the people go to sacrifice to the Lord." So Moses and Aaron went out from Pharaoh; and Moses cried to the Lord concerning the frogs, as he had agreed with Pharaoh. And the Lord did according to the word of Moses; the frogs died out of the houses and the courtyards and out of the fields. And they gathered them together in heaps, and the land stank. But when Pharaoh saw that there was a respite, he hardened his heart, and would not listen to them; as the Lord had said.

MOSES: JUDGMENTS OF GOD—GNATS

Exodus 8:16–19

Then the Lord said to Moses, "Say to Aaron, 'Stretch out your rod and strike the dust of the earth, that it may become gnats throughout all the land of Egypt.' " And they did so; Aaron stretched out his hand with his rod, and struck the dust of the earth, and there came gnats on man and beast; all the dust of the earth became gnats throughout all the land of Egypt. The magicians tried by their secret arts to bring forth gnats, but they could not. So there were gnats on man and beast. And the magicians said to Pharaoh, "This is the finger of God." But Pharaoh's heart was hardened, and he would not listen to them; as the Lord had said.

MOSES: JUDGMENTS OF GOD—FLIES

Exodus 8:20–21, 24, 28–32

Then the Lord said to Moses, "Rise up early in the morning and wait for Pharaoh, as he goes out to the water, and say to him, 'Thus says the Lord, "Let my people go, that they may serve me. Else, if you will not let my people go, behold, I will send swarms of flies on you and your servants and your people, and into your houses; and the houses of the Egyptians shall be filled with swarms of flies, and also the ground on which they stand." ' " And the Lord did so; there came great swarms of flies into the house of Pharaoh and into his servants' houses, and in all the land of Egypt the land was ruined by reason of the flies.

So Pharaoh said, "I will let you go, to sacrifice to the Lord your God in the wilderness; only you shall not go very far away. Make entreaty for me." And Moses said, "Behold, I am going out from you and I will pray to the Lord that the swarms of flies may depart from Pharaoh, from his servants, and from his people, tomorrow; only let not Pharaoh deal falsely again by not letting the people go to sacrifice to the Lord." So Moses went out from Pharaoh and prayed to the Lord. And the Lord did as Moses asked, and removed the swarms of flies from Pharaoh, from his servants, and from his people; not one remained. But Pharaoh hardened his heart this time also, and did not let the people go.

MOSES: JUDGMENTS OF GOD—THE CATTLE DIE

Exodus 9:1–7

Then the Lord said to Moses, "Go in to Pharaoh and say to him, 'Thus says the Lord, the God of the Hebrews, "Let my people go, that they may serve me. For if you refuse to let them go and still hold them, behold, the hand of the Lord will fall with a severe plague upon your cattle which are in the field, the horses, the asses, the camels, the herds, and the flocks. But the Lord will make a distinction between the cattle of Israel and the cattle of Egypt, so that nothing shall die of all that belongs to the people of Israel." ' " And the Lord set a time, saying, "Tomorrow the Lord will do this thing in the land." And on the morrow the Lord did this thing; all the cattle of the Egyptians died, but of the cattle of the Israelites not one died. And Pharaoh sent, and behold, not one of the cattle of the Israelites was dead. But the heart of Pharaoh was hardened, and he did not let the people go.

MOSES: JUDGMENTS OF GOD—BOILS

Exodus 9:8–12

And the Lord said to Moses and Aaron, "Take handfuls of ashes from the kiln, and let Moses throw them toward heaven in the sight of Pharaoh. And it shall become fine dust over all the land of Egypt, and become boils breaking out in the sores of man and beast. And the magicians could not stand before Moses because of the boils, for the boils were upon the magicians and upon all the Egyptians. But the Lord hardened the heart of Pharaoh, and he did not listen to them; as the Lord had spoken to Moses.

MOSES: JUDGMENTS OF GOD—HAIL

Exodus 9:22–30, 33–35

And the Lord said to Moses, "Stretch forth your hand toward heaven, that there may be hail in all the land of Egypt, upon man and beast and every plant of the field, throughout the land of Egypt." Then Moses stretched forth his rod toward heaven; and the Lord sent thunder and hail, and fire ran down to the earth. And the Lord rained down hail upon the land of Egypt; there was hail and fire flashing continually in the midst of the hail, very heavy hail, such as had never been in all the land of Egypt since it became a nation. The hail struck down everything that was in the field throughout all the land of Egypt, both man and beast; and the hail struck down every plant of the field, and shattered every tree of the field. Only in the land of Goshen, where the people of Israel were, there was no hail.

Then Pharaoh sent, and called Moses and Aaron, and said to them, "I have sinned this time; the Lord is in the right, and I and my people are in the wrong. Entreat the Lord; for there has been enough of this thunder and hail; I will let you go, and you shall stay no longer." Moses said to him, "As soon as I have gone out of the city, I will stretch out my hands to the Lord; the thunder will cease, and then there will be no more hail, that you may know that the earth is the Lord's. But as for you and your servants, I know that you do not yet fear the Lord God." So Moses went out of the city from Pharaoh, and stretched out his hands to the Lord; and the thunder and the hail ceased, and the rain no longer poured upon the earth. But when Pharaoh saw that the rain and the hail and the thunder had ceased, he sinned yet again, and hardened his heart, he and his servants. So the heart of Pharaoh was hardened, and he did not let the people of Israel go; as the Lord had spoken through Moses.

MOSES: JUDGMENTS OF GOD—LOCUSTS

Exodus 10:12–20

Then the Lord said to Moses, "Stretch out your hand over the land of Egypt for the locusts, that they may come upon the land of Egypt, and eat every plant in the land, all that the hail has left." So Moses stretched forth his rod over the land of Egypt, and the Lord brought an east wind upon the land all that day and all that night; and when it was morning the east wind had brought the locusts. And the locusts came up over the land of Egypt, and settled on the whole country of Egypt, such a dense swarm of locusts as had never been before, nor ever shall be again. For they covered the face of the whole land, so that the land was darkened, and they ate all the plants in the land and all the fruit of the trees which the hail had left; not a green thing remained, neither tree nor plant of the field, through all the land of Egypt. Then Pharaoh called Moses and Aaron in haste, and said, "I have sinned against the Lord your God, and against you. Now therefore, forgive my sin, I pray you, only this once, and entreat the Lord your God only to remove this death from me." So he went out from Pharaoh, and entreated the Lord. And the Lord turned a very strong west wind, which lifted the locusts and drove them into the Red Sea; not a single locust was left in all the country of Egypt. But the Lord hardened Pharaoh's heart, and he did not let the children of Israel go.

MOSES: JUDGMENTS OF GOD—DARKNESS
Exodus 10:21–29

Then the Lord said to Moses, "Stretch out your hand toward heaven that there may be darkness over the land of Egypt, a darkness to be felt." So Moses stretched out his hand toward heaven, and there was thick darkness in all the land of Egypt three days; they did not see one another, nor did any rise from his place for three days; but all the people of Israel had light where they dwelt. Then Pharaoh called Moses, and said, "Go, serve the Lord; your children also may go with you; only let your flocks and your herds remain behind." But Moses said, "You must also let us have sacrifices and burnt offerings, that we may sacrifice to the Lord our God. Our cattle also must go with us; not a hoof shall be left behind, for we must take of them to serve the Lord our God, and we do not know with what we must serve the Lord until we arrive there." But the Lord hardened Pharaoh's heart, and he would not let them go. Then Pharaoh said to him, "Get away from me; take heed to yourself; never see my face again; for in the day that you see my face you shall die." Moses said, "As you say! I will not see your face again."

MOSES: JUDGMENTS OF GOD—THE PASSOVER
Exodus 12:1–13, 29–32

The Lord said to Moses and Aaron in the land of Egypt, "This month shall be for you the beginning of months; it shall be the first month of the year for you. Tell all the congregation of Israel that on the tenth day of this month they shall take every man a lamb according to their fathers' house, a lamb for a household; and if the household is too small for a lamb, then a man and his neighbor next to his house shall take according to the number of persons; according to what each can eat you shall make your count for the lamb. Your lamb shall be without blemish, a male a year old; you shall take it from the sheep or from the goats; and you shall keep it until the fourteenth day of this month, when the whole assembly of the congregation of Israel shall kill their lambs in the evening. Then they shall take some of the blood, and put it on the two doorposts and the lintel of the houses in which they eat them. They shall eat the flesh that night, roasted; with unleavened bread and bitter herbs they shall eat it. Do not eat any of it raw or boiled with water, but roasted, its head with its legs and its inner parts. And you shall let none of it remain until the morning, anything that remains until morning you shall burn. In this manner you shall eat it; your loins girded, your sandals on your feet, your staff in your hand; and you shall eat it in haste. It is the Lord's passover. For I will pass through the land of Egypt that night, and I will smite all the first-born in the land of Egypt, both man and beast; and on all the gods of Egypt I will execute judgments: I am the Lord. The blood shall be a sign for you, upon the houses where you are; and when I see the blood, I will pass over you, and no plague shall fall upon you or destroy you, when I smite the land of Egypt.

At midnight the Lord smote all the first-born in the land of Egypt, from the first-born of Pharaoh who sat at his throne to the first-born of the captive who was in the dungeon, and all the first-born of the cattle. And Pharaoh rose up in the night, he, and all his servants, and all the Egyptians; and there was a great cry in Egypt, for there was not a house where one was not dead. And he summoned Moses and Aaron by night, and said, "Rise up, go forth from among my people, both you and the people of Israel; and go, serve the Lord, as you have said. Take your flocks and your herds, as you have said, and be gone; and bless me also!"

MOSES: WILDERNESS EXPEDITION—THE JOURNEY

Exodus 13:17–22

When Pharaoh let the people go, God did not lead them by way of the land of the Philistines, although that was near; for God said, "Lest the people repent when they see war, and return to Egypt." But God lead the people round by the way of the wilderness toward the Red Sea. And the people of Israel went up out of the land of Egypt equipped for battle. And Moses took the bones of Joseph with him; for Joseph had solemnly sworn the people of Israel, saying, "God will visit you; then you must carry my bones with you from here." And they moved on from Succoth, and encamped at Etham, on the edge of the wilderness. And the Lord went before them by day in a pillar of cloud to lead them along the way, and by night in a pillar of fire to give them light, that they might travel by day and by night; the pillar of cloud by day and the pillar of fire by night did not depart from before the people.

MOSES: WILDERNESS EXPEDITION—PHARAOH PURSUES ISRAEL

Exodus 14:8–12

And the Lord hardened the heart of Pharaoh king of Egypt and he pursued the people of Israel as they went forth defiantly. The Egyptians pursued them, all Pharaoh's horses and chariots and his horsemen and his army, and overtook them encamped at the sea, by Pi-ha-hiroth, in front of Baal-zephon.

When Pharaoh drew near, the people of Israel lifted up their eyes, and behold, the Egyptians were marching after them; and they were in great fear. And the people of Israel cried out to the Lord; and they said to Moses, "Is it because there are no graves in Egypt that you have taken us away to die in the wilderness? What have you done to us, in bringing us out of Egypt? Is not this what we said to you in Egypt, 'Let us alone, and let us serve the Egyptians'? For it would have been better for us to have served the Egyptians than to die in the wilderness."

MOSES: WILDERNESS EXPEDITION—THE RED SEA OPENS

Exodus 14:13–31

And Moses said to the people, "Fear not, stand firm, and see the salvation of the Lord, which he will work for you today; for the Egyptians whom you see today, you will never see again. The Lord will fight for you, and you have only to be still." The Lord said to Moses, "Why do you cry to me? Tell the people of Israel to go forward. Lift up your rod, and stretch out your hand over the sea and divide it, that the people of Israel may go on dry ground through the sea. And I will harden the hearts of the Egyptians so that they shall go in after them, and I will get glory over Pharaoh and all his host, his chariots, and his horsemen. And the Egyptians shall know that I am the Lord, when I have gotten glory over Pharaoh, his chariots, and his horsemen."

Then the angel of God who went before the host of Israel moved and went behind them; and the pillar of cloud moved from before them and stood behind them, coming between the host of Egypt and the host of Israel. And there was the cloud and the darkness; and the night passed without one coming near the other all night.

Then Moses stretched out his hand over the sea; and the Lord drove the sea back by a strong east wind all night, and made the sea dry land, and the waters were divided. And the people of Israel went into the midst of the sea on dry ground, the waters being a wall to them on their right hand and on their left. The Egyptians pursued, and went in after them into the midst of the sea, all Pharaoh's horses, his chariots, and his horsemen. And in the morning watch the Lord in the pillar of fire and of cloud looked down upon the host of the Egyptians, and discomforted the host of the Egyptians, clogging their chariot wheels so that they drove heavily; and the Egyptians said, "Let us flee from before Israel; for the Lord fights for them against the Egyptians."

Then the Lord said to Moses, "Stretch out your hand over the sea, that the water may come back upon the Egyptians, upon their chariots, and upon their horsemen." So Moses stretched forth his hand over the sea, and the sea returned to its wonted flow when the morning appeared; and the Egyptians fled into it, and the Lord routed the Egyptians in the midst of the sea. The waters returned and covered the chariots and the horsemen and all the host of Pharaoh that had followed them into the sea; not so much as one of them remained. But the people of Israel walked on dry ground through the sea, the waters being a wall to them on their right hand and on their left.

Thus the Lord saved Israel that day from the hand of the Egyptians; and Israel saw the Egyptians dead upon the seashore. And Israel saw the great work which the Lord did against the Egyptians, and the people feared the Lord; and they believed in the Lord and in his servant Moses.

MOSES: WILDERNESS EXPEDITION—AARON'S ROD BUDS

Numbers 17:1–12; 18:1–5

The Lord said to Moses, "Speak to the people of Israel, and

get from them rods, one for each fathers' house, from all their leaders according to their fathers' houses, twelve rods. Write each man's name upon his rod, and write Aaron's name upon the rod of Levi. For there shall be one rod for the head of each fathers' house. Then you shall deposit them in the tent of meeting before the testimony, where I meet with you. And the rod of the man whom I choose shall sprout; thus I will make to cease from me the murmurings of the people of Israel, which they murmur against you." Moses spoke to the people of Israel; and all their leaders gave him rods, one for each leader, according to their fathers' houses, twelve rods; and the rod of Aaron was among their rods. And Moses deposited the rods before the Lord in the tent of the testimony.

And on the morrow Moses went into the tent of the testimony; and behold, the rod of Aaron for the house of Levi had sprouted and put forth buds, and produced blossoms, and it bore ripe almonds. Then Moses brought out all the rods from before the Lord to all the people of Israel; and they looked, and each man took his rod. And the Lord said to Moses, "Put back the rod of Aaron before the testimony, to be kept as a sign for the rebels, that you may make an end of their murmurings against me, lest they die." Thus did Moses; as the Lord commanded him, so he did.

So the Lord said to Aaron, "You and your sons and your fathers' house with you shall bear iniquity in connection with the sanctuary; and you and your sons with you shall bear iniquity in connection with your priesthood. And with you bring your brethren also, the tribe of Levi, the tribe of your father, that they may join you, and minister to you while you and your sons with you are before the tent of the testimony. They shall attend you and attend to all duties of the tent; but shall not come near to the vessels of the sanctuary or the altar, lest they, and you, die. They shall join you and attend to the tent of the meeting, for all the service of the tent; and no one else shall come near you. And you shall attend to the duties of the sanctuary and the duties of the altar, that there be wrath no more upon the people of Israel.

MOSES: SINAI EXPERIENCE

Exodus 19:20; 20:1–20

And the Lord came down upon Mount Sinai, to the top of the mountain; and the Lord called Moses to the top of the mountain, and Moses went up.

And God spoke all these words, saying, "I am the Lord your

God, who brought you out of the land of Egypt, out of the house of bondage.

"You shall have no other gods before me.

"You shall not make for yourself a graven image, or any likeness of anything that is in heaven above, or that is in the earth beneath, or that is in the water under the earth; you shall not bow down to them or serve them; for I the Lord your God am a jealous God, visiting the iniquity of the fathers upon the children to the third and the fourth generation of those who hate me, but showing steadfast love to thousands of those who love me and keep my commandments.

"You shall not take the name of the Lord your God in vain; for the Lord will not hold him guiltless who takes his name in vain.

"Remember the sabbath day, to keep it holy. Six days you shall labor, and do all your work; but the seventh day is a sabbath to the Lord your God; in it you shall not do any work, you, or your son, or your daughter, your manservant, or your maidservant, or your cattle, or the sojourner who is within your gates; for in six days the Lord made heaven and earth, the sea, and all that is in them, and rested the seventh day; therefore the Lord blessed the sabbath day and hallowed it.

"Honor your father and your mother, that your days may be long in the land which the Lord your God gives you.

"You shall not kill.

"You shall not commit adultery.

"You shall not steal.

"You shall not bear false witness against your neighbor.

"You shall not covet your neighbor's house; you shall not covet your neighbor's wife, or his manservant, or his maidservant, or his ox, or his ass, or anything that is your neighbor's."

Now when all the people perceived the thunderings and the lightnings and the sound of the trumpet and the mountain smoking, the people were afraid and trembled; and they stood afar off, and said to Moses, "You speak to us, and we will hear; but let not God speak to us, lest we die." And Moses said to the people, "Do not fear; for God has come to prove you, and that the fear of him may be before your eyes, that you may not sin."

MOSES: A SPECIAL REQUEST OF GOD

Exodus 33:18–23; 34:28–35

Moses said, "I pray thee, show me thy glory." And he said, "I will make all my goodness pass before you, and will proclaim before you my name 'The Lord'; and I will be gracious to whom I will be gracious, and will show mercy on whom I will show mercy. But," he said, "you cannot see my face; for man shall not see me and live." And the Lord said, "Behold, there is a place by me where you shall stand upon the rock; and while my glory passes by I will put you in a cleft of the rock, and I will cover you with my hand until I have passed by; then I will take away my hand, and you shall see my back; but my face shall not be seen."

And he was there with the Lord forty days and forty nights; he neither ate bread nor drank water. And he wrote upon the tables the words of the covenant, the ten commandments.

When Moses came down from Mount Sinai, with the two tables of the testimony in his hand as he came down from the mountain, Moses did not know that the skin of his face shone because he had been talking with God. And when Aaron and all the people of Israel saw Moses, behold, the skin of his face shone, and they were afraid to come near him. But Moses called to them; and Aaron and all the leaders of the congregation returned to him, and Moses talked with them. And afterward all the people of Israel came near, and he gave them in commandment all that the Lord had spoken with him in Mount Sinai. And when Moses had finished speaking with them, he put a veil on his face; but whenever Moses went in before the Lord to speak with him, he took the veil off, until he came out; and when he came out, and told the people of Israel what he was commanded, the people of Israel saw the face of Moses, that the skin of Moses' face shone; and Moses would put the veil upon his face again, until he went in to speak with him.

MOSES: WATER FROM THE ROCK—DISOBEDIENCE
Numbers 20:7-13; 27:12-19

And the glory of the Lord appeared to them, and the Lord said to Moses, "Take the rod, and assemble the congregation, you and Aaron your brother, and tell the rock before their eyes to yield its water; so you shall bring water out of the rock for them; so you shall give drink to the congregation and their cattle." And Moses took the rod before the Lord, as he commanded him.

And Moses and Aaron gathered the assembly together before the rock, and he said to them, "Hear now, you rebels; shall we bring forth water for you out of this rock?" And Moses lifted up his hand and struck the rock with his rod twice; and water came forth abundantly, and the congregation drank, and their cattle.

And the Lord said to Moses and Aaron, "Because you did not believe in me, to sanctify me in the eyes of the people of Israel, therefore you shall not bring this assembly into the land which I have given them." These are the waters of Meribah, where the people of Israel contended with the Lord, and he showed himself holy among them.

The Lord said to Moses, "Go up into this mountain of Abarim, and see the land which I have given to the people of Israel. And when you have seen it, you shall be gathered to your people, as your brother Aaron was gathered, because you rebelled against my word in the wilderness of Zin during the strife of the congregation, to sanctify me at the waters before their eyes. (These are the waters of Meribah of Kadesh in the wilderness of Zin.) Moses said to the Lord, "Let the Lord, the God of the spirits of all flesh, appoint a man over the congregation, who shall go out before them and come in before them, who shall lead them out and bring them in; that the congregation of the Lord shall not be as sheep which have no shepherd." And the Lord said to Moses, "Take Joshua the son of Nun, a man in whom is the spirit, and lay your hand upon him; cause him to stand before Eleazar the priest and all the congregation, and you shall commission him in their sight."

MOSES: FORBIDDEN TO ENTER THE PROMISED LAND

Deuteronomy 3:18–28

"And I commanded you at that time, saying, 'The Lord your God has given you this land to possess; all your men of valor shall pass over armed before your brethren the people of Israel. But your wives, your little ones, and your cattle (I know that you have many cattle) shall remain in the cities which I have given you, until the Lord gives rest to your brethren, as to you, and they also occupy the land which the Lord your God gives them beyond the Jordan; then you shall return every man to his possession which I have given you.' And I commanded Joshua at that time, 'Your eyes have seen all that the Lord your God has done to these two kings; so will the Lord do to all the kingdoms in which you are going over. You shall not fear them; for it is the Lord your God who fights for you.'

"And I besought the Lord at that time, saying, 'O Lord God, thou hast only begun to show thy servant thy greatness and thy mighty hand; for what god is there in heaven or on earth who can do such works and mighty acts as thine? Let me go over, I pray, and see the good land beyond the Jordan, that goodly hill country, and Lebanon.' But the Lord was angry with me on your account, and would not hearken to me; and the Lord said to me, 'Let it suffice you; speak no more to me of this matter. Go up to the top of Pisgah, and lift up your eyes westward and northward and southward and eastward, and behold it with your eyes; for you shall not go over this Jordan. But charge Joshua, and encourage and strengthen him; for he shall go over at the head of this people, and he shall put them in possession of the land which you shall see.' "

MOSES: COMPLETING THE TABERNACLE

Exodus 40:1–38

The Lord said to Moses, "On the first day of the month you shall erect the tabernacle of the tent of meeting. And you shall put in it the ark of the testimony, and you shall screen the ark with the veil. And you shall bring in the table, and set its arrangements in order; and you shall bring in the lamp stand, and set up its lamps. And you shall put the golden altar for incense before the ark of the testimony, and set up the screen before the door of the tabernacle. You shall set the altar of burnt offering before the door of the tabernacle of the tent of meeting, and place the laver between the tent of the meeting and the altar, and put water in it. And you shall set up the court round about, and hang up the screen for the gate of the court. Then you shall take the anointing oil, and anoint the tabernacle and all that is in it, and consecrate it and all its furniture; and it shall become holy. You shall also anoint the laver and its base, and consecrate it. Then you shall bring Aaron and his sons to the door of the tent of meeting, and shall wash them with water, and put upon Aaron the holy garments, and you shall anoint him and consecrate him, that he may serve me as priest. You shall bring his sons also and put coats on them, and anoint them, as you anointed their father, that they may serve me as priests: and their anointing shall admit them to a perpetual priesthood throughout their generations."

Thus did Moses; according to all that the Lord commanded him, so he did. And in the first month in the second year, on the first day of the month, the tabernacle was erected. Moses erected the tabernacle; he laid its bases, and set up its frames, and put in its poles, and raised up its pillars; and he spread the tent over the tabernacle, and put the covering of the tent over it, as the Lord had commanded Moses. And he took the testimony and put it into the ark, and put the poles on the ark, and set the mercy seat above on the ark; and he brought the ark into the tabernacle, and set up the veil of the screen, and screened the ark of the testimony; as the Lord had commanded Moses. And he put the table in the tent of meeting, on the north side of the tabernacle, outside the veil, and set the bread in order on it before the Lord; as the Lord had commanded Moses. And he put the lamp stand in the tent of meeting, opposite the table on the south side of the tabernacle, and set up the lamps before the Lord; as the Lord had commanded Moses. And he put the golden altar in the tent of meeting before the veil, and burnt fragrant incense upon it; as the Lord had commanded Moses. And he put in place the screen for the door of the tabernacle. And he set the altar of burnt offering at the door of the tabernacle of the tent of meeting, and offered upon it the burnt offering and the cereal offering; as the Lord had commanded Moses. And he set the laver between the tent of meeting and the altar, and put water in it for washing, with which Moses and Aaron and his sons washed their hands and their feet; and they went into the tent of meeting, and when they approached the altar, they washed; as the Lord commanded Moses. And he erected the court round the tabernacle and the altar, and set up the screen at the gate of the court. So Moses finished the work.

Then the cloud covered the tent of meeting, and the glory of the Lord filled the tabernacle. And Moses was not able to enter the tent of meeting, because the cloud abode upon it, and the glory of the Lord filled the tabernacle. Throughout all their journeys, whenever the cloud was taken up from over the tabernacle, the people of Israel would go onward; but if the cloud was not taken up, when they did not go onward till the day that it was taken up. For throughout all their journeys the cloud of the Lord was upon the tabernacle by day, and fire was in it by night, in the sight of all the house of Israel.

MOSES: HIS DEATH

Deuteronomy 34:1–12

And Moses went up from the plains of Moab to Mount Nebo, to the top of Pisgah, which is opposite Jericho. And the Lord showed him all the land, Gilead as far as Dan, all Naphtali, the land of Ephraim and Manasseh, all the land of Judah as far as the Western Sea, the Negeb, and the Plain, that is, the valley of Jericho the city of palm trees, as far as Zoar. And the Lord said to him, "This is the land which I swore to Abraham, to Isaac, and to

Jacob, 'I will give it to your descendants.' I have let you see it with your eyes, but you shall not go over there." So Moses the servant of the Lord died there in the land of Moab, according to the word of the Lord, and he buried him in the valley of the land of Moab opposite Beth-peor; but no man knows the place of his burial to this day. Moses was a hundred and twenty years old when he died; his eye was not dimmed, nor his natural force abated. And the people of Israel wept for Moses in the plains of Moab thirty days; then the days of weeping and mourning for Moses were ended.

And Joshua the son of Nun was full of the spirit of wisdom, for Moses had laid his hand upon him; so the people of Israel obeyed him, and did as the Lord had commanded Moses. And there has not arisen a prophet since in Israel like Moses, whom the Lord knew face to face, none like him for all the signs and the wonders which the Lord sent him to do in the land of Egypt, to Pharaoh, and to all his servants and to all his land, and for all the mighty power and all the great and terrible deeds which Moses wrought in the sight of all Israel.

RUTH

The book of Ruth presents a beautiful story about a lovely woman. During the years of the great Judges of Israel, the Israelites were constantly at war. But the story of Ruth is far removed from these turbulent scenes. She lived in a place of peace and order, and her story unveils a delightful and charming picture of domestic, rural life. Hers is also a story of a beautiful friendship between two women. And the love story between Ruth and Boaz as a type is still supreme in literature.

At first glance, the story of Ruth may not seem of epic proportion; however, a thousand years earlier, Abraham had been called by God to begin a new nation for the purpose of someday bringing a Messiah to mankind. In the story of Ruth a family within that nation is founded through which the Messiah is to come: Ruth is the grandmother of King David, around whom the Old Testament centers in its historical development.

THE BOOK OF RUTH

In the days when the judges ruled there was a famine in the land, and a certain man of Bethlehem in Judah went to sojourn in the country of Moab, he and his wife and his two sons. The name of the man was Elimelech and the name of his wife Naomi, and the names of his two sons were Mahlon and Chilion; they were Ephrathites from Bethlehem in Judah. They went into the country of Moab and remained there. But Elimelech, the husband of Naomi, died, and she was left with her two sons. These took Moabite wives; the name of the one was Orpah and the name of the other Ruth. They lived there about ten years; and both Mahlon and Chilion died, so that the woman was bereft of her two sons and her husband.

Then she started with her daughters-in-law to return to the country of Moab, for she had heard in the country of Moab that the Lord had visited the people and given them food. So she set out from the place where she was, with her two daughters-in-law, and they went on the way to return to the land of Judah. But Naomi said to her two daughters-in-law, "Go, return each of you to her mother's house. May the Lord deal kindly with you, as you have dealt with the dead and with me. The Lord grant that you may find a home, each of you in the house of her husband!" Then she kissed them, and they lifted up their voices and wept. And they said to her, "No, we will return with you to your people." But Naomi said, "Turn back, my daughters, why will you go with me? Have I yet sons in my womb that they may become your husbands? Turn back, my daughters, go your way, for I am too old to have a husband. If I should say I have hope, even if I should have a husband this night and should bear sons, would you therefore wait until they were grown? Would you therefore refrain from marrying? No, my daughters, for it is exceedingly bitter to me for your sake that the hand of the Lord has gone forth against me." Then they lifted up their voices and wept again; and Orpah kissed her mother-in-law, but Ruth clung to her.

And she said, "See, your sister-in-law has gone back to her people and to her gods; return after your sister-in-law." But Ruth said, "Entreat me not to leave you, or to return from following you; for where you go I will go, and where you lodge I will lodge; your people shall be my people, and your God my God; where you die I will die, and there will I be buried. May the Lord do so to me and more also if even death parts me from you." And when Naomi saw that she was determined to go with her, she said no more.

So the two of them went on until they came to Bethlehem. And when they came to Bethlehem, the whole town was stirred because of them; and the women said, "Is this Naomi?" She said to them, "Do not call me Naomi, call me Mara, for the Almighty has dealt very bitterly with me. I went away full, and the Lord has brought me back empty. Why call me Naomi, when the Lord has afflicted me and the Almighty has brought calamity upon me?"

So Naomi returned, and Ruth the Moabitess her daughter-in-law with her, who returned from the country of Moab. And they came to Bethlehem at the beginning of barley harvest.

Now Naomi had a kinsman of her husband's, a man of wealth, of the family of Elimelech, whose name was Boaz. And Ruth the Moabitess said to Naomi, "Let me go to the field, and glean among the ears of grain after him in whose sight I shall find favor." And she said to her, "Go, my daughter." So she set forth and went and gleaned in the field after the reapers; and she happened to come to the part of the field belonging to Boaz, who was of the family of Elimelech. And behold, Boaz came from Bethlehem; and he said to the reapers, "The Lord be with you!" And they answered, "The Lord bless you." Then Boaz said to his servant who was in charge of the reapers, "Whose maid is this?" And the servant who was in charge of the reapers answered, "It is the Moabite maiden, who came back with Naomi from the country of Moab. She said, 'Pray, let me gather among the sheaves after the reapers.' So she came, and she has continued from early morning until now, without resting for even a moment."

Then Boaz said to Ruth, "Now, listen, my daughter, do not go to glean in another field or leave this one, but keep close to my maidens. Let your eyes be upon the field which they are reaping, and go after them. Have I not charged the young men not to molest you? And when you are thirsty, go to the vessels and drink what the young men have drawn." Then she fell on her face, bowing to the ground, and said to him, "Why have I found favor in your eyes, that you should take notice of me, when I am a foreigner?" But Boaz answered her, "All that you have done for your mother-in-law since the death of your husband has been fully told me, and how you left your father and mother and your native land and came to a people that you did not know before. The Lord recompense you for what you have done, and a full reward be given you by the Lord, the God of Israel, under whose wings you have come to take refuge!" Then she said, "You are most gracious to me, my lord, for you have comforted me and spoken kindly to your maidservant, though I am not of your maidservants."

And at mealtime Boaz said to her, "Come here, and eat some

bread, and dip your morsel in the wine." So she sat beside the reapers, and he passed to her parched grain; and she ate until she was satisfied, and she had some left over. When she rose to glean, Boaz instructed his young men, saying "Let her glean even among the sheaves, and do not reproach her. And also pull some out from the bundles for her, and leave it for her to glean, and do not rebuke her."

So she gleaned in the field until evening; then she beat out what she had gleaned, and it was about an ephah of barley. And she took it up and went into the city; she showed her mother-in-law what she had gleaned, and she also brought out and gave her what food she had left over after being satisfied. And her mother-in-law said to her, "Where did you glean today? And where have you worked? Blessed be the man who took notice of you." She told her mother-in-law with whom she had worked, and said, "The man's name with whom I worked today is Boaz." And Naomi said to her daughter-in-law, "Blessed be he by the Lord, whose kindness has not forsaken the living or the dead!" Naomi also said to her, "The man is a relative of ours, one of our nearest kin." And Ruth the Moabitess said, "Besides, he said to me, 'You shall keep close by my servants, till they have finished all my harvests.'" And Naomi said to Ruth, her daughter-in-law, "It is well, my daughter, that you go out with his maidens, lest in another field you be molested." So she kept close to the maidens of Boaz, gleaning until the end of the barley and wheat harvests; and she lived with her mother-in-law.

Then her mother-in-law said to her, "My daughter, should I not seek a home for you, that it may be well with you? Now is not Boaz our kinsman, with whose maidens you were? See, he is winnowing barley tonight at the threshing floor. Wash therefore and anoint yourself, and put on your best clothes and go down to the threshing floor; but do not make yourself known to the man until he finishes eating and drinking. But when he lies down, observe the place where he lies; then, go and uncover his feet and lie down; and he will tell you what to do." And she she said, "All that you say I will do."

So she went down to the threshing floor and did just as her mother-in-law had told her. And when Boaz had eaten and drunk, and his heart was merry, he went to lie down at the end of a heap of grain. Then she came softly, and uncovered his feet, and lay down. At midnight the man was startled, and turned over, and behold, a woman lay at his feet! He said, "Who are you?'' And she answered, "I am Ruth, your maidservant; spread your skirt over your maidservant, for you are next of kin." And he said, "May you be blessed by the Lord, my daughter; you have made the last kindness greater than the first, in that you have not gone after young men, whether poor or rich. And now, my daughter, do not fear, I will do for you all that you ask, for all my fellow townsmen know that you are a woman of worth. And now it is true that I am a near kinsman, yet there is a kinsman nearer than I. Remain this night, and in the morning, if he will do the part of the next of kin for you, well; let him do it; but if he is not willing to do the part of the next of kin for you, then, as the Lord lives, I will do the part of the next of kin for you. Lie down until the morning."

So she lay at his feet until the morning, but arose before one could recognize another, and he said, "Let it be known that the woman came to the threshing floor." And he said, "Bring the mantle you are wearing and hold it out." So she held it, and he measured out six measures of barley, and laid it upon her; then she went into the city. And when she came to her mother-in-law, she said, "How did you fare, my daughter?" Then she told her all that the man had done for her, saying, "These six measures of barley he gave to me, for he said, 'You must not go back empty-handed to your mother-in-law.' " She replied, "Wait, my daughter, until you learn how the matter turns out, for the man will not rest, but will settle the matter today."

And Boaz went up to the gate and sat down there; and behold, the next of kin, of whom Boaz had spoken, came by. So Boaz said, "Turn aside, friend; sit down here"; and he turned aside and sat down. And he took ten men of the elders of the city, and said, "Sit down here"; so they sat down. Then he said to the next of kin, "Naomi, who has come back from the country of the Moab, is selling the parcel of land which belonged to our kinsman Elimelech. So I thought I would tell you of it, and say, Buy it in the presence of those sitting here, and in the presence of the elders of my people. If you will redeem it, redeem it; but if you will not, tell me, that I may know, for there is no one besides you to redeem it, and I come after you." And he said, "I will redeem it." Then Boaz said, "The day you buy the field from the hand of Naomi, you are also buying Ruth the Moabitess, the widow of the dead, in order to restore the name of the dead to his inheritance." Then the next of kin said, "I cannot redeem it for myself, lest I impair my own inheritance. Take my right of redemption yourself, for I cannot redeem it."

Now this was the custom in former times in Israel concerning redeeming and exchanging: to confirm a transaction, the one drew off his sandal and gave it to the other, and this was the manner of attesting in Israel. So when the next of kin said, to Boaz, "Buy it for yourself," he drew off his sandal. Then Boaz said to the elders and all the people, "You are witnesses this day that I have bought from the hand of Naomi all that belonged to Elimelech and all that belonged to Chilion and to Mahlon. Also, Ruth the Moabitess, the widow of Mahlon, I have bought to be my wife, to perpetuate the name of the dead in his inheritance, that the name of the dead might not be cut off from among his brethren and from the gate of his native place; you are witnesses this day." Then all the people who were at the gate, and the elders, said, "We are witnesses. May the Lord make the woman, who is coming into your house, like Rachel and Leah, who together built up the house of Israel. May you prosper in Ephrathah and be renowned in Bethlehem; and may your house be like the house of Perez, whom Tamar bore to Judah, because of the children that the Lord will give you by this young woman."

So Boaz took Ruth and she became his wife; and he went in to her, and the Lord gave her conception, and she bore a son. Then the women said to Naomi, "Blessed be the Lord, who has not left you this day without next of kin; and may his name be renowned in Israel!" He shall be to you a restorer of life and a nourisher of your old age; for your daughter-in-law who loves you, who is more to you than seven sons, has borne him." Then Naomi took the child and laid him in her bosom, and became his nurse. And the women of the neighborhood gave him a name, saying, "A son has been born to Naomi." They named him Obed; he was the father of Jesse, the father of David.

SPECIAL HISTORY

The New Testament counterpart of Old Testament ecclesiastical history is the Gospels and the Acts of the Apostles. The Old Testament developed the concept of a single God and a single set of laws governing all men. The New Testament continues this theistic concept, but with an important ramification, Christ, Whose teaching and life help man to understand God and His laws. The four Gospels, Matthew, Mark, Luke, and John, all narrate, from a different point of view, the life and work of Jesus. The book of Acts is sort of a companion volume and carries on the story of Jesus' followers after the crucifixion.

The Gospels and the Acts are definitely not intended to be biographical, for a biography based upon them would be full of gaps. They are simply some of the acts and words of Christ and His followers. The selections in the following unit are arranged in historical order and the various Gospels are merged in an attempt to provide continuity.

The Acts, as the first history of the Christian Church, show the fusion of Jewish and Gentile thought and belief into one body through a common religious experience. Thus, these writings may be considered as a specific literary form. On one hand, they chronicle the life of Christ and are history. On the other hand, they are looked upon by many churches as supreme law and example and are dogma. Hence the label of Special History.

Probably no other figure has attracted as many serious writers as has Christ. In fact, whole schools of criticism have devoted pages to finding the Christ-like figure in works as diverse as *Hamlet* and John Millington Synge's *Playboy of the Western World*. The Christ-like hero may be easily seen in a work like *The Greek Passion* by Nikos Kanzantzakis where his hero is literally and figuratively crucified. In Hemingway's *Old Man and the Sea* the old man staggers up the hill carrying the heavy mast across his shoulders, stumbling several times, and finally collapses on his bed with his arms outstretched and his hands and forehead showing his recent wounds. Charles Dickens did much to inculcate the Christian virtues of love and good will toward men. It is safe to say that no other figure has appeared in as many major works of literature as has Christ.

THE GOSPELS

The period of history following the coming of Christ was one of great literary activity. Within a single generation the story of Jesus spread over the whole known world and enlisted countless thousands of devoted followers. Naturally there arose a great demand for written narratives of Christ's life. The Gospels answered this demand.

The four Gospels are four parallel accounts, narrating the same story, but with different emphases. Only Matthew and Luke tell of the birth and childhood of Jesus. Matthew and Mark dwell on His Galilean ministry; Luke, the Perean ministry; and John, the Judean. The week preceding the crucifixion of Jesus takes up one-third of Matthew's and Mark's Gospels, one-fourth of Luke's, and one-half of John's. In fact, John devoted one-third of his book to the Crucifixion Day, from sunset to sunset.

The following passages illustrate some of the more dramatic incidents in the Gospels and highlight the life and work of Christ.

JOHN, THE BAPTIZER: FORERUNNER OF CHRIST
Luke 1:5–17, 57–80

In the days of Herod, king of Judea, there was a priest named Zechariah, of the division of Abijah; and he had a wife of the daughters of Aaron, and her name was Elizabeth. And they were both righteous before God, walking in all the commandments and ordinances of the Lord blameless. But they had no child, because Elizabeth was barren, and both were advanced in years.

Now while he was serving as priest before God when his division was on duty, according to the custom of the priesthood, it fell to him by lot to enter the temple of the Lord and burn incense. And the whole multitude of the people were praying outside at the hour of incense. And there appeared to him an angel of the Lord standing on the right side of the altar of incense. And Zechariah was troubled when he saw him, and fear fell upon him. But the angel said to him, "Do not be afraid, Zechariah, for your prayer is heard, and your wife Elizabeth will bear you a son, and you shall call his name John.

And you will have joy and gladness,
and many will rejoice at his birth;
for he will be great before the Lord,
and he shall drink no wine or strong drink,
and he will be filled with the Holy Spirit,
even from his mother's womb.
And he will turn many of the sons of Israel to the Lord their
God,
and he will go before him in the spirit and power of Elijah,
to turn the hearts of the fathers to the children,
and the disobedient to the wisdom of the just,
to make ready for the Lord a people prepared."

Now the time came for Elizabeth to be delivered, and she gave birth to a son. And her neighbors and kinsfolk heard that the Lord had shown great mercy to her, and they rejoiced with her. And on the eighth day they came to circumcise the child; and they would have named him Zechariah after his father, but his mother said, "Not so; he shall be called John." And they said to her, "None of your kindred is called by this name." And they made signs to his father, inquiring what he would have him called. And he asked for a writing tablet, and wrote, "His name is John." And they all marveled. And immediately his mouth was opened and his tongue loosed, and he spoke, blessing God. And fear came on all their neighbors. And all these things were talked about all through the hill country of Judea; and all who heard them laid them up in their hearts, saying, "What then will this child be?" For the hand of the Lord was with him.

And his father Zechariah was filled with the Holy Spirit, and prophesied, saying,

> "Blessed be the Lord God of Israel,
> for he has visited and redeemed his people,
> and has raised up a horn of salvation for us
> in the house of his servant David,
> as he spoke by the mouths of his holy prophets from of old,
> that we should be saved from our enemies,
> and from the hand of all who hate us;
> to perform the mercy promised to our fathers,
> and to remember his holy covenant,
> the oath which he swore to our father Abraham, to grant us
> that we, being delivered from the hand of our enemies,
> might serve him without fear,
> in holiness and righteousness before him all the days of our
>   life.
> And you, child, will be called the prophet of the Most High;
> for you will go before the Lord to prepare his ways,
> to give knowledge of salvation to his people,
> in the forgiveness of their sins,
> through the tender mercy of our God,
> when the day shall dawn upon us from on high
> to give light to those who sit in darkness and in the shadow of
>   death,
> to guide our feet into the way of peace."

And the child grew and became strong in spirit, and he was in the wilderness till the day of his manifestation to Israel.

BIRTH OF JESUS

Luke 1:26–56; 2:1–21; Matthew 2:1–23

The angel Gabriel was sent from God to a city of Galilee named Nazareth, to a virgin betrothed to a man whose name was Joseph, of the house of David; and the virgin's name was Mary. And he came to her and said, "Hail, O favored one, the Lord is with you!" But she was greatly troubled at the saying, and considered in her mind what sort of greeting this might be. And the angel said to her, "Do not be afraid, Mary, for you have found favor with God. And behold, you shall conceive in your womb and bear a son, and you shall call his name Jesus.

> He will be great, and will be called the Son of the Most High;
> and the Lord will give to him the throne of his father David,
> and he will reign over the house of Jacob forever;
> and of his kingdom there will be no end."

And Mary said to the angel, "How can this be, since I have no husband?" And the angel said to her,

> "The Holy Spirit will come upon you,
> and the power of the Most High will overshadow you;
> therefore, the child to be born will be called holy,
> the Son of God.

And behold your kinswoman Elizabeth in her old age has also conceived a son; and this is the sixth month with her who was called barren. For with God nothing will be impossible." And Mary said, "Behold, I am the handmaiden of the Lord; let it be to me according to your word." And the angel departed from her.

In those days Mary arose and went with haste into the hill country, to a city of Judah, and she entered the house of Zechariah and greeted Elizabeth. And when Elizabeth heard the greeting of Mary, the babe leaped in her womb; and Elizabeth was filled with the Holy Spirit and she exclaimed with a loud cry, "Blessed are you among women, and blessed is the fruit of your womb! And why is this granted me, that the mother of my Lord should come to me? For behold, when the voice of your greeting came to my ears, the babe in my womb leaped for joy. And blessed is she who believed that there would be a fulfilment of what was spoken to her from the Lord."

And Mary said,

> "My soul magnifies the Lord,
> and my spirit rejoices in God my Savior,
> for he has regarded the low estate of his handmaiden.
> For behold, henceforth all generations will call me blessed;
> for he who is mighty has done great things for me,

and holy is his name.
And his mercy is on those who fear him
from generation to generation.
He has shown strength with his arm,
he has scattered the proud in the imagination of their hearts,
he has put down the mighty from their thrones,
and exalted those of low degree;
he has filled the hungry with good things,
and the rich he has sent empty away.
He has helped his servant Israel,
in remembrance of his mercy,
as he spoke to our fathers,
to Abraham and to his posterity forever."

And Mary remained with her about three months, and returned to her home.

In those days a decree went out from Caesar Augustus that all the world should be enrolled. This was the first enrollment, when Quirinius was governor of Syria. And all went to be enrolled, each to his own city. And Joseph also went up from Galilee, from the city of Nazareth, to Judea, the city of David, which is called Bethlehem, because he was of the house and lineage of David, to be enrolled with Mary, his betrothed, who was with child. And while they were there the time came for her to be delivered. And she gave birth to her first-born son and wrapped him in swaddling clothes, and laid him in a manger, because there was no place for them in the inn.

And in that region there were shepherds out in the field, keeping watch over their flock by night. And the angel of the Lord appeared to them, and the glory of the Lord shone around them, and they were filled with fear. And the angel said to them, "Be not afraid; for behold, I bring you good news of a great joy which will come to all the people; for to you is born this day in the city of David a Savior, who is Christ the Lord. And this will be a sign for you: you will find a babe wrapped in swaddling clothes and lying in a manger." And suddenly there was with the angel a multitude of the heavenly host praising God and saying,

"Glory to God in the highest,
and on earth peace among men with whom he is pleased!"

When the angels went away from them into heaven, the shepherds said to one another, "Let us go over to Bethlehem and see this thing that has happened, which the Lord has made known to us." And they went with haste, and found Mary and Joseph, and the babe lying in a manger. And when they saw it they made known the saying which had been told them concerning this child; and all who heard it wondered at what the shepherds told them. But Mary kept all these things, pondering them in her heart. And the shepherds returned, glorifying and praising God for all they had heard and seen, as it had been told them.

And at the end of eight days, when he was circumcised, he was called Jesus, the name given by the angel before he was conceived in the womb.

Now when Jesus was born in Bethlehem of Judea in the days of Herod the king, behold, wise men from the East came to Jerusalem, saying, "Where is he who has been born king of the Jews? For we have seen his star in the East, and have come to worship him." When Herod the king heard this, he was troubled, and all Jerusalem with him; and assembling all the chief priests and scribes of the people, he inquired of them where the Christ was to be born. They told him, "In Bethlehem of Judea; for so it is written by the prophet:

'And you, O Bethlehem, in the land of Judah,
are by no means least among the rulers of Judah;
for from you shall come a ruler
who will govern my people Israel.'"

Then Herod summoned the wise men secretly and ascertained from them what time the star appeared; and he sent them to Bethlehem, saying, "Go and search diligently for the child, and when you have found him bring me word, that I too may come and worship him." When they had heard the king they went their way; and lo, the star which they had seen in the East went before them, till it came to rest over the place where the child was. When they saw the star they rejoiced exceedingly with great joy; and going into the house they saw the child with Mary his mother, and they fell down and worshipped him. Then opening their treasures, they offered him gifts, gold and frankincense and myrrh. And being warned in a dream not to return to Herod, they departed to their own country by another way.

Now when they had departed, behold, an angel of the Lord appeared unto Joseph in a dream and said, "Rise, take the child and his mother, and flee to Egypt, and remain there till I tell you; for Herod is about to search for the child, to destroy him." And he arose and took the child and his mother by night, and departed to Egypt, and remained there until the death of Herod. This was to fulfil what the Lord had spoken by the prophet, "Out of Egypt have I called my son."

Then Herod, when he saw that he had been tricked by the wise men, was in a furious rage, and he sent and killed all the male children in Bethlehem and in all that region who were two years old or under, according to the time which he had ascertained from the wise men. Then was fulfilled what was spoken by the prophet Jeremiah:

"A voice was heard in Ramah,
wailing and loud lamentation,
Rachel weeping for her children;
she refused to be consoled,
because they were no more."

But when Herod died, behold, an angel of the Lord appeared in a dream to Joseph in Egypt, saying, "Rise, take the child and his mother, and go to the land of Israel, for those who sought the child's life are dead." And he rose and took the child and his mother, and went to the land of Israel. But when he heard that Archelaus reigned over Judea in place of his father Herod, he was afraid to go there, and being warned in a dream he withdrew to the district of Galilee. And he went and dwelt in a city called Nazareth, that what was spoken by the prophet might be fulfilled, "He shall be called a Nazarene."

BOYHOOD VISIT TO THE TEMPLE

Luke 2:41–52

Now his parents went to Jerusalem every year at the feast of the Passover. And when he was twelve years old, they went up according to custom; and when the feast was ended, as they were returning, the boy stayed behind in Jerusalem. His parents did not know it, but supposing him to be in the company they went a day's journey, and they sought him among their kinsfolk and acquaintances; and when they did not find him, they returned to Jerusalem seeking him. After three days they found him in the temple, sitting among the teachers, listening to them, and asking them questions; and all who heard him were amazed at his understanding and his answers. And when they saw him they were astonished; and his mother said to him, "Son, why have you treated us so? Behold, your father and I have been looking for you anxiously." and he said to them, "How is it that you sought me? Did you not know that I must be in my Father's house?" And they did not understand the saying which he spoke to them. And he went down with them and came to Nazareth, and was obedient to them; and his mother kept all these things in her heart.

And Jesus increased in wisdom and in stature, and in favor with God and man.

JESUS IS BAPTIZED OF JOHN

Luke 3:2–22

The word of God came to John the son of Zechariah in the wilderness; and he went into all the region about the Jordan, preaching a baptism of repentance for the forgiveness of sins. As it is written in the book of the words of Isaiah the prophet,

"The voice of one crying in the wilderness:
Prepare the way of the Lord,
make his paths straight.
Every valley shall be filled,
and every mountain and hill shall be brought low,
and the crooked shall be made straight,
and the rough ways shall be made smooth;
and all flesh shall see the salvation of God."

He said therefore to the multitudes that came out to be baptized by him, "You brood of vipers! Who warned you to flee from the wrath to come? Bear fruits that befit repentance, and do not begin to say to yourselves, 'We have Abraham as our father'; for I tell you, God is able from these stones to raise up children to Abraham. Even now the axe is laid to the root of the trees; every tree therefore that does not bear good fruit is cut down and thrown into the fire."

And the multitudes asked him, "What then shall we do?" And he answered them, "He who has two coats, let him share with him who has none; and he who has food, let him do likewise." Tax collectors also came to be baptized, and said to him, "Teacher, what shall we do?" And he said to them, "Collect no more than is appointed you." Soldiers also asked him, "And we, what shall we do?" And he said to them, "Rob no one by violence or by false accusation, and be content with your wages."

As the people were in expectation, and all men questioned in their hearts concerning John, whether perhaps he were the Christ, John answered them all, "I baptize you with water; but he who is mightier than I is coming, the thong of whose sandals I am not worthy to untie; he will baptize you with the Holy Spirit and with fire. His winnowing fork is in his hand, to clear his threshing floor, and to gather the wheat into his granary, but the chaff he will burn with unquenchable fire."

So, with many other exhortations, he preached good news to the people. But Herod the tetrarch, who had been reproved by him for Herodi-as, his brother's wife, and for all the evil things that Herod had done, added this to them all, that he shut up John in prison.

Now when all the people were baptized, and when Jesus had been baptized and was praying, the heaven was opened, and the Holy Spirit descended upon him in bodily form, as a dove, and a voice came from heaven, "Thou art my beloved Son; with whom I am well pleased."

TEMPTATION OF JESUS BY SATAN

Luke 4:1–13

And Jesus, full of the Holy Spirit, returned from the Jordan, and was led by the Spirit for forty days in the wilderness, tempted by the devil. And he ate nothing in those days; and when they were ended, he was hungry. The devil said to him, "If you are the Son of God, command this stone to become bread." And Jesus answered him, "It is written, 'Man shall not live by bread alone.'" And the devil took him up, and showed him all the kingdoms of the world in a moment of time, and said to him, "To you I will give all this authority and their glory; for it has been delivered to me, and I give it to whom I will. If you, then, will worship me, it shall all be yours." And Jesus answered him, "It is written,

'You shall worship the Lord your God,
and him only shall you serve.'"

And he took him to Jerusalem, and set him on the pinnacle of the temple, and said to him, "If you are the Son of God, throw yourself down from here; for it is written,

'He will give his angels charge over you, to guard you,'
and

'On their hands they will bear you up,
lest you strike you foot against a stone.'"

And Jesus answered him, "It is said, 'You shall not tempt the Lord
your God." And when the devil had ended every temptation, he
departed from him until an opportune time.

CALL FOR DISCIPLESHIP: SIMON PETER

Luke 5:1–11

While the people pressed upon him to hear the word of God,
he was standing by the lake of Gennesaret. And he saw two boats
by the lake; but the fishermen had gone out of them, and were
washing their nets. Getting into one of the boats, which was
Simon's, he asked him to put out a little from the land. And he
sat down and taught the people from the boat. And when he had
ceased speaking, he said to Simon, "Put out into the deep and
put down your nets for a catch." And Simon answered, "Master,
we toiled all night and took nothing! But at your word I will let
down the nets." And when they had done this they enclosed a
great shoal of fish; and as their nets were breaking, they beckoned
to their partners in the other boat to come and help them. And
they came and filled both boats, so that they began to sink. But
when Simon Peter saw it, he fell down at Jesus' knees, saying,
"Depart from me, for I am a sinful man, O Lord." For he was
astonished, and all that were with him, at the catch of fish which
they had taken; and so also were James and John, sons of Zebe-
dee, who were partners with Simon. And Jesus said to Simon,
"Do not be afraid; henceforth you will be catching men." And
when they had brought their boats to land, they left everything and
followed him.

MATTHEW

Luke 5:27–32

After this he went out, and saw a tax collector, named Levi,
sitting at the tax office; and he said to him, "Follow me." And he
left everything, and rose and followed him.

And Levi made a great feast in his house; and there was a large
company of tax collectors and others sitting at the table with them.
And the Pharisees and their scribes murmured against his disciples,
saying, "Why do you eat and drink with tax collectors and sinners?" And Jesus answered them, "Those who are well have no

need of a physician, but those who are sick; I have not come to call the righteous, but sinners to repentance."

TEST OF DISCIPLESHIP

Luke 9:57–62

As they were going along the road, a man said to him, "I will follow you wherever you go." And Jesus said to him, "Foxes have holes, and birds of the air have nests; but the Son of man has nowhere to lay his head." To another he said, "Follow me." But he said, "Lord, let me first go and bury my father." But he said to him, "Leave the dead to bury their own dead; but as for you, go and proclaim the kingdom of God." Another said, "I will follow you, Lord; but let me first say farewell to those at my home." Jesus said to him, "No one who puts his hand to the plow and looks back is fit for the kingdom of God."

FIVE THOUSAND PEOPLE FED

Matthew 14:13–21

He withdrew there in a boat to a lonely place apart. But when the crowds heard it, they followed him on foot from the towns. As he went ashore he saw a great throng; and he had compassion on them, and healed their sick. When it was evening, the disciples came to him and said, "This a lonely place and the day is now over; send the crowds away to go into the villages and buy food for themselves." Jesus said, "They need not go away; you give them something to eat." They said to him, "We have only five loaves here and two fish." And he said, "Bring them here to me." Then he ordered the crowds to sit down on the grass; and taking the five loaves and the two fish he looked up to heaven, and blessed, and broke and gave the loaves to the disciples, and the disciples gave them to the crowds. And they all ate and were satisfied. And they took up twelve baskets full of the broken pieces left over. And those who ate were about five thousand men, besides women and children.

JESUS WALKS ON THE WATER

Matthew 14:22–33

Then he made the disciples get into the boat and go before him to the other side, while he dismissed the crowds. And after he had dismissed the crowds, he went up into the hills by himself to pray. When evening came, he was there alone, but the boat by this time was many furlongs distant from the land, beaten by the waves; for the wind was against them. And in the fourth watch of the night he came to them, walking on the sea. But when the disciples saw him walking on the sea, they were terrified, saying, "It is a ghost!" And they cried out for fear. But immediately he spoke to them, saying, "Take heart, it is I; have no fear."

And Peter answered him, "Lord, if it is you, bid me come to you on the water." He said, "Come." So Peter got out of the boat and walked on the water and came to Jesus; but when he saw the wind, he was afraid, and beginning to sink he cried out, "Lord, save me." Jesus immediately reached out his hand and caught him, saying to him, "O man of little faith, why did you doubt?" And when he got into the boat, the wind ceased. And those in the boat worshipped him, saying, "Truly you are the Son of God."

DISCOURSE ON HUMILITY

Matthew 18:1–14

At that time the disciples came to Jesus, saying, "Who is the greatest in the kingdom of heaven?" And calling to him a child, he put him in the midst of them, and said, "Truly, I say to you, unless you turn and become like children, you will never enter the kingdom of heaven. Whoever humbles himself like this child, he is the greatest in the kingdom of heaven.

"Whoever receives one such child in my name receives me; but whoever causes one of these little ones who believe in me to sin, it would be better for him to have a great millstone fastened round his neck and to be drowned in the depth of the sea.

"Woe to the world for temptations to sin. For it is necessary that temptations come, but woe to the man by whom the temptation comes! And if your hand or your foot causes you to sin, cut it off and throw it from you; it is better for you to enter life maimed or lame than with two hands or two feet to be thrown into eternal fire. And if your eye causes you to sin, pluck it out and throw it from you; it is better for you to enter life with one eye than with two eyes to be thrown into the hell of fire.

"See that you do not despise one of these little ones; for I tell you that in heaven their angels always hold the face of my Father who is in heaven. What do you think? If a man has a hundred sheep, and one of them has gone astray, does he not leave the ninety-nine on the hills and go in search of the one that went astray? And if he finds it, truly, I say to you, he rejoices over it more than over the ninety-nine that never went astray. So it is not the will of my Father who is in heaven that one of these little ones should perish.

PETER'S CONFESSION

Matthew 16:13–20

Now when Jesus came into the district of Caesarea Philippi, he asked his disciples, "Who do men say that the Son of man is?" And they said, "Some say John the Baptist, others say Elijah, and others Jeremiah or one of the prophets." He said to them, "But who do you say that I am?" Simon Peter replied, "You are the Christ, the Son of the living God." And Jesus answered him, "Blessed are you, Simon Bar-Jona! For flesh and blood has not revealed this to you, but my Father who is in heaven. And I tell you, you are Peter, and on this rock I will build my church, and powers of death shall not prevail against it. I will give you the keys of the kingdom of heaven, and whatever you bind on earth shall be bound in heaven, and whatever you loose on earth shall be loosed in heaven." Then he strictly charged the disciples to tell no one that he was the Christ.

THE RICH MAN AND LAZARUS

Luke 16:19–31

"There was a rich man, who was clothed in purple and fine linen and who feasted sumptuously every day. And at his gate lay a poor man named Lazarus, full of sores, who desired to be fed with what fell from the rich man's table; moreover the dogs came and licked his sores. The poor man died and was carried by the angels to Abraham's bosom. The rich man also died and was buried; and in Hades, being in torment, he lifted up his eyes, and saw Abraham afar off and Lazarus in his bosom. And he called out 'Father Abraham, have mercy upon me, and send Lazarus to dip the end of his finger in water and cool my tongue; for I am in anguish in this flame.' But Abraham said, 'Son, remember that you in your lifetime received your good things, and Lazarus in like manner evil things; but now he is comforted here, and you are in anguish. And besides all this, between us and you a great chasm has been fixed, in order that those who would pass from here to you may not be able, and none may cross from there to us.' And he said, 'Then I beg you, father, to send him to my father's house, for I have five brothers, so that he may warn them, lest they also come to this place of torment.' But Abraham said, 'They have Moses and the prophets; let them hear them.' And he said, 'No, father Abraham; but if someone goes to them from the dead, they will repent.' He said to him, 'If they do not hear Moses and the prophets, neither will they be convinced if someone should rise from the dead.' "

THE RICH YOUNG RULER

Matthew 19:16-30

And behold, one came to him, saying, "Teacher, what good deed must I do, to have eternal life?" And he said to him, "Why do you ask me about what is good? One there is who is good. If you would enter life, keep the commandments." He said to him, "Which?" And Jesus said, "You shall not kill, You shall not commit adultery, You shall not steal, You shall not bear false witness, Honor your father and mother, and, You shall love your neighbor as yourself." The young man said to him. "All these I have observed; what do I still lack?" Jesus said to him, "If you would be perfect, go, sell what you possess and give to the poor, and you will have treasure in heaven; and come, follow me." When the young man heard this he went away sorrowful; for he had great possessions.

And Jesus said to his disciples, "Truly, I say to you, it will be hard for a rich man to enter the kingdom of heaven. Again I tell you, it is easier for a camel to go through the eye of a needle than for a rich man to enter the kingdom of God." When the disciples heard this they were greatly astonished, saying, "Who then can be saved?" But Jesus looked at them and said to them, "With men this is impossible, but with God all things are possible." Then Peter said in reply, "Lo, we have left everything and followed you. What then shall we have?" Jesus said to them, "Truly, I say to you, in the new world, when the Son of man shall sit on his glorious throne, you who have followed me will also sit on twelve thrones, judging the twelve tribes of Israel. And every one who has left houses or brothers or sisters or father or mother or children or lands, for my name's sake, shall receive a hundredfold, and inherit eternal life. But many that are first will be last, and the last first."

THE RAISING OF LAZARUS

John 11:1-53

Now a certain man was ill, Lazarus of Bethany, the village of Mary and her sister Martha. It was Mary who anointed the Lord with ointment and wiped his feet with her hair, whose brother

Lazarus was ill. So the sisters sent to him, saying, "Lord, he whom you love is ill." But when Jesus heard it he said, "This illness is not unto death; it is for the glory of God, so that the Son of God may be glorified by means of it."

Now Jesus loved Martha and her sister and Lazarus. So when he heard that he was ill, he stayed two days longer in the place where he was. Then after this he said to his disciples, "Let us go to Judea again." The disciples said to him, "Rabbi, the Jews were but seeking to stone you, and are you going there again?" Jesus answered, "Are there not twelve hours in the day? If anyone walks in the day, he does not stumble, because he sees the light of this world. But if anyone walks in the night, he stumbles, because the light is not in him." Thus he spoke, and then he said to them, "Our friend Lazarus has fallen asleep, but I go to waken him out of sleep." The disciples said to him, "Lord, if he has fallen asleep, he will recover." Now Jesus had spoken of his death, but they thought that he meant taking rest in sleep. Then Jesus told them plainly, "Lazarus is dead; and for your sake I am glad that I was not there, so that you may believe. But let us go to him." Thomas, called the Twin, said to his fellow disciples, "Let us also go, that we may die with him."

Now when Jesus came, he found that Lazarus had already been in the tomb four days. Bethany was near Jerusalem, about two miles off, and many of the Jews had come to Martha and Mary to console them concerning their brother. When Martha heard that Jesus was coming, she went and met him, while Mary sat in the house. Martha said to Jesus, "Lord, if you had been here, my brother would not have died. And even now I know that whatever you ask from God, God will give you." Jesus said to her, "Your brother will rise again." Martha said to him, "I know that he will rise again in the resurrection at the last day." Jesus said to her, "I am the resurrection and the life; he who believes in me, though he die, yet shall he live, and whoever lives and believes in me shall never die. Do you believe this?" She said to him, "Yes, Lord, I believe that you are the Christ, the Son of God, he who is coming into the world."

When she had said this, she went and called her sister Mary, saying quietly, "The Teacher is here and is calling for you." And when she heard it, she rose quickly and went to him. Now Jesus had not yet come to the village, but was still in the place where Martha had met him. When the Jews who were with her in the house, consoling her, saw Mary rise quickly and go out, they followed her, supposing that she was going to the tomb to weep there. Then Mary, when she came to where Jesus was and saw him, fell at his feet, saying to him, "Lord, if you had been here, my brother would not have died." When Jesus saw her weeping, and the Jews who came with her also weeping, he was deeply moved in spirit and troubled; and he said, "Where have you laid him?" They said to him, "Lord, come and see." Jesus wept. So the Jews said, "See how he loved him!" But some of them said, "Could not he who opened the eyes of the blind man have kept this man from dying?"

Then Jesus, deeply moved again, came to the tomb; it was a cave, and a stone lay upon it. Jesus said, "Take away the stone." Martha, the sister of the dead man, said to him, "Lord, by this time there will be an odor, for he has been dead four days." Jesus said to her, "Did I not tell you that if you would believe you would see the glory of God?" So they took away the stone. And Jesus lifted up his eyes and said, "Father, I thank thee that thou hast heard me. I knew that thou hearest me always, but I have said this on account of the people standing by, that they might believe that thou didst send me." When he had said this, he cried with a loud voice, "Lazarus, come out." The dead man came out, his hands and feet bound with bandages, and his face wrapped with a cloth. Jesus said, "Unbind him, and let him go."

Many of the Jews therefore, who had come with Mary and had seen what he did, believed in him; but some of them went to the Pharisees and told them what Jesus had done. So the chief priests and the Pharisees gathered the council, and said, "What are we to do? For this man performs many signs. If we let him go thus, everyone will believe in him, and the Romans will come and destroy both our holy place and our nation." But one of them, Caiaphas, who was high priest that year, said to them, "You know nothing at all; you do not understand that it is expedient for you that one man should die for the people, and that the whole nation should not perish." He did not say this of his own accord, but being high priest that year he prophesied that Jesus should die for the nation, and not for the nation only, but to gather into one the children of God who are scattered abroad. So from that day on they took counsel how to put him to death.

TRIUMPHAL ENTRY INTO JERUSALEM

Luke 19:28–48

He went on ahead, going up to Jerusalem. When he drew near to Bethphage and Bethany, at the mount that is called Olivet, he sent two of the disciples, saying, "Go into the village opposite, where on entering you will find a colt tied, on which no one has ever yet sat; unite it and bring it here. If anyone asks you, 'Why are you untying it?' you shall say, 'The Lord has need of it.'" So those who were sent went away and found it as he had told them. And as they were untying the colt, its owners said to them, "Why are you untying the colt?" And they said, "The Lord has need of it." And they brought it to Jesus, and throwing their garments on the colt they set Jesus upon it. And as he rode along, they spread their garments on the road. As he was drawing near, at the descent of the Mount of Olives, the whole multitude of the disciples began to rejoice and praise God with a loud voice for all the mighty works that they had seen, saying, "Blessed is the King who comes in the name of the Lord! Peace in heaven and glory in the highest!" And some of the Pharisees in the multitude said to him, "Teacher, rebuke your disciples." He answered, "I tell you, if these were silent, the very stones would cry out."

And when he drew near and saw the city he wept over it, saying, "Would that even today you knew the things that make for peace! But now they are hid from your eyes. For the days shall come upon you, when your enemies will cast up a bank about you and surround you, and hem you in on every side, and dash you to the ground, you and your children within you, and they will not leave one stone upon another in you; because you did not know the time of your visitation."

And he entered the temple and began to drive out those who sold, saying to them, "It is written, 'My house shall be a house of prayer'; but you have made it a den of robbers."

And he was teaching daily in the temple. The chief priests and the principal men of the people sought to destroy him; but they did not find anything they could do, for all the people hung upon his words.

BETRAYAL OF JUDAS

Luke 22:1–22; John 18:1–5; Matthew 26:48–49;
Luke 22:48; John 18:10; Matthew 26:52–57; 27:3–5

Now the feast of Unleavened Bread drew near, which is called the Passover. And the chief priests and the scribes were seeking how to put him to death; for they feared the people.

Then Satan entered into Judas called Iscariot, who was of the number of the twelve; and he went away and conferred with the chief priests and the captains how he might betray him to them. And they were glad, and engaged to give him money. So he agreed, and sought an opportunity to betray him to them in the absence of the multitude.

Then came the day of Unleavened Bread, on which the passover lamb had to be sacrificed. So Jesus sent Peter and John, saying, "Go and prepare the passover for us, that we may eat it." They said to him, "Where will you have us prepare it?" He said to them, "Behold, when you have entered the city, a man carrying a jar of water will meet you; follow him into the house which he enters, and tell the householder, 'The teacher says to you, Where is the guest room, where I am to eat the passover with my disciples?' And he will show you a large upper room furnished; there make ready." And they went, and found it as he had told them; and they prepared the passover.

And when the hour came, he sat at table, and the apostles with him. And he said to them, "I have earnestly desired to eat this passover with you before I suffer; for I tell you I shall not eat it until it is fulfilled in the kingdom of God. And he took a cup, and when he had given thanks he said, "Take this, and divide it among yourselves; for I tell you that from now on I shall not drink of the fruit of the vine until the kingdom of God comes." And he took bread, and when he gave thanks he broke it, and gave it to them, saying, "This is my body. But behold the hand of him who betrays me is with me on the table. For the Son of man goes as it has been determined; but woe to that man by whom he is betrayed!"

When Jesus had spoken these words, he went forth with his disciples across the Kidron valley, where there was a garden, which he and his disciples entered. Now Judas, who betrayed him, also knew the place; for Jesus often met there with his disciples. So Judas, procuring a band of soldiers and some officers from the chief priest and the Pharisees, went there with lanterns and torches and weapons. Then Jesus, knowing all that would befall him, came forward and said to them, "Whom do you seek?" They answered him, "Jesus of Nazareth." Now the betrayer had given them a sign, saying, "The one I shall kiss is the man; seize him." And he came up to Jesus at once and said, "Hail, Master!" And he kissed him. Jesus said to him, "Judas, would you betray the Son of man with a kiss?" Then Simon Peter, having a sword, drew it and struck the high priest's slave and cut off his right ear. The slave's name was Malchus. Then Jesus said to him, "Put your sword back into its place; for all who take the sword shall perish by the sword. Do you think that I cannot appeal to my father, and he will at once send me more than twelve legions of angels? But how then shall the scriptures be fulfilled, that it must be so?" At that hour Jesus said to the crowds, "Have you come out as against a robber, with swords and clubs to capture me? Day after day I sat in the temple teaching, and you did not seize me. But all this has taken place, that the scriptures of the prophets might be fulfilled." Then all the disciples forsook him and fled.

Then those who had seized Jesus led him to Caiaphas the high priest, where the scribes and the elders had gathered.

When Judas, his betrayer, saw that he was condemmed, he repented and brought back the thirty pieces of silver to the chief priests and the elders, saying, "I have sinned in betraying innocent blood." They said, "What is that to us. See to it yourself." And throwing down the pieces of silver in the temple, he departed; and he went and hanged himself.

THE CRUCIFIXION OF JESUS

Luke 22:63–71; John 18:28–40; Luke 23:6–12;
John 19:1–17; Luke 23:26–47; John 19:31–37;
Luke 23:50–56

Now the men who were holding Jesus mocked him and beat him; they also blindfolded him and asked him, "Prophesy! Who is it that struck you?" And they spoke many other words against him, reviling him.

When day came, the assembly of the elders of the people gathered together, both chief priests and scribes; and they led him away to their council, and they said, "If you are you the Christ, tell us." But he said to them, "If I tell you, you will not believe; and if I ask you, you will not answer. But from now on the Son of man shall be seated at the right hand of the power of God." And they all said, "Are you the Son of God, then?" And he said to them, "You say that I am." And they said, "What further testimony do we need? We have heard it ourselves from his own lips."

Then they led Jesus from the house of Caiaphas to the praetorium. It was early. They themselves did not enter the praetorium, so that they might not be defiled, but might eat the passover. So Pilate went out to them, and said, "What accusation do you bring against this man?" They answered him, "If this man were not an evildoer, we would not have handed him over." Pilate said to them, "Take him yourselves and judge him by your own law." The Jews said to him, "It is not lawful for us to put any man to death." This was to fulfill the word which Jesus had spoken to show by what death he was to die.

Pilate entered the praetorium again and called Jesus, and said to him, "Are you the King of the Jews?" Jesus answered, "Do you say this of your own accord, or did others say it to you about me?" Pilate answered, "Am I a Jew? Your own nation and the chief priests have handed you over to me; what have you done?" Jesus answered, "My kingship is not of this world; if my kingship were of this world, my servants would fight, that I might not be handed over to the Jews; but my kingship is not from the world." Pilate said to him, "So you are a king?" Jesus answered, "You say that I am a king. For this I was born, and for this I have come into the world, to bear witness to the truth. Everyone who is of the truth hears my voice." Pilate said to him, "What is truth?"

After he had said this, he went out to the Jews again, and told them, "I find no crime in him. But you have a custom that I should release one man for you at the Passover; will you have me release for you the King of the Jews?" They cried out again, "Not this man, but Barabbas!" Now Barabbas was a robber.

He asked whether the man was a Galilean. And when he learned that he belonged to Herod's jurisdiction, he sent him over to Herod, who was himself in Jerusalem at that time. When Herod saw Jesus, he was very glad, for he had long desired to see him, because he had heard about him, and he was hoping to see some sign done by him. So he questioned him at some length; but he made no answer. The chief priests and the scribes stood by, vehemently accusing him. And Herod with his soldiers treated him with contempt and mocked him; then, arraying him in gorgeous apparel, he sent him back to Pilate. And Herod and Pilate became friends with each other that very day, for before this they had been at enmity with each other.

Then Pilate took Jesus and scourged him. And the soldiers plaited a crown of thorns, and put it on his head, and arrayed him in a purple robe; they came up to him, saying, "Hail, King of the Jews!" and struck him with their hands. Pilate went out again, and said to them, "Behold, I am bringing him out to you, that you may know that I find no crime in him." So Jesus came out, wearing the crown of thorns and the purple robe. Pilate said to them, "Here is the man!" When the chief priests and the officers saw him, they cried out, "Crucify him, crucify him!" Pilate said to them, "Take him yourselves and crucify him, for I find no crime in him." The Jews answered him, "We have a law, and by that law he ought to die, because he has made himself the Son of God." When Pilate heard these words, he was the more afraid; he entered the prae-torium again and said to Jesus, "Where are you from?" But Jesus gave no answer. Pilate therefore said to him, "You will not speak to me? Do you not know that I have power to release you, and power to crucify you?" Jesus answered him, "You would have no power over me unless it had been given you from above; therefore he who delivered me to you has the greater sin."

Upon this Pilate sought to release him, but the Jews cried out, "If you release this man, you are not Caesar's friend; everyone who makes himself a king sets himself against Caesar." When Pilate heard these words, he brought Jesus out and sat down on the judgment seat at a place called The Pavement, and in Hebrew, Gabbatha. Now it was the day of Preparation of the Passover; it was about the sixth hour. He said to the Jews, "Here is your King!" They cried out, "Away with him, away with him, crucify him!" Pilate said to them, "Shall I crucify your King?" The chief priests answered, "We have no king but Caesar." Then he handed him over to them to be crucified.

So they took Jesus, and he went out, bearing his own cross, to the place called the place of the skull, which is called in Hebrew Golgotha. And as they led him away, they seized one Simon of Cyrene, who was coming in from the country, and laid on him the cross, to carry it behind Jesus. And there followed him a great multitude of the people, and of women who bewailed and lamented him. But Jesus turning to them said, "Daughters of Jerusalem, do not weep for me, but weep for yourselves, and for your children. For behold, the days are coming when they will say, 'Blessed are the barren, and the wombs that never bore, and the breasts that never gave suck!' Then they will begin to say to the mountains, 'Fall on us'; and to the hills, 'Cover us.' For if they do this when the wood is green, what will happen when it is dry?"

Two others also, who were criminals, were led away to be put to death with him. And when they came to the place which is called The Skull, there they crucified him, and the criminals, one on the right and one on the left. And Jesus said, "Father, forgive them; for they know not what they do." And they cast lots to divide his garments. And the people stood by, watching; but the rulers scoffed at him, saying, "He saved others; let him save himself, if he is the Christ of God, his Chosen One!" The soldiers also mocked him, coming up and offering him vinegar, and saying, "If you are the King of the Jews, save yourself!" There was also an inscription over him, "This is the King of the Jews."

One of the criminals who were hanged railed at him, saying, "Are you not the Christ? Save yourself and us!" But the other rebuked him, saying, "Do you not fear God, since you are under the same sentence of condemnation? And we indeed justly; for we are receiving the due reward of our deeds; but this man has done nothing wrong." And he said, "Jesus, remember me when you come in your kingly power." And he said to him, "Truly, I say to you, today you will be with me in Paradise."

It was now about the sixth hour, and there was darkness over the whole land until the ninth hour, while the sun's light failed; and the curtain of the temple was torn in two. Then Jesus, crying with a loud voice, said, "Father, into thy hands I commit my spirit!" And having said this, he breathed his last. Now when the centurion saw what had taken place, he praised God, and said, "Certainly this man was innocent!"

Since it was the day of Preparation, in order to prevent the bodies from remaining on the cross on the sabbath (for that sabbath was a high day), the Jews asked Pilate that their legs might be broken, and that they might be taken away. So the soldiers came and broke the legs of the first, and of the other who had been crucified with him; but when they came to Jesus and saw that he was already dead, they did not break his legs. But one of the soldiers pierced his side with a spear, and at once there came out blood and water. He who saw it has borne witness—his testimony is true, and he knows that he tells the truth —that you may also believe. For these things took place that the scripture might be fulfilled, "Not a bone of him shall be broken." And again another scripture says, "They shall look on him whom they have pierced."

Now there was a man named Joseph from the Jewish town of Arimathea. He was a member of the council, a good and righteous man, who had not consented to their purpose and deed, and he was looking for the kingdom of God. This man went to Pilate and asked for the body of Jesus. Then he took it down and wrapped it in a linen shroud, and laid him in a rock-hewn tomb, where no one had ever yet been laid. It was the day of Preparation, and the sabbath was beginning. The women who had come with him from Galilee followed, and saw the tomb, and how his body was laid; then they returned, and prepared spices and ointments.

PETER'S DENIAL

Luke 22:31–34, 54–62

"Simon, Simon, behold, Satan demanded to have you, that he might sift you like wheat, but I have prayed for you that your faith may not fail; and when you have turned again, strengthen your brethren." And he said to him, "Lord, I am ready to go with you to prison and to death." He said, "I tell you, Peter, the cock will not crow this day, until you three times deny that you know me."

They seized him and led him away, bringing him into the high priest's house. Peter followed at a distance; and when they had kindled a fire in the middle of the courtyard and sat down together, Peter sat among them. Then a maid, seeing him as he sat in the light and gazing at him, said, "This man also was with him." But he denied it, saying, "Woman, I do not know him." And a little later someone else saw him and said, "You also are one of them." But Peter said, "Man, I am not." And after an interval of about an hour still another insisted, saying, "Certainly this man also was with him; for he is a Galilean." But Peter said, "Man, I do not know what you are saying." And immediately, while he was still speaking, the cock crowed. And the Lord turned and looked at Peter. And Peter remembered the word of the Lord, how he had said to him, "Before the cock crows today, you will deny me three times." And he went out and wept bitterly.

THE RESURRECTION OF JESUS

John 20:1–5, 7–18; Luke 24:13–35;
John 20:19–23

Now on the first day of the week Mary Magdalene came to the tomb early, while it was still dark, and saw that the stone had been taken away from the tomb. So she ran, and went to Simon Peter and the other disciple, the one whom Jesus loved, and said to them, "They have taken the Lord out of the tomb, and we do not know where they have laid him." Peter then came out with the other disciple, and they went toward the tomb. They both ran, but the other disciple outran Peter and reached the tomb first; and stopping to look in, he saw the linen cloths lying there, and the napkin, which had been on his head, not lying with the linen cloths but rolled up in a place by itself. Then the other disciple, who reached the tomb first, also went in, and he saw and believed; for as yet they did not know the scripture, that he must rise from the dead. Then the disciples went back to their homes.

But Mary stood weeping outside the tomb, and as she wept she stooped to look into the tomb; and she saw two angels of white, sitting where the body of Jesus had lain, one at the head and one at the feet. They said to her, "Woman, why are you weeping?" She said to them, "Because they have taken away my Lord, and I do not know where they have laid him." Saying this, she turned round and saw Jesus standing, but she did not know that it was Jesus. Jesus said to her, "Woman, why are you weeping? Whom do you seek?" Supposing him to be the gardener, she said to him, "Sir, if you have carried him away, tell me where you have laid him, and I will take him away." Jesus said to her, "Mary." She turned and said to him in Hebrew, "Rab-boni!" (which means Teacher). Jesus said to her, "Do not hold me, for I have not yet ascended to the Father; but go to my brethren and say to them, I am ascending to my Father and your Father, to my God and your God." Mary Magdalene went and said to the disciples, "I have seen the Lord"; and she told them that he had said these things to her.

That very day two of them were going to a village named Emmaus, about seven miles from Jerusalem, and talking to each other about all these things that had happened. While they were talking and discussing together, Jesus himself drew near and went with them. But their eyes were kept from recognizing him. And he said to them, "What is this conversation which you are holding with each other as you walk?" And they stood still, looking sad. Then one of them, named Cleopas, answered him, "Are you the only visitor to Jerusalem who does not know the things that have happened there in these days?" And he said to them, "What things?" And they said to him, "Concerning Jesus of Nazareth, who was a prophet mighty in deed and word before God and all the people, and how our chief priests and rulers delivered him up to be condemned to death, and crucified him. But we had hoped that he was the one to redeem Israel. Yes, and besides all this, it is now the third day since this happened. Moreover, some women of our company amazed us. They were at the tomb early in the morning and did not find his body; and they came back saying that they had even seen a vision of angels, who said that he was alive. Some of those who were with us went to the tomb, and found it just as the women had said; but him they did not see." And he said to them, "O foolish men, and slow of heart to believe all that the prophets have spoken! Was it not necessary that the Christ should suffer these things and enter into his glory?" And beginning with Moses and all the prophets, he interpreted to them in all the scriptures the things concerning himself.

So they drew near the village to which they were going. He appeared to be going further, but they constrained him, saying, "Stay with us, for it is toward evening and the day is now spent." So he went in to stay with them. When he was at table with them, he took the bread and blessed, and broke it, and gave it to them. And their eyes were opened, and they recognized him; and he vanished out of their sight. They said to each other, "Did not our hearts burn within us while he talked to us on the road, while he opened to us the scriptures?" And they rose the same hour and returned to Jerusalem; and they found the eleven gathered together and those who were with them, who said, "The Lord has risen indeed, and has appeared to Simon!" Then they told what had happened on the road, and how he was known to them in the breaking of the bread.

On the evening of that day, the first day of the week, the doors being shut where the disciples were, for fear of the Jews, Jesus came and stood among them and said to them, "Peace be with you." When he had said this, he showed them his hands and his side. Then the disciples were glad when they saw the Lord. Jesus said to them again, "Peace be with you. As the Father has sent me, even so I send you." And when he had said this, he breathed on them, and said to them, "Receive the Holy Spirit. If you forgive the sins of any, they are forgiven; if you retain the sins of any, they are retained."

JESUS CONVINCES THOMAS

John 20:24–31

Now Thomas, one of the twelve, called the Twin, was not with them when Jesus came. So the other disciples told him, "We have seen the Lord." But he said to them, "Unless I see in his hands the print of the nails, and place my finger in the mark of the nails, and place my hand in his side, I will not believe."

Eight days later, his disciples were again in the house, and Thomas was with them. The doors were shut, but Jesus came and stood among them, and said, "Peace be with you." Then he said to Thomas, "Put your finger here, and see my hands; and put out your hand, and place it in my side; do not be faithless, but believing." Thomas answered him, "My Lord and my God!" Jesus said to him, "Have you believed because you have seen me? Blessed are those who have not seen and yet believe."

And Jesus did many other signs in the presence of the disciples, which are not written in this book; but these are written that you may believe that Jesus is the Christ, the Son of God, and that believing you may have life in his name.

THE ACTS OF THE APOSTLES

The authorship of the Acts is not known with certainty; however, it is generally recognized to be the same author as the book of Luke. It is, therefore, an extension of the Gospels. The book primarily traces the spread of the Gospel of Christ from Jerusalem to Rome through the two apostles Peter and Paul. Christianity is viewed as it passed from a purely national affair to an international affair. The conversion and work of the apostle Paul comprise the major portion of the book.

THE RESURRECTION, MINISTRY, AND ASCENSION OF CHRIST

Acts 1:1–11

In the first book, O The-ophilus, I dealt with all that Jesus began to do and teach, until the day he was taken up, after he had given commandment through the Holy Spirit to the apostles whom he had chosen. To them he presented himself alive after his passion by many proofs, appearing to them during forty days, and speaking of the kingdom of God. And while staying with them he charged them not to depart from Jerusalem, but to wait for the promise of the Father, which, he said, "you heard from me, for John baptized with water, but before many days you shall be baptized with the Holy Spirit."

So when they had come together, they asked him, "Lord, will you at this time restore the kingdom of Israel?" He said to them, "It is not for you to know times or seasons which the Father has fixed by his own authority. But you shall receive power when the Holy Spirit has come upon you; and you shall be my witnesses in Jerusalem and in all Judea and Samaria and to the end of the earth." And when he had said this, as they were looking on, he was lifted up, and a cloud took him out of their sight. And while they were gazing into heaven as he went, behold, two men stood by them in white robes, and said, "Men of Galilee, why do you stand looking into heaven? This Jesus, who was taken up from you into heaven, will come in the same way as you saw him go into heaven."

SAUL PERSECUTES THE CHURCH

Acts 6:7–15; 7:1–2, 51–60; 8:1–4

And the word of God increased; and the number of the disciples multiplied greatly in Jerusalem, and a great many of the priests were obedient to the faith.

And Stephen, full of grace and power, did great wonders and signs among the people. Then some of those who belonged to the synagogue of the Freedmen (as it was called), and of the Cyrenians, and of the Alexandrians, and of those from Cilicia and Asia, arose and disputed with Stephen. But they could not withstand the wisdom and the Spirit with which he spoke. Then they secretly instigated men, who said, "We have heard him speak blasphemous words against Moses and God." And they stirred up the people and the elders and the scribes, and they came upon him and seized him, and brought him before the council, and set up false witnesses who said, "This man never ceases to speak words against this holy place and the law; for we have heard him say that this Jesus of Nazareth will destroy this place, and change the customs which Moses delivered to us." And gazing at him, all who sat in the council saw that his face was like the face of an angel.

And the high priest said, "Is this so?" And Stephen said; "You stiff-necked people, uncircumcised in heart and ears, you always resist the Holy Spirit. As your father did, so do you. Which of the prophets did not your fathers persecute? And they killed those who announced beforehand the coming of the Righteous One, whom you have now betrayed and murdered, you who received the law as delivered by angels and did not keep it."

Now when they heard these things they were enraged, and they ground their teeth against him. But he, full of the Holy Spirit, gazed into heaven and saw the glory of God, and Jesus standing at the right hand of God; and he said, "Behold, I see the heavens opened, and the Son of man standing at the right hand of God." But they cried out with a loud voice and stopped their ears and rushed together upon him. Then they cast him out of the city and stoned him; and the witnesses laid down their garments at the feet of a young man named Saul. And as they were stoning Stephen, he prayed, "Lord Jesus, receive my spirit." And he knelt down and cried with a loud voice, "Lord, do not hold this sin against them." And when he had said this, he fell asleep. And Saul was consenting to his death.

And on that day a great persecution arose against the church in Jerusalem; and they were all scattered throughout the region of Judea and Samaria, except the apostles. Devout men buried Stephen, and made great lamentation over him. But Saul laid waste the church in Jerusalem, and entering house after house, he dragged off men and women and committed them to prison.

Now those who were scattered went about preaching the word.

CONVERSION OF SAUL

Acts 9:1–22

But Saul, still breathing threats and murder against the disciples of the Lord, went to the high priest and asked him for letters to the synagogues at Damascus, so that if he found any belonging to the Way, men or women, he might bring them bound to Jerusalem. Now as he journeyed he approached Damascus, and suddenly a light from heaven flashed about him. And he fell to the ground and heard a voice saying to him, "Saul, Saul, why do you persecute me?" And he said, "Who are you, Lord?" And he said, "I am Jesus, whom you are persecuting; but rise and enter the city, and you will be told what you are to do." The men who were traveling with him stood speechless, hearing the voice but seeing no one. Saul arose from the ground; and when his eyes were opened, he could see nothing; so they led him by the hand and brought him into Damascus. And for three days he was without sight, and neither ate nor drank.

Now there was a disciple at Damascus named Ananias. The Lord said to him in a vision, "Ananias." And he said, "Here I am, Lord." And the Lord said to him, "Rise and go to the street called Straight, and inquire in the house of Judas for a man of Tarsus named Saul; for behold, he is praying, and he has seen a man named Ananias come in and lay his hands on him so that he might regain his sight." But Ananias answered, "Lord, I have heard from many about this man, how much evil he has done to thy saints at Jerusalem; and here he has authority from the chief priests to bind all who call upon thy name." But the Lord said to him, "Go, for he is a chosen instrument of mine to carry my name before the Gentiles and kings and the sons of Israel; for I will show him how much he must suffer for the sake of my name." So Ananias departed and entered the house. And laying his hands on him he said, "Brother Saul, the Lord Jesus who appeared to you on the road by which you came, has sent me that you may regain your sight and be filled with the Holy Spirit." And immediately something like scales fell from his eyes and he regained his sight. Then he rose and was baptized, and took food and was strengthened.

For several days he was with the disciples at Damascus. And in the synagogues immediately he proclaimed Jesus, saying, "He is the Son of God." And all who heard him were amazed, and said, "Is this not the man who made havoc in Jerusalem of those who called on this name? And he has come here for this purpose, to bring them bound before the chief priests." But Saul increased all the more in strength, and confounded the Jews who lived in Damascus by proving that Jesus was the Christ.

PAUL AND BARNABAS CALLED GODS

Acts 14:8–18

Now at Lystra there was a man sitting, who could not use his feet; he was a cripple from birth, who had never walked. He listened to Paul speaking; and Paul looked intently at him and seeing that he had faith to be made well, said in a loud voice, "Stand upright on your feet." And he sprang up and walked. And when the crowds saw what Paul had done, they lifted up their voices, saying in Lycaonian, "The gods have come down to us in the likeness of men!" Barnabas they called Zeus, and Paul, because he was the chief speaker, they called Hermes. And the priest of Zeus, whose temple was in front of the city, brought oxen and garlands to the gates and wanted to offer sacrifice with the people. But when the apostles Barnabas and Paul heard of it, they tore their garments and rushed out among the multitude, crying, "Men, why are you doing this? We also are men, of like nature with you, and bring you good news, that you should turn from these vain things to a living God who made the heaven and the earth and the sea and all that is in them. In past generations he allowed all the nations to walk in their own ways; yet he did not leave himself without witness, for he did good and gave you from heaven rains and fruitful seasons, satisfying your hearts with food and gladness." With these words they scarcely restrained the people from offering sacrifices to them.

PAUL AND SILAS IN JAIL

Acts 16:16–40

As we were going to the place of prayer, we were met by a slave girl who had a spirit of divination and brought her owners much gain by soothsaying. She followed Paul and us, crying,

"These men are servants of the Most High God, who proclaim to you the way of salvation." And this she did for many days. But Paul was annoyed, and turned and said to the spirit, "I charge you in the name of Jesus Christ to come out of her." And it came out that very hour.

But when the owners saw that their hope of gain was gone, they seized Paul and Silas and dragged them into the market place before the rulers; and when they had brought them to the magistrates they said, "These men are Jews and they are disturbing our city. They advocate customs which it is not lawful for us Romans to accept or practice." The crowd joined in attacking them; and the magistrates tore the garments off them and gave orders to beat them with rods. And when they had inflicted many blows upon them, they threw them into prison, charging the jailer to keep them safely. Having received this charge, he put them into the inner prison and fastened their feet in the stocks.

But about midnight Paul and Silas were praying and singing hymns to God, and the prisoners were listening to them, and suddenly there was a great earthquake, so that the foundations of the prison were shaken; and immediately all of the doors were opened and everyone's fetters were unfastened. When the jailer woke and saw that the prison doors were open, he drew his sword and was about to kill himself, supposing that the prisoners had escaped. But Paul cried with a loud voice, "Do not harm yourself, for we are all here." And he called for lights and rushed in, and trembling with fear he fell down before Paul and Silas, and brought them out and said, "Men, what must I do to be saved?" And they said, "Believe in the Lord Jesus, and you will be saved, you and your household." And they spoke the word of the Lord to him and to all that were in his house. And he took them the same hour of the night, and washed their wounds, and he was baptized at once, with all his family. Then he brought them up into his house, and set food before them; and he rejoiced with all his household that he had believed in God.

So when it was day, the magistrates sent the police, saying, "Let those men go." And the jailer reported the words to Paul, saying, "The magistrates have sent to let you go; now therefore come out and go in peace." But Paul said to them, "They have beaten us publicly, uncondemned, men who are Roman citizens, and have thrown us into prison; and do they now cast us out secretly? No! let them come themselves and take us out." The police reported these words to the magistrates, and they were afraid when they heard that they were Roman citizens; so they came and apologized to them. And they took them out and asked them to leave the city. So they went out of the prison, and visited Lydia; and when they had seen the brethren, they exhorted them and departed.

PAUL IN ATHENS

Acts 17:15–34

Those who conducted Paul brought him as far as Athens; and receiving a command for Silas and Timothy to come to him as soon as possible, they departed.

Now while Paul was waiting for them in Athens, his spirit was provoked within him as he saw that the city was full of idols. So he argued in the synagogue with the Jews and the devout persons, and in the market place every day with those who chanced to be there. Some also of the Epicurean and Stoic philosophers met him. And some said, "What would this babbler say?" Others said, "He seems to be a preacher of foreign divinities"—because he preached Jesus and the resurrection. And they took hold of him and brought him to the Are-opagus, saying, "May we know what this new teaching is which you present? For you bring some strange things to our ears; we wish to know therefore what these things mean." Now all the Athenians and the foreigners who lived there spent their time in nothing except telling or hearing something new.

So Paul, standing in the middle of the Are-opagus, said, "Men of Athens, I perceive that in every way you are very religious. For as I passed along, and observed the objects of your worship, I found also an altar with this inscription, 'To an unknown god.' What therefore you worship as unknown, this I proclaim to you. The God who made the world and everything in it, being Lord of heaven and earth, does not live in shrines made by man, nor is he served by human hands, as though he needed anything, since he himself gives to all men life and breath and everything. And he made from one every nation of men to live on all the face of the earth, having determined allotted periods and the boundaries of their habitation, that they should seek God, in the hope that they might feel after him and find him. Yet he is not far from each one of us, for

'In him we live and move and have our being';

as even some of your poets have said,

'For we are indeed his offspring.'

Being then God's offspring, we ought not to think that the Deity is like gold, or silver, or stone, a representation by the art and imagination of man. The times of ignorance God overlooked, but now he commands all men everywhere to repent, because he has fixed a day on which he will judge the world in righteousness by a man whom he has appointed, and of this he has given assurance to all men by raising him from the dead."

Now when they heard of the resurrection of the dead, some mocked; but others said, "We will hear you again about this." So Paul went out from among them. But some men joined him and believed.

PAUL SUMMARIZES HIS MINISTRY TO KING AGRIPPA

Acts 26:1–32

Agrippa said to Paul, "You have permission to speak for yourself." Then Paul stretched out his hand and made his defense:

"I think myself fortunate that it is before you, King Agrippa, I am about to make my defense today against all the accusation of the Jews; therefore I beg you to listen to me patiently.

"My manner of life from my youth, spent from the beginning among my own nation and at Jerusalem, is known by all the Jews. They have known for a long time, if they are willing to testify, that according to the strictest party of our religion I have lived as a Pharisee. And now I stand here on trial for hope in the promise made by God to our fathers, to which our twelve tribes hope to attain, as they earnestly worship night and day. And for this hope I am accused by Jews, O King! Why is it thought incredible by any of you that God raises the dead?

"I myself was convinced that I ought to do many things in opposing the name of Jesus of Nazareth. And I did so in Jerusalem; I not only shut up many of the saints in prison, by authority from the chief priests, but when they were put to death I cast my vote against them. And I punished them often in all the synagogues and tried to make them blaspheme; and in raging fury against them, I persecuted them even to foreign cities.

"Thus I journeyed to Damascus with the authority and commission of the chief priests. At midday, O king, I saw on the way a light from heaven, brighter than the sun, shining round me and those who journeyed with me. And when we had all fallen to the ground, I heard a voice saying to me in the Hebrew language, 'Saul, Saul, why do you persecute me? It hurts you to kick against the goads.' And I said, 'Who are you, Lord?' And the Lord said, 'I am Jesus whom you are persecuting. But rise and stand upon your feet; for I have appeared to you for this purpose, to appoint you to serve and bear witness to the things in which you have seen me and to those things in which I will appear to you, delivering you from the people and from the Gentiles—to whom I send you to open their eyes, that they may turn from darkness to light, and from the power of Satan to God, that they may receive forgiveness of sins and a place among those who are sanctified by faith in me.'

"Wherefore, O King Agrippa, I was not disobedient to the heavenly vision, but declared first to those at Damascus, then at Jerusalem and throughout all the country of Judea, and also to the Gentiles, that they should repent and turn to God and perform deeds worthy of their repentance. For this reason the Jews seized me in the temple and tried to kill me. To this day I have had the help that comes from God, and so I stand here testifying to both small and great, saying nothing but what the prophets and Moses said would come to pass: that the Christ must suffer, and that, by being the first to rise from the dead, he would proclaim light both to the people and to the Gentiles."

And as he thus made his defense, Festus said with a loud voice, "Paul, you are mad; your great learning is turning you mad." But Paul said, "I am not mad, most excellent Festus, but I am speaking the sober truth. For the king knows about these things, and to him I speak freely; for I am persuaded that none of these things has escaped his notice, for this was not done in a corner. King Agrippa, do you believe the prophets? I know that you believe." And Agrippa said to Paul, "In a short time you think to make me a Christian!" And Paul said, "Whether short or long, I would to God that not only you but also all who hear me this day might become such as I am—except for these chains."

Then the king rose, and the governor and Bernice and those who were sitting with them; and when they had withdrawn, they said to one another, "This man is doing nothing to deserve death or imprisonment." And Agrippa said to Festus, "This man could have been set free if he had not appealed to Caesar."

PAUL IN ROME

Acts 28:14–31

And so we came to Rome. And the brethren there, when they heard of us, came as far as the Forum of Appius and Three Taverns to meet us. On seeing them Paul thanked God and took courage. And when we came into Rome, Paul was allowed to stay by himself, with the soldier that guarded him.

After three days he called together the local leaders of the Jews; and when they had gathered, he said to them, "Brethren, though I had done nothing against the people or the customs of our fathers, yet I was delivered prisoner from Jerusalem into the hands of the Romans. When they had examined me, they wished to set me at liberty, because there was no reason for the death penalty in my case. But when the Jews objected, I was compelled to appeal to Caesar—though I had no charge to bring against my nation. For this reason therefore I have asked to see you and speak with you, since it is because of the hope of Israel that I am bound with this chain."

And they said to him, "We have received no letters from Judea about you, and none of the brethren coming here has reported or spoken evil about you. But we desire to hear from you what your views are; for with regard to this sect we know that everywhere it is spoken against."

When they appointed a day for him, they came to him at his lodging in great numbers. And he expounded the matter to them from morning till evening, testifying to the kingdom of God and trying to convince them about Jesus both from the law of Moses and from the prophets. And some were convinced by what he said, while others disbelieved. So, as they agreed among themselves, they departed, after Paul had made one statement: "The Holy Spirit was right in saying to your fathers through Isaiah the prophet:

'Go to this people, and say,
You shall indeed hear but never understand,
and you shall indeed see but never perceive.

For this people's heart has grown dull,
and their ears are heavy of hearing,
and their eyes they have closed;
lest they should perceive with their eyes,
and hear with their ears,
and understand with their heart,
and turn for me to heal them.'

Let it be known to you then that this salvation of God has been sent to the Gentiles; they will listen."

And he lived there two whole years at his own expense, and welcomed all who came to him, preaching the kingdom of God and teaching about the Lord Jesus Christ quite openly and unhindered.

Lyric
Poetry

*P*OETRY IS AMONG every people the earliest form of literary expression. There are reasons why poetry antedates prose. Among primitive people emotion has always tended to find expression in song. There were many occasions for emotional expression, such as a feast to celebrate a victory or marriage. Most occasions were celebrated with music and dancing, and the words that were developed naturally followed the rhythm of dance. In primitive times, when writing was still unknown, poetry was also an aid to memory rather than an expression of beauty.

As Hebrew poetry developed, it was admired by many races and generations. Hebrew poetry is simple and concrete. The emotions most common to all men are expressed in appropriate imagery and diction and transcend the limitations of race and nationality. As in all great art, the temporal is lost in the eternal. The occasions producing such poetry are merged in the meaning and emotion.

Poetry and religion get along well together. In those moments of religious experience when the soul was in closest harmony with God, the utterances of its spokesmen were obsessed with God's glory and sang His praises with joyful abandonment to their emotions. They were not interested in enumerating His attributes in a dull, mechanical manner, but poured forth wholeheartedly their gladness of His majesty and splendor. They found prose inadequate to express the inspiration and joy which they felt. Only poetry could properly express these praises.

Therefore, Hebrew literature is very largely poetical; even much of its prose is prose poetry. It is sometimes hard to distinguish between the prose and poetic forms. More and more translations present much of the Old Testament as poetry.

Lyric poetry is filled with imagery. It is characteristic of Hebrew lyrics to crowd images together in rapid succession. Several minor images are often used to illustrate a single major image in full detail. Numerous similes are used, such as:

Like as a father pitieth his children,
So the Lord pitieth them that fear him.

Whole passages are often built on metaphor, as in the following passage where the psalmist himself is the sparrow who has found a home.

Yea, the sparrow hath found her an house,
And the swallow a nest for herself,
    where she may lay her young.
Even thine altars, O Lord of hosts, my King
    and my God.

Original Bible verse, unlike English verse, was not made primarily by rhythm, the numbering of syllables, or rhyme, but by the symmetry or balance of clauses in a verse or stanza. This resemblance or correspondence, commonly called *parallelism,* takes several forms. The simplest form is the couplet, where a pair of lines form a verse.

He that is slow to anger is better than the mighty,
And he that ruleth his spirit than he that taketh a city.

The triplet is three successive lines that form a verse.

O give thanks unto the Lord,
For he is good:
For his mercy endureth forever.

The quartrain is four successive lines that form a verse.

I will lift up mine eyes unto the hills,
From whence cometh my help.
My help cometh from the Lord,
Which made heaven and earth.

The sextet and octet and other successive numbers of lines vary accordingly.

The ultimate source of the Hebrew form of parallelism is unknown. Suggestions are made that it came directly from nature. Life itself is rhythmical: walking, breathing, the heartbeat. External nature has parallel rhythm: the ebb and flow of the tide or the rapid strokes of alternate wings of a bird in flight. The parallelism of Hebrew verse is suited to express this natural rhythm.

When the early English translators labored with ancient Bible transcripts, they did not suspect that much of the book was poetry. The reason is evident, for in the manuscripts the words succeeded one another with little to indicate the length of the sentences. The meter was not that of the classics or English poetry with which the translators were familiar. Also, the translators found no indication of rhyme. By the middle 1700's attention was drawn to the fact that Bible poetry was based on a rather elaborate system of parallelism. English poetry had depended largely for its effects upon the recurrence of sounds; Hebrew poetry cultivated the recurrence of thought.

This parallel rhythm of thought consisted of a relation of thought between two or more consecutive lines of verse. Four kinds of parallelism are generally recognized. *Synonymous parallelism* expresses the same thought in two or more lines.

> The earth is the Lord's, and the fullness thereof;
> The world, and they that dwell therein.
>> or
> What is man that thou art mindful of him,
> And the son of man that thou dost care for him.

Antithetic parallelism expresses contrasting thoughts.

> Jehovah knoweth the way of the righteous,
> But the way of the wicked shall perish.

Synthetic parallelism completes the thought of the first line by continuing into the second.

> Though war shall rise against me
> Even then will I be confident.
>> or
> As a hart longs for flowing streams,
> So longs my soul for thee, O God.

Climatic parallelism is expressed when the second line takes up the words of the first and adds to the thought.

Give unto Jehovah, O ye sons of the mighty,
Give unto Jehovah glory and strength.

or

The law of the Lord is perfect,
    reviving the soul;
The testimony of the Lord is sure,
    making wise the simple;
The precepts of the Lord are right,
    rejoicing the heart;
The commandment of the Lord is pure,
    enlightening the eyes;
The fear of the Lord is clean,
    enduring forever;
The ordinances of the Lord are true,
    and righteous altogether.

The emphasis of Hebrew poetry upon parallelism of thought has a great advantage over that of European literature. The natural rhythm of thought made it possible to keep the essential poetic forms of the Hebrew poetry even in translation. In a literature designed for worldwide use this is a great asset. Meter or rhyme or alliteration cannot be transferred from one language to another. These are mechanical devices. But Hebrew poetry lost little in translation.

There is also a parallelism of interpretation, sometimes called *higher parallelism*. Higher parallelism has design largely through meaning, as in the following example, which has the commandments on the left and the rewards on the right.

My son, forget not my law;
But let thine heart keep my commandments:
    For length of days, and long life,
    And peace, shall they add to thee;
Let not mercy and truth forsake thee;
Bind them about thy neck:
Write them upon the tables of thine heart:
    So shalt thou find favor and good understanding
    In the sight of God and man.
Trust in the Lord with all thine heart,
And lean not to thine own understanding:
In all thy ways acknowledge him,
    And he shall direct thy paths.

Fortunately, the lower and higher parallelisms do not clash.

Also in the Hebrew tradition it was common that the speakers or singers of the verse would utter a statement and then expand the statement or answer themselves. The first utterance is called a *strophe* (from the Greek word meaning "a turning") and the expanding or answering statement of the pair is called an *antistrophe*. Many of these verses can be distinguished by the disposition of stanzas in pairs.

> Blessed is the man that walketh not in the counsel of the
>   ungodly,
>   Nor standeth in the way of sinners,
>   Nor sitteth in the seat of the scornful.
> But his delight is in the law of the Lord;
>   And in his law doth he meditate day and night.

or

> The heavens declare the glory of God;
>   And the firmament showeth his handiwork.
> Day unto day uttereth speech,
>   And night unto night showeth knowledge.

or

> Wash me thoroughly from mine iniquity,
>   And cleanse me from my sin.
> For I acknowledge my transgressions:
>   And my sin is ever before me.

However, some well-marked divisions have no similarity with regard to length or parallelism. Sometimes refrains, repetition of clauses, give aid in determining form.

> Therefore, whosoever heareth these sayings of mine,
>   and doeth them,
> I will liken him to a wise man,
> which built his house upon a rock:
>   And the rain descended,
>   and the floods came,
>   and the winds blew,
>   and beat upon the house;
> and it fell not:
> for it was founded upon the rock.

And everyone that heareth these sayings of mine,
    and doeth them not,
shall be likened unto a foolish man,
which built his house upon the sand:
    And the rain descended,
    and the floods came,
    and the winds blew,
    and beat upon the house;
and it fell:
and great was the fall of it.

An ear for rhythm is helpful for the appreciation of Biblical poetry, but it is no more essential than for the appreciation of music. The restructuring in this text of portions of the Bible by rhythm or interpretation should add to the understanding of and enjoyment in reading the Bible.

Parallelism of large sections containing several verses usually takes two basic forms, the *envelope figure* and the *pendulum figure.* Note the envelope figure in the first two samples, where a general statement is made concrete by exact detail.

Fruits

You will know them by their fruits.
    Are grapes gathered from thorns,
    or figs from thistles?
    So every sound tree bears good fruit,
    but the bad tree bears evil fruit.

    A sound tree cannot bear evil fruit,
    nor can a bad tree bear good fruit.
    Every tree that does not bear good fruit is cut down
    and thrown into the fire.
Thus you will know them by their fruits.

Who Shall Abide?

O Lord, who shall sojourn in thy tent?
Who shall dwell on thy holy hill?

    He who walks blamelessly,
    and does what is right,
    and speaks truth from his heart;

    Who does not slander with his tongue,

and does no evil to his friend,
nor takes up a reproach against his neighbor;

In whose eyes a reprobate is despised,
but who honors those who fear the Lord;

Who swears to his own hurt and does not change,
who does not put out his money at interest,
and does not take a bribe against the innocent.

He who does these things shall never be moved.

The pendulum figure surges to and fro between two thoughts, and thus adjustments in form are made frequently.

God, Our Refuge

God is our refuge and strength,
    a very present help in trouble.
Therefore we will not fear
    though the earth should change,
    though the mountains shake in the heart of the sea;
    though its waters roar and foam,
    though the mountains tremble with its tumult. *Selah.*

There is a river whose streams make glad the city of God,
    the holy habitation of the Most High.
        God is in the midst of her,
            she shall not be moved;
        God will help her right early.

The nations rage, the kingdoms totter;
    he utters his voice, the earth melts.
        The Lord of hosts is with us;
            the God of Jacob is our refuge. *Selah.*

Come, behold the works of the Lord,
    how he has wrought desolations in the earth.
He makes wars cease to the end of the earth;
    he breaks the bow, and shatters the spear,
    he burns the chariots with fire!
"Be still, and know that I am God.
    I am exalted among the nations,
    I am exalted in the earth!"

The Lord of hosts is with us;
   the God of Jacob is our refuge. *Selah.*

The Deliverer

O give thanks to the Lord,
   for he is good;
   for his steadfast love endures forever!
Let the redeemed of the Lord say so,
whom he has redeemed from trouble
and gathered in from the lands,
   from the east
   and from the west,
   from the north
   and from the south.

Some wandered in desert wastes,
finding no way to a city to dwell in;
hungry and thirsty,
their soul fainted within them.
   Then they cried unto the Lord in their trouble,
   and he delivered them out of their distresses;
   he led them by a straight way,
   till they reached a city to dwell in.
Let them thank the Lord for his steadfast love,
for his wonderful works to the sons of men!
for he satisfies him who is thirsty,
and the hungry he fills with good things.

Some sat in darkness and in gloom,
prisoners in afflictions and in irons,
for they had rebelled against the words of God,
and spurned the counsel of the Most High.
Their hearts were bowed down with hard labor;
they fell down, with none to help.
   Then they cried unto the Lord in their trouble,
   and he delivered them in their distress;
   he brought them out of darkness and gloom,
   and broke their bonds asunder.
Let them thank the Lord for his steadfast love,
for his wonderful works to the sons of men!
For he shatters the doors of bronze,
And cuts in two the bars of iron.

Some were sick through their sinful ways,
and because of their iniquities suffered affliction;
they loathed any kind of food,
and they drew near to the gates of death.
    And they cried to the Lord in their trouble,
    and he delivered them from their distress;
    he sent forth his word, and healed them,
    and delivered them from destruction.
Let them thank the Lord for his steadfast love,
for his wonderful works to the sons of men!
And let them offer sacrifices of thanksgiving,
and tell of his deeds in songs of joy!

To further demonstrate how the effect of Hebrew verse is bound up in parallelism of clauses, note the following experiment with the 105th Psalm, beginning with verse 8. The first example will omit the second line of each couplet: it would make excellent historic prose.

He is mindful of his covenant forever, the covenant which he made with Abraham, which he confirmed to Jacob as a statute, saying, "To you I will give the land of Canaan." When they were few in number, wandering from nation to nation, he allowed no one to oppress them, saying, "Touch not my anointed ones!"

Now read the passage again, putting in the omitted lines. The prose is transformed into verse.

He is mindful of his covenant forever,
    of the word which he commanded, for a thousand genera-
        tions,
the covenant which he made with Abraham,
    his sworn promise to Isaac,
which he confirmed to Jacob as a statute,
    to Israel as an everlasting covenant,
saying, "To you I will give the land of Canaan
    as your portion for an inheritance."

When they were few in number,
    of little account, and sojourners in it,
wandering from nation to nation,
    from one kingdom to another people,
he allowed no one to oppress them;

he rebuked kings on their account,
saying, "Touch not my anointed ones,
do my prophets no harm!"

There is appeal in Bible poetry through its musical quality, but it is in the special function of reflection and meditation that its greatest appeal lies. In the following readings notice how easily lyric poetry passes into the epic and the drama without losing its own distinctive character. The forms of lyric poetry to be illustrated are the song, the ode, the elegy, meditation, monody, dramatic lyrics, ritual lyrics, and lyric idyl.

Although Bible poetry did not generally affect the form of English poetry as it developed, it did have a dramatic affect upon the content of both English and American poetry and prose. Hebrew poetry is possibly the most commonly quoted and read of all national poetries.

THE SONG

The song is the simplest of lyric types and the one that is most varied in its application. It is used to celebrate particular occasions and themes. The songs embody a peculiar national consciousness of the Hebrew people, who felt that God had given the nation a unique confidence in its destiny. This concept served to draw religion and patriotism into closest union.

Hebrew songs view nature anthropomorphically. Nature is described in human terms. The poets may describe the sun as a bridegroom coming out of his chamber and rejoicing as a strong man to run his course. The valleys, covered with corn, shout for joy; they also sing. Nature shares with man in the joy and marvels of creation. Taken one step further, nature shares in and sympathizes with man's joys. It is interesting that nature is never sorrowful or cruel. Thus, the poet's view of nature is simple, direct, and instinctive. The most obvious is what strikes him—vast expanses and great movements. He revels in grandeur, in the God who makes the winds His messengers. Where sound is noticed, it is its grandeur and not its beauty that attracts attention—the floods lifting up their voice, the crash of thunder, the roaring of the beasts of prey.

Many songs are devoted to more personal themes of faith and trust, of confession and penitence, and of hope and love. The major portion of the Psalms is made up of these themes.

THE UNIVERSAL KING

Psalms 2:1–6

Why do the nations conspire,
    and the people plot in vain?
The kings of the earth set themselves,
    and the rulers take counsel together,
        against the Lord
        and his anointed, saying,
"Let us burst their bonds asunder,
    and cast their cords from us."

He who sits in the heavens laughs;
    the Lord has them in derision.
Then he will speak to them in his wrath,
    and terrify them in his fury, saying,
"I have set my king
    on Zion, my holy hill."

THE MESSIAH

Psalms 110:1–4

The Lord says to my lord:
    "Sit at my right hand,
till I make your enemies
    your footstool."

The Lord sends forth from Zion
    your mighty scepter.
Rule in the midst
    of your foes!

Your people will offer themselves freely
    on the day you lead your host
    upon the holy mountains.
From the womb of the morning
    like dew your youth
    will come to you.

The Lord has sworn
    and will not change his mind,
"You are a priest forever
    after the order of Melchizedek."

JEHOVAH'S IMMOVABLE THRONE

Psalms 93:1–5

The Lord reigns;
    he is robed in majesty;
The Lord is robed,
    he is girded with strength.
Yea, the world is established;
    it shall never be moved;
Thy throne is established from of old;
    thou art from everlasting.

The floods have lifted up, O Lord,
    the floods have lifted up their voice,
    the floods lift up their roaring.
Mightier than the thunders of many waters,
    mightier than the waves of the sea,
    the Lord on high is mighty.
Thy decrees are very sure;
    holiness befits thy house,
    O Lord, for evermore.

THE GREAT DELIVERER

Psalms 40:1–5

I waited patiently for the Lord;
he inclined to me
and heard my cry.

    He drew me up from the desolate pit,
    out of the miry bog,
    and set my feet upon a rock,
    making my steps secure.
    He put a new song in my mouth,
    a song of praise to our God.

Many will see
and fear,
and put their trust in the Lord.

Blessed is the man who makes the Lord his trust,
who does not turn to the proud,
to those who go astray after false gods!

Thou hast multiplied, O Lord my God,
thy wondrous deeds
and thy thoughts toward us;
none can compare with thee!
Were I to proclaim and tell of them,
they would be more than can be numbered.

THIRSTING AFTER GOD

Psalms 42:1–6

As the hart longs for flowing streams,
　　so longs my soul for thee, O God.
My soul thirsts for God, for the living God.
　　When shall I come and behold the face of God?
My tears have been my food day and night,
　　while men say to me continually,
　　　"Where is your God?"

These things I remember,
　　as I pour out my soul:
how I went with the throng,
　　and led them in procession to the house of God,
with glad shouts and songs of thanksgiving,
　　a multitude keeping festival.
Why are you cast down, O my soul,
　　and why are you disquieted within me?
Hope in God; for I shall again praise him,
　　my help and my God.

CONFIDENCE IN GOD

Psalms 91

He who dwells in the shelter of the Most High,
　　who abides in the shadow of the Almighty,
will say to the Lord,
　　"My refuge
　　　and my fortress;
　　　my God,
　　in whom I trust."
For he will deliver you
　　from the snare of the fowler
　　and from the deadly pestilence;
he will cover you with his pinions,

and under his wings you will find refuge;
    his faithfulness is a shield and buckler.
You will not fear the terror of the night,
    nor the arrow that flies by day,
    nor the pestilence that stalks in darkness,
    nor the destruction that wastes at noonday.
A thousand may fall at your side,
    ten thousand at your right hand;
    but it will not come near you.
You will only look with your eyes
    and see the recompense of the wicked.

Because you have made the Lord your refuge,
    the Most High your habitation,
no evil shall befall you,
    no scourge come near your tent.

For he will give his angels charge of you
    to guard you in all your ways.
On their hands they will bear you up,
    lest you dash your foot against a stone.
You will tread on the lion and the adder,
    the young lion
    and the serpent
    you will trample under foot.

Because he cleaves to me in love,
    I will deliver him;
    I will protect him,
because he knows my name.
When he calls to me,
    I will answer him;
    I will be with him in trouble,
    I will rescue him and honor him.
With long life I will satisfy him,
    and show him my salvation.

HALLELUJAH

Psalms 148

Praise the Lord!
    Praise the Lord from the heavens,
praise him in the heights!

Praise him, all his angels,
praise him, all his host!

Praise him, sun and moon,
praise him, all you shining stars!
Praise him, you highest heavens,
and you waters above the heavens!

Let them praise the name of the Lord!
For he commanded
and they were created.
And he established them for ever and ever;
he fixed their bounds which cannot be passed.

Praise the Lord from the earth,
you sea monsters, and all deeps,
fire and hail,
snow and frost,
stormy wind fulfilling his command!
Mountains and all hills,
fruit trees and all cedars!
Beasts and all cattle,
creeping things and flying birds!
Kings of the earth and all peoples,
princes and all rulers of the earth!
Young men and maidens together,
old men and children!
Let them praise the name of the Lord,
for his name alone is exalted;
his glory is above earth and heaven.
He has raised up a horn for his people,
praise for all his saints,
for the people of Israel who are near to him.
Praise the Lord!

RECALLING DELIVERANCE FROM EGYPT

Psalms 114

When Israel went forth from Egypt,
the house of Jacob from a people of strange language,
Judah became his sanctuary,
Israel his dominion.

The sea looked and fled,
Jordan turned back.
The mountains skipped like rams,
the hills like lambs.

What ails you, O sea, that you flee?
O Jordan, that you turn back?
O mountains, that you skip like rams?
O hills, like lambs?

Tremble, O earth, at the presence of the Lord,
at the presence of the God of Jacob,
who turns the rock into a pool of water,
the flint into a spring of water.

HALLELUJAH HYMN

Psalms 150

Praise the Lord!

Praise God in his sanctuary;
 praise him in his mighty firmament!
Praise him for his mighty deeds;
 praise him according to his exceeding greatness!

Praise him with trumpet sound;
 praise him with lute and harp!
Praise him with timbrel and dance;
 praise him with strings and pipe!
Praise him with sounding cymbals;
 praise him with loud clashing cymbals!
Let everything that breathes praise the Lord!

Praise the Lord!

EVERLASTING SALVATION

Isaiah 55:1–13

*(Note: This is one of the Songs of Zion in
the great Isaiahan Rhapsody: an address to
the nations with recitative passages which
interrupt and make God the speaker. The
two forms differentiate the two speakers.)*

"Ho, every one who thirsts, come to the waters;
    and he who has no money, come, buy and eat!
Come, buy wine and milk
    without money and without price.

Why do you spend your money for that which is not bread,
    and your labor for that which does not satisfy?
Hearken diligently to me, and eat what is good,
    and delight yourself in fatness.

Incline your ear, and come to me;
    hear, that your soul may live;
I will make with you an everlasting covenant,
    my steadfast, sure love for David."

Behold, I made him a witness to the peoples, a leader and commander for the peoples. Behold, you shall call nations that you know not, and nations that knew you not shall run to you, because of the Lord your God, and of the Holy One of Israel, for he has glorified you.

"Seek you that Lord while he may be found,
    call upon him while he is near;
let the wicked forsake his way,
    and the unrighteous man his thoughts;

Let him return to the Lord,
    that he may have mercy on him,
and to our God,
    for he will abundantly pardon."

For my thoughts are not your thoughts, neither are your ways my ways, says the Lord. For as the heavens are higher than the earth, so are my ways higher than your ways and my thoughts than your thoughts. For as the rain and the snow come down from heaven, and return not thither but water the earth, making it bring forth the sprout, giving seed to the sower and bread to the eater, so shall my word be that goes forth from my mouth; it shall not return to me empty, but it shall accomplish that which I purpose, and prosper in the thing for which I sent it.

"For you shall go out in joy,
    and be led forth in peace;
the mountains and the hills before you shall break forth
        into singing,

and all the trees of the field shall clap their hands.

Instead of the thorn shall come up the cypress;
    instead of the brier shall come up the myrtle;
and it shall be to the Lord for a memorial,
    for an everlasting sign which shall not be cut off."

THE THUNDERSTORM SONG

Psalms 29

Ascribe to the Lord, O heavenly beings,
ascribe to the Lord glory and strength.
Ascribe to the Lord the glory of his name;
worship the Lord in holy array.

The voice of the Lord is upon the waters,
    the God of glory thunders,
    the Lord, upon many waters.
The voice of the Lord is powerful,
the voice of the Lord is full of majesty.

The voice of the Lord breaks the cedars,
the Lord breaks the cedars of Lebanon.
He makes Lebanon to skip like a calf,
and Sirion like a young wild ox.

The voice of the Lord flashes forth flames of fire.
The voice of the Lord shakes the wilderness,
    the Lord shakes the wilderness of Kadesh.
The voice of the Lord makes the oaks to whirl,
    and strips the forests bare;
    and in his temple all cry, "Glory!"

The Lord sits enthroned over the flood;
the Lord sits enthroned as king for ever.
May the Lord give strength to his people!
May the Lord bless his people with peace!

GOD'S MAJESTY IN THE STORM

Job 36:24–33; 37:1–22

"Remember to extol his work,
    of which men have sung.
All men have looked on it;

man beholds it from afar.
Behold, God is great, and we know him not;
 the number of his years is unsearchable.
For he draws up the drops of water,
 he distils his mist in rain
which the skies pour down,
 and drop upon man abundantly.
Can any one understand the spreading of the clouds,
 the thunderings of his pavilion?
Behold, he scatters his lightning about him,
 and covers the roots of the sea.
For by these he judges peoples;
 he gives food in abundance.
He covers his hands with the lightning,
 and commands it to strike the mark.
Its crashing declares concerning him,
 who is jealous with anger against iniquity.

"At this also my heart trembles,
 and leaps out of its place.
Hearken to the thunder of his voice
 and the rumbling that comes from his mouth.
Under the whole heaven he lets it go,
 and his lightning to the corners of the earth.
After it his voice roars;
 he thunders with his majestic voice
 and he does not restrain the lightnings when his voice is
 heard.
God thunders wondrously with his voice;
 he does great things which we cannot comprehend.
For to the snow he says, 'Fall on the earth;'
 and to the shower and the rain, 'Be strong.'
He seals up the hand of every man,
 that all men may know his work.
Then the beasts go into their lairs,
 and remain in their dens.
From its chamber comes the whirlwind,
 and cold from the scattering winds.
By the breath of God ice is given,
 and the broad waters are frozen fast.
He loads the thick cloud with moisture,
 the clouds scatter his lightning.
They turn round and round by his guidance,

to accomplish all that he commands them
    on the face of the habitable world.
Whether for correction, or for his land,
    or for love, he causes it to happen.

"Hear this, O Job;
    stop and consider the wondrous works of God.
Do you know how God lays his command upon them,
    and causes the lightning of his cloud to shine?
Do you know the balancings of the clouds,
    the wondrous works of him who is perfect in knowledge,
you whose garments are hot
    when the earth is still because of the south wind?
Can you, like him, spread out the skies,
    hard as a molten mirror?
Teach us what we shall say to him;
    we cannot draw up our case because of darkness.
Shall it be told him that I would speak?
    Did a man ever wish that he would be swallowed up?
And now men cannot look on the light
    when it is bright in the skies,
    when the wind has passed and cleared them.
Out of the north comes golden splendor;
    God is clothed with terrible majesty."

SONG OF THE PRINCE OF PEACE

Isaiah 9:2–7

The people who walked in darkness
    have seen a great light;
those who dwell in a land of deep darkness,
    on them has light shined.
Thou hast multiplied the nation,
    thou hast increased its joy;
they rejoice before thee
    as witn joy at the harvest,
    as men rejoice when they divide the spoil.
For the yoke of his burden,
    and the staff for his shoulder,
    the rod of his oppressor,
    thou hast broken as on the day of Midian.
For every boot of the tramping warrior in battle tumult
    and every garment rolled in blood

will be burned as fuel for the fire.
For to us a child is born,
    to us a son is given;
and the government shall be upon his shoulder,
    and his name will be called
        "Wonderful Counselor,
        Mighty God,
        Everlasting Father,
        Prince of Peace."
Of the increase of his government and of peace
    there will be no end,
upon the throne of David, and over his kingdom,
    to establish it, and to uphold it
with justice and with righteousness
    from this time forth and for evermore.
The zeal of the Lord of hosts will do this.

MOSES CELEBRATES THE ESCAPE

Exodus 15:1–2, 9–11

I will sing to the Lord, for he has triumphed gloriously;
the horse and his rider he has thrown into the sea.
The Lord is my strength and my song,
and he has become my salvation;
this is my God, and I will praise him,
my father's God, and I will exalt him.

The enemy said,
    "I will pursue,
    I will overtake,
    I will divide the spoil,
    my desire shall have its fill of them.
    I will draw my sword,
    my hand shall destroy them."

Thou didst blow with thy wind,
the sea covered them;
they sank as lead in the mighty waters.

Who is like thee, O Lord, among the gods?
Who is like thee,
    majestic in holiness,
    terrible in glorious deeds,
    doing wonders?

MARY, SINGING TO ELIZABETH

Luke 1:46–55

And Mary said,
"My soul magnifies the Lord,
and my spirit rejoices in God my Savior,
for he has regarded the low estate of his handmaiden.
For behold, henceforth all generations will call me blessed;
for he who is mighty has done great things for me,
and holy is his name.
And his mercy is on those who fear him
from generation to generation.
He has shown strength with his arm,
he has scattered the proud in the imagination of their
           hearts,
he has put down the mighty from their thrones,
and exalted those of low degree;
he has filled the hungry with good things,
and the rich he has sent empty away.
He has helped his servant Israel,
in remembrance of his mercy,
as he spoke to our fathers,
to Abraham and to his posterity for ever."

SONG OF THE IDEAL OF WORLD JUSTICE

Isaiah 2:2–4

It shall come to pass in the latter days
    that the mountain of the house of the Lord
shall be established as the highest of the mountains,
    and it shall be raised above the hills;
and all the nations shall flow to it,
    and many peoples shall come, and say:
"Come, let us go up to the mountain of the Lord,
    to the house of the God of Jacob;
that he may teach us his ways
    and that we may walk in his paths."
For out of Zion shall go forth the law,
    and the word of the Lord from Jerusalem.
He shall judge between the nations,
    and shall decide for many peoples;
and they shall beat their swords into plowshares,
    and their spears into pruning hooks;

nation shall not lift up sword against nation,
neither shall they learn war any more.

THE IDEAL RULER

Isaiah 11:1–10

There shall come forth a shoot from the stump of Jesse,
and a branch shall grow out of his roots.
And the Spirit of the Lord shall rest upon him,
the spirit of wisdom and understanding,
the spirit of counsel and might,
the spirit of knowledge and the fear of the Lord.
And his delight shall be in the fear of the Lord.

He shall not judge by what his eyes see,
or decide by what his ears hear;
but with righteousness he shall judge the poor,
and decide with equity for the meek of the earth;
and he shall smite the earth with the rod of his mouth,
and with the breath of his lips he shall slay the wicked.
Righteousness shall be the girdle of his waist,
and faithfulness the girdle of his loins.

The wolf shall dwell with the lamb,
and the leopard shall lie down with the kid,
and the calf and the lion and the fatling together,
and a little child shall lead them.
The cow and the bear shall feed;
their young shall lie down together;
and the lion shall eat straw like the ox.
The suckling child shall play over the hole of the asp,
and the weaned child shall put his hand on the adder's
den.
They shall not hurt or destroy
in all my holy mountain;
for the earth shall be full of the knowledge of the Lord
as the waters cover the sea.

In that day the root of Jesse shall stand as an ensign to the
peoples; him shall the nations seek, and his dwellings shall be
glorious.

THE ODE

Although the English Romantic poets are more closely akin to the classical writers than to the Biblical authors, one can find suggestions and overtones of the Biblical ode in Shelley's "Ode to the West Wind" and Keats' "Ode on a Grecian Urn." Probably closer in spirit and language is Henry Timrod's "Ode on the Graves of the Confederate Dead."

Etymologically the word *ode* means "song." It is the furthest removed from the ordinary speech and the nearest to pure music. The ode is distinguished from the other lyrics by greater elaboration and more defined structure.

The ode in Psalm 30 was performed by a body of singers whose evolutions as they sang carried them from a central altar toward the right: then turning around they performed the answering stanza, repeating the movements, until the close brought them to the altar from which they had started. Then a stanza would take them to the left of the altar, and the answering stanza would bring them back to the starting point. The first stanza was called a *strophe* and the answering stanza an *antistrophe.* The two stanzas of a pair usually agree in number of parallel lines.

DEDICATION

Psalms 30

Strophe I

I will extol thee, O Lord;
for thou hast drawn me up,
and hast not let my foes rejoice over me.
O Lord, my God, I cried to thee for help,
and thou hast healed me.
O Lord, thou hast brought up my soul from Sheol,
restored me to life among those gone down to the Pit.

Antistrophe I

Sing praises to the Lord, O you his saints,
and give thanks to his holy name.
for his anger is but for a moment,
and his favor is for a lifetime.
Weeping may tarry for the night,
but joy comes with the morning.

Strophe II

As for me, I said in my prosperity,
"I shall never be moved."
By thy favor, O Lord,
thou hadst established me as a strong mountain.

Antistrophe II

Thou didst hide thy face,
I was dismayed.
To thee, O Lord, I cried;
and to the Lord I made supplication.

Strophe III

"What profit is there in my death,
if I go down to the Pit?
Will the dust praise thee?
Will it tell of thy faithfulness?
Hear, O Lord, and be gracious to me!
O Lord, be thou my helper!"

Antistrophe III

Thou hast turned for me my mourning into dancing;
thou hast loosed my sackcloth
and girded me with gladness,
that my soul may praise thee
and not be silent.
O Lord my God, I will give thanks to thee for ever.

In Proverbs 4 note how the strophe describes the path of the
just and the antistrophe the path of the wicked. The brief conclusion
blends the two ideas in a common image.

THE TWO PATHS

Proverbs 4:10–19

Hear, my son, and accept my words,
that the years of your life may be many.
I have taught you the way of wisdom;
I have led you in the paths of uprightness.
When you walk, your step will not be hampered;
and if you run, you will not stumble.
    Keep hold of instruction,

do not let go;
guard her,
for she is your life.
Do not enter the path of the wicked,
and do not walk in the way of evil men.
Avoid it;
do not go on it;
turn away from it
and pass on.
For they cannot sleep unless they have done wrong;
they are robbed of sleep unless they have made some one
stumble.
For they eat the bread of wickedness
and drink the wine of violence.

But the path of the righteous is like the light of dawn,
which shines brighter and brighter until full day.
The way of the wicked is like deep darkness;
they do not know over what they stumble.

The most elaborate of the Biblical odes is "Deborah's Song" in the book of Judges, Chapter 5. Three devices distinguish this poem: (1) a whole story concentrated into a few luminous details; (2) narrative delayed or broken by refrains called *apostrophes,* in which the singers turn aside from the story to address heaven or bystanders or one another; and (3) the antiphonal performance, in which one singer or set of singers is answered by another.

In the song of Deborah and Barak, the two individuals sing a song to each other or Deborah leads a chorus of women and Barak leads a chorus of men. The titles and parentheses in the ode are not in the original but are added to clarify structure.

Following the song of Deborah and Barak, a second song, "The Song of Moses and Miriam," is presented for comparison.

DEBORAH'S SONG

Judges 5:3–31

Prelude

MEN:
Hear, O kings;
WOMEN:
give ear, O princes;

MEN:

to the Lord I will sing,

WOMEN:

I will make melody to the Lord, the God of Israel.

BOTH:

Lord, when thou didst go forth from Seir,
when thou didst march from the region of Edom,
the earth trembled,
and the heavens dropped,
yea, the clouds dropped water.
The mountains quaked before the Lord,
yon Sinai before the Lord, the God of Israel.

The Desolation

(The men lead off with a description of the oppression.)

MEN:

In the days of Shamgar, son of Anath,
in the days of Jael,
caravans ceased
and travelers kept to the byways.
The peasantry ceased in Israel,
they ceased.

(Deborah and the women break in with a return to ordinary language.)

WOMEN:

Until you arose, Deborah,
arose as a mother in Israel.
When new gods were chosen,
then war was in the gates.
Was shield or spear to be seen
among forty thousand in Israel?

Refrain
(Singers bid publish glad tidings of victory.)

MEN:

My heart goes out to the commanders of Israel,

WOMEN:

who offered themselves willingly among the people.

BOTH:

Bless the Lord.

MEN:

> Tell of it, you who ride on tawny asses,
>> you who sit on rich carpets
>> and you who walk by the way.

WOMEN:

> To the sound of musicians
>> at the watering places,

BOTH:

> there they repeat the triumphs of the Lord,
>> the triumphs of his peasantry in Israel.

The Mustering of the Tribes

BOTH:

> Then down to the gates
>> marched the people of the Lord.

MEN:

> Awake, awake, Deborah!
> Awake, awake, utter a song!

WOMEN:

> Arise, Barak, lead away your captives,
>> O son of Abino-am.

BOTH:

> Then down marched the remnant of the noble;
>> the people of the Lord marched down for him against the
>> mighty.

(Tribes of Israel called off)

WOMEN:

> From Ephraim they set out thither
>> into the valley,

MEN:

> following you, Benjamin,
>> with your kinsmen;

WOMEN:

> from Machir marched down the commanders,

MEN:

> and from Zebulun those who bear the marshal's staff;

WOMEN:

> the princes of Issachar came with Deborah,

MEN:

> and Issachar faithful to Barak;

BOTH:

> into the valley they rushed forth at his heels.

MEN:
> Among the clans of Reuben
>> there were great searchings of heart.

WOMEN:
> Why did you tarry among the sheepfolds,
>> to hear the piping for the flocks?

MEN:
> Among the clans of Reuben
>> there were great searchings of heart.

WOMEN:
> Gilead stayed beyond the Jordan;

MEN:
> and Dan, why did he abide with the ships?

WOMEN:
> Asher sat still at the coast of the sea,
>> settling down by his landings.

MEN:
> Zebulun is a people that jeoparded their lives to the death;
> Naphtali too, on the heights of the field.

The Battle and the Rout

(The men picture the actual murder of Sisera; the women add the feminine touch of the mother and her ladies awaiting the dead warrior's return.)

MEN:
> The kings came, they fought;
>> then fought the kings of Canaan,
> at Taanach, by the waters of Megiddo;
>> they got no spoils of silver.

WOMEN:
> From heaven fought the stars,
>> from their courses they fought against Sisera.
> The torrent Kishon swept them away,
>> the onrushing torrent, the torrent Kishon.

MEN:
> March on, my soul,
>> with might!
> Then loud beat the horses' hoofs
>> with the galloping, galloping of his steeds.

WOMEN:
> Curse Meroz, says the angel of the Lord,
>> curse bitterly its inhabitants,

because they come not to the help of the Lord,
    to the help of the Lord against the mighty.

The Retribution

MEN:
    Most blessed of women be Jael,
        the wife of Heber the Kenite,
        of tent-dwelling women most blessed.
    He asked water and she gave him milk,
        she brought him curds in a lordly bowl.
    She put her hand to the tent peg
        and her right hand to the workman's mallet;
    she struck Sisera a blow,
        she crushed his head,
        she shattered and pierced his temple.
    He sank, he fell,
        he lay still at her feet;
    at her feet he sank, he fell;
        where he sank, there he fell dead.
WOMEN:
    Out of the window she peered,
        the mother of Sisera gazed through the lattice:
    "Why is his chariot so long in coming?
        Why tarry the hoofbeats of his chariots?"
    Her wisest ladies make answer,
        nay, she gives answer to herself,
    "Are they not finding and dividing the spoil?—
        a maiden or two for every man;
        spoil of dyed stuffs for Sisera,
        spoil of dyed stuffs embroidered,
        two pieces of dyed work embroidered
        for my neck as spoil?"
BOTH:
    So perish all thine enemies, O Lord!
        But thy friends be like the sun
    as he rises in his might.

And the land had rest for forty years.

SONG OF MOSES AND MIRIAM

Exodus 15:1–21

MEN AND WOMEN:

I will sing to the Lord, for he has triumphed gloriously;
  the horse and his rider he has thrown into the sea.
The Lord is my strength and my song,
  and he has become my salvation;
this is my God, and I will praise him,
  my father's God, and I will exalt him.

MEN:

The Lord is a man of war;
  the Lord is his name.
Pharaoh's chariots and his host he cast into the sea;
  and his picked officers are sunk in the Red Sea.
The floods cover them;
  they went down into the depths like a stone.

MEN:

Thy right hand, O Lord, glorious in power,
  thy right hand, O Lord, shatters the enemy.
In the greatness of thy majesty thou overthrowest thy
      adversaries;
  thou sendest forth thy fury, it consumes them like
      stubble.
At the blast of thy nostrils the waters piled up,
  the floods stood up in a heap;
  the deeps congealed in the heart of the sea.
The enemy said, "I will pursue, I will overtake,
  I will divide the spoil,
  my desire shall have its fill of them.
  I will draw my sword,
  my hand shall destroy them."
Thou didst blow with thy wind, the sea covered them;
  they sank as lead in the mighty waters.

MEN:

Who is like thee, O Lord, among the gods?
  Who is like thee, majestic in holiness,
  terrible in glorious deeds, doing wonders?
Thou didst stretch out thy right hand,
  the earth swallowed them.
Thou hast led in thy steadfast love the people whom thou
      hast redeemed,
  thou hast guided them by thy strength to thy holy
      abode.
The people have heard, they tremble;
  pangs have seized on the inhabitants of Philistia.
Now are the chiefs of Edom dismayed;

the leaders of Moab, trembling seizes them;
all the inhabitants of Canaan have melted away.
Terror and dread fall upon them;
because of the greatness of thy arm,
they are as still as a stone,
till thy people, O Lord, pass by,
till the people pass by whom thou hast purchased.
Thou wilt bring them in, and plant them on thy own
mountain,
the place, O Lord, which thou hast made for thy
abode,
the sanctuary, O Lord, which thy hands have established.

WOMEN:
The Lord will reign for ever and ever.
For when the horses of Pharaoh with his chariots
and his horsemen went into the sea,
the Lord brought back the waters of the sea upon them;
but the people of Israel walked on dry ground
in the midst of the sea.
MEN:
Then Miriam, the prophetess, the sister of Aaron,
took a timbrel in her hand;
and all the women went out after her
with timbrels and dancing.
MEN AND WOMEN:
And Miriam sang to them:
"Sing to the Lord, for he has triumphed gloriously;
the horse and his rider
he has thrown into the sea."

THE ELEGY

This particular form of poetry is not as fashionable as it once was. It is hard to conceive of a twentieth-century poet writing an elegy in the Biblical sense. Earlier writers, however, made use of this form; and certainly one of the most widely read poems in the English language, Thomas Gray's "Elegy Written in a Country Churchyard," owes much to the Bible. Milton's elegy "Lycidas," although classical in form, is Biblical in tone, and Alfred Tennyson's "In Memoriam" comes even closer to the Biblical model.

Elegy rests upon professional mourning. The rhythm is the ordinary couplet with the second member weakened either by being shortened or without strong parallelism, so much so that the second member is often printed on the same line as the first member.

CAPTIVES WEEPING BY THE RIVERS OF BABYLON

Psalms 137:1–4

By the waters of Babylon, there we sat down and wept,
    when we remembered Zion.
On the willows there we hung up our lyres.
    For there our captors required of us songs,
and our tormentors, mirth, saying,
    "Sing us one of the songs of Zion!"
How shall we sing the Lord's song
    in a foreign land?

LAMENTATION OF DAVID OVER SAUL AND JONATHAN

2 Samuel 1:19–27

Thy glory, O Israel, is slain upon thy high places!
    How are the mighty fallen!
Tell it not in Gath,
    publish it not in the streets of Ashkelon;
lest the daughters of the Philistines rejoice,
    lest the daughters of the uncircumcised exult.

Ye mountains of Gilboa,
    let there be no dew or rain upon you,
nor upsurging of the deep!
    For there the shield of the mighty was defiled,
the shield of Saul,
    not anointed with oil.

From the blood of the slain,
    from the fat of the mighty,
the bow of Jonathan turned not back,
    and the sword of Saul returned not empty.

Saul and Jonathan, beloved and lovely!
    In life and in death they were not divided;
They were swifter than eagles,
    they were stronger than lions.

Ye daughters of Israel, weep over Saul,
    who clothed you daintily in scarlet,
who put ornaments of gold
    upon your apparel.
How are the mighty fallen,
    in the midst of the battle!

Jonathan lies slain upon thy high places.
    I am distressed for you, my brother Jonathan;
very pleasant have you been to me;
    your love for me was wonderful,
    passing the love of women.
How are the mighty fallen,
    and the weapons of war perished!

LAMENT OVER GLORY DEPARTED

Lamentations 3:22–33

The steadfast love of the Lord never ceases,
    his mercies never come to an end;
they are new every morning;
    great is thy faithfulness.
"The Lord is my portion," says my soul,
    "therefore I will hope in him."

The Lord is good to those who wait for him,
    to the soul that seeks him.
It is good that one should wait quietly
    for the salvation of the Lord.
It is good for a man that he bear
    the yoke in his youth.

Let him sit alone in silence
    when he has laid it on him;
let him put his mouth in the dust—
    there may yet be hope;
let him give his cheek to the smiter,
    and be filled with insults.

For the Lord will not
    cast off for ever,
but, though he cause grief, he will have compassion

according to the abundance of his steadfast love;
for he does not willingly afflict
or grieve the sons of men.

MEDITATION POETRY

Unfortunately, today, most meditation poetry has degenerated into sloppy, sentimental mush aimed at a mass market. However, a poem such as "Pied Beauty" by Gerard Manley Hopkins demonstrates how a skillful modern poet can approximate the intense feeling of the poetry in this section. Meditation poetry differs from songs in that a song celebrates a theme while meditation poetry reflects upon a theme.

THE BLESSEDNESS OF RIGHTEOUSNESS

Psalms 1

Blessed is the man who walks not in the counsel of the wicked,
    nor stands in the way of sinners,
    nor sits in the seat of scoffers;
but his delight is in the law of the Lord,
    and on his law he meditates day and night.

He is like a tree planted by streams of water,
    that yields its fruit in its season,
and its leaf does not wither.
    In all that he does, he prospers.

The wicked are not so, but are like chaff which the wind drives
    away.
    Therefore the wicked will not stand in the judgment,
    nor sinners in the congregation of the righteous;
for the Lord knows the way of the righteous,
    but the way of the wicked will perish.

GLORIES OF CREATION AND PERFECTION OF GOD'S LAWS

Psalms 19

The heavens are telling the glory of God;
    and the firmament proclaims his handiwork.
Day to day pours forth speech,
    and night to night declares knowledge.
There is no speech, nor are there words;

their voice is not heard;
yet their voice goes through all the earth,
    and their words to the end of the world.

In them he has set a tent for the sun,
    which comes forth like a bridegroom leaving his chamber,
    and like a strong man runs its course with joy.
Its rising is from the end of the heavens,
    and its circuit to the end of them;
    and there is nothing hid from its heat.

The law of the Lord is perfect, reviving the soul;
the testimony of the Lord is sure, making wise the simple;
the precepts of the Lord are right, rejoicing the heart;
the commandment of the Lord is pure, enlightening the eyes;
the fear of the Lord is clean, enduring for ever;
the ordinances of the Lord are true, and righteous altogether.

More to be desired are they than gold, even much fine gold;
    sweeter also than honey and drippings of the honeycomb.
Moreover by them is thy servant warned;
    in keeping them there is great reward.
But who can discern his errors?
    Clear thou me from hidden faults.

Keep back thy servant also from presumptuous sins;
    let them not have dominion over me!
Then I shall be blameless,
    and innocent of great transgression.

Let the words of my mouth
    and the meditation of my heart
be acceptable in thy sight,
    O Lord, my rock and my redeemer.

THE SHEPHERD SONG

Psalms 23

The Lord is my shepherd,
I shall not want;

    He makes me lie down in green pastures.
    He leads me beside still waters;

he restores my soul.
He leads me in paths of righteousness for his name's sake.

Even though I walk through the valley of the shadow of death,
I fear no evil;
for thou art with me;
thy rod and thy staff, they comfort me.

Thou preparest a table before me
in the presence of my enemies;
thou anointest my head with oil,
my cup overflows.

Surely goodness and mercy shall follow me all the days of my
        life;
and I shall dwell in the house of the Lord for ever.

THE IMPORTANCE OF GOD'S WORD

Psalms 119:9–16

How can a young man keep his way pure?
    By guarding it according to thy word.
    With my whole heart I see thee;
        let me not wander from thy commandments!
    I have laid up thy word in my heart,
        that I might not sin against thee.

Blessed be thou, O Lord;
teach me thy statutes!
With my lips I declare all the ordinances of thy mouth.

In the way of thy testimonies I delight
    as much as in all riches.
I will meditate on thy precepts,
    and fix my eyes on thy ways.
I will delight in thy statutes;
    I will not forget thy word.

THE INADEQUACY OF MAN

Psalms 14:1–3

The fool says in his heart, "There is no God."

They are corrupt,
    they do abominable deeds,
there is none that does good.

The Lord looks down from heaven
    upon the children of men,
to see if there are any that act wisely,
    that seek after God.

They have all gone astray,
    they are all alike corrupt;
there is none that does good,
    no, not one.

THE SUFFICIENCY OF GOD

Psalms 107:1–9

O give thanks to the Lord,
for he is good;
for his steadfast love endures for ever!

Let the redeemed of the Lord say so,
    whom he has redeemed from trouble
and gathered in from the lands,
    from the east
    and from the west,
    from the north
    and from the south.

Some wandered in desert wastes,
finding no way to a city to dwell in.
Hungry and thirsty, their soul fainted within them.

Then they cried to the Lord in their trouble,
    and he delivered them from their distress;
he led them by a straight way,
    till they reached a city to dwell in.

Let them thank the Lord for his steadfast love,
    for his wonderful works to the sons of men!
For he satisfies him who is thirsty,
    and the hungry he fills with good things.

A SEASON FOR EVERYTHING

Ecclesiastes 3:1–8

For everything there is a season,
and a time for every matter under heaven:

> A time to be born,
>   and a time to die;
> A time to plant,
>   and a time to pluck up what is planted;
> A time to kill,
>   and a time to heal;
> A time to break down,
>   and a time to build up;
> A time to weep,
>   and a time to laugh;
> A time to mourn,
>   and a time to dance;
> A time to cast away stones,
>   and a time to gather stones together;
> A time to embrace,
>   and a time to refrain from embracing;
> A time to seek,
>   and a time to lose;
> A time to keep,
>   and a time to cast away;
> A time to rend,
>   and a time to sew;
> A time to keep silence,
>   and a time to speak;
> A time to love,
>   and a time to hate;
> A time for war,
>   and a time for peace.

MONODIES

Like meditation poetry, most contemporary monodies are mawkishly dull and aimed at those who read poetry to "feel good" rather than to think. For an example of the really introspective monody similar to the biblical type, one has to read a poem such as Keats' "When I Have Fears" or Milton's sonnet "On His Blindness."

Monodies are founded on special, personal experience, usually narrated. They are addressed either to God or to the poet himself.

HYMN OF TRUST IN GOD

Psalms 4

Answer me when I call, O God of my right!
    Thou hast given me room when I was in distress.
Be gracious to me,
    and hear my prayer.

O men, how long shall my honor suffer shame?
    How long will you love vain words, and seek after lies?
        Selah.
But know that the Lord has set apart the godly for himself;
    the Lord hears when I call to him.

Be angry, but sin not;
    commune with your own hearts on your beds, and be silent.
        Selah.
Offer right sacrifices,
    and put your trust in the Lord.

There are many who say, "O that we might see some good!
    Lift up the light of thy countenance upon us, O Lord!"
Thou hast put more joy in my heart
    than they have when their grain and wine abound.

In peace I will both lie down
    and sleep;
for thou alone, O Lord,
    makest me dwell in safety.

MAN TO BE LORD OVER GOD'S CREATION

Psalms 8

O Lord, our Lord,
how majestic is thy name in all the earth!

    Thou whose glory above the heavens is chanted
    by the mouth of babes and infants,
    thou hast founded a bulwark because of thy foes,
    to still the enemy and the avenger.

When I look at thy heavens, the work of thy fingers,
the moon and the stars which thou hast established;
what is man that thou art mindful of him,
and the son of man that thou dost care for him?

Yet thou hast made him little less than God,
and dost crown him with glory and honor.
Thou hast given him dominion over the works of thy hands;
thou hast put all things under his feet,
    all sheep and oxen,
    and also the beasts of the field,
    the birds of the air,
    and the fish of the sea,
    whatever passes along the paths of the sea.

O Lord, our Lord,
how majestic is thy name in all the earth!

GOD, OUR DWELLING PLACE

Psalms 90

Lord, thou hast been our dwelling place
in all generations.

Before the mountains were brought forth,
    or ever thou hadst formed the earth and the world,
from everlasting to everlasting,
    thou art God.

Thou turnest man back to the dust,
    and sayest, "Turn back, O children of men!"
For a thousand years in thy sight
    are but as yesterday when it is past,
    or as a watch in the night.

Thou dost sweep men away; they are like a dream,
    like grass which is renewed in the morning:
in the morning it flourishes and is renewed;
    in the evening it fades and withers.

For we are consumed by thy anger;
    by thy wrath we are overwhelmed.
Thou hast set our iniquities before thee,
    our secret sins in the light of thy countenance.

For all our days pass away under thy wrath,
  our years come to an end like a sigh.
The years of our life are threescore and ten,
  or even by reason of strength fourscore;
yet their span is but toil and trouble;
  they are soon gone, and we fly away.

Who considers the power of thy anger,
  and thy wrath according to the fear of thee?
So teach us to number our days
  that we may get a heart of wisdom.

Return, O Lord! How long?
  Have pity on thy servants!
Satisfy us in the morning with thy steadfast love,
  that we may rejoice and be glad all our days.
Make us glad as many days as thou hast afflicted us,
  and as many years as we have seen evil.
Let thy work be manifest to thy servants,
  and thy glorious power to their children.
Let the favor of the Lord our God be upon us,
  and establish thou the work of our hands upon us,
  yea, the work of our hands establish thou it.

BLESS THE LORD, O MY SOUL

Psalms 103

Bless the Lord, O my soul;
  and all that is within me, bless his holy name!
Bless the Lord, O my soul,
  and forget not all his benefits,
who forgives all your iniquity,
  who heals all your diseases,
who redeems your life from the Pit,
  who crowns you with steadfast love and mercy,
who satisfies you with good as long as you live
  so that your youth is renewed like the eagle's.

The Lord works vindication
  and justice for all who are oppressed.
He made known his ways to Moses,
  his acts to the people of Israel.
The Lord is merciful and gracious,

slow to anger and abounding in steadfast love.
He will not always chide,
    nor will he keep his anger for ever.
He does not deal with us according to our sins,
    nor requite us according to our iniquities.
For as the heavens are high above the earth,
    so great is his steadfast love toward those who fear him;
as far as the east is from the west,
    so far does he remove our transgressions from us.
As a father pities his children,
    so the Lord pities those who fear him.
For he knows our frame;
    he remembers that we are dust.

As for man, his days are like grass;
    he flourishes like a flower of the field;
for the wind passes over it, and it is gone,
    and its place knows it no more.
But the steadfast love of the Lord is from everlasting to ever-
        lasting upon those who fear him,
    and his righteousness to children's children,
to those who keep his covenant
    and remember to do his commandments.

The Lord has established his throne in the heavens,
    and his kingdom rules over all.
Bless the Lord, O you his angels,
    you mighty ones who do his word,
    hearkening to the voice of his word!
Bless the Lord, all his hosts,
    his ministers that do his will!
Bless the Lord, all his works,
    in all places of his dominion.
Bless the Lord, O my soul!

PILGRIM'S PSALM

Psalms 121

I lift up my eyes to the hills.
From whence does my help come?
My help comes from the Lord,
who made heaven and earth.

He will not let your foot be moved,
he who keeps you will not slumber.
Behold, he who keeps Israel
will neither slumber nor sleep.

The Lord is your keeper;
the Lord is your shade on your right hand.
The sun shall not smite you by day,
nor the moon by night.

The Lord will keep you from all evil;
he will keep your life.
The Lord will keep your going out and your coming in
from this time forth and for evermore.

INFINITE KNOWLEDGE OF GOD

Psalms 139

O Lord, thou hast searched me and known me!
  Thou knowest when I sit down and when I rise up;
  thou discernest my thoughts from afar.
  Thou searchest out my path and my lying down,
  and art acquainted with all my ways.
  Even before a word is on my tongue,
  lo, O Lord, thou knowest it altogether.
  Thou dost beset me behind and before,
  and layest thy hand upon me.
  Such knowledge is too wonderful for me;
  it is high, I cannot attain it.
  Whither shall I go from thy Spirit?
  Or whither shall I flee from thy presence?
  If I ascend to heaven, thou art there!
  If I make my bed in Sheol, thou art there!
  If I take the wings of the morning
  and dwell in the uttermost parts of the sea,
  even there thy hand shall lead me,
  and thy right hand shall hold me.
  If I say, "Let only darkness cover me,
  and the light above me be night,"
  even the darkness is not dark to thee,
  the night is bright as the day;
  for darkness is as light with thee.

For thou didst form my inward parts,
thou didst knit me together in my mother's womb.

I praise thee, for thou art fearful and wonderful.
Wonderful are thy works!
Thou knowest me right well;
my frame was not hidden from thee,
when I was being made in secret,
intricately wrought in the depths of the earth.
Thy eyes beheld my unformed substance;
in thy book were written, every one of them,
the days that were formed for me,
when as yet there was none of them.

How precious to me are thy thoughts, O God!
How vast is the sum of them!
If I would count them, they are more than the sand.
When I awake, I am still with thee.

O that thou wouldst slay the wicked, O God,
and that men of blood would depart from me,
men who maliciously defy thee,
who lift themselves up against thee for evil!
Do I not hate them that hate thee, O Lord?
And do I not loathe them that rise up against thee?
I hate them with perfect hatred;
I count them my enemies.

Search me, O God, and know my heart!
Try me and know my thoughts!
And see if there be any wicked way in me,
and lead me in the way everlasting!

PLEA FOR CLEANSING

Psalms 51:1–13

Have mercy on me, O God,
according to thy steadfast love;
according to thy abundant mercy
blot out my transgressions.
Wash me thoroughly from my iniquity,
and cleanse me from my sin!
For I know my transgressions,

and my sin is ever before me.
Against thee, thee only, have I sinned,
    and done that which is evil in thy sight,
so that thou art justified in thy sentence
    and blameless in thy judgment.
Behold, I was brought forth in iniquity,
    and in sin did my mother conceive me.

Behold, thou desirest truth in the inward being;
    therefore teach me wisdom in my secret heart.
Purge me with hyssop, and I shall be clean;
    wash me, and I shall be whiter than snow.
Fill me with joy and gladness;
    let the bones which thou hast broken rejoice.
Hide thy face from my sins,
    and blot out all my iniquities.

Create in me a clean heart, O God,
    and put a new and right spirit within me.
Cast me not away from thy presence,
    and take not thy holy Spirit from me.
Restore to me the joy of thy salvation,
    and uphold me with a willing spirit.
Then I will teach transgressors thy ways,
    and sinners will return to thee.

APPROACH TO GOD
Psalms 100

Make a joyful noise to the Lord, all the lands!
    Serve the Lord with gladness!
    Come into his presence with singing!

Know that the Lord is God!
    It is he that made us, and we are his;
    we are his people, and the sheep of his pasture.

Enter his gates with thanksgiving,
    and his courts with praise!
    Give thanks to him, bless his name!

For the Lord is good;
    his steadfast love endures for ever,
    and his faithfulness to all generations.

THE LORD'S PRAYER

Matthew 6:9-13

Our Father who art in heaven,
  Hallowed be thy name.
  Thy kingdom come,
    thy will be done,
On earth as it is in heaven.
  Give us this day our daily bread;
  and forgive us our debts,
as we also have forgiven our debtors;
  and lead us not into temptation,
    but deliver us from evil.

DRAMATIC LYRICS

Dramatic lyrics represent a single moment and, like the follow-ing section dealing with ritual lyrics, are likely to seem somewhat mechanical unless one is a participant in a religious ceremony. Much metaphysical poetry of the seventeenth century is similar in ap-proach, particularly that of John Donne and Edward Taylor.

DEVOTION TO GOD'S HOUSE

Psalms 27

The Lord is my light and my salvation;
  whom shall I fear?
The Lord is the stronghold of my life;
  of whom shall I be afraid?

When evildoers assail me,
  uttering slanders against me,
my adversaries and foes,
  they shall stumble and fall.

Though a host encamp against me,
  my heart shall not fear;
though war arise against me,
  yet I will be confident.

One thing have I asked of the Lord,

that will I seek after;
that I may dwell in the house of the Lord
    all the days of my life,
to behold the beauty of the Lord,
    and to inquire in his temple.
For he will hide me in his shelter
    in the day of trouble;
he will conceal me under the cover of his tent,
    he will set me high upon a rock.

And now my head shall be lifted up
    above my enemies round about me;
and I will offer in his tent
    sacrifices with shouts of joy;
I will sing and make melody to the Lord.

Hear, O Lord, when I cry aloud,
    be gracious to me and answer me!
Thou hast said, "Seek ye my face."
    My heart says to thee,
"Thy face, Lord, do I seek."
    Hide not thy face from me.

Turn not thy servant away in anger,
    thou who hast been my help.
Cast me not off, forsake me not,
    O God of my salvation!
For my father and my mother have forsaken me,
    but the Lord will take me up.

Teach me thy way, O Lord;
    and lead me on a level path
    because of my enemies.
Give me not up to the will of my adversaries;
    for false witnesses have risen against me,
    and they breathe out violence.

I believe that I shall see
    the goodness of the Lord
    in the land of the living!
Wait for the Lord;
    be strong, and let your heart take courage;
    yea, wait for the Lord.

CALL FOR MERCY

Psalms 85

Lord, thou wast favorable to thy land;
thou didst restore the fortunes of Jacob.
Thou didst forgive the iniquity of thy people;
thou didst pardon all their sin. Selah.
Thou didst withdraw all thy wrath;
thou didst turn from thy hot anger.

Restore us again, O God of our salvation,
and put away thy indignation toward us!
Wilt thou be angry with us for ever?
Wilt thou prolong thy anger to all generations?
Wilt thou not revive us again,
that thy people may rejoice in thee?
Show us thy steadfast love, O Lord,
and grant us thy salvation.

Let me hear what God the Lord will speak,
for he will speak peace to his people,
to his saints, to those who turn to him in their hearts.
Surely his salvation is at hand for those who fear him,
that glory may dwell in our land.

Steadfast love and faithfulness will meet;
righteousness and peace will kiss each other.
Faithfulness will spring up from the ground,
and righteousness will look down from the sky.
Yea, the Lord will give what is good,
and our land will yield its increase.
Righteousness will go before him,
and make his footsteps a way.

RITUAL LYRICS

Ritual lyrics are connected with elaborate ceremony. The classic example of this today, outside of the church, is the singing of the national anthem before a ball game.

GOD'S POSITION IN THE UNIVERSE

Psalms 24

*(Note: This psalm was intended for cere-
monial reading by a procession standing outside the massive walls.)*

The earth is the Lord's
    and the fulness therof,
    the world
    and those who dwell therein;
for he has founded it upon the seas,
    and established it upon the rivers.

Who shall ascend the hill of the Lord?
    And who shall stand in his holy place?
He who has clean hands
    and a pure heart,
    who does not lift up his soul to what is false,
    and does not swear deceitfully.
He will receive blessing from the Lord,
    and vindication from the God of his salvation.
Such is the generation of those who seek him,
    who seek the face of the God of Jacob. Selah.

Lift up your heads, O gates!
And be lifted up, O ancient doors!
That the King of glory may come in.

Who is the King of glory?

The Lord, strong and mighty,
the Lord, mighty in battle!

Lift up your heads, O gates!
And be lifted up, O ancient doors!
That the King of glory may come in.

Who is this King of glory?

The Lord of hosts,
he is the King of glory! Selah.

BENEDICTION

Psalms 67

*(Note: This psalm is a response to the High
Priestly Benediction.)*

1. The High Priest

May God be gracious to us
    and bless us
and make his face
    to shine upon us, Selah.
That thy way may be known upon the earth,
    thy saving power among all nations.

2. The People

Let the peoples praise thee, O God;
let all the peoples praise thee!
Let the nations be glad and sing for joy,
for thou dost judge
    the peoples with equity
and guide
    the nations upon earth. Selah.

Let the peoples praise thee, O God;
let all the peoples praise thee!
The earth has yielded its increase;
    God, our God, has blessed us.
God has blessed us;
    let all the ends of the earth fear him!

LYRIC IDYL

The "Song of Solomon" is distinctive among Bible units in that
its form, grasp of matter, and spirit are lyric idyl.

Lyric idyl is similar to drama, with exceptions. Drama is pure
presentation, and its author can never go back. In lyric idyl the
story is not acted, but assumed or alluded to, and allusions can be
made to the different parts of the story in any order. A pure dramati-
zation of a love story would begin with the first meeting of the
lovers, would proceed with the circumstances of growing intimacy,
and end with marriage. But the series of idyls making Solomon's
Song commences with the wedding day, goes back to the day of
betrothal and reminiscences of the courtship, and then goes forward
to the close of the honeymoon.

In drama every speech is referred to personal speakers, either an individual or a chorus. Lyric idyl also makes use of the reciting chorus, which is impersonal and is a device for carrying on the story not presented dramatically.

Every speech in drama must be spoken in a definite place or scene, but refrains in lyric idyl may be, and usually are, parenthetic —they may not be attached to their context, but may refer to the poem as a whole.

The passionate nature of the Oriental people accounts for the amatory warmth of their poetry's language. Western poetry rests mainly upon imagery, but the poetry of the East adds to imagery symbolism in analytical comparisons, importing ideas such as "His head is as the most fine gold."

The background of the poem includes King Solomon's visit to his vineyard at Mount Lebanon when he comes upon a beautiful Shulammite maiden. She flees from him, and he visits her in disguise as a shepherd and wins her as his queen; they are being wedded in the Royal Palace when the poem opens.

The difficulty in reading lyric idyl, as compared to drama, is that speakers and scenes change readily without indication. The poem, however, may be broken into several divisions:

The wedding day (1:1–2:7)
The bride's reminiscences of the courtship (2:8–3:5)
The day of betrothal (3:6–5:1)
The troubled dream of the bride (5:2–6:3)
The king's meditation on his bride (6:4–7:9)
The bride's longing for her home in Lebanon (7:10–8:4)
The renewal of love in the vineyard of Lebanon (8:5–14)

THE SONG OF SONGS, WHICH IS SOLOMON'S

THE BRIDE:
O that you would kiss me with the kisses
of your mouth!
For your love is better than wine,
your anointing oils are fragrant,
your name is oil poured out;
therefore the maidens love you.

(To the bridegroom)

Draw me after you,
*(Part of the ceremony was lifting the bride
over the threshold of her future house.)*

ATTENDING CHORUS:
  Let us make haste.
        (Bridegroom lifts bride across the threshold.)

THE BRIDE:
  The king has brought me into his chambers.
ATTENDING CHORUS:
  We will exult and rejoice in you;
      we will extol your love more than wine;
THE BRIDE:
  Rightly do they love you.
  (she apologizes to him for her homely beauty)
  I am very dark, but comely,
      O daughters of Jerusalem,
  like the tents of Kedar,
      like the curtains of Solomon.
  Do not gaze at me because I am swarthy,
      because the sun has scorched me.
  My mother's sons were angry with me,
      they made me keeper of the vineyards;
      but, my own vineyard I have not kept!

THE BRIDEGROOM:
  Tell me, you whom my soul loves,
      where you pasture your flock,
      where you make it lie down at noon;
  for why should I be like one who wanders
      beside the flocks of your companions?
  If you do not know, O fairest among women,
      follow in the tracks of the flock,
  and pasture your kids
      beside the shepherds' tents.
  I compare you, my love,
      to a mare of Pharaoh's chariots.
  Your cheeks are comely with ornaments,
      your neck with strings of jewels.
  We will make you ornaments of gold,
      studded with silver.

THE BRIDE:
  While the king is on his couch,
      my nard gave forth its fragrance.
  My beloved is to me a bag of myrrh,
      that lies between my breasts.
  My beloved is to me a cluster of henna blossoms
      in the vineyard of Engedi.

THE BRIDEGROOM:
  Behold, you are beautiful, my love;
    Behold, you are beautiful,
    your eyes are doves.
THE BRIDE:
  Behold, you are beautiful, my beloved, truly lovely.
    Our couch is green;
  the beams of our house are cedar,
    our rafters are pine.
  I am a rose of Sharon,
    a lily of the valleys.
THE BRIDEGROOM:
  As a lily among brambles,
    so is my love among maidens.
THE BRIDE:
  As an apple tree among the trees of the wood,
    so is my beloved among young men.
  With great delight I sat in his shadow,
    and his fruit was sweet to my taste.
  He brought me to the banqueting house,
    and his banner over me was love.
  Sustain me with raisins,
    refresh me with apples;
    for I am sick with love.
  O that his left hand were under my head,
    and that his right hand embraced me!

> *(The procession reaches the bridal chamber
> and the refrain is heard, terminating the first
> song, calling upon all to leave the lovers.)*

  I adjure you, O daughters of Jerusalem,
    by the gazelles or the hinds of the field,
  that you stir not up nor awaken love
    until it please.
THE BRIDE:

> *(Standing outside the bridal chamber, the
> bride reminisces about the courtship along
> with the attending chorus.)*

  The voice of my beloved!
    Behold, he comes,
  leaping upon the mountains,
    bounding over the hills.
  My beloved is like a gazelle,
    or a young stag.

ATTENDING CHORUS:
   Behold, there he stands
      behind our wall,
   gazing in at the windows,
      looking through the lattice.
THE BRIDE:
   My beloved speaks and says to me:
      "Arise, my love, my fair one, and come away;
   for lo, the winter is past,
      the rain is over and gone.
   The flowers appear on the earth,
      the time of singing has come,
   and the voice of the turtledove
      is heard in our land.
   The fig tree puts forth its figs,
      and the vines are in blossom;
      and they give forth fragrance.
   Arise, my love, my fair one,
      and come away.
   O my dove, in the clefts of the rock,
      in the covert of the cliff,
   let me see your face,
      let me hear your voice,
   for your voice is sweet,
      and your face is comely.
   Catch us the foxes,
      the little foxes,
   that spoil the vineyards,
      for our vineyards are in blossom."

   My beloved is mine and I am his,
      he pastures his flock among the lilies.
   Until the day breathes
      and the shadows flee,
   turn, my beloved, be like a gazelle,
      or a young stag upon rugged mountains.

                  (Bride continues her reminiscence.)

   Upon my bed by night
      I sought him whom my soul loves;
   I sought him, but found him not;
      I called him, but he gave no answer.

"I will rise now and go about the city,
    in the streets and in the squares;
I will seek him whom my soul loves."
    I sought him, but found him not.
The watchmen found me,
    as they went about the city.
"Have you seen him whom my soul loves?"
    Scarcely had I passed them,
when I found him whom my soul loves.
    I held him, and would not let him go
until I had brought him into my mother's house,
    and into the chamber of her that conceived me.

(To the attending chorus)

I adjure you, O daughters of Jerusalem,
    by the gazelles or the hinds of the field,
that you stir not up nor awaken love
    until it please.

THE ATTENDING CHORUS:

(Continuing the reminiscence)

What is that coming up from the wilderness,
    like a column of smoke,
perfumed with myrrh and frankincense,
    with all the fragrant powders of the merchant?
Behold, it is the litter of Solomon!
    About it are sixty mighty men of the mighty men of Israel,
all girt with swords
    and expert in war,
each with his sword at his thigh,
    against alarms by night.
King Solomon made himself a palanquin
    from the wood of Lebanon.
He made its posts of silver,
    its back of gold, its seat of purple;
it was lovingly wrought within
    by the daughters of Jerusalem.

THE BRIDE:

(To the attending chorus)

Go forth, O daughters of Zion,
    and behold King Solomon,
with the crown with which his mother crowned him

on the day of his wedding,
on the day of the gladness of his heart.

THE BRIDEGROOM:

*(Likewise the bridegroom reminisces about
the courtship period.)*

Behold, you are beautiful, my love,
behold, you are beautiful!
Your eyes are doves
behind your veil.
Your hair is like a flock of goats,
moving down the slopes of Gilead.
Your teeth are like a flock of shorn ewes
that have come up from the washing,
all of which bear twins,
and not one among them is bereaved.
Your lips are like a scarlet thread,
and your mouth is lovely.
Your cheeks are like halves of a pomegranate
behind your veil.
Your neck is like the tower of David,
built for an arsenal,
whereon hang a thousand bucklers,
all of them shields of warriors.
Your two breasts are like two fawns,
twins of a gazelle,
that feed upon the lilies.
Until the day breathes
and the shadows flee,
I will hie me to the mountain of myrrh
and the hill of frankincense.
You are all fair, my love;
there is no flaw in you.
Come with me from Lebanon, my bride;
come with me from Lebanon.
Depart from the peak of Amana,
from the peak of Senir and Hermon,
from the dens of lions,
from the mountains of leopards.

You have ravished my heart, my sister, my bride,
you have ravished my heart with a glance of your eyes,
with one jewel of your necklace.
How sweet is your love, my sister, my bride!

How much better is your love than wine,
and the fragrance of your oils than any spice!
Your lips distil nectar, my bride;
honey and milk are under your tongue;
the scent of your garments is like the scent of Lebanon.
A garden locked is my sister, my bride,
a garden locked, a fountain sealed.
Your shoots are an orchard of pomegranates
with all choicest fruits,
henna with nard,
nard and saffron, calamus and cinnamon,
with all trees of frankincense,
myrrh and aloes,
with all chief spices—
a garden fountain, a well of living water,
and flowing streams from Lebanon.

THE BRIDE:
Awake, O north wind,
and come, O south wind!
Blow upon my garden,
let its fragrance be wafted abroad.
Let my beloved come to his garden,
and eat its choicest fruits.

THE BRIDEGROOM:
I come to my garden, my sister, my bride,
I gather my myrrh with my spice.
I eat my honeycomb with my honey,
I drink my wine with my milk.

THE ATTENDING CHORUS:
Eat, O friends, and drink:
drink deeply, O lovers!

THE BRIDE:

*(The day of betrothal is past, and the bride
has a troubled dream.)*

I slept, but my heart was awake.
Hark! my beloved is knocking.
"Open to me, my sister, my love,
my dove, my perfect one;
for my head is wet with dew,
my locks with the drops of the night."
I had put off my garment,
how could I put it on?
I had bathed my feet,

how could I soil them?
My beloved put his hand to the latch,
　　and my heart was thrilled within me.
I arose to open to my beloved,
　　and my hands dripped with myrrh,
my fingers with liquid myrrh,
　　upon the handles of the bolt.
I opened to my beloved,
　　but my beloved had turned and gone.
My soul failed me when he spoke.
I sought him, but found him not;
　　I called him, but he gave no answer.

THE BRIDEGROOM:

The watchmen found me,
　　as they went about in the city;
they beat me, they wounded me,
　　they took away my mantle,
　　those watchmen of the walls.

THE BRIDE:

(To the attending chorus)

I adjure you, O daughters of Jerusalem,
　　if you find my beloved,
that you tell him
　　I am sick with love.

THE ATTENDING CHORUS:

What is your beloved more than another beloved,
　　O fairest among women?
What is your beloved more than another beloved,
　　that you thus adjure us?

THE BRIDE:

My beloved is all radiant and ruddy,
　　distinguished among ten thousand,
His head is the finest gold;
　　his locks are wavy,
　　black as a raven.
His eyes are like doves
　　beside springs of water,
bathed in milk,
　　fitly set.
His cheeks are like beds of spices,
　　yielding fragrance.
His lips are lilies,

distilling liquid myrrh.
His arms are rounded gold,
    set with jewels.
His body is ivory work,
    encrusted with sapphires.
His legs are alabaster columns,
    set upon bases of gold.
His appearance is like Lebanon,
    choice as the cedars.
His speech is most sweet,
    and he is altogether desirable.
This is my beloved and this is my friend,
    O daughters of Jerusalem.

THE ATTENDING CHORUS:

Whither has your beloved gone,
    O fairest among women?
Whither has your beloved turned,
    that we may seek him with you?

THE BRIDE:

My beloved has gone down to his garden,
    to the beds of spices,
to pasture his flock in the gardens,
    and to gather lilies.
I am my beloved's and my beloved is mine;
    he pastures his flock among the lilies.

THE BRIDEGROOM:

(At the garden site)

You are beautiful as Tirzah, my love,
    comely as Jerusalem,
    terrible as an army with banners.
Turn away your eyes from me,
    for they disturb me—
Your hair is like a flock of goats,
    moving down the slopes of Gilead.
Your teeth are like a flock of ewes,
    that have come up from the washing,
all of them bear twins,
    not one among them is bereaved.
Your cheeks are like the halves of a pomegranate
    behind your veil.
There are sixty queens and eighty concubines,
    and maidens without number.

My dove, my perfect one, is only one,
    the darling of her mother,
    flawless to her who bore her.
The maidens saw her and called her happy;
    the queens and concubines also, and they praised her.
"Who is this that looks forth like the dawn,
    fair as the moon, bright as the sun,
    terrible as an army with banners?"

THE BRIDE:

I went down to the nut orchard,
    to look at the blossoms of the valley,
to see whether the vines had budded,
    whether the pomegranates were in bloom.
Before I was aware, my fancy set me
    in a chariot beside my prince.

THE ATTENDING CHORUS:

Return, return, O Shulammite,
    return, return, that we may look upon you.

THE BRIDE:

(To the attending chorus)

Why should you look upon the Shulammite,
    as upon a dance before two armies?

THE BRIDEGROOM:

(The bridegroom, still at the garden, con-
tinues to meditate on his bride.)

How graceful are your feet in sandals,
    O queenly maiden!
Your rounded thighs are like jewels,
    the work of a master's hand.
Your navel is a round bowl
    that never lacks mixed wine.
Your belly is a heap of wheat,
    encircled with lilies.
Your two breasts are like two fawns,
    twins of a gazelle.
Your neck is like an ivory tower.
Your eyes are pools in Heshbon,
    by the gate of Bath-rabbim.
Your nose is like a tower of Lebanon,
    overlooking Damascus.
Your head crowns you like Carmel,

and your flowing locks are like purple;
    a king is held captive in the tresses.

How fair and pleasant you are,
    O loved one, delectable maiden!
You are stately as a palm tree,
    and your breasts are like its clusters.
I say I will climb the palm tree
    and lay hold of its branches.
Oh, may your breasts be like clusters of the vine,
    and the scent of your breath like apples,
and your kisses like the best wine
    that goes down smoothly,
        gliding over lips and teeth.

THE BRIDE:
I am my beloved's,
    and his desire is for me.
Come, my beloved,
    let us go forth into the fields,
    and lodge in the villages;
let us go out early to the vineyards,
    and see whether the vines have budded,
whether the grape blossoms have opened
    and the pomegranates are in bloom.
There I will give you my love.
The mandrakes give forth fragrance,
    and over our doors are all choice fruits,
new as well as old,
    which I have laid up for you, O my beloved.
O that you were like a brother to me,
    that nursed at my mother's breast!
If I met you outside, I would kiss you,
    and none would despise me.
I would lead you and bring you
    into the house of my mother,
        and into the chamber of her that conceived me.
I would give you spiced wine to drink,
    the juice of my pomegranates.
O that his left hand were under my head,
    and that his right hand embraced me!
                (To the attending chorus)
I adjure you, O daughters of Jerusalem,
    that you stir not up nor awaken love

until it please.

THE ATTENDING CHORUS:

Who is coming up from the wilderness,
leaning upon her beloved?

THE BRIDEGROOM:

Under the apple tree I awakened you.
There your mother was in travail with you,
there she who bore you was in travail.

THE BRIDE:

Set me as a seal upon your heart,
as a seal upon your arm;
for love is strong as death,
jealousy is cruel as the grave.
Its flashes are flashes of fire,
a most vehement flame.
Many waters cannot quench love,
neither can floods drown it.
If a man offered for love
all the wealth of his house,
it would be utterly scorned.

THE ATTENDING CHORUS:

We have a little sister,
and she has no breasts.
What shall we do for our sister,
on the day when she is spoken for?
If she is a wall,
we will build upon her a battlement of silver;
but if she is a door,
we will enclose her with boards of cedar.

THE BRIDE:

I was a wall,
and my breasts were like towers;
then I was in his eyes
as one who brings peace.

Solomon had a vineyard at Baal-hamon;
he let out the vineyard to keepers;
each one was to bring for its fruit a thousand pieces of silver.
My vineyard, my very own, is for myself;
you, O Solomon, may have the thousand,
and the keepers of the fruit two hundred.

O you who dwell in the gardens,

my companions are listening for your voice;
let me hear it.

Make haste, my beloved,
and be like a gazelle
or a young stag
upon the mountains of spices.

Rhetoric

*R*HETORIC IS BASICALLY the literature of address. It is usually divided into two classes: the *epistle*, written addresses found mostly in the New Testament, and *oratory*, spoken addresses found scattered throughout the Bible.

EPISTOLARY LITERATURE

New Testament epistles have immense historical importance. They provide a many-sided reflection on the vitally important formative period of Christianity. Their highest importance is their subject matter rather than their form.

The epistle is distinguished from letters, since it is the product of a much more conscious art than the letter. It is meant usually for a wide public and has something of the character of a written speech. It is designed for presentation, whereas a letter is individual and intimate and has passing interest.

The whole of the New Testament was written in colloquial Greek, such as was commonly spoken at that time around the Mediterranean Sea. A colloquial language is especially suitable for use in epistles because it is flexible and expressive and widely readable.

EPISTLES OF PASTORAL INTERCOURSE

Epistles of pastoral intercourse, sent usually to specific people or specific groups, include greetings from the writer to the person or group, a special message, and then instructions about particular circumstances. The epistles in this category include the following books: 1 Corinthians, Galatians, Philippians, 1 Thessalonians, 2 Timothy, Titus, and Philemon. The selected passages used from each book illustrate the theme of the book.

For example, in *Corinthians,* after tidings to the church at Corinth, Paul proceeds to talk of moral laxity, ecclesiastical policy, relation of the sexes in the place of worship, diverse spiritual gifts, and love.

THE SUPREMACY OF LOVE

1 Corinthians 13

If I speak in the tongues of men and of angels, but have not love, I am a noisy gong or a clanging cymbal. And if I have prophetic powers, and understand all mysteries and all knowledge, and if I have all faith, so as to remove mountains, but have not love, I am nothing. If I give away all I have, and if I deliver my body to be burned, but have not loved, I gain nothing.

Love is patient and kind; love is not jealous or boastful; it is not arrogant or rude. Love does not insist on its own way; it is not irritable or resentful; it does not rejoice at wrong, but rejoices in the right. Love bears all things, believes all things, hopes all things, endures all things.

Love never ends; as for prophecies, they will pass away; as for tongues, they will cease; as for knowledge, it will pass away. For our knowledge is imperfect and our prophecy is imperfect; but when the perfect comes, the imperfect will pass away. When I was a child, I spoke like a child, I thought like a child, I reasoned like a child; when I became a man, I gave up childish ways. For now we see in a mirror dimly, but then face to face. Now I know in part; then I shall understand fully, even as I have been fully understood. So faith, hope, love abide, these three; but the greatest of these is love.

IMMORTALITY

1 Corinthians 15

Now I would remind you, brethren, in what terms I preached to you the gospel, which you received, in which you stand, by which you are saved, if you hold it fast—unless you believed in vain.

For I delivered to you as of first importance what I also received, that Christ died for our sins in accordance with the scriptures, that he was buried, that he was raised on the third day in accordance with the scriptures, and that he appeared to Cephas, then to the twelve. Then he appeared to more than five hundred brethren at one time, most of whom are still alive, though some have fallen asleep. Then he appeared to James, then to all the apostles. Last of all, as to one untimely born, he appeared also to me. For I am the least of the apostles, unfit to be called an apostle, because I persecuted the church of God. But by the grace of God I am what I am, and his grace toward me was not in vain. On the contrary, I worked harder than any of them, though it was not I, but the grace of God which is with me. Whether then it was I or they, so we preach and so you believed.

Now if Christ is preached as raised from the dead, how can some of you say that there is no resurrection of the dead? But if there is no resurrection of the dead, then Christ has not been raised; if Christ has not been raised, then our preaching is in vain and your faith is in vain. We are even found to be misrepresenting God, because we testified of God that he raised Christ, whom he did not raise if it is true that the dead are not raised. For if the dead are not raised, then Christ has not been raised. If Christ has not been raised, your faith is futile and you are still in your sins. Then those also who have fallen asleep in Christ have perished. If for this life only we have hoped in Christ, we are of all men most to be pitied.

But in fact Christ has been raised from the dead, the first fruits of those who have fallen asleep. For as by a man came death, by a man has come also the resurrection of the dead. For as in Adam all die, so also in Christ shall all be made alive. But each in his own order: Christ the first fruits, then at his coming those who belong to Christ. Then comes the end, when he delivers the kingdom to God the Father after destroying every rule and every authority and power. For he must reign until he has put all his enemies under his feet. The last enemy to be destroyed is death. "For God has put all things in subjection under his feet." But when it says, "All things are put in subjection under him," it is plain that he is excepted who put all things under him. When all things are subjected to him, then the Son himself will also be subjected to him who put all things under him, that God may be everything to every one.

Otherwise, what do people mean by being baptized on behalf of the dead? If the dead are not raised at all, why are people baptized on their behalf? Why am I in peril every hour?

I protest, brethren, by my pride in you which I have in Christ Jesus our Lord, I die every day! What do I gain if, humanly speaking, I fought with beasts at Ephesus? If the dead are not raised,

"Let us eat and drink, for tomorrow we die." Do not be deceived: "Bad company ruins good morals." Come to your right mind, and sin no more. For some have no knowledge of God. I say this to your shame.

But some one will ask, "How are the dead raised? With what kind of body do they come?" You foolish man! What you sow does not come to life unless it dies. And what you sow is not the body which is to be, but a bare kernel, perhaps of wheat or of some other grain. But God gives it a body as he has chosen, and to each kind of seed its own body. For not all flesh is alike, but there is one kind for men, another for animals, another for birds, and another for fish. There are celestial bodies and there are terrestrial bodies; but the glory of the celestial is one, and the glory of the terrestrial is another. There is one glory of the sun, and another glory of the moon, and another glory of the stars; for star differs from star in glory.

So is it with the resurrection of the dead. What is sown is perishable, what is raised is imperishable. It is sown in dishonor, it is raised in glory. It is sown in weakness, it is raised in power. It is sown a physical body, it is raised a spiritual body. If there is a physical body, there is also a spiritual body. Thus it is written, "The first man Adam became a living being"; the last Adam became a life-giving spirit. But it is not the spiritual which is first but the physical, and then the spiritual. The first man was from the earth, a man of dust; the second man is from heaven. As was the man of dust, so are those who are of the dust; and as is the man of heaven, so are those who are of heaven. Just as we have borne the image of the man of dust, we shall also bear the image of the man of heaven. I tell you this, brethren: flesh and blood cannot inherit the kingdom of God, nor does the perishable inherit the imperishable.

Lo! I tell you a mystery. We shall not all sleep, but we shall all be changed, in a moment, in the twinkling of an eye, at the last trumpet. For the trumpet will sound, and the dead will be raised imperishable, and we shall be changed. For this perishable nature must put on the imperishable, and this mortal nature must put on immortality. When the perishable puts on the imperishable, and the mortal puts on immortality, then shall come to pass the saying that is written:

"Death is swallowed up in victory."
"O death, where is thy victory?
O death, where is thy sting?"

The sting of death is sin, and the power of sin is the law. But thanks be to God, who gives us the victory through our Lord Jesus Christ.

Therefore, my beloved brethren, be steadfast, immovable, always abounding in the work of the Lord, knowing that in the Lord your labor is not in vain.

In *Galatians*, following greetings to the church at Galatia, Paul discusses the special bond of intimacy which has been disturbed by Judaising tendencies.

FULFILLING THE LAW OF CHRIST

Galatians 6

Brethren, if a man is overtaken in any trespass, you who are spiritual should restore him in a spirit of gentleness. Look to yourself, lest you too be tempted. Bear one another's burdens, and so fulfill the law of Christ. For if any one thinks he is something, when he is nothing, he deceives himself. But let each one test his own work, and then his reason to boast will be in himself alone and not in his neighbor. For each man will have to bear his own load.

Let him who is taught the word share all good things with him who teaches.

Do not be deceived; God is not mocked, for whatever a man sows, that he will also reap. For he who sows to his own flesh will from the flesh reap corruption; but he who sows to the Spirit will from the Spirit reap eternal life. And let us not grow weary in well-doing, for in due season we shall reap, if we do not lose heart. So then, as we have opportunity, let us do good to all men, and especially to those who are of the household of faith.

See with what large letters I am writing to you with my own hand. It is those who want to make a good showing in the flesh that would compel you to be circumcised, and only in order that they may not be persecuted for the cross of Christ. For even those who receive circumcision do not themselves keep the law, but they desire to have you circumcised that they may glory in your flesh. But far be it from me to glory except in the cross of our Lord Jesus Christ, by which the world has been crucified to me, and I to the world. For neither circumcision counts for anything, nor uncircumcision, but a new creation. Peace and mercy be upon all who walk by this rule, upon the Israel of God.

Henceforth let no man trouble me; for I bear on my body the marks of Jesus.

The grace of our Lord Jesus Christ be with your spirit, brethren. Amen.

Paul's letter to the church at *Philippi* is intended to heal local differences by pointing out the common bond in Christ.

Philippians 2:5–16

Have this mind among yourselves, which you have in Christ Jesus, who, though he was in the form of God, did not count equality with God a thing to be grasped, but emptied himself, taking the form of a servant, being born in the likeness of men. And being found in human form he humbled himself and became obedient unto death, even death on a cross. Therefore God has highly exalted him and bestowed on him the name which is above every name, that at the name of Jesus every knee should bow, in heaven and on earth and under the earth, and every tongue confess that Jesus Christ is Lord, to the glory of God the Father.

Therefore, my beloved, as you have always obeyed, so now, not only as in my presence but much more in my absence, work out your own salvation with fear and trembling; for God is at work in you, both to will and to work for his good pleasure.

Do all things without grumbling or questioning, that you may be blameless and innocent, children of God without blemish in the midst of a crooked and perverse generation, among whom you shine as lights in the world, holding fast the word of life, so that in the day of Christ I may be proud that I did not run in vain or labor in vain.

Paul's letter to Thessalonica discusses the "near coming of Christ."

1 Thessalonians 4:13–18

But we would not have you ignorant, brethren, concerning those who are asleep, that you may not grieve as others do who have no hope. For since we believe that Jesus died and rose again, even so, through Jesus, God will bring with him those who have fallen asleep. For this we declare to you by the word of the Lord, that we who are alive, who are left until the coming of the Lord, shall not precede those who have fallen asleep. For the Lord himself will descend from heaven with a cry of command, with the archangel's call, and with the sound of the trumpet of God. And the dead in Christ will rise first; then we who are alive, who are left, shall be caught up together with them in the clouds to meet the Lord in the air; and so we shall always be with the Lord. Therefore comfort one another with these words.

In *Timothy*, Paul appeals to the young fellow-worker, touching his personal character as a teacher, and advises him on questions he is likely to dispute.

2 Timothy 1:1–18; 3:1–17; 4:1–22

Paul, an apostle of Christ Jesus by the will of God according to the promise of the life which is in Christ Jesus,

To Timothy, my beloved child: Grace, mercy, and peace from God the Father and Christ Jesus our Lord.

I thank God whom I serve with a clear conscience, as did my fathers, when I remember you constantly in my prayers. As I remember your tears, I long night and day to see you, that I may be filled with joy. I am reminded of your sincere faith, a faith that dwelt first in your grandmother Lois and your mother Eunice and now, I am sure, dwells in you. Hence I remind you to rekindle the gift of God that is within you through the laying on of my hands; for God did not give us a spirit of timidity but a spirit of power and love and self-control.

Do not be ashamed then of testifying to our Lord, nor of me his prisoner, but take your share of suffering for the gospel in the power of God, who saved us and called us with a holy calling, not in virtue of our works but in virtue of his own purpose and the grace which he gave us in Christ Jesus ages ago, and now has manifested through the appearing of our Savior Christ Jesus, who abolished death and brought life and immortality to light through the gospel. For this gospel I was appointed a preacher and apostle and teacher, and therefore I suffer as I do. But I am not ashamed, for I know whom I have believed, and I am sure that he is able to guard until that Day what has been entrusted to me. Follow the pattern of the sound words which you have heard from me, in the faith and love which are in Christ Jesus; guard the truth that has been entrusted to you by the Holy Spirit who dwells within us.

You are aware that all who are in Asia turned away from me, and among them Phygelus and Hermogenes. May the Lord grant mercy to the household of Onesiphorus, for he often refreshed me; he was not ashamed of my chains, but when he arrived in

Rome he searched for me eagerly and found me—may the Lord grant him to find mercy from the Lord on that Day—and you well know all the service he rendered at Ephesus.

But understand this, that in the last days there will come times of stress. For men will be lovers of self, lovers of money, proud, arrogant, abusive, disobedient to their parents, ungrateful, unholy, inhuman, implacable, slanderers, profligates, fierce, haters of good, treacherous, reckless, swollen with conceit, lovers of pleasure rather than lovers of God, holding the form of religion but denying the power of it. Avoid such people. For among them are those who make their way into households and capture weak women, burdened with sins and swayed by various impulses, who will listen to anybody and can never arrive at a knowledge of the truth. As Jannes and Jambres opposed Moses, so these men also oppose the truth, men of corrupt mind and counterfeit faith; but they will not get very far, for their folly will be plain to all, as was that of those two men.

Now you have observed my teaching, my conduct, my aim in life, my faith, my patience, my love, my steadfastness, my persecutions, my sufferings, what befell me at Antioch, at Iconium, and at Lystra, what persecutions I endured; yet from them all the Lord rescued me. Indeed all who desire to live a godly life in Christ Jesus will be persecuted, while evil men and impostors will go on from bad to worse, deceivers and deceived. But as for you, continue in what you have learned and have firmly believed, knowing from whom you learned it and how from childhood you have been acquainted with the sacred writings which are able to instruct you for salvation through faith in Christ Jesus. All scripture is inspired by God and profitable for teaching, for reproof, for correction, and for training in righteousness, that the man of God may be complete, equipped for every good work.

I charge you in the presence of God and of Christ Jesus who is to judge the living and the dead, and by his appearing and his kingdom: preach the word, be urgent in season and out of season, convince, rebuke, and exhort, be unfailing in patience and in teaching. For the time is coming when people will not endure sound teaching, but having itching ears they will accumulate for themselves teachers to suit their own likings, and will turn away from listening to the truth and wander into myths. As for you, always be steady, endure suffering, do the work of an evangelist, fulfil your ministry.

For I am already on the point of being sacrificed; the time of my departure has come. I have fought the good fight, I have finished the race, I have kept the faith. Henceforth there is laid up for me the crown of righteousness, which the Lord, the righteous judge, will award to me on that Day, and not only to me but also to all who have loved his appearing.

Do your best to come to me soon. For Demas, in love with this present world, has deserted me and gone to Thessalonica; Crescens has gone to Galatia, Titus to Dalmatia. Luke alone is with me. Get Mark and bring him with you; for he is very useful in serving me. Tychicus I have sent to Ephesus. When you come, bring the cloak that I left with Carpus at Troas, also the books, and above all the parchments. Alexander the coppersmith did me great harm; the Lord will requite him for his deeds. Beware of him yourself, for he strongly opposed our message. At my first defense no one took my part; all deserted me. May it not be charged against them! But the Lord stood by me and gave me strength to proclaim the word fully, that all the Gentiles might hear it. So I was rescued from the lion's mouth. The Lord will rescue me from every evil and save me for his heavenly kingdom. To him be the glory for ever and ever. Amen.

Greet Prisca and Aquila, and the household of Onesiphorus. Erastus remained at Corinth; Trophimus I left ill at Miletus. Do your best to come before winter. Eubulus sends greetings to you, as do Pudens and Linus and Claudia and all the brethren.

The Lord be with your spirit. Grace be with you.

In *Titus*, Paul summarizes the instructions to one left in charge of a distant district where much organization was to be done.

ORDER IN THE CHURCH
Titus 2

But as for you, teach what befits sound doctrine. Bid the older men be temperate, serious, sensible, sound in faith, in love, and in steadfastness. Bid the older women likewise to be reverent in behavior, not to be slanderers or slaves to drink; they are to teach what is good, and so train the young women to love their husbands and children, to be sensible, chaste, domestic, kind, and submissive to their husbands, that the word of God may not be discredited. Likewise urge the younger men to control themselves. Show yourself in all respects a model of good deeds, and in your teaching show integrity, gravity, and sound speech that cannot be censured, so that an opponent may be put to shame, having nothing evil to say of us. Bid slaves to be submissive to their masters and to give satisfaction in every respect; they are not to be refractory, nor to pilfer, but to show entire and true fidelity, so that in everything they may adorn the doctrine of God our Savior.

For the grace of God has appeared for the salvation of all men, training us to renounce irreligion and wordly passions, and to live sober, upright, and godly lives in this world, awaiting our blessed hope, the appearing of the glory of our great God and Savior Jesus Christ, who gave himself for us to redeem us from all iniquity and to purify for himself a people of his own who are zealous for good deeds.

Declare these things; exhort and reprove with all authority. Let no one disregard you.

In *Philemon*, Paul appeals personally to a runaway slave, now Christianized and desiring to return to his master.

Philemon 1:1-9

Paul, a prisoner for Christ Jesus, and Timothy our brother,
To Philemon our beloved fellow worker and Apphia our sister and Archippus our fellow soldier, and the church in your house:
Grace to you and peace from God our Father and the Lord Jesus Christ.

I thank my God always when I remember you in my prayers, because I hear of your love and of the faith which you have toward the Lord Jesus and all the saints, and I pray that the sharing of your faith may promote the knowledge of all the good that is ours in Christ. For I have derived much joy and comfort from your love, my brother, because the hearts of the saints have been refreshed through you.

Accordingly, though I am bold enough in Christ to command you to do what is required, yet for love's sake I prefer to appeal to you—I, Paul, an ambassador and now a prisoner also for Christ Jesus—

EPISTOLARY TREATIES

Epistolary treaties are letters intended for several churches. They were to be circulated by the churches or a messenger responsible for delivery. Epistolary treaties include the following books: Romans, Hebrews, James, and Revelation.

In *Romans*, although addressed to a particular church, it is the church of the world's metropolis that is intended. Included are Paul's concepts of "righteousness by faith" and the Gospels realized in practical life.

SPIRITUAL SERVICE

Romans 12

I appeal to you therefore, brethren, by the mercies of God, to present your bodies as a living sacrifice, holy and acceptable to God, which is your spiritual worship. Do not be conformed to this world but be transformed by the renewal of your mind, that you may prove what is the will of God, what is good and acceptable and perfect.

For by the grace given to me I bid every one among you not to think of himself more highly than he ought to think, but to think with sober judgment, each according to the measure of faith which God has assigned him.

For as in one body we have many members, and all the members do not have the same function, so we, though many, are one body in Christ, and individually members one of another. Having gifts that differ according to the grace given to us, let us use them: if prophecy, in proportion to our faith; if service, in our serving; he who teaches, in his teaching; he who exhorts, in his exhortation; he who contributes, in liberality; he who gives aid, with zeal; he who does acts of mercy, with cheerfulness.

Let love be genuine; hate what is evil, hold fast to what is good; love one another with brotherly affection; outdo one another in showing honor.

Never flag in zeal, be aglow with the Spirit, serve the Lord. Rejoice in your hope, be patient in tribulation, be constant in prayer. Contribute to the needs of the saints, practice hospitality.

Bless those who persecute you; bless and do not curse them. Rejoice with those who rejoice, weep with those who weep. Live in harmony with one another; do not be haughty, but associate with the lowly; never be conceited. Repay no one evil for evil, but take thought for what is noble in the sight of all. If possible, so far as it depends upon you, live peaceably with all. Beloved, never avenge yourselves, but leave it to the wrath of God; for it is written, "Vengeance is mine, I will repay, says the Lord."

No, "If your enemy is hungry, feed him; if he is thirsty, give him drink; for by so doing you will heap burning coals upon his head." Do not be overcome by evil, but overcome evil with good.

Paul's letter to Hebrew Christians scattered throughout the world purports that the Law must give place to the Gospels as a higher and fuller dispensation.

HEROES OF FAITH

Hebrews 11:1–40; 12:1–3

Now faith is the assurance of things hoped for, the conviction of things not seen. For by it the men of old received divine approval. By faith we understand that the world was created by the word of God, so that what is seen was made out of things which do not appear.

By faith Abel offered to God a more acceptable sacrifice than Cain, through which he received approval as righteous, God bearing witness by accepting his gifts; he died, but through his faith he is still speaking. By faith Enoch was taken up so that he should not see death; and he was not found, because God had taken him. Now before he was taken he was attested as having pleased God. And without faith it is impossible to please him. For whoever would draw near to God must believe that he exists and that he rewards those who seek him. By faith Noah, being warned by God concerning events as yet unseen, took heed and constructed an ark for the saving of his household; by this he condemned the world and became an heir of the righteousness which comes by faith.

By faith Abraham obeyed when he was called to go out to a place which he was to receive as an inheritance; and he went out, not knowing where he was to go. By faith he sojourned in the land of promise, as in a foreign land, living in tents with Isaac and Jacob, heirs with him of the same promise. For he looked forward to the city which has foundations, whose builder and maker is God. By faith Sarah herself received power to conceive, even when she was past the age, since she considered him faithful who had promised. Therefore from one man, and him as good as dead, were born decendants as many as the stars of heaven and as the innumerable grains of sand by the seashore.

These all died in faith, not having received what was promised, but having seen it and greeted it from afar, and having acknowledged that they were strangers and exiles on the earth. For people who speak thus make it clear that they are seeking a homeland. If they had been thinking of that land from which they had gone out, they would have had opportunity to return. But as it is, they desire a better country, a heavenly one. Therefore God is not ashamed to be called their God, for he has prepared for them a city.

By faith Abraham, when he was tested, offered up Isaac, and he who had received the promises was ready to offer up his only son, of whom it was said, "Through Isaac shall your descendants be named." He considered that God was able to raise men even from the dead; hence, figuratively speaking, he did receive him back. By faith Isaac invoked future blessings on Jacob and Esau. By faith Jacob, when dying, blessed each of the sons of Joseph, bowing in worship over the head of his staff. By faith Joseph, at the end of his life, made mention of the exodus of the Israelites and gave directions concerning his burial.

By faith Moses, when he was born, was hid for three months by his parents, because they saw that the child was beautiful; and they were not afraid of the king's edict. By faith Moses, when he was grown up, refused to be called the son of Pharaoh's daughter, choosing rather to share ill-treatment with the people of God than to enjoy the fleeting pleasures of sin. He considered abuse suffered for the Christ greater wealth than the treasures of Egypt, for he looked to the reward. By faith he left Egypt, not being afraid of the anger of the king; for he endured as seeing him who is invisible. By faith he kept the Passover and sprinkled the blood, so that the Destroyer of the first-born might not touch them.

By faith the people crossed the Red Sea as if on dry land; but the Egyptians, when they attempted to do the same, were drowned. By faith the walls of Jericho fell down after they had been encircled for seven days. By faith Rahab the harlot did not perish with those who were disobedient, because she had given friendly welcome to the spies.

And what more shall I say? For time would fail me to tell of Gideon, Barak, Samson, Jephthah, of David and Samuel and the prophets—who through faith conquered kingdoms, enforced justice, received promises, stopped the mouths of lions, quenched raging fire, escaped the edge of the sword, won strength out of weakness, became mighty in war, put foreign armies to flight. Women received their dead by resurrection. Some were tortured, refusing to accept release, that they might rise again to a better life.

Others suffered mocking and scourging, and even chains and imprisonment. They were stoned, they were sawn in two, they were killed with the sword; they went about in skins of sheep and goats, destitute, afflicted, ill-treated—of whom the world was not worthy—wandering over deserts and mountains, and in dens and caves of the earth.

And all these, though well attested by their faith, did not receive what was promised, since God had foreseen something better for us, that apart from us they should not be made perfect.

Therefore, since we are surrounded by so great a cloud of witnesses, let us also lay aside every weight, and sin which clings so closely, and let us run with perseverance the race that is set before us, looking to Jesus the pioneer and perfecter of our faith, who for the joy that was set before him endured the cross, despising the shame, and is seated at the right hand of the throne of God.

Consider him who endured from sinners such hostility against himself, so that you may not grow weary or fainthearted.

James' letter to the Hebrews contrasts the two important elements of Christianity, faith and works.

FAITH WITHOUT WORKS IS DEAD

James 2

My brethren, show no partiality as you hold the faith of our Lord Jesus Christ, the Lord of glory. For if a man with gold rings and in fine clothing comes into your assembly, and a poor man in shabby clothing also comes in, and you pay attention to the one who wears the fine clothing and say, "Have a seat here, please," while you say to the poor man, "Stand there," or, "Sit at my feet," have you not made distinctions among yourselves, and become judges with evil thoughts? Listen, my beloved brethren. Has not God chosen those who are poor in the world to be rich in faith and heirs of the kingdom which he has promised to those who love him? But you have dishonored the poor man. Is it not the rich who oppress you, is it not they who drag you into court? Is it not they who blaspheme that honorable name by which you are called?

If you really fulfil the royal law, according to the scripture, "You shall love your neighbor as yourself," you do well. But if you show partiality, you commit sin, and are convicted by the law as transgressors. For whoever keeps the whole law but fails in one point has become guilty of all of it. For he who said, "Do not commit adultery," said also, "Do not kill." If you do not commit adultery but do kill, you have become a transgressor of the law. So speak and so act as those who are to be judged under the law of liberty. For judgment is without mercy to one who has shown no mercy; yet mercy triumphs over judgment.

What does it profit, my brethren, if a man says he has faith but has not works? Can his faith save him? If a brother or sister is ill-clad and in lack of daily food, and one of you says to them, "Go in peace, be warmed and filled," without giving them the things needed for the body, what does it profit? So faith by itself, if it has no works, is dead.

But some one will say, "You have faith and I have works." Show me your faith apart from your works, and I by my works will show you my faith. You believe that God is one; you do well. Even the demons believe—and shudder. Do you want to be shown, you foolish fellow, that faith apart from works is barren? Was not Abraham our father justified by works, when he offered his son Isaac upon the altar? You see that faith was active along with his works, and faith was completed by works, and the scripture was fulfilled which says, "Abraham believed God, and it was reckoned to him as righteousness"; and he was called the friend of God. You see that a man is justified by works and not by faith alone. And in the same way was not also Rahab the harlot justified by works when she received the messengers and sent them out another way? For as the body apart from the spirit is dead, so faith apart from works is dead.

In *Revelation*, John, the apostle, wrote this letter to the seven churches of Asia about the vision he had of future events.

CHRIST OF THE FUTURE

Revelation 1:1–19

The revelation of Jesus Christ, which God gave him to show to his servants what must soon take place; and he made it known by sending his angel to his servant John, who bore witness to the word of God and to the testimony of Jesus Christ, even to all that he saw. Blessed is he who reads aloud the words of the prophecy, and blessed are those who hear, and who keep what is written therein; for the time is near.

John to the seven churches that are in Asia:

Grace to you and peace from him who is and who was and who is to come, and from the seven spirits who are before his throne, and from Jesus Christ the faithful witness, the first-born of the dead, and the ruler of kings on earth.

To him who loves us and has freed us from our sins by his blood and made us a kingdom, priests to his God and Father, to him be glory and dominion for ever and ever. Amen. Behold, he is coming with clouds, and every eye will see him, every one who pierced him; and all tribes of the earth will wail on account of him. Even so. Amen.

"I am the Alpha and the Omega," says the Lord God, who is and who was and who is to come, the Almighty.

I John, your brother, who share with you in Jesus the tribulation and the kingdom and the patient endurance, was on the island called Patmos on account of the word of God and the testimony of Jesus. I was in the Spirit on the Lord's day, and I heard behind me a loud voice like a trumpet saying, "Write what you see in a book and send it to the seven churches, to Ephesus and to Smyrna and to Pergamum and to Thyatira and to Sardis and to Philadelphia and to La-odicea."

Then I turned to see the voice that was speaking to me, and on turning I saw seven golden lampstands, and in the midst of the lampstands one like a son of man, clothed with a long robe and with a golden girdle round his breast; his head and his hair were white as white wool, white as snow; his eyes were like a flame of fire, his feet were like burnished bronze, refined as in a furnace, and his voice was like the sound of many waters; in his right hand he held seven stars, from his mouth issued a sharp two-edged sword, and his face was like the sun shining in full strength.

When I saw him, I fell at his feet as though dead. But he laid his right hand upon me, saying, "Fear not, I am the first and the last, and the living one; I died, and behold I am alive for evermore, and I have the keys of Death and Hades. Now write what you see, what is and what is to take place hereafter.

FINAL WORDS

Revelation 22

Then he showed me the river of the water of life, bright as crystal, flowing from the throne of God and of the Lamb through the middle of the street of the city; also, on either side of the river, the tree of life with its twelve kinds of fruit, yielding its fruit each month; and the leaves of the tree were for the healing of the nations. There shall no more by anything accursed, but the throne of God and of the Lamb shall be in it, and his servants shall worship him; they shall see his face, and his name shall be on their foreheads. And night shall be no more; they need no light of lamp or sun, for the Lord God will be their light, and they shall reign for ever and ever.

And he said to me, "These words are trustworthy and true. And the Lord, the God of the spirits of the prophets, has sent his angel to show his servants what must soon take place. And behold, I am coming soon."

Blessed is he who keeps the words of the prophecy of this book.

I John am he who heard and saw these things. And when I heard and saw them, I fell down to worship at the feet of the angel who showed them to me; but he said to me, "You must not do that! I am a fellow servant with you and your brethren the prophets, and with those who keep the words of this book. Worship God."

And he said to me, "Do not seal up the words of the prophecy of this book, for the time is near. Let the evildoer still do evil, and the filthy still be filthy, and the righteous still do right, and the holy still be holy."

"Behold, I am coming soon, bringing my recompense, to repay every one for what he has done. I am the Alpha and the Omega, the first and the last, the beginning and the end."

Blessed are those who wash their robes, that they may have the right to the tree of life and that they may enter the city by the gates. Outside are the dogs and sorcerers and fornicators and murderers and idolaters, and every one who loves and practices falsehood.

"I Jesus have sent my angel to you with this testimony for the churches. I am the root and the offspring of David, the bright morning star."

The Spirit and the Bride say, "Come." And let him who hears say, "Come." And let him who is thirsty come, let him who desires take the water of life without price.

I warn every one who hears the words of the prophecy of this book: if any one adds to them, God will add to him the plagues described in this book, and if any one takes away from the words the book of this prophecy, God will take away his share in the tree of life and in the holy city, which are described in this book.

He who testifies to these things says, "Surely I am coming soon." Amen. Come, Lord Jesus!

The grace of the Lord Jesus be with all the saints. Amen.

EPISTOLARY MANIFESTOS

These letters are addressed to special groups or Christians in general. They do not normally discuss specific issues but, rather, include the writer's conception of Truth and the life to which he is consecrated. Epistolary manifestos include the following books: Colossians, Ephesians, 1 Peter, 2 Peter, 1 John, and Jude.

In *Colossians* and *Ephesians*, rivalry of some other systems of truth seems to have inspired these letters, and Paul's purpose is to present the Christian faith and life as satisfying every capacity of man.

WARNING AGAINST ERROR

Colossians 3:1–24

If then you have been raised with Christ, seek the things that are above, where Christ is, seated at the right hand of God. Set your minds on things that are above, not on things that are on earth. For you have died, and your life is hid with Christ in God. When Christ who is our life appears, then you also will appear with him in glory.

Put to death therefore what is earthly in you: immorality, impurity, passion, evil desire, and covetousness, which is idolatry. On account of these the wrath of God is coming. In these you once walked, when you lived in them. But now put them all away: anger, wrath, malice, slander, and foul talk from your mouth. Do not lie to one another, seeing that you have put off the old nature with its practices and have put on the new nature, which is being renewed in knowledge after the image of its creator. Here there cannot be Greek and Jew, circumcised and uncircumcised, barbarian, Scythian, slave, free man, but Christ is all, and in all.

Put on then, as God's chosen ones, holy and beloved, compassion, kindness, lowliness, meekness, and patience, forbearing one another and, if one has a complaint against another, forgiving each other; as the Lord has forgiven you, so you also must forgive. And above all these put on love, which binds everything together in perfect harmony. And let the peace of Christ rule in your hearts, to which indeed you were called in the one body. And be thankful. Let the word of Christ dwell in you richly as you teach and admonish one another in all wisdom, and as you sing psalms and hymns and spiritual songs with thankfulness in your hearts to God. And whatever you do, in word or deed, do everything in the name of the Lord Jesus, giving thanks to God the Father through him.

Wives, be subject to your husbands, as is fitting in the Lord. Husbands, love your wives, and do not be harsh with them. Children, obey your parents in everything, for this pleases the Lord. Fathers, do not provoke your children, lest they become discouraged. Slaves, obey in everything those who are your earthly masters, not with eyeservice, as men-pleasers, but in single-ness of heart, fearing the Lord. Whatever your task, work heartily, as serving the Lord and not men, knowing that from the Lord you will receive the inheritance as your reward; you are serving the Lord Christ.

SPIRITUAL WELFARE

Ephesians 6

Children, obey your parents in the Lord, for this is right. "Honor your father and mother" (this is the first commandment with a promise), "that it may be well with you and that you may live long on the earth." Fathers, do not provoke your children to anger, but bring them up in the discipline and instruction of the Lord.

Slaves, be obedient to those who are your earthly masters, with fear and trembling, in singleness of heart, as to Christ; not in the way of eyeservice, as men-pleasers, but as servants of Christ, doing the will of God from the heart, rendering service with a good will as to the Lord and not to men, knowing that whatever good any one does, he will receive the same again from the Lord, whether he is a slave or free. Masters, do the same to them, and forbear threatening, knowing that he who is both their Master and yours is in heaven, and that there is no partiality with him.

Finally, be strong in the Lord and in the strength of his might. Put on the whole armor of God, that you may be able to stand against the wiles of the devil. For we are not contending against flesh and blood, but against the principalities, against the powers, against the world rulers of this present darkness, against the spiritual hosts of wickedness in the heavenly places. Therefore take the whole armor of God, that you may be able to withstand in the evil day, and having done all, to stand. Stand therefore, having girded your loins with truth, and having put on the breastplate of righteousness, and having shod your feet with the equipment of the gospel of peace; above all taking the shield of faith, with which you can quench all the flaming darts of the evil one. And take the helmet of salvation, and the sword of the Spirit, which is the word of God. Pray at all times in the Spirit, with all prayer and supplication. To that end keep alert with all perseverance, making supplication for all the saints, and also for me, that utterance may be given me in opening my mouth boldly to proclaim the mystery of the gospel, for which I am an ambassador in chains; that I may declare it boldly, as I ought to speak.

Now that you also may know how I am and what I am doing, Tychicus the beloved brother and faithful minister in the Lord will tell you everything. I have sent him to you for this very purpose, that you may know how we are, and that he may encourage your hearts.

Peace be to the brethren, and love with faith, from God the Father and the Lord Jesus Christ. Grace be with all who love our Lord Jesus Christ with love undying.

This is the apostle Peter's address to the Hebrew Christians dispersed because of the terrible persecution to test the foundation of their faith.

ATONEMENT

1 Peter 4

Since therefore Christ suffered in the flesh, arm yourselves with the same thought, for whoever has suffered in the flesh has ceased from sin, so as to live for the rest of the time in the flesh no longer by human passions but by the will of God. Let the time that is past suffice for doing what the Gentiles like to do, living in licentiousness, passions, drunkenness, revels, carousing, and lawless idolatry. They are surprised that you do not now join them in the same wild profligacy, and they abuse you; but they will give account to him who is ready to judge the living and the dead. For this is why the gospel was preached even to the dead, that though judged in the flesh like men, they might live in the spirit like God.

The end of all things is at hand; therefore keep sane and sober for your prayers. Above all hold unfailing your love for one another, since love covers a multitude of sins. Practice hospitality ungrudgingly to one another. As each has received a gift, employ it for one another, as good stewards of God's varied grace: whoever speaks, as one who utters oracles of God; whoever renders service, as one who renders it by the strength which God supplies; in order that in everything God may be glorified through Jesus Christ. To him belong glory and dominion for ever and ever. Amen.

Beloved, do not be surprised at the fiery ordeal which comes upon you to prove you, as though something strange were happening to you. But rejoice in so far as you share Christ's sufferings, that you may also rejoice and be glad when his glory is revealed. If you are reproached for the name of Christ, you are blessed, because the spirit of glory and of God rests upon you. But let none of you suffer as a murderer, or a thief, or a wrong-doer, or a mischief-maker; yet if one suffers as a Christian, let him not be ashamed, but under that name let him glorify God. For the time has come for judgment to begin with the household of God; and if it begins with us, what will be the end of those who do not obey the gospel of God? And

"If the righteous man is scarcely saved,
where will the impious and sinner appear?"

Therefore let those who suffer according to God's will do right and entrust their souls to a faithful Creator.

Jude and *2 Peter* were written because of the perversion of the doctrine of "liberty" and the attack of evil upon the church.

COMMON SALVATION

Jude

Jude, a servant of Jesus Christ and brother of James,
To those who are called, beloved in God the Father and kept for Jesus Christ:
May mercy, peace, and love be multiplied to you.
Beloved, being very eager to write to you of our common salvation, I found it necessary to write appealing to you to contend for the faith which was once for all delivered to the saints. For admission has been secretly gained by some who long ago were designated for this condemnation, ungodly persons who pervert the grace of our God into licentiousness and deny our only Master and Lord, Jesus Christ.
Now I desire to remind you, though you were once for all fully informed, that he who saved a people out of the land of Egypt, afterward destroyed those who did not believe. And the angels that did not keep their own position but left their proper dwelling have been kept by him in eternal chains in the nether gloom until the judgment of the great day; just as Sodom and Gomorrah and the surrounding cities, which likewise acted immorally and indulged in unnatural lust, serve as an example by undergoing a punishment of eternal fire.
Yet in like manner these men in their dreamings defile the flesh, reject authority, and revile the glorious ones. But when the archangel Michael, contending with the devil, disputed about the body of Moses, he did not presume to pronounce a reviling judgment upon him, but said, "The Lord rebuke you." But these men revile whatever they do not understand, and by those things that they know by instinct as irrational animals do, they are destroyed. Woe to them! For they walk in the way of Cain, and abandon them-

selves for the sake of gain to Balaam's error, and perish in Korah's rebellion. These are blemishes on your love feasts, as they boldly carouse together, looking after themselves; waterless clouds, carried along by winds; fruitless trees in late autumn, twice dead, uprooted; wild waves of the sea, casting up the foam of their own shame; wandering stars for whom the nether gloom of darkness has been reserved for ever.

It was of these also that Enoch in the seventh generation from Adam prophesied, saying, "Behold, the Lord came with his holy myriads, to execute judgment on all, and to convict all the ungodly of all their deeds of ungodliness which they have committed in such an ungodly way, and of all the harsh things which ungodly sinners have spoken against him." These are grumblers, malcontents, following their own passions, loud-mouthed boasters, flattering people to gain advantage.

But you must remember, beloved, the predictions of the apostles of our Lord Jesus Christ; they said to you, "In the last time there will be scoffers, following their own ungodly passions." It is these who set up divisions, wordly people, devoid of the Spirit. But you, beloved, build yourselves up on your most holy faith; pray in the Holy Spirit; keep yourselves in the love of God; wait for the mercy of our Lord Jesus Christ unto eternal life. And convince some, who doubt; save some, by snatching them out of the fire; on some have mercy with fear, hating even the garment spotted by the flesh.

Now to him who is able to keep you from falling and to present from falling and to present you without blemish before the presence of his glory with rejoicing, to the only God, our Savior through Jesus Christ our Lord, be glory, majesty, dominion, and authority, before all time and now and for ever. Amen.

REMEMBRANCE

2 Peter 3

This is now the second letter that I have written to you, beloved, and in both of them I have aroused your sincere mind by way of reminder; that you should remember the predictions of the holy prophets and the commandment of the Lord and Savior through your apostles. First of all you must understand this, that scoffers will come in the last days with scoffing, following their own passions and saying, "Where is the promise of his coming? For ever since the fathers fell asleep, all things have continued as they were from the beginning of creation." They deliberately ignore this fact, that by the word of God heavens existed long ago and an earth formed out of water and by means of water, through which the world that then existed was deluged with water and perished. But by the same word the heavens and earth that now exist have been stored up for fire, being kept until the day of judgment and destruction of ungodly men.

But do not ignore this one fact, beloved, that with the Lord one day is a thousand years, and a thousand years as one day. The Lord is not slow about his promise as some count slowness, but is forbearing toward you, not wishing that any should perish, but that all should reach repentance. But the day of the Lord will come like a thief, and then the heavens will pass away with a loud noise, and the elements will be dissolved with fire, and the earth and the works that are upon it will be burned up.

Since all these things are thus to be dissolved, what sort of persons ought you to be in lives of holiness and godliness, waiting for and hastening the coming of the day of God, because of which the heavens will be kindled and dissolved, and the elements will melt with fire! But according to his promise we wait for new heavens and a new earth in which righteousness dwells.

Therefore, beloved, since you wait for these, be zealous to be found by him without spot or blemish, and at peace. And count the forbearance of our Lord as salvation. So also our beloved brother Paul wrote to you according to the wisdom given him, speaking of this as he does in all his letters. There are some things in them hard to understand, which the ignorant and unstable twist to their own destruction, as they do the other scriptures. You therefore, beloved, knowing this beforehand, beware lest you be carried away with the error of lawless men and lose your own stability. But grow in the grace and knowledge of our Lord and Savior Jesus Christ. To him be the glory both now and to the day of eternity. Amen.

1 John was written to stress the idea of Christ's love, the quality which overcomes all evil.

THE OLD COMMANDMENT

1 John 2:7–17

Beloved, I am writing you no new commandment, but an old commandment which you had from the beginning; the old commandment is the word which you have heard. Yet I am writing you a new commandment, which is true in him and in you, because the darkness is passing away and the true light is already shining. He who says he is in the light and hates his brother is in the darkness still. He who loves his brother abides in the light, and in it there is no cause for stumbling. But he who hates his brother is in the darkness and walks in the darkness, and does not know where he is going, because the darkness has blinded his eyes.

I am writing to you, little children, because your sins are forgiven for his sake. I am writing to you, fathers, because you know him who is from the beginning. I am writing to you, young men, because you have overcome the evil one. I write to you, children, because you know the Father. I write to you, fathers, because you know him who is from the beginning. I write to you, young men, because you are strong, and the word of God abides in you, and you have overcome the evil one.

Do not love the world or the things in the world. If any one loves the world, love for the Father is not in him. For all that is in the world, the lust of the flesh and the lust of the eyes and the pride of life, is not of the Father but is of the world. And the world passes away, and the lust of it; but he who does the will of God abides for ever.

ORATORY (SPOKEN RHETORIC)

Oratory in the Bible is usually an elaborate speech with flowing eloquence. It usually possesses the characteristics of directness, clear logic, concise argument, and a keen dramatic sense. The speakers had the conviction of the worth of their message—the first secret of convincing oratory.

The purpose of the speaker was usually to cause a realignment of ideas and feelings. He was successful whether he gained cheers or hisses, for he had made the people listen and convicted them, convinced them, or converted them. Most of the Bible speakers were hissed off the stage. Elijah had to run down to Horeb for refuge; Amos was told to return home and dared not return to Bethel again; Isaiah was listened to by a minority; Jeremiah was put in the stocks and then a miry cistern; Peter was charged not to speak at all and then put into prison; Paul was chained and packed off to Rome; and Jesus was crucified.

Many modern speeches reflect Biblical speeches. Lincoln's "Gettysburg Address" and Wendell Phillips' "The War for the Union" both have Biblical echoes.

Oratory in the Bible includes addresses to persons, addresses to God, and formal prayers.

FORMAL SPEECHES

Bible literature only records "snatches" of Elijah's speeches on Mount Carmel. Hebrew law and justice, Hebrew religion and character were brushed aside as they tamely surrendered to foreign influences. King Ahab's son had married the princess of Sidon, who sought to establish her own customs and heathen gods and priests of Baalim. Mount Carmel became the meeting place of conflict between Elijah and the prophets of Baal.

1 Kings 18:17–40

When Ahab saw Elijah, Ahab said to him, "Is it you, you troubler of Israel?" And he answered, "I have not troubled Israel; but you have, and your father's house, because you have forsaken the commandments of the Lord and followed the Baals. Now therefore send and gather all Israel to me at Mount Carmel, and the four hundred and fifty prophets of Baal and the four hundred prophets of Asherah, who eat at Jezebel's table."

So Ahab sent to all the people of Israel, and gathered the prophets together at Mount Carmel. And Elijah came near to all the people, and said, "How long will you go limping with two different opinions? If the Lord is God, follow him; but if Baal, then follow him." And the people did not answer him a word. Then Elijah said to the people, "I, even I only, am left a prophet of the Lord; but Baal's prophets are four hundred and fifty men. Let two bulls be given to us; and let them choose one bull for themselves, and cut it in pieces and lay it on the wood, and put no fire to it; and I will prepare the other bull and lay it on the wood, and put no fire to it. And you call on the name of your god and I will call on the name of the Lord; and the God who answers by fire, he is God." And all the people answered, "It is well spoken." Then Elijah said to the prophets of Baal, "Choose for yourselves one bull and prepare it first, for you are many; and call on the name of your god, but put no fire to it." And they took the bull which was given them, and they prepared it, and called on the name of Baal from morning until noon, saying, "O Baal, answer us!" But there was no voice, and no one answered. And they limped about the altar which they had made. And at noon Elijah mocked them, saying, "Cry aloud, for he is a god; either he is musing, or he has gone aside, or he is on a journey, or perhaps he is asleep and must be awakened." And they cried aloud, and cut themselves after their custom with swords and lances, until the blood gushed out upon them. And as midday passed, they raved on until the time of the offering of the oblation, but there was no voice; no one answered, no one heeded.

Then Elijah said to all the people, "Come near to me"; and all the people came near to him. And he repaired the altar of the Lord that had been thrown down; Elijah took twelve stones, according to the number of the tribes of the sons of Jacob, to whom the word of the Lord came, saying, "Israel shall be your name"; and with the stones he built an altar in the name of the Lord. And he made a trench about the altar, as great as would contain two measures of seed. And he put the wood in order, and cut the bull in pieces and laid it on the wood. And he said, "Fill four jars with water, and pour it on the burnt offering, and on the wood." And he said, "Do it a second time"; and they did it a second time. And he said, "Do it a third time"; and they did it a third time. And the water ran round about the altar, and filled the trench also with water.

And at the time of the offering of the oblation, Elijah the prophet came near and said, "O Lord, God of Abraham, Isaac, and Israel, let it be known this day that thou art God in Israel, and that I am thy servant, and that I have done all these things at thy word. Answer me, O Lord, answer me, that this people may know that thou hast turned their hearts back." Then the fire of the Lord fell, and consumed the burnt offering, and the wood, and the stones, and the dust, and licked up the water that was in the trench. And when all the people saw it, they fell on their faces; and they said, "The Lord, he is God; the Lord, he is God." And Elijah said to them, "Seize the prophets of Baal; let not one of them escape." And they seized them; and Elijah brought them down to the brook Kishon, and killed them there.

Amos's maiden speech is a gathering up of present conditions with an outlook to the future. Amos wished to set the Hebrews straight as to their own place in the eyes of the Lord in connection with other nations.

Amos 1:1–15; 2:1–16

The words of Amos, who was among the shepherds of Tekoa, which he saw concerning Israel in the days of Uzziah king of Judah and in the days of Jeroboam the son of Joash, king of Israel, two years before the earthquake. And he said:

The Lord roars from Zion,
    and utters his voice from Jerusalem;

the pastures of the shepherds mourn,
    and the top of Carmel withers."

Thus says the Lord:
"For three transgressions of Damascus,
    and for four, I will not revoke the punishment;
because they have threshed Gilead
    with threshing sledges of iron.
So I will send a fire upon the house of Hazael,
    and it shall devour the strongholds of Benhadad.
I will break the bar of Damascus,
    and cut off the inhabitants from the Valley of Aven,
and him that holds the scepter from Betheden;
    and the people of Syria shall go into exile to Kir,"
                                                says the Lord.

Thus says the Lord:
"For three transgressions of Gaza,
    and for four, I will not revoke the punishment;
because they carried into exile a whole people
    to deliver them up to Edom.
So I will send a fire upon the wall of Gaza,
    and it shall devour her strongholds.
I will cut off the inhabitants from Ashdod,
    and him that holds the scepter from Ashkelon;
I will turn my hand against Ekron;
    and the remnant of the Philistines shall perish,"
                                            says the Lord God.

Thus says the Lord:
"For three transgressions of Tyre,
    and for four, I will not revoke the punishment;
because they delivered up a whole people to Edom,
    and did not remember the covenant of brotherhood
So I will send a fire upon the wall of Tyre,
    and it shall devour her strongholds."

Thus says the Lord:
"For three transgressions of Edom,
    and for four, I will not revoke the punishment;
because he pursued his brother with the sword,
    and cast off all pity,
and his anger tore perpetually,

and he kept his wrath for ever.
So I will send a fire upon Teman,
   and it shall devour the strongholds of Bozrah.''

Thus says the Lord:
"For three transgressions of the Ammonites,
   and for four, I will not revoke the punishment;
because they have ripped up women with child in Gilead,
   that they might enlarge their border.
So I will kindle a fire in the wall of Rabbah,
   and it shall devour her strongholds,
with shouting in the day of battle,
   with a tempest in the day of the whirlwind;
and their king shall go into exile,
   he and his princes together,"
                             says the Lord.

Thus says the Lord:
"For three transgressions of Moab,
   and for four, I will not revoke the punishment;
because he burned to lime
   the bones of the king of Edom.
So I will send a fire upon Moab,
   and it shall devour the strongholds of Kerioth,
and Moab shall die amid uproar,
   amid shouting and the sound of the trumpet;
I will cut off the ruler from its midst,
   and will slay all its princes with him,"
                             says the Lord.

Thus says the Lord:
"For three transgressions of Judah,
   and for four, I will not revoke the punishment;
because they have rejected the law of the Lord,
   and have not kept his statutes,
but their lies have led them astray,
   after which their fathers walked.
So I will send a fire upon Judah,
   and it shall devour the strongholds of Jerusalem.''

Thus says the Lord:
"For three transgressions of Israel,
   and for four, I will not revoke the punishment;

because they sell the righteous for silver,
    and the needy for a pair of shoes—
they that trample the head of the poor into the dust of the earth,
    and turn aside the way of the afflicted;
a man and his father go in to the same maiden,
    so that my holy name is profaned;
they lay themselves down beside every altar
    upon garments taken in pledge;
and in the house of their God they drink
    the wine of those who have been fined.

"Yet I destroyed the Amorite before them,
    whose height was like the height of the cedars,
    and who was as strong as the oaks;
I destroyed his fruit above,
    and his roots beneath.
Also I brought you up out of the land of Egypt,
    and led you forty years in the wilderness,
    to possess the land of the Amorite.
And I raised up some of your sons for prophets,
    and some of your young men for Nazirites.
    Is it not indeed so, O people of Israel?"

                                                    says the Lord.

"But you made the Nazirites drink wine,
    and commanded the prophets,
    saying, 'You shall not prophesy.'

"Behold, I will press you down in your place,
    as a cart full of sheaves presses down.
Flight shall perish from the swift,
    and the strong shall not retain his strength,
    nor shall the mighty save his life;
he who handles the bow shall not stand,
    and he who is swift of foot shall not save himself,
    nor shall he who rides the horse save his life;
and he who is stout of heart among the mighty
    shall flee away naked in that day,"

                                                    says the Lord.

Peter's speech at Pentecost was prompted by the miraculous
happenings in Jerusalem on the special occasion of the gathering
of devout Hebrews from many nations. The unseasonal strong
winds, the appearance of tongues of fire that seemed to settle on

many Christians, and the disciples' sudden ability to speak in other languages in order to present the Gospel to the many visitors to Jerusalem perplexed the multitudes. Peter rose to provide the explanation.

Acts 2:5–42

Now there were dwelling in Jerusalem Jews, devout men from every nation under heaven. And at this sound the multitude came together, and they were bewildered, because each one heard them speaking in his own language. And they were amazed and wondered, saying, "Are not all these who are speaking Galileans? And how is it that we hear, each of us in his own native language? Parthians and Medes and Elamites and residents of Mesopotamia, Judea and Cappadocia, Pontus and Asia, Phrygia and Pamphylia, Egypt and the parts of Libya belonging to Cyrene, and visitors from Rome, both Jews and proselytes, Cretans and Arabians, we hear them telling in our own tongues the mighty works of God." And all were amazed and perplexed, saying to one another, "What does this mean?" But others mocking said, "They are filled with new wine."

But Peter, standing with the eleven, lifted up his voice and addressed them, "Men of Judea and all who dwell in Jerusalem, let this be known to you, and give ear to my words. For these men are not drunk, as you suppose, since it is only the third hour of the day; but this is what was spoken by the prophet Joel:

'And in the last days it shall be, God declares,
that I will pour out my Spirit upon all flesh,
and your sons and your daughters shall prophesy,
and your young men shall see visions,
and your old men shall dream dreams;
yea, and on my menservants and my maidservants in those
   days
I will pour out my Spirit; and they shall prophesy.
And I will show wonders in the heaven above
and signs on the earth beneath,
blood, and fire, and vapor of smoke;
the sun shall be turned into darkness
and the moon into blood,
before the day of the Lord comes,
the great and manifest day.
And it shall be that whoever calls on the name of the Lord shall
   be saved.'

"Men of Israel, hear these words: Jesus of Nazareth, a man attested to you by God with mighty works and wonders and signs which God did through him in your midst, as you yourselves know—this Jesus, delivered up according to the definite plan and foreknowledge of God, you crucified and killed by the hands of lawless men. But God raised him up, having loosed the pangs of death, because it was not possible for him to be held by it. For David says concerning him,

'I saw the Lord always before me,
for he is at my right hand that I may not be shaken;
therefore my heart was glad, and my tongue rejoiced;
moreover my flesh will dwell in hope.
For thou wilt not abandon my soul to Hades,
nor let thy Holy One see corruption.
Thou hast made known to me the ways of life;
thou wilt make me full of gladness with thy presence.'

"Brethren, I may say to you confidently of the patriarch David that he both died and was buried, and his tomb is with us to this day. Being therefore a prophet, and knowing that God had sworn with an oath to him that he would set one of his descendants upon his throne, he foresaw and spoke of the resurrection of the Christ, that he was not abandoned to Hades, nor did his flesh see corruption.

This Jesus God raised up, and of that we all are witnesses. Being therefore exalted at the right hand of God, and having received from the Father the promise of the Holy Spirit, he has poured out this which you see and hear. For David did not ascend into the heavens; but he himself says,

'The Lord said to my Lord, Sit at my right hand,
till I make thy enemies a stool for thy feet.'

Let all the house of Israel therefore know assuredly that God has made him both Lord and Christ, this Jesus whom you crucified."
Now when they heard this they were cut to the heart, and said to Peter and the rest of the apostles, "Brethren, what shall we do?" And Peter said to them, "Repent, and be baptized every one of you in the name of Jesus Christ for the forgiveness of your sins; and you shall receive the gift of the Holy Spirit. For the promise is to you and to your children and to all that are far off, every one

whom the Lord our God calls to him." And he testified with many other words and exhorted them, saying, "Save yourselves from this crooked generation." So those who received his word were baptized, and there were added that day about three thousand souls. And they devoted themselves to the apostles' teaching and fellowship, to the breaking of bread and the prayers.

Paul's speech at Athens was prompted by certain philosophers who encountered Paul and brought him to the hill Areopagus underneath the great temple of Athena, the Parthenon. The whole city of Athens was given over to idolatry. There was no danger of mob violence or persecution, so Paul plunged straight into his subject.

Acts 17:16–34

Now while Paul was waiting for them at Athens, his spirit was provoked within him as he saw that the city was full of idols. So he argued in the synagogue with the Jews and the devout persons, and in the market place every day with those who chanced to be there. Some also of the Epicurean and Stoic philosophers met him. And some said, "What would this babbler say?" Others said, "He seems to be a preacher of foreign divinities"—because he preached Jesus and the resurrection. And they took hold of him and brought him to the Are-opagus, saying, "May we know what this new teaching is which you present? For you bring some strange things to our ears; we wish to know therefore what these things mean." Now all the Athenians and the foreigners who lived there spent their time in nothing except telling or hearing something new.

So Paul, standing in the middle of the Are-opagus, said: "Men of Athens, I perceive that in every way you are very religious. For as I passed along, and observed the objects of your worship, I found also an altar with this inscription, 'To an unknown god.' What therefore you worship as unknown, this I proclaim to you. The God who made the world and everything in it, being Lord of heaven and earth, does not live in shrines made by man, nor is he served by human hands, as though he needed anything, since he himself gives to all men life and breath and everything. And he made from one every nation of men to live on all the face of the earth, having determined allotted periods and the boundaries of their habitation, that they should seek God, in the hope that they might feel after him and find him. Yet he is not far from each one of us, for

'In him we live and move and have our being';
as even some of your poets have said,
'For we are indeed his offspring.'
Being then God's offspring, we ought not to think that the Deity is like gold, or silver, or stone, a representation by the art and imagination of man. The times of ignorance God overlooked, but now he commands all men everywhere to repent, because he has fixed a day on which he will judge the world in righteousness by a man whom he has appointed, and of this he has given assurance to all men by raising him from the dead."

Now when they heard of the resurrection of the dead, some mocked; but others said, "We will hear you again about this." So Paul went out from among them. But some men joined him and believed.

In Paul's speech of defense before Agrippa, Paul's liberty, not his life, is at stake. He reminds King Agrippa that he is happy to come before one so learned in Jewish customs and bases his arguments on familiar Jewish tradition.

Acts 26

Agrippa said to Paul, "You have permission to speak for yourself." Then Paul stretched out his hand and made his defense:

"I think myself fortunate that it is before you, King Agrippa, I am to make my defense today against all the accusations of the Jews, because you are especially familiar with all customs and controversies of the Jews; therefore I beg you to listen to me patiently.

"My manner of life from my youth, spent from the beginning among my own nation and at Jerusalem, is known by all the Jews. They have known for a long time, if they are willing to testify, that according to the strictest party of our religion I have lived as a Pharisee. And now I stand here on trial for hope in the promise made by God to our fathers, to which our twelve tribes hope to attain, as they earnestly worship night and day. And for this hope I am accused by Jews, O king! Why is it thought incredible by any of you that God raises the dead?

"I myself was convinced that I ought to do many things in opposing the name of Jesus of Nazareth. And I did so in Jerusalem; I not only shut up many of the saints in prison, by authority from the chief priests, but when they were put to death I cast my vote against them. And I punished them often in all the synagogues and tried to make them blaspheme; and in raging fury against them, I persecuted them even to foreign cities.

"Thus I journeyed to Damascus with the authority and commission of the chief priests. At midday, O king, I saw on the way a light from heaven, brighter than the sun, shining round me and those who journeyed with me. And when we had all fallen to the ground, I heard a voice saying to me in the Hebrew language, 'Saul, Saul, why do you persecute me? It hurts you to kick against the goads.' And I said, 'Who are you, Lord?' And the Lord said, 'I am Jesus whom you are persecuting. But rise and stand upon your feet; for I have appeared to you for this purpose, to appoint you to serve and bear witness to the things in which you have seen me and to those in which I will appear to you, delivering you from the people and from the Gentiles—to whom I send you to open their eyes, that they may turn from darkness to light and from the power of Satan to God, that they may receive forgiveness of sins and a place among those who are sanctified by faith in me.'

"Wherefore, O King Agrippa, I was not disobedient to the heavenly vision, but declared first to those at Damascus, then at Jerusalem and throughout all the country of Judea, and also to the Gentiles, that they should repent and turn to God and perform deeds worthy of their repentance. For this reason the Jews seized me in the temple and tried to kill me. To this day I have had the help that comes from God, and so I stand here testifying both to small and great, saying nothing but what the prophets and Moses said would come to pass: that the Christ must suffer, and that, by being the first to rise from the dead, he would proclaim light both to the people and to the Gentiles."

And as he thus made his defense, Festus said with a loud voice, "Paul, you are mad; your great learning is turning you mad." But Paul said, "I am not mad, most excellent Festus, but I am speaking the sober truth. For the king knows about these things, and to him I speak freely; for I am persuaded that none of these things has escaped his notice, for this was not done in a corner. King Agrippa, do you believe the prophets? I know that you believe." And Agrippa said to Paul, "In a short time you think to make me a Christian!" And Paul said, "Whether short or long, I would to God that not only you but also all who hear me this day might become such as I am—except for these chains."

Then the king rose, and the governor and Bernice and those who were sitting with them; and when they had withdrawn, they said to one another, "This man is doing nothing to deserve death or imprisonment." And Agrippa said to Festus, "This man could have been set free if he had not appealed to Caesar."

The book of Deuteronomy is filled with spoken rhetoric and is most quoted in this respect. The following sample will illustrate the style of the book.

Deuteronomy 6:4–12; 7:6–8; 8:1–20

"Hear, O Israel: The Lord our God is one Lord; and you shall love the Lord your God with all your heart, and with all your soul, and with all your might. And these words which I command you this day shall be upon your heart; and you shall teach them diligently to your children, and shall talk of them when you sit in your house, and when you walk by the way, and when you lie down, and when you rise. And you shall bind them as a sign upon your hand, and they shall be as frontlets between your eyes. And you shall write them on the doorposts of your house and on your gates.

"And when the Lord your God brings you into the land which he swore to your fathers, to Abraham, to Isaac, and to Jacob, to give you, with great and godly cities, which you did not build, and houses full of all good things, which you did not fill, and cisterns hewn out, which you did not hew, and vineyards and olive trees, which you did not plant, and when you eat and are full, then take heed lest you forget the Lord, who brought you out of the land of Egypt, out of the house of bondage.

"For you are a people holy to the Lord your God; the Lord your God has chosen you to be a people for his own possession, out of all the peoples that are on the face of the earth. It was not because you were more in number than any other people that the Lord set his love upon you and chose you, for you were the fewest of all peoples; but it is because the Lord loves you, and is keeping the oath which he swore to your fathers, that the Lord has brought you out with a mighty hand, and redeemed you from the house of bondage, from the hand of Pharaoh king of Egypt.

"All the commandment which I command you this day you shall be careful to do, that you may live and multiply, and go in and possess the land which the Lord swore to give to your fathers. And you shall remember all the way which the Lord your God has led you these forty years in the wilderness, that he might humble you, testing you to know what was in your heart, whether you would keep his commandments, or not. And he humbled you and let you hunger and fed you with manna, which you did not know, nor did your fathers know; that he might make you know that man does not live by bread alone, but that man lives by everything that proceeds out of the mouth of the Lord. Your clothing did not wear out upon you, and your foot did not swell, these forty years. Know then in your heart that, as a man disciplines his son, the Lord your God disciplines you. So you shall keep the commandments of the Lord your God, by walking in his ways and by fearing him. For the Lord your God is bringing you into a good land, a land of brooks of water, of fountains and springs, flowing forth in valleys and hills, a land of wheat and barley, of vines and fig trees and pomegranates, a land of olive trees and honey, a land in which you will eat bread without scarcity, in which you will lack nothing, a land whose stones are iron, and out of whose hills you can dig copper. And you shall eat and be full, and you shall bless the Lord your God for the good land he has given you.

"Take heed lest you forget the Lord your God, by not keeping his commandments and his ordinances and his statutes, which I command you this day: lest, when you have eaten and are full, and have built goodly houses and live in them, and when your herds and flocks multiply, and your silver and gold is multiplied, and all that you have is multiplied, then your heart be lifted up, and you forget the Lord your God, who brought you out of the land of Egypt, out of the house of bondage, who led you through the great and terrible wilderness, with its fiery serpents and scorpions and thirsty ground where there was no water, who brought you water out of the flinty rock, who fed you in the wilderness with manna which your fathers did not know, that he might humble you and test you, to do you good in the end. Beware lest you say in your heart, 'My power and the might of my hand have gotten me this wealth.' You shall remember the Lord your God, for it is he who gives you power to get wealth; that he may confirm his covenant which he swore to your fathers, as at this day. And if you forget the Lord your God and go after other gods and serve them and worship them, I solemnly warn you this day that you shall surely perish. Like the nations that the Lord makes to perish before you, so shall you perish, because you would not obey the voice of the Lord your God."

The sermon on the mount, like most speeches of the Old and New Testaments, was presented in the open air—this time on a mountain side. The style of the speech is more like the Old Testament prophetic style rather than like Peter's or Paul's speeches.

Matthew apparently regarded the Sermon as the epitome of Jesus' teaching, of which his whole ministry was an illustration.

Two sections near the beginning and end appear to unfold in orderly themes, but the rest is more like a group of proverbial sayings about various unrelated subjects.

Matthew 5–7

Seeing the crowds, he went up on the mountain, and when he sat down his disciples came to him. And he opened his mouth and taught them,

"Blessed are the poor in spirit, for theirs is the kingdom of heaven.

"Blessed are those who mourn, for they shall be comforted.

"Blessed are the meek, for they shall inherit the earth.

"Blessed are those who hunger and thirst for righteousness, for they shall be satisfied.

"Blessed are the merciful, for they shall obtain mercy.

"Blessed are the pure in heart, for they shall see God.

"Blessed are the peacemakers, for they shall be called sons of God.

"Blessed are those who are persecuted for righteousness' sake, for theirs is the kingdom of heaven.

"Blessed are you when men revile you and persecute you and utter all kinds of evil against you falsely on my account. Rejoice and be glad, for your reward is great in heaven, for so men persecuted the prophets who were before you.

"You are the salt of the earth; but if salt has lost its taste, how shall its saltness be restored? It is no longer good for anything except to be thrown out and trodden under foot by men.

"You are the light of the world. A city set on a hill cannot be hid. Nor do men light a lamp and put it under a bushel, but on a stand, and it gives light to all in the house. Let your light so shine before men, that they may see your good works and give glory to your Father who is in heaven.

"Think not that I have come to abolish the law and the prophets; I have come not to abolish them but to fulfil them. For truly, I say to you, till heaven and earth pass away, not an iota, not a dot, will pass from the law until all is accomplished. Whoever then relaxes one of the least of these commandments and teaches men so, shall be called least in the kingdom of heaven; but he who does them and teaches them shall be called great in the kingdom of heaven. For I tell you, unless your righteousness exceeds that of the scribes and Pharisees, you will never enter the kingdom of heaven.

"You have heard that it was said to the men of old, 'You shall not kill; and whoever kills shall be liable to judgment.' But I say to you that every one who is angry with his brother shall be liable to judgment; whoever insults his brother shall be liable to the council, and whoever says, 'You fool!' shall be liable to the hell of fire. So if you are offering your gift at the altar, and there remember that your brother has something against you, leave your gift there before the altar and go; first be reconciled to your brother, and then come and offer your gift. Make friends quickly with your accuser, while you are going with him to court, lest your accuser hand you over to the judge, and the judge to the guard, and you be put in prison; truly, I say to you, you will never get out till you have paid the last penny.

"You have heard that it was said, 'You shall not commit adultery.' But I say to you that every one who looks at a woman lustfully has already committed adultery with her in his heart. If your right eye causes you to sin, pluck it out and throw it away; it is better that you lose one of your members than that your whole body be thrown into hell. And if your right hand causes you to sin, cut it off and throw it away; it is better than you lose one of your members than that your whole body go into hell.

"It was also said, 'Whoever divorces his wife, let him give her a certificate of divorce. But I say to you that every one who divorces his wife, except on the ground of unchastity, makes her an adulteress; and whoever marries a divorced woman commits adultery.

"Again you have heard that it was said to the men of old, 'You shall not swear falsely, but shall perform to the Lord what you have sworn.' But I say to you, Do not swear at all, either by heaven, for it is the throne of God, or by the earth, for it is his footstool, or by Jerusalem, for it is the city of the great King. And do not swear by your head, for you cannot make one hair white or black. Let what you say be simply 'Yes' or 'No'; anything more than this comes from evil.

"You have heard that it was said, 'An eye for an eye and a tooth for a tooth.' But I say to you. Do not resist one who is evil. But if any one strikes you on the right cheek, turn to him the other also; and if any one would sue you and take your coat, let him have your cloak as well; and if any one forces you to go one mile, go with him two miles. Give to him who begs from you, and do not refuse him who would borrow from you.

"You have heard that it was said, 'You shall love your neighbor and hate your enemy.' But I say to you, Love your enemies and pray for those who persecute you, so that you may be sons of your Father who is in heaven; for he makes his sun rise on the evil and on the good, and sends rain on the just and on the unjust. For if you love those who love you, what reward have you? Do not even the tax collectors do the same? And if you salute only your brethren, what more are you doing than others? Do not even the Gentiles do the same? You, therefore, must be perfect, as your heavenly Father is perfect.

"Beware of practicing your piety before men in order to be seen by them; for then you will have no reward from your Father who is in heaven.

"Thus, when you give alms, sound no trumpet before you, as the hypocrites do in the synagogues and in the streets, that they may be praised by men. Truly, I say to you, they have their reward. But when you give alms, do not let your left hand know what your right hand is doing, so that your alms may be in secret; and your Father who sees in secret will reward you.

"And when you pray, you must not be like the hypocrites; for they love to stand and pray in the synagogues and at the street corners, that they may be seen by men. Truly, I say to you, they have their reward. But when you pray, go into your room and shut the door and pray to your Father who is in secret; and your Father who sees in secret will reward you.

"And in praying do not heap up empty phrases as the Gentiles do; for they think that they will be heard for their many words. Do not be like them, for your Father knows what you need before you ask him. Pray then like this:

> Our Father who art in heaven,
> Hallowed be thy name.
> Thy kingdom come,
> Thy will be done,
>   On earth as it is in heaven.
> Give us this day our daily bread;
> And forgive us our debts,
>   As we also have forgiven our debtors;
> And lead us not into temptation,
>   But deliver us from evil.

For if you forgive men their trespasses, your heavenly Father also will forgive you; but if you do not forgive men their trespasses, neither will your Father forgive your trespasses.

"And when you fast, do not look dismal, like the hypocrites, for they disfigure their faces that their fasting may be seen by men. Truly, I say to you, they have their reward. But when you fast, anoint your head and wash your face, that your fasting may not be seen by men but by your Father who is in secret; and your Father who sees in secret will reward you.

"Do not lay up for yourselves treasures on earth, where moth and rust consume and where thieves break in and steal, but lay up for yourselves treasures in heaven, where neither moth nor rust consumes and where thieves do not break in and steal. For where your treasure is, there will your heart be also.

"The eye is the lamp of the body. So, if your eye is sound, your whole body will be full of light; but if your eye is not sound, your whole body will be full of darkness. If then the light in you is darkness, how great is the darkness!

"No one can serve two masters; for either he will hate the one and love the other, or he will be devoted to the one and despise the other. You cannot serve God and mammon.

"Therefore I tell you, do not be anxious about your life, what you shall eat or what you shall drink, nor about your body, what you shall put on. Is not life more than food, and the body more than clothing? Look at the birds of the air; they neither sow nor reap nor gather into barns, and yet your heavenly Father feeds them. Are you not of more value than they? And which of you by being anxious can add one cubit to his span of life? And why are you anxious about clothing? Consider the lilies of the field, how they grow; they neither toil nor spin; yet I tell you, even Solomon in all his glory was not arrayed like one of these. But if God so clothes the grass of the field, which today is alive and tomorrow is thrown into the oven, will he not much more clothe you, O men of little faith? Therefore do not be anxious, saying, 'What shall we eat?' or 'What shall we drink?' or 'What shall we wear?' For the Gentiles seek all these things; and your heavenly Father knows that you need them all. But seek first his kingdom and his righteousness, and all these things shall be yours as well.

"Therefore do not be anxious about tomorrow, for tomorrow will be anxious for itself. Let the day's own trouble be sufficient for the day.

"Judge not, that you be not judged. For with the judgment you pronounce you will be judged, and the measure you give will be the measure you get. Why do you see the speck that is in your brother's eye, but do not notice the log that is in your own eye? Or how can you say to your brother, 'Let me take the speck out of your eye,' when there is the log in your own eye? You hypocrite, first take the log out of your own eye, and then you will see clearly to take the speck out of your brother's eye.

"Do not give dogs what is holy; and do not throw your pearls before swine, lest they trample them under foot and turn to attack you.

"Ask, and it will be given you; seek, and you will find; knock, and it will be opened to you. For every one who asks receives, and he who seeks finds, and to him who knocks it will be opened. Or what man of you, if his son asks him for bread, will give him a stone? Or if he asks for a fish, will give him a serpent? If you then, who are evil, know how to give good gifts to your children, how much more will your Father who is in heaven give good things to those who ask him! So whatever you wish that men would do to you, do so to them; for this is the law and the prophets.

"Enter by the narrow gate; for the gate is wide and the way is easy, that leads to destruction, and those who enter by it are many. For the gate is narrow and the way is hard, that leads to life, and those who find it are few.

"Beware of false prophets, who come to you in sheep's clothing but inwardly are ravenous wolves. You will know them by their fruits. Are grapes gathered from thorns, or figs from thistles? So, every sound tree bears good fruit, but the bad tree bears evil fruit. A sound tree cannot bear evil fruit, nor can a bad tree bear good fruit. Every tree that does not bear good fruit is cut down and thrown into the fire. Thus you will know them by their fruits.

"Not every one who says to me, 'Lord, Lord,' shall enter the kingdom of heaven, but he who does the will of my Father who is in heaven. On that day many will say to me, 'Lord, Lord, did we not prophesy in your name, and cast out demons in your name, and do many mighty works in your name?' And then will I declare to them, 'I never knew you; depart from me, you evildoers.'

"Every one then who hears these words of mine and does them will be like a wise man who built his house upon the rock; and the rain fell, and the floods came, and the winds blew and beat upon that house, but it did not fall, because it had been founded on the rock. And every one who hears these words of mine and does not do them will be like a foolish man who built his house upon the sand; and the rain fell, and the floods came, and the winds blew and beat against that house, and it fell; and great was the fall of it."

And when Jesus finished these sayings, the crowds were astonished at his teaching, for he taught them as one who had authority, and not as their scribes.

FABLES, ALLEGORIES, AND PARABLES

Instruction is more readily received by primitive and uneducated people in the form of a story than in the bare, didactic form of a sermon or essay. This method is also effective among the cultured. People with strong prejudices are often best awakened to a truth in this way.

Fables and parables are both lengthy similes. These is a resemblance between the animals or plants or natural objects to the human beings to whom they are likened. Usually the lesson of the fable is drawn from a lower level than a parable. The fable deals with wordly wisdom, an understanding of natural law for its moral. The parable is on a more spiritual plane. In the fable animals and trees are made to act in human fashion; human motives are attributed to them; there is no distinction made between the spirits of nature and the spirit of man. In a parable there is a strict truthfulness; facts of nature are set over against facts in human life—the laws of nature and the laws of spiritual life are in perfect harmony. The fable is usually in a very light vein; the parable is always serious. The fable may be a jest, but there is no jest in a parable. There may be contrasts in a parable that reveal a humorous situation, but the story is not told for the sake of humor; it is told with a most serious moral earnestness.

As the fable and parable are lengthy similes, the allegory is a lengthened metaphor. Instead of the resemblance between the natural objects and human nature being plainly marked by a *like* or *as*, the likeness is taken for granted. Jesus did not first tell a story of a good shepherd and then say that he was like him. He said "I am the good shepherd" and then went on to tell what the good shepherd did, assuming that he did the same thing for his sheep, human beings. Bible allegories are on the same high spiritual level as parables.

The Bible is filled with fables, parables, and allegories. They are among the most common sources of allusions in literature.

Following are two examples of the *fable*.

JOTHAM'S FABLE
Judges 9:7–15

When it was told to Jotham, he went and stood on the top of Mount Gerizim, and cried aloud and said to them, "Listen to me, you men of Shechem, that God may listen to you. The trees once went forth to anoint a king over them; and they said to the olive tree, 'Reign over us.' But the olive tree said to them, 'Shall I leave my fatness, by which gods and men are honored, and go to sway over the trees?' And the trees said to the fig tree, 'Come you, and reign over us.' But the fig tree said to them, 'Shall I leave my sweetness and my good fruit, and go to sway over the trees?' And the trees said to the vine, 'Come you, and reign over us.' But the vine said to them, 'Shall I leave my wine which cheers gods and men, and go to sway over the trees?' Then all the trees said to the bramble, 'Come you, and reign over us.' And the bramble said to the trees, 'If in good faith you are anointing me king over you, then come and take refuge in my shade; but if not, let fire come out of the bramble and devour the cedars of Lebanon.'

THE MEMBERS AND THE BODY

1 Corinthians 12:12–30

For just as the body is one and has many members, and all the members of the body, though many, are one body, so it is with Christ. For by one Spirit we were all baptized into one body—Jews or Greeks, slaves or free—and all were made to drink of one Spirit.

For the body does not consist of one member but of many. If the foot should say, "Because I am not a hand, I do not belong to the body," that would not make it any less a part of the body. And if the ear should say, "Because I am not an eye, I do not belong to the body," that would not make it any less a part of the body. If the whole body were an eye, where would be the hearing? If the whole body were an ear, where would be the sense of smell? But as it is, God arranged the organs in the body, each one of them, as he chose. If all were a single organ, where would the body be? As it is, there are many parts, yet one body. The eye cannot say to the hand, "I have no need of you," nor again the head to the feet, "I have no need of you." On the contrary, the parts of the body which seem to be weaker are indispensable, and those parts of the body which we think less honorable we invest with the greater honor, and our unpresentable parts are treated with greater modesty, which our more presentable parts do not require. But God has so adjusted the body, giving the greater honor to the inferior part, that there may be no discord in the body, but that the members may have the same care for one another. If one member suffers, all suffer together; if one member is honored, all rejoice together.

Now you are the body of Christ and individually members of it. And God has appointed in the church first apostles, second prophets, third teachers, then workers of miracles, then healers, helpers, administrators, speakers in various kinds of tongues. Are all apostles? Are all prophets? Are all teachers? Do all work miracles? Do all possess gifts of healing? Do all speak with tongues? Do all interpret? But earnestly desire the higher gifts.

Following are examples of *allegories*.

ISAIAH'S VINEYARD

Isaiah 5:1–10

Let me sing for my beloved
    a love song concerning his vineyard:
My beloved had a vineyard
    on a very fertile hill.
He digged it and cleared it of stones,
    and planted it with choice vines;
he built a watchtower in the midst of it,
    and hewed out a wine vat in it;
and he looked for it to yield grapes
    but it yielded wild grapes.

And now, O inhabitants of Jerusalem
    and men of Judah,
judge, I pray you, between me
    and my vineyard.
What more was there to do for my vineyard,
    that I have not done in it?
When I looked for it to yield grapes,
    why did it yield wild grapes?

And now I will tell you
    what I will do to my vineyard.
I will remove its hedge,
    and it shall be devoured;
I will break down its wall,
    and it shall be trampled down.
I will make it a waste;
    it shall not be pruned or hoed,
    and briers and thorns shall grow up;
I will also command the clouds
    that they rain no rain upon it.

For the vineyard óf the Lord of hosts
    is the house of Israel,
and the men of Judah
    are his pleasant planting;
and he looked for justice,
    but behold, bloodshed;
for righteousness,
    but behold, a cry!

Woe to those who join house to house,
    who add field to field,
until there is no more room,
    and you are made to dwell alone
    in the midst of the land.
The Lord of hosts has sworn in my hearing:
"Surely many houses shall be desolate,
    large and beautiful houses, without inhabitant.
For ten acres of vineyard shall yield but one bath,
    and a homer of seed shall yield but an ephah."

WATER TURNED TO WINE

John 2:1–11

On the third day there was a marriage at Cana in Galilee, and the mother of Jesus was there; Jesus also was invited to the marriage, with his disciples. When the wine failed, the mother of Jesus said to him, "They have no wine." And Jesus said to her, "O woman, what have you to do with me? My hour has not yet come." His mother said to the servants, "Do whatever he tells you." Now six stone jars were standing there, for the Jewish rites of purification, each holding twenty or thirty gallons. Jesus said to them, "Fill the jars with water." And they filled them up to the brim. He said to them, "Now draw some out, and take it to the steward of the feast." So they took it. When the steward of the feast tasted the water now become wine, and did not know where it came from (though the servants who had drawn the water knew), the steward of the feast called the bridegroom and said to him, "Every man serves the good wine first; and when men have drunk freely, then the poor wine; but you have kept the good wine until now." This, the first of his signs, Jesus did at Cana in Galilee, and manifested his glory; and his disciples believed in him.

THE VINE

John 15:1–8

"I am the true vine, and my Father is the vinedresser. Every branch of mine that bears no fruit, he takes away, and every branch that does bear fruit he prunes that it may bear more fruit. You are already made clean by the word which I have spoken to you. Abide in me, and I in you. As the branch cannot bear fruit by itself, unless it abides in the vine, neither can you, unless you abide in me. I am the vine, you are the branches. he who abides in me, and I in him, he it is that bears much fruit, for apart from me you can do nothing. If a man does not abide in me, he is cast forth as a branch and withers; and the branches are gathered, thrown into the fire and burned. If you abide in me, and my words abide in you, ask whatever you will, and it shall be done for you. By this my Father is glorified, that you bear much fruit, and so prove to be my disciples."

THE SHEEPFOLD

John 10:1–21

"Truly, truly, I say to you, he who does not enter the sheepfold by the door but climbs in by another way, that man is a thief and a robber; but he who enters by the door is the shepherd of the sheep. To him the gatekeeper opens; the sheep hear his voice, and he calls his own sheep by name and leads them out. When he has brought out all his own, he goes before them, and the sheep follow him, for they know his voice. A stranger they will not follow, but they will flee from him, for they do not know the voice of strangers." This figure Jesus used with them, but they did not understand what he was saying to them.

So Jesus again said to them, "Truly, truly, I say to you, I am the door of the sheep. All who came before me are thieves and robbers; but the sheep did not heed them. I am the door; if any one enters by me, he will be saved, and will go in and out and find pasture. The thief comes only to steal and kill and destroy; I came that they may have life, and have it abundantly. I am the good shepherd. The good shepherd lays down his life for the sheep. He who is a hireling and not a shepherd, whose own the sheep are not, sees the wolf coming and leaves the sheep and flees; and the wolf snatches them and scatters them. He flees because he is a hireling and cares nothing for the sheep. I am the good shepherd; I know my own and my own know me, as the Father knows me and I know the Father; and I lay down my life for the sheep. And I have other sheep, that are not of this fold; I must bring them also, and they will heed my voice. So there shall be one flock, one shepherd. For this reason the Father loves me, because I lay down my life, that I may take it again. No one takes it from me, but I lay it down of my own accord. I have power to lay it down, and I have power to take it again; this charge I have received from my Father."

There was again a division among the Jews because of these words. Many of them said, "He has a demon, and he is mad; why listen to him?" Others said, "These are not the sayings of one who has a demon. Can a demon open the eyes of the blind?"

Finally, we see examples of the *parable*.

TARES AMONG THE WHEAT

Matthew 13:24–30, 36–43

Another parable he put before them, saying, "The kingdom of heaven may be compared to a man who sowed good seed in his field; but while men were sleeping, his enemy came and sowed weeds among the wheat, and went away. So when the plants came up and bore grain, then the weeds appeared also. And the servants of the householder came and said to him, 'Sir, did you not sow good seed in your field? How then has it weeds?' He said to them, 'An enemy has done this.' The servants said to him, 'Then do you want us to go and gather them?' But he said, 'No; lest in gathering the weeds you root up the wheat along with them. Let both grow together until the harvest; and at harvest time I will tell the reapers, Gather the weeds first and bind them in bundles to be burned, but gather the wheat into my barn.' "

Then he left the crowds and went into the house. And his disciples came to him, saying, "Explain to us the parable of the weeds of the field." He answered, "He who sows the good seed is the Son of man; the field is the world, and the good seed means the sons of the kingdom; the weeds are the sons of the evil one, and the enemy who sowed them is the devil; the harvest is the close of the age, and the reapers are angels. Just as the weeds are gathered and burned with fire, so will it be at the close of the age. The Son of man will send his angels, and they will gather out of his kingdom all causes of sin and all evildoers, and throw them into the furnace of fire; there men will weep and gnash their teeth. Then the righteous will shine like the sun in the kingdom of their Father. He who has ears, let him hear."

GRAIN AND THE MUSTARD SEED

Matthew 13:31–32

Another parable he put before them, saying, "The kingdom of heaven is like a grain of mustard seed which a man took and sowed in his field; it is the smallest of all seeds, but when it has grown it is the greatest of shrubs and becomes a tree, so that the birds of the air come and make nests in its branches."

LEAVEN

Matthew 13:33–35

He told them another parable. "The kingdom of heaven is like leaven which a woman took and hid in three measures of meal, till it was all leavened."

All this Jesus said to the crowds in parables; indeed he said nothing to them without a parable. This was to fulfil what was spoken by the prophet:

"I will open my mouth in parables,
I will utter what has been hidden since
    the foundation of the world."

HIDDEN TREASURE

Matthew 13:44

"The kingdom of heaven is like treasure hidden in a field, which a man found and covered up; then in his joy he goes and sells all that he has and buys that field."

THE PEARL

Matthew 13:45–46

"Again, the kingdom of heaven is like a merchant in search of fine pearls, who, on finding one pearl of great value, went and sold all that he had and bought it."

DRAGNET

Matthew 13:47–50

"Again, the kingdom of heaven is like a net which was thrown into the sea and gathered fish of every kind; when it was full, men drew it ashore and sat down and sorted the good into vessels but threw away the bad. So it will be at the close of the age. The angels will come out and separate the evil from the righteous, and throw them into the furnace of fire; there men will weep and gnash their teeth.''

THE MARRIAGE FEAST

Matthew 22:1–14

And again Jesus spoke to them in parables, saying, ''The kingdom of heaven may be compared to a king who gave a marriage feast for his son, and sent his servants to call those who were invited to the marriage feast; but they would not come. Again he sent other servants, saying, 'Tell those who are invited, Behold, I have made ready my dinner, my oxen and my fat calves are killed, and everything is ready; come to the marriage feast.' But they made light of it and went off, one to his farm, another to his business, while the rest seized his servants, treated them shamefully, and killed them. The king was angry, and he sent his troops and destroyed those murderers and burned their city. Then he said to his servants, 'The wedding is ready, but those invited were not worthy. Go therefore to the thoroughfares, and invite to the marriage feast as many as you find.' And those servants went out into the streets and gathered all whom they found, both bad and good; so the wedding hall was filled with guests.

''But when the king came in to look at the guests, he saw there a man who had no wedding garment; and he said to him, 'Friend, how did you get in here without a wedding garment?' And he was speechless. Then the king said to the attendants, 'Bind him hand and foot, and cast him into the outer darkness; there men will weep and gnash their teeth.' For many are called, but few are chosen.''

THE SOWER

Matthew 13:1–9, 18–23

That same day Jesus went out of the house and sat beside the sea. And great crowds gathered about him, so that he got into a boat and sat there; and the whole crowd stood on the beach. And he told them many things in parables, saying: ''A sower went out to sow. And as he sowed, some seeds fell along the path, and the birds came and devoured them. Other seeds fell on rocky ground, where they had not much soil, and immediately they sprang up, since they had no depth of soil, but when the sun rose they were scorched; and since they had no root they withered away. Other seeds fell upon thorns, and the thorns grew up and choked them. Other seeds fell on good soil and brought forth grain, some a hundredfold, some sixty, some thirty. He who has ears, let him hear."

"Hear then the parable of the sower. When any one hears the word of the kingdom and does not understand it, the evil one comes and snatches away what is sown in his heart; this is what was sown along the path. As for what was sown on rocky ground, this is he who hears the word and immediately receives it with joy; yet he has no root in himself, but endures for a while, and when tribulation or persecution arises on account of the word, immediately he falls away. As for what was sown among thorns, this is he who hears the word, but the cares of the world and the delight in riches choke the word, and it proves unfruitful. As for what was sown on good soil, this is he who hears the word and understands it; he indeed bears fruit, and yields, in one case a hundredfold, in another sixty, and in another thirty."

THE LOST SHEEP

Luke 15:3–7

So he told them this parable: "What man of you, having a hundred sheep, if he has lost one of them, does not leave the ninety-nine in the wilderness, and go after the one which is lost, until he finds it? And when he has found it, he lays it on his shoulders, rejoicing. And when he comes home, he calls together his friends and his neighbors, saying to them, 'Rejoice with me, for I have found my sheep which was lost.' Just so, I tell you, there will be more joy in heaven over one sinner who repents than over ninety-nine righteous persons who need no repentance."

THE LOST COIN

Luke 15:8–10

"Or what woman, having ten silver coins, if she loses one coin, does not light a lamp and sweep the house and seek diligently until she finds it? And when she has found it, she calls together her friends and neighbors, saying, 'Rejoice with me, for I have found the coin which I had lost.' Just so, I tell you, there is joy before the angels of God over one sinner who repents."

THE PRODICAL SON

Luke 15:11–32

And he said, "There was a man who had two sons; and the younger of them said to his father, 'Father, give me the share of property that falls to me.' And he divided his living between them. Not many days later, the younger son gathered all he had and took his journey into a far country, and there he squandered his property in loose living. And when he had spent everything, a great famine arose in that country, and he began to be in want. So he went and joined himself to one of the citizens of that country, who sent him into his fields to feed swine. And he would gladly have fed on the pods that the swine ate; and no one gave him anything. But when he came to himself he said, 'How many of my father's hired servants have bread enough and to spare, but I perish here with hunger! I will arise and go to my father, and I will say to him, "Father, I have sinned against heaven and before you; I am no longer worthy to be called your son; treat me as one of your hired servants.'" And he arose and came to his father. But while he was yet at a distance, his father saw him and had compassion, and ran and embraced him and kissed him. And the son said to him, 'Father, I have sinned against heaven and before you; I am no longer worthy to be called your son.' But the father said to his servants, 'Bring quickly the best robe, and put it on him; and put a ring on his hand, and shoes on his feet; and bring the fatted calf and kill it, and let us eat and make merry; for this my son was dead, and is alive again; he was lost, and is found.' And they began to make merry.

"Now his elder son was in the field; and as he came and drew near to the house, he heard music and dancing. And he called one of the servants and asked what this meant. And he said to him. 'Your brother has come, and your father has killed the fatted calf, because he has received him safe and sound.' But he was angry and refused to go in. His father came out and entreated him, but he answered his father, 'Lo, these many years I have served you, and I never disobeyed your command; yet you never gave me a kid, that I might make merry with my friends. But when this son of yours came, who has devoured your living with harlots, you killed for him the fatted calf!' And he said to him, 'Son, you are always with me, and all that is mine is yours. It was fitting to make merry and be glad, for this your brother was dead, and is alive; he was lost, and is found.' "

THE RICH MAN AND LAZARUS

Luke 16:19–31

"There was a rich man, who was clothed in purple and fine linen and who feasted sumptuously every day. And at his gate lay a poor man named Lazarus, full of sores, who desired to be fed with what fell from the rich man's table; moreover the dogs came and licked his sores. The poor man died and was carried by the angels to Abraham's bosom. The rich man also died and was buried; and in Hades, being in torment, he lifted up his eyes, and saw Abraham far off and Lazarus in his bosom. And he called out, 'Father Abraham, have mercy upon me, and send Lazarus to dip the end of his finger in water and cool my tongue; for I am in anguish in this flame.' But Abraham said, 'Son, remember that you in your lifetime received your good things, and Lazarus in like manner evil things; but now he is comforted here, and you are in anguish. And besides all this, between us and you a great chasm has been fixed, in order that those who would pass from here to you may not be able, and none may cross from there to us.' And he said, 'Then I beg you, father, to send him to my father's house, for I have five brothers, so that he may warn them, lest they also come into this place of torment.' But Abraham said, 'They have Moses and the prophets; let them hear them.' And he said, 'No, father Abraham; but if some one goes to them from the dead, they will repent.' He said to him, 'If they do not hear Moses and the prophets, neither will they be convinced if some one should rise from the dead.' "

THE POUNDS

Luke 19:11–27

As they heard these things, he proceeded to tell a parable, because he was near to Jerusalem, and because they supposed that the kingdom of God was to appear immediately. He said therefore, "A nobleman went into a far country to receive kingly power and then return. Calling ten of his servants, he gave them ten pounds, and said to them, 'Trade with these till I come.' But his citizens hated him and sent an embassy after him, saying, 'We do not want this man to reign over us.' When he returned, having received the kingly power, he commanded these servants, to whom he had given the money, to be called to him, that he might know what they had gained by trading. The first came before him, saying, 'Lord, your pound has made ten pounds more.' And he said to him, 'Well done, good servant! Because you have been faithful in a very little, you shall have authority over ten cities.' And the second came, saying, 'Lord, your pound has made five pounds.' And he said to him, 'And you are to be over five cities.' Then another came, saying, 'Lord, here is your pound, which I kept laid away in a napkin; for I was afraid of you, because you are a severe man; you take up what you did not lay down, and reap what you did not sow.' He said to him, 'I will condemn you out of your own mouth, you wicked servant! You knew that I was a severe man, taking up what I did not lay down and reaping what I did not sow? Why then did you not put my money into the bank, and at my coming I should have collected it with interest?' And he said to those who stood by, 'Take the pound from him, and give it to him who has the ten pounds.' (And they said to him, 'Lord, he has ten pounds!') 'I tell you, that to every one who has will more be given; but from him who has not, even what he has will be taken away. But as for these enemies of mine, who did not want me to reign over them, bring them here and slay them before me.' ''

THE GARMENT AND THE BOTTLE

Luke 5:33-39

And they said to him, ''The disciples of John fast often and offer prayers, and so do the disciples of the Pharisees, but yours eat and drink.'' And Jesus said to them, ''Can you make wedding guests fast while the bridegroom is with them? The days will come, when the bridegroom is taken away from them, and then they will fast in those days.'' He told them a parable also: ''No one tears a piece from a new garment and puts it upon an old garment; if he does, he will tear the new, and the piece from the new will not match the old. And no one puts new wine into old wineskins; if he does, the new wine will burst the skins and it will be spilled, and the skins will be destroyed. But new wine must be put into fresh wineskins. And no one after drinking old wine desires new; for he says, 'The old is good.' ''

LABORERS IN THE VINEYARD

Matthew 20:1–16

''For the kingdom of heaven is like a householder who went out early in the morning to hire laborers for his vineyard. After agreeing with the laborers for a denarius a day, he sent them into his_vineyard. And going out about the third hour he saw others standing idle in the market place; and to them he said, 'You go into the vineyard too, and whatever is right I will give you.' So they went. Going out again about the sixth hour and the ninth hour, he did the same. And about the eleventh hour he went out and found others standing; and he said to them, 'Why do you stand there idle all day?' They said to him, 'Because no one has hired us.' He said to them, 'You go into the vineyard too.' And when evening came, the owner of the vineyard said to his steward, 'Call the laborers and pay them their wages, beginning with the last, up to the first.' And when those hired about the eleventh hour came, each of them received a denarius. Now when the first came, they thought they would receive more; but each of them also received a denarius. And on receiving it they grumbled at the householder, saying, 'These last worked only one hour, and you have made them equal to us who have borne the burden of the day and the scorching heat.' But he replied to one of them, 'Friend, I am doing you no wrong; did you not agree with me for a denarius? Take what belongs to you, and go; I choose to give to this last as I give to you. Am I not allowed to do what I choose with what belongs to me? Or do you begrudge my generosity? So the last will be first, and the first last.'"

THE FIG TREE

Matthew 24:32–51

"From the fig tree learn its lesson: as soon as its branch becomes tender and puts forth its leaves, you know that summer is near. So also, when you see all these things, you know that he is near, at the very gates. Truly, I say to you, this generation will not pass away till all these things take place. Heaven and earth will pass away, but my words will not pass away.

"But of that day and hour no one knows, not even the angels of heaven, nor the Son, but the Father only. As were the days of Noah, so will be the coming of the Son of man. For as in those days before the flood they were eating and drinking, marrying and giving in marriage, until the day when Noah entered the ark, and they did not know until the flood came and swept them all away, so will be the coming of the Son of man. Then two men will be in the field; one is taken and one is left. Two women will be grinding at the mill; one is taken and one is left.

Watch therefore, for you do not know on what day your Lord is coming. But know this, that if the householder had known in what part of the night the thief was coming, he would have watched and would not have let his house be broken into. Therefore you also must be ready; for the Son of man is coming at an hour you do not expect.

"Who then is the faithful and wise servant, whom his master has set over his household, to give them their food at the proper time? Blessed is that servant whom his master when he comes will find so doing. Truly, I say to you, he will set him over all his possessions. But if that wicked servant says to himself, 'My master is delayed,' and begins to beat his fellow servants, and eats and drinks with the drunken, the master of that servant will come on a day when he does not expect him and at an hour he does not know, and will punish him, and put him with the hypocrites; there men will weep and gnash their teeth."

WISDOM
LITERATURE

WISDOM LITERATURE is the counterpart of modern philosophy and science. But it is not philosophical in the technical sense of the word. The writers were not concerned with the central problem of the universe, but, rather, with the particular problems of practical life. In the mind of the writer there was no conflict between science and religion, because to him all knowledge had its source in God. Reason and revelation were not mutually opposed to him. His writings dealt with the results of observation of human life.

Wisdom writers began with the assumption that the law is the way that leads to God. They accepted these laws and customs as they found them, and they examined man's life to draw practical conclusions as to what is good and what is bad and why one goal should be pursued and the other avoided. Practical ethics, then, became the writer's principal field of work. His purpose was to understand God's works and ways and to turn one's knowledge of them to practical account. Reason and conscience were as important to the wisdom writer as inspiration.

Wisdom literature concerns itself with everything. It has specific observations or precepts in matters of the administration of the law, the training of the family, the ordering of the household, industry and management, honesty, sobriety, public policy, friendship, the problem of suffering, the question of whether life is worth while, and many other subjects. It gives good common-sense advice. Although wisdom literature is religious in spirit, it deals largely with secular subjects. The ethical ideas are not stated as demands but as maxims.

The primary sources of Bible wisdom literature are the books of Job, Proverbs, Ecclesiastes, Song of Solomon, and Lamentations. Two writers in particular are distinguished in this area, David and Solomon.

THE RIDDLE

The simplest form of wisdom literature is the riddle. It is simply a difficult question to be interpreted. The most notable of Bible riddles is Samson's riddle in Judges.

Judges 14:1–20

Samson went down to Timnah, and at Timnah he saw one of the daughters of the Philistines. Then he came up, and told his father and mother, "I saw one of the daughters of the Philistines at Timnah; now get her for me as my wife." But his father and mother said to him, "Is there not a woman among the daughters of your kinsmen, or among all our people, that you must go to take a wife from the uncircumcised Philistines?" But Samson said to his father, "Get her for me; for she pleases me well."

His father and mother did not know that it was from the Lord; for he was seeking an occasion against the Philistines. At that time the Philistines had dominion over Israel.

Then Samson went down with his father and mother to Timnah. And behold, a young lion roared against him; and the Spirit of the Lord came mightily upon him, and he tore the lion asunder as one tears a kid; and he had nothing in his hand. But he did not tell his father or his mother what he had done. Then he went down and talked with the woman; and she pleased Samson well. And after a while he returned to take her; and he turned aside to see the carcass of the lion, and behold, there was a swarm of bees in the body of the lion, and honey. He scraped it out into his hands, and went on, eating as he went; and he came to his father and mother, and gave some to them, and they ate. But he did not tell them that he had taken the honey from the carcass of the lion.

And his father went down to the woman, and Samson made a feast there; for so the young men used to do. And when the people saw him, they brought thirty companions to be with him. And Samson said to them, "Let me now put a riddle to you; if you can tell me what it is, within the seven days of the feast, and find it out, then I will give you thirty linen garments and thirty festal garments; but if you cannot tell me what it is, then you

shall give me thirty linen garments and thirty festal garments."
And they said to him, "Put your riddle, that we may hear it." And
he said to them,

> "Out of the eater came something to eat.
> Out of the strong came something sweet."

And they could not in three days tell what the riddle was.

On the fourth day they said to Samson's wife, "Entice your
husband to tell us what the riddle is, lest we burn you and your
father's house with fire. Have you invited us here to impoverish
us?" And Samson's wife wept before him, and said, "You only
hate me, you do not love me; you have put a riddle to my countrymen, and you have not told me what it is." And he said to her,
"Behold, I have not told my father nor my mother, and shall I
tell you?" She wept before him the seven days that their feast
lasted; and on the seventh day he told her, because she pressed
him hard. Then she told the riddle to her countrymen. And the
men of the city said to him on the seventh day before the sun went
down,

> "What is sweeter than honey?
> What is stronger than a lion?"

And he said to them,

> "If you had not plowed with my heifer,
> you would not have found out my riddle."

And the Spirit of the Lord came mightily upon him, and he went
down to Ashkelon and killed thirty men of the town, and took
their spoil and gave the festal garments to those who had told
the riddle. In hot anger he went back to his father's house. And
Samson's wife was given to his companion, who had been his
best man.

THE UNIT PROVERB

The book of Proverbs is considered the earliest form of Hebrew
wisdom literature. It is a practical manual for the guidance of life,
a prescription for living safely and sanely here on earth, and a code
of ethics.

Collections of aphorisms, like Proverbs, are highly prized by Orientals, but are not common among Western writers. However, they are comparable to Benjamin Franklin's *Poor Richard's Almanac.* Francis Bacon has a strong proverbial element in his essays, as does William Penn's *Some Fruits of Solitude.* And Cowper's poem "Wisdom" is a paraphrase and expansion of Proverbs 8:22–31.

The whole book of Proverbs is largely a mass of unit proverbs, without any attempt to arrange them. The unit proverb is usually a couplet: a first line that contains all the philosophical reflections required, and a second line that is supplementary and fills out the dimensions. The importance of the unit proverb is that it is the germ of the foundation of several forms of poetry (the epigram and the sonnet) and prose (the maxim and the essay).

THE COUPLET

The following couplets are excerpts from the book of Proverbs.

He that is slow to anger is better than the mighty,
And he that ruleth his spirit than he that taketh a city.

The Lord hath made everything for its own end;
Yea, even the wicked for the day of evil.

A rebuke entereth deeper into one that hath understanding
Than a hundred stripes into a fool.

Seven days are the days of mourning for the dead.
But for a fool and an ungodly man, all the days of his life.

Everyone that is proud in heart is an abomination to the Lord.
Though hand join in hand, he shall not be unpunished.

The crucible is for silver, and the furnace for gold,
And a man is judged by his praise.

THE EPIGRAM

The following epigrams illustrate how the couplet is extended into longer and more detailed forms of poetry. Notice how two of the lines contain the germ thought and the rest the expansion.

Proverbs 24:13–14

My son, eat honey, for it is good,
and the drippings of the honeycomb are sweet to your taste.
    Know that wisdom is such to your soul;
      if you find it, there will be a future,
      and your hope will not be cut off.

Proverbs 24:15–16

Lie not in wait as a wicked man against the dwelling of the
          righteous;
    do not violence to his home;
for a righteous man falls seven times, and rises again;
    but the wicked are overthrown by calamity.

Proverbs 1:8–9

Hear, my son, your father's instructions,
    and reject not your mother's teaching;
for they are a fair garland for your head,
    and pendants for your neck.

Proverbs 23:19–21

Hear, my son, and be wise,
and direct your mind in the way.
Be not among winebibbers,
or among gluttonous eaters of meat;
    for the drunkard and the glutton will come to poverty,
    and drowsiness will clothe a man with rags.

Proverbs 23:6–8

Do not eat the bread of a man who is stingy;
do not desire his delicacies;
    for he is like one who is inwardly reckoning.
    "Eat and drink!" he says to you;
    but his heart is not with you.
    You will vomit up the morsels which you have eaten,
    and waste your pleasant words.

Proverbs 6:20–35

My son, keep your father's commandment,
and forsake not your mother's teaching.
Bind them upon your heart always;
tie them about your neck.
When you walk, they will lead you;
when you lie down, they will watch over you;
and when you wake, they will talk with you.
    For the commandment is a lamp and the teaching a light,
    and the reproofs of discipline are the way of life,
    to preserve you from the evil woman,
    from the smooth tongue of the adventuress.
Do not desire her beauty in your heart,
and do not let her capture you with her eyelashes;
    for a harlot may be hired for a loaf of bread,
    but an adulteress stalks a man's very life.
Can a man carry fire in his bosom
and his clothes not be burned?
Or can one walk upon hot coals
and his feet not be scorched?
    So is he who goes in to his neighbor's wife;
    none who touches her will go unpunished.
Do not men despise a thief if he steals
to satisfy his appetite when he is hungry?
    And if he is caught, he will pay sevenfold;
    he will give all the goods of his house.
He who commits adultery has no sense;
he who does it destroys himself.
    Wounds and dishonor will he get,
    and his disgrace will not be wiped away.
    For jealousy makes a man furious,
    and he will not spare when he takes revenge.
    He will accept no compensation,
    nor be appeased though you multiply gifts.

In the following selection notice that the basic form appears to
be a listing, and the themes change frequently.

Proverbs 10:1–12

A wise son makes a glad father,
    but a foolish son is a sorrow to his mother.

Treasures gained by wickedness do not profit,
    but righteousness delivers from death.
The Lord does not let the righteous go hungry,
    but he thwarts the craving of the wicked.
A slack hand causes poverty,
    but the hand of the diligent makes rich.
A son who gathers in summer is prudent,
    but a son who sleeps in harvest brings shame.
Blessings are in the head of the righteous,
    but the mouth of the wicked conceals violence.
The memory of the righteous is a blessing,
    but the name of the wicked will rot.
The wise of heart will heed commandments,
    but a prating fool will come to ruin.
He who walks in integrity walks securely,
    but he who perverts his ways will be found out.
He who winks the eye causes trouble,
    but he who boldly reproves makes peace.
The mouth of the righteous is a fountain of life,
    but the mouth of the wicked conceals violence.
Hatred stirs up strife,
    but love covers all offenses.

Notice how the following passage in Matthew seems very much like the book of Proverbs in structure.

Matthew 5:1–10

Seeing the crowds, he went up on the mountain, and when he sat down his disciples came to him. And he opened his mouth and taught them, saying:

"Blessed are the poor in spirit,
    for theirs is the kingdom of heaven.
"Blessed are those who mourn,
    for they shall be comforted.
"Blessed are the meek,
    for they shall inherit the earth.
"Blessed are those who hunger and thirst for righteousness,
    for they shall be satisfied.
"Blessed are the merciful,
    for they shall obtain mercy.

"Blessed are the pure in heart,
    for they shall see God.
"Blessed are the peacemakers,
    for they shall be called sons of God.
"Blessed are those who are persecuted for righteousness' sake,
    for theirs is the kingdom of heaven."

BIBLE SONNETS

Bible sonnets, also extensions of the couplet, are not fixed by numbers of lines but by parallelism of rhythm or interpretation. Bible sonnets are made up of miscellaneous thoughts gathered around a common theme.

Proverbs 30:24–28

Four things on earth are small,
    but they are exceedingly wise:
the ants are a people not strong,
    yet they provide their food in the summer;
the badgers are people not mighty,
    yet they make their homes in the rocks;
the locusts have no king,
    yet all of them march in rank;
the lizard you can take in your hands,
    yet it is in kings' palaces.

Proverbs 30:18–19

Three things are too wonderful for me;
four I do not understand:
    the way of an eagle in the sky,
    the way of a serpent on a rock,
    the way of a ship on the high seas,
    and the way of a man with a maiden.

Proverbs 30:7–9

Two things I ask of thee;
deny them not to me before I die:
    Remove from me falsehood and lying;
        give me neither poverty nor riches;
            feed me with food that is needful for me,
            lest I be full and deny thee, and say, "Who is
            the Lord?"

or lest I be poor, and steal,
and profane the name of my God.

Proverbs 6:6–11

Go to the ant, O sluggard;
consider her ways, and be wise.
    Without having any chief, officer or ruler,
        she prepares her food in summer,
        and gathers her sustenance in harvest.
How long will you lie there, O sluggard?
When will you arise from your sleep?
    A little sleep, a little slumber,
    a little folding of the hands to rest,
        and poverty will come upon you like a vagabond,
        and want like an armed man.

Notice in the following excerpt that the commandments are on the left and the rewards on the right.

Proverbs 3:1–10

My son, do not forget my teaching,
but let your heart keep my commandments;
    for length of days and years of life
    and abundant welfare will they give you.
Let not loyalty and faithfulness forsake you;
bind them about your neck,
write them on the table of your heart.
    So you will find favor and good repute
    in the sight of God and man.
Trust in the Lord with all your heart,
and do not rely on your own insight.
In all your ways acknowledge him,
    and he will make straight your paths.
Be not wise in your own eyes;
fear the Lord and turn away from evil.
    It will be healing to your flesh
    and refreshment to your bones.
Honor the Lord with your substance
and with the first fruits of all your produce;
    then your barns will be filled with plenty,
    and your vats will be bursting with wine.

Ecclesiastes 12:1–7

Remember also your Creator in the days of your youth,

before the evil days come,
and the years draw nigh,
when you will say, "I have no pleasure in them";

before the sun
and the light
and the moon
and the stars
are darkened
and the clouds return after the rain;

in the day when the keepers of the house tremble,
and the strong men are bent,
and the grinders cease because they are few,
and those that look through the windows are dimmed,
and the doors on the street are shut;

when the sound of the grinding is low,
and one rises up at the voice of a bird,
and all the daughters of song are brought low;

they are afraid also of what is high,
and terrors are in the way;
the almond tree blossoms,
the grasshopper drags itself along
and desire fails

because man goes to his eternal home,
and the mourners go about the streets;

before the silver cord is snapped,
or the golden bowl is broken,
or the pitcher is broken at the fountain,
or the wheel broken at the cistern,

and the dust returns to the earth
as it was,
and the spirit returns to God
who gave it.

The book of Amos is the classic example of structural beauty in the combination of poetry and prose on the same theme.

Amos 1:3–8, 11–15

1

Thus says the Lord:

"For three transgressions of Damascus,
and for four,
  I will not revoke the punishment;

because they have threshed Gilead with threshing sledges of iron.

So I will send a fire upon the house of Hazael,
and it shall devour the strongholds of Ben-hadad.

I will break the bar of Damascus, and cut off the inhabitants from the Valley of Aven, and him that holds the scepter from Beth-eden; and the people of Syria shall go into exile to Kir," says the Lord.

2

Thus says the Lord:

"For three transgressions of Gaza,
and for four,
  I will not revoke the punishment;

because they carried into exile a whole people to deliver them up to Edom.

So I will send a fire upon the wall of Gaza,
and it shall devour her strongholds.

I will cut off the inhabitants from Ashdod, and him that holds the scepter from Ashkelon; I will turn my hand against Ekron; and the remnant of the Philistines shall perish," says the Lord God.

3

Thus says the Lord:

"For three transgressions of Edom,
and for four,
  I will not revoke the punishment;

286 / THE BIBLE AS LITERATURE

because he pursued his brother with the sword, and cast off all
pity, and his anger tore perpetually, and he kept his wrath for ever.

> So I will send a fire upon Teman,
> and it shall devour the strongholds of Bozrah."

4

Thus says the Lord:

> "For three transgressions of the Ammonites,
> and for four,
>   I will not revoke the punishment;

because they have ripped up women with child in Gilead, that
they might enlarge their border.

> So I will kindle a fire in the wall of Rabbah,
> and it shall devour her strongholds,

with shouting in the day of battle, with tempest in the day of the
whirlwind; and their king shall go into exile, he and his princess
together," says the Lord.

THE MAXIM

Notice that the couplet is still distinguishable in the maxim, the
prose counterpart of the poetic epigram. The germ proverb is merely
merged into the prose expansion.

Ecclesiastes 4:9–12

Two are better than one, because they have a good reward for
their toil. For if they fall, one will lift up his fellow; but woe to him
who is alone when he falls and has not another to lift him up.
Again, if two lie together, they are warm; but how can one be
warm alone? And though a man might prevail against one who is
alone, two will withstand him. A threefold cord is not quickly
broken.

Ecclesiastes 6:1–6

There is an evil which I have seen under the sun, and it lies
heavy upon men: a man to whom God gives wealth, possessions,
and honor, so that he lacks nothing of all that he desires, yet

God does not give him power to enjoy them, but a stranger enjoys them; this is vanity; it is a sore affliction. If a man begets a hundred children, and lives many years, so that the days of his years are many, but he does not enjoy life's good things, and also has no burial, I say that an untimely birth is better off than he. For it comes into vanity and goes into darkness, and in darkness its name is covered; moreover, it has not seen the sun or known anything; yet it finds rest rather than he. Even though he should live a thousand years twice told, yet enjoy no good—do not all go to the one place?

Ecclesiastes 2:18–23

I hated all my toil in which I had toiled under the sun, seeing that I must leave it to the man who will come after me; and who knows whether he will be a wise man or a fool? Yet he will be master of all for which I toiled and used my wisdom under the sun. This also is vanity. So I turned about and gave my heart up to despair over all the toil of my labors under the sun, because sometimes a man who has toiled with wisdom and knowledge and skill must leave all to be enjoyed by a man who did not toil for it. This also is vanity and a great evil. What has a man from all the toil and strain with which he toils beneath the sun? For all his days are full of pain, and his work is a vexation; even in the night his mind does not rest. This also is vanity.

Ecclesiastes 8:10–13

Then I saw the wicked buried; they used to go in and out of the holy place, and were praised in the city where they had done such things. This also is vanity. Because sentence against an evil deed is not executed speedily, the heart of the sons of men is fully set to do evil. Though a sinner does evil a hundred times and prolongs his life, yet I know that it will be well with those who fear God, because they fear before him; but it will not be well with the wicked, neither will he prolong his days like a shadow, because he does not fear before God.

THE ESSAY

The essay is a natural extension of the maxim. It is considered a most important form in wisdom literature.

Critics for many years sought to find essays in the Bible that demonstrated all the common characteristics of the modern essay with its logically arranged thoughts based on the philosophical method. The Hebrew writer, however, attempted to give a picture of his mind as he reflected upon some subject that interested him, rather than present a formal treatise. He treated his subject in the manner of a man who gives us the results of his own individual living and thinking. The Hebrew essay, then, is a series of notes on one theme, possessing some of the charm and intimacy of a personal diary. It is as if the reader were privileged to listen in while a cultivated man, worth listening to, thinks aloud. His thoughts are often miscellaneous but are collected around a common theme. The thoughts often run together without a break.

Most Bible essays avoid symbolism in the presentation of material, similar to some of Shakespeare's works, such as Scene 7, Act II of *As You Like It*, which sounds very much like a chapter in Ecclesiastes. Holmes' "The Last leaf" has the same quality. Christina Rossetti's poem "The Testimony" is full of echoes from Ecclesiastes.

In the following two examples, notice how the proverb cluster is simply a group of sayings bearing upon the general subject and that any one of the sayings could be removed without affecting the unity of the whole. Notice also that the essay retains a connectiveness of thought that prevails completely over the independence of sentences or paragraphs.

Proverbs 12:17–22

He who speaks the truth gives honest evidence,
    but a false witness utters deceit.
There is one whose rash words are like sword thrusts,
    but the tongue of the wise brings healing.
Truthful lips endure for ever,
    but a lying tongue is but for a moment.
Deceit is in the heart of those who devise evil,
    but those who plan good have joy.
No ill befalls the righteous,
    but the wicked are filled with trouble.
Lying lips are an abomination to the Lord,
    but those who act faithfully are his delight.

THE RESPONSIBILITY OF SPEECH

James 3:1–18

Let not many of you become teachers, my brethren, for you know that we who teach shall be judged with greater strictness.

For we all make many mistakes, and if any one makes no mistakes in what he says he is a perfect man, able to bridle the whole body also. If we put bits into the mouths of horses that they may obey us, we guide their whole bodies. Look at the ships also; though they are so great and are driven by strong winds, they are guided by a very small rudder wherever the will of the pilot directs. So the tongue is a little member and boasts of great things. How great a forest is set ablaze by a small fire!

And the tongue is a fire. The tongue is an unrighteous world among our members, staining the whole body, setting on fire the cycle of nature, and set on fire by hell. For every kind of beast and bird, of reptile and sea creature, can be tamed and has been tamed by humankind, but no human being can tame the tongue— a restless evil, full of deadly poison. With it we bless the Lord and Father, and with it we curse men, who are made in the likeness of God. From the same mouth come blessing and cursing. My brethren, this ought not to be so. Does a spring pour forth from the same opening fresh water and brackish? Can a fig tree, my brethren, yield olives, or a grapevine figs? No more can salt water yield fresh.

Who is wise and understanding among you? By his good life let him show his works in the meekness of wisdom. But if you have bitter jealousy and selfish ambition in your hearts, do not boast and be false to the truth. This wisdom is not such as comes down from above, but is earthly, unspiritual, devilish. For where jealousy and selfish ambition exist, there will be disorder and every vile practice. But the wisdom from above is first pure, then peaceable, gentle, open to reason, full of mercy and good fruits, without uncertainty or insincerity. And the harvest of righteousness is sown in peace by those who make peace.

The essay is most prominent in three books of the Bible: Ecclesiastes, James, and 1 John. These books are sometimes called wisdom "epistles." They are unlike the epistles of Paul in that there is no connective line of thought. They should be read as a series of independent essays.

SOLOMON'S SEARCH FOR WISDOM
Ecclesiastes 1:12–18; 2:1–26

I the Preacher have been king over Israel in Jerusalem. And I applied my mind to seek and to search out by wisdom all that is done under heaven; it is an unhappy business that God has given to the sons of men to be busy with. I have seen everything that is done under the sun; and behold, all is vanity and a striving after wind.

What is crooked cannot be made straight,
and what is lacking cannot be numbered.

I said to myself, "I have acquired great wisdom, surpassing all who were over Jerusalem before me; and my mind has had great experience of wisdom and knowledge." And I applied my mind to know wisdom and to know madness and folly. I perceived that this also is but a striving after wind.

For in much wisdom is much vexation,
and he who increases knowledge increases sorrow.

I said to myself, "Come now, I will make a test of pleasure; enjoy yourself." But behold, this also was vanity. I said of laughter, "It is mad," and of pleasure, "What use is it?" I searched with my mind how to cheer my body with wine—my mind still guiding me with wisdom—and how to lay hold on folly, till I might see what was good for the sons of men to do under heaven during the few days of their life. I made great works; I built houses and planted vineyards for myself; I made myself gardens and parks, and planted in them all kinds of fruit trees. I made myself pools from which to water the forest of growing trees. I bought male and female slaves, and had slaves who were born in my house; I had also great possessions of herds and flocks, more than any who had been before me in Jerusalem. I also gathered for myself silver and gold and the treasure of kings and provinces; I got singers, both men and women, and many concubines, man's delight.

So I became great and surpassed all who were before me in Jerusalem; also my wisdom remained with me. And whatever my eyes desired I did not keep from them; I kept my heart from no pleasure, for my heart found pleasure in all my toil, and this was my reward for all my toil. Then I considered all that my hands had done and the toil I had spent in doing it, and behold, all was vanity and a striving after wind, and there was nothing to be gained under the sun.

So I turned to consider wisdom and madness and folly; for what can the man do who comes after the king? Only what he has already done. Then I saw that wisdom excels folly as light excels darkness. The wise man has his eyes in his head, but the fool walks in darkness; and yet I perceived that one fate comes to all of them. Then I said to myself, "What befalls the fool will befall me also; why then have I been so very wise?" And I said to myself that this also is vanity. For of the wise man as of the fool there is no enduring remembrance, seeing that in the days to come all will have been long forgotten. How the wise man dies just like the fool! So I hated life, because what is done under the sun was grievous to me; for all is vanity and a striving after wind.

I hated all my toil in which I had toiled under the sun, seeing that I must leave it to the man who will come after me; and who knows whether he will be a wise man or a fool? Yet he will be master of all for which I toiled and used my wisdom under the sun. This also is vanity. So I turned about and gave my heart up to despair over all the toil of my labors under the sun, because sometimes a man who has toiled with wisdom and knowledge and skill must leave all to be enjoyed by a man who did not toil for it. This also is vanity and a great evil. What has a man from all the toil and strain with which he toils beneath the sun? For all his days are full of pain, and his work is a vexation; even in the night his mind does not rest. This also is vanity.

There is nothing better for a man than that he should eat and drink, and find enjoyment in his toil. This also, I saw, is from the hand of God; for apart from him who can eat or who can have enjoyment? For to the man who pleases him God gives wisdom and knowledge and joy; but to the sinner he gives the work of gathering and heaping, only to give to one who pleases God. This also is vanity and a striving after wind.

THE VANITY OF DESIRE

Ecclesiastes 5:10–20; 6:1–12

He who loves money will not be satisfied with money; nor he who loves wealth, with gain: this also is vanity.

When goods increase, they increase who eat them; and what gain has their owner but to see them with his eyes?

Sweet is the sleep of a laborer, whether he eats little or much; but the surfeit of the rich will not let him sleep.

There is a grievous evil which I have seen under the sun: riches were kept by their owner to his hurt, and those riches were lost in a bad venture; and he is father of a son, but he has nothing in his hand. As he came from his mother's womb he shall go again, naked as he came, and shall take nothing for his toil, which he may carry away in his hand. This also is a grievous evil: just as he came, so shall he go; and what gain has he that he toiled for the wind, and spent all his days in darkness and grief, in much vexation and sickness and resentment?

Behold, what I have seen to be good and to be fitting is to eat and drink and find enjoyment in all the toil with which one toils under the sun the few days of his life which God has given him, for this is his lot. Every man also to whom God has given wealth and possessions and power to enjoy them, and to accept his lot and find enjoyment in his toil—this is the gift of God. For he will not much remember the days of his life because God keeps him occupied with joy in his heart.

There is an evil which I have seen under the sun, and it lies heavy upon men: a man to whom God gives wealth, possessions, and honor, so that he lacks nothing of all that he desires, yet God does not give him power to enjoy them, but a stranger enjoys them; this is vanity; it is a sore affliction. If a man begets a hundred children, and lives many years, so that the days of his years are many, but he does not enjoy life's good things, and also has no burial, I say that an untimely birth is better off than he. For it comes into vanity and goes into darkness, and in darkness its name is covered; moreover it has not seen the sun or known anything; yet it finds rest rather than he. Even though he should live a thousand years twice told, yet enjoy no good—do not all go to the one place?

All the toil of man is for his mouth, yet his appetite is not satisfied. For what advantage has the wise man over the fool? And what does the poor man have who knows how to conduct himself before the living? Better is the sight of the eyes than the wandering of desire; this also is vanity and a striving after wind.

Whatever has come to be has already been named, and it is known what man is, and that he is not able to dispute with one stronger than he. The more words, the more vanity, and what is man the better? For who knows what is good for man while he lives the few days of his vain life, which he passes like a shadow? For who can tell man what will be after him under the sun?

SOURCES OF EVIL AND GOOD

James 1:12–27

Blessed is the man who endures trial, for when he has stood the test he will receive the crown of life which God has promised to those who love him. Let no one say when he is tempted, "I am tempted by God"; for God cannot be tempted with evil and he himself tempts no one; but each person is tempted when he is lured and enticed by his own desire. Then desire when it has conceived gives birth to sin; and sin when it is full-grown brings forth death.

Do not be deceived, my beloved brethren. Every good endowment and every perfect gift is from above, coming down from the Father of lights with whom there is no variation or shadow due to change. Of his own will he brought us forth by the word of truth that we should be a kind of first fruits of his creatures.

Know this, my beloved brethren. Let every man be quick to hear, slow to speak, slow to anger, for the anger of man does not work the righteousness of God. Therefore put away all filthiness and rank growth of wickedness and receive with meekness the implanted word, which is able to save your souls.

But be doers of the word, and not hearers only, deceiving yourselves. For if any one is a hearer of the word and not a doer, he is like a man who observes his natural face in a mirror; for he observes himself and goes away and at once forgets what he was like. But he who looks into the perfect law, the law of liberty, and perseveres, being no hearer that forgets but a doer that acts, he shall be blessed in his doing.

If any one thinks he is religious, and does not bridle his tongue but deceives his heart, this man's religion is vain. Religion that is pure and undefiled before God and the Father is this: to visit orphans and widows in their affliction, and to keep oneself unstained from the world.

ON RESPECT OF PERSONS

James 2:1–13

My brethren, show no partiality as you hold the faith of our Lord Jesus Christ, the Lord of glory. For if a man with gold rings and in fine clothing comes into your assembly, and a poor man in shabby clothing also comes in, and you pay attention to the one who wears the fine clothing and say, "Have a seat here, please," while you say to the poor man, "Stand there," or, "Sit at my feet," have you not made distinctions among yourselves, and become judges with evil thoughts? Listen, my beloved brethren. Has not God chosen those who are poor in the world to be rich in faith and heirs of the kingdom which he has promised to those who love him? But you have dishonored the poor man. Is it not the rich who oppress you, is it not they who drag you into court? Is it not they who blaspheme that honorable name by which you are called?

If you really fulfil the royal law, according to the scripture, "You shall love your neighbor as yourself," you do well. But if you show partiality you commit sin, and are convicted by the law as transgressors. For whoever keeps the whole law but fails in one point has become guilty of all of it. For he who said, "Do not commit adultery," said also, "Do not kill." If you do not commit adultery but do kill, you have become a transgressor of the law. So speak and so act as those who are to be judged under the law of liberty. For judgment is without mercy to one who has shown no mercy; yet mercy triumphs over judgment.

CLEANSING FROM SIN

1 John 1:5–10; 2:1–2

This is the message we have heard from him and proclaim to you, that God is light and in him is no darkness at all. If we say we have fellowship with him while we walk in darkness, we lie and do not live according to the truth; but if we walk in the light, as he is in the light, we have fellowship with one another, and the blood of Jesus his Son cleanses us from all sin. If we say we have no sin, we deceive ourselves, and the truth is not in us. If we confess our sins, he is faithful and just, and will forgive our sins and cleanse us from all unrighteousness. If we say we have not sinned, we make him a liar, and his word is not in us.

My little children, I am writing this to you so that you may not sin; but if any one does sin, we have an advocate with the Father, Jesus Christ the righteous; and he is the expiation for our sins, and not for ours only but also for the sins of the whole world.

OLD AND NEW COMMANDMENTS

1 John 2:7–11

Beloved, I am writing you no new commandment, but an old commandment which you had from the beginning; the old commandment is the word which you have heard. Yet I am writing you a new commandment, which is true in him and in you, because the darkness is passing away and the true light is already shining. He who says he is in the light and hates his brother is in the darkness still. He who loves his brother abides in the light, and in it there is no cause for stumbling. But he who hates his brother is in the darkness and walks in the darkness, and does not know where he is going, because the darkness has blinded his eyes.

LOVE OF THE WORLD

1 John 2:15–17

Do not love the world or the things in the world. If any one loves the world, love for the Father is not in him. For all that is in the world, the lust of the flesh and the lust of the eyes and the pride of life, is not of the Father but is of the world. And the world passes away, and the lust of it; but he who does the will of God abides for ever.

LOVE OF THE BRETHREN

1 John 3:13–23

Do not wonder, brethren, that the world hates you. We know that we have passed out of death into life, because we love the brethren. He who does not love remains in death. Any one who hates his brother is a murderer, and you know that no murderer has eternal life abiding in him. By this we know love, that he laid down his life for us; and we ought to lay down our lives for the brethren. But if any one has the world's goods and sees his brother in need, yet closes his heart against him, how does God's love abide in him? Little children, let us not love in word or speech but in deed and in truth.

By this we shall know that we are of the truth, and reassure our hearts before him whenever our hearts condemn us; for God is greater than our hearts, and he knows everything. Beloved, if our hearts do not condemn us, we have confidence before God; and we receive from him whatever we ask, because we keep his commandments and do what pleases him. And this is his commandment, that we should believe in the name of his Son Jesus Christ and love one another, just as he has commanded us.

LOVE

1 John 4:7–21

Beloved, let us love one another; for love is of God, and he who loves is born of God and knows God. He who does not love does not know God; for God is love. In this the love of God was made manifest among us, that God sent his only Son into the world, so that we might live through him. In this is love, not that we loved God but that he loved us and sent his Son to be the expiation for our sins. Beloved, if God so loved us, we also ought to love one another. No man has ever seen God; if we love one another, God abides in us and his love is perfected in us.

By this we know that we abide in him and he in us, because he has given us of his own Spirit. And we have seen and testify that the Father has sent his Son as the Savior of the world. Whoever confesses that Jesus is the Son of God, God abides in him, and he in God. So we know and believe the love God has for us. God is love, and he who abides in love abides in God, and God abides in him. In this is love perfected with us, that we may have confidence for the day of judgment, because as he is so are we in this world. There is no fear in love, but perfect love casts out fear. For fear has to do with punishment, and he who fears is not perfected in love. We love, because he first loved us. If any one says, "I love God," and hates his brother, he is a liar; for he who does not love his brother whom he has seen, cannot love God whom he has not seen. And this commandment we have from him, that he who loves God should love his brother also.

FAITH

1 John 5:1–5

Every one who believes that Jesus is the Christ is a child of God, and every one who loves the parent loves the child. By this we know that we love the children of God, when we love God and obey his commandments. For this is the love of God, that we keep his commandments. And his commandments are not burdensome. For whatever is born of God overcomes the world; and this is the victory that overcomes the world, our faith. Who is it that overcomes the world but he who believes that Jesus is the Son of God?

THE BOOK OF JOB

Some people would call the book of Job the greatest piece of literature in the Bible and rank it with the best of the world classics. The reason for this praise is twofold: its profound thought and its elevated style. Some of the passages rise to the heights of the very finest poetry, and its dramatic setting is skillfully arranged. It is the writing in the Bible nearest to a drama.

The note it strikes is that of the universal, age-long problem, the meaning of suffering. Along with the problem of suffering the theme of disinterested love is ever-recurring. These are the vital problems, an issue in every home that is started, in every friendship pledged, in every public position accepted, and in every national relationship. In literature these problems lie at the heart of almost every good novel or play, and furnish the fascination for many good histories or biographies.

The book has influenced a number of writers. H. G. Wells' *The Undying Fire* translates the book of Job into the terms of modern life, and Wells suggests a solution to Job's problem. Milton modeled *Paradise Regained* after the book of Job. "In Memoriam" compares favorably to Job's progress through moods of doubt, despair, anguished questioning, faith, hope, and fortitude. Robert Browning's "Rabbi Ben Ezra" and "Saul" discuss the ministry of pain. Josiah Royce's *Studies in Good and Evil* and John Fiske's *Through Nature to God* also have much to say about the problem.

The structure of the book is not difficult. It is primarily a series of speeches between Job, his friends, and God. In order to facilitate understanding, introductory comments about structure and content precede each portion of text. The speeches have been reduced and certain portions of the text eliminated because of the sheer volume of the book.

Prologue

Chapters 1 and 2 present background data simply and directly with little detail. There are two scenes in heaven and two scenes on earth. There is no attempt to describe God or to overwhelm the reader with the glories of His court or to contrast God and satan. The object of the prologue is to tell the reader what Job himself does not know, the reason for his suffering.

Job 1:1–22; 2:1–13

There was a man in the land of Uz, whose name was Job; and that man was blameless and upright, one who feared God, and turned away from evil. There were born to him seven sons and three daughters. He had seven thousand sheep, three thousand camels, five hundred yoke of oxen, and five hundred she-asses, and very many servants; so that this man was the greatest of all the people of the east. His sons used to go and hold a feast in the house of each on his day; and they would send and invite their three sisters to eat and drink with them. And when the days of the feast had run their course, Job would send and sanctify them, and he would rise early in the morning and offer burnt offerings according to the number of them all; for Job said, "It may be that my sons have sinned, and cursed God in their hearts." Thus Job did continually.

Now there was a day when the sons of God came to present themselves before the Lord, and Satan also came among them. The Lord said to Satan, "Whence have you come?" Satan answered the Lord, "From going to and fro on the earth, and from walking up and down on it." And the Lord said to Satan, "Have you considered my servant Job, that there is none like him on the earth, a blameless and upright man, who fears God and turns away from evil?" Then Satan answered the Lord, "Does Job fear God for nought? Hast thou not put a hedge about him and his house and all that he has, on every side? Thou hast blessed the work of his hands, and his possessions have increased in the land. But put forth thy hand now, and touch all that he has, and he will curse thee to thy face." And the Lord said to Satan. "Behold, all that he has is in your power; only upon himself do not put forth your hand." So Satan went forth from the presence of the Lord.

Now there was a day when his sons and daughters were eating and drinking wine in their eldest brother's house; and there came a messenger to Job, and said, "The oxen were plowing and the asses feeding beside them; and the Sabeans fell upon them and took them, and slew the servants with the edge of the sword; and I alone have escaped to tell you." While he was yet speaking, there came another, and said, "The fire of God fell from heaven and burned up the sheep and the servants, and consumed them; and I alone have escaped to tell you." While he was yet speaking, there came another, and said, "The Chaldeans formed three companies, and made a raid upon the camels and took them, and slew the servants with the edge of the sword; and I alone have escaped to tell you." While he was yet speaking, there came another, and said, "Your sons and daughters were eating and drinking wine in their eldest brother's house; and behold, a great wind came across the wilderness, and struck the four corners of the house, and it fell upon the young people, and they are dead; and I alone have escaped to tell you."

Then Job arose, and rent his robe, and shaved his head, and fell upon the ground, and worshipped. And he said, "Naked I came from my mother's womb, and naked shall I return; the Lord gave, and the Lord has taken away; blessed be the name of the Lord."

In all this Job did not sin or charge God with wrong.

Again there was a day when the sons of God came to present themselves before the Lord, and Satan also came among them to present himself before the Lord. And the Lord said to Satan, "Whence have you come?" Satan answered the Lord, "From going to and fro on the earth, and from walking up and down on it."

And the Lord said to Satan, "Have you considered my servant Job, that there is none like him on the earth, a blameless and upright man, who fears God and turns away from evil? He still holds fast his integrity, although you moved me against him, to destroy him without cause." Then Satan answered the Lord, "Skin for skin! All that a man has he will give for his life. But put forth thy hand now, and touch his bone and his flesh, and he will curse thee to thy face." And the Lord said to Satan, "Behold, he is in your power; only spare his life."

So Satan went forth from the presence of the Lord, and afflicted Job with loathsome sores from the sole of his foot to the crown of his head. And he took a potsherd with which to scrape himself, and sat among the ashes.

Then his wife said to him, "Do you still hold fast your integrity? Curse God, and die." But he said to her, "You speak as one of the foolish women would speak. Shall we receive good at the hand of God, and shall we not receive evil?" In all this Job did not sin with his lips.

Now when Job's three friends heard of all this evil that had come upon him, they came each from his own place, Eliphaz the Temanite, Bildad the Shuhite, and Zophar the Naamathite. They made an appointment together to come to condole with him and comfort him. And when they saw him from afar, they did not recognize him; and they raised their voices and wept; and they rent their robes and sprinkled dust upon their heads toward heaven. And they sat with him on the ground seven days and seven nights, and no one spoke a word to him, for they saw that his suffering was very great.

Job's Introductory Speech

This speech is Job's outburst developing out of his friends' attitude and is the prelude to dialogue. His friends sit in silence and do not wish to say that his sufferings show him to be a great sinner.

Job 3:1–26

After this Job opened his mouth and cursed the day of his birth. And Job said:

"Let the day perish wherein I was born,
    and the night which said,
    'A man-child is conceived.'

Let that day be darkness!
May God above not seek it,
   nor light shine upon it.
Let gloom and deep darkness claim it.
   Let clouds dwell upon it;
   let the blackness of the day terrify it.
That night—let thick darkness seize it!
   let it not rejoice among the days of the year,
   let it not come into the number of the months.
Yea, let that night be barren;
   let no joyful cry be heard in it.
Let those curse it who curse the day,
   who are skilled to rouse up Leviathan.
Let the stars of its dawn be dark;
   let it hope for light, but have none,
   nor see the eyelids of the morning;
because it did not shut the doors of my mother's womb,
   nor hide trouble from my eyes.

"Why did I not die at birth,
   come forth from the womb and expire?
Why did the knees receive me?
   Or why the breasts, that I should suck?
For then I should have lain down and been quiet;
   I should have slept; then I should have been at rest,
with kings and counselors of the earth
   who rebuilt ruins for themselves,
or with princes who had gold,
   who filled their houses with silver.
Or why was I not as a hidden untimely birth,
   as infants that never see the light?
There the wicked cease from troubling,
   and there the weary are at rest.
There the prisoners are at ease together;
   they hear not the voice of the taskmaster.
The small and the great are there,
   and the slave is free from his master.

"Why is light given to him that is in misery,
   and life to the bitter in soul,
who long for death, but it comes not,
   and dig for it more than for hid treasures;
who rejoice exceedingly,

and are glad, when they find the grave?
Why is light given to a man whose way is hid,
   whom God has hedged in?
For my sighing comes as my bread,
   and my groanings are poured out like water.
For the thing that I fear comes upon me,
   and what I dread befalls me.
I am not at ease, nor am I quiet;
   I have no rest; but trouble comes."

In Chapters 4–31 there are three cycles, composed of speeches by Job's friends and Job's answering speeches.

Eliphaz's First Speech

Eliphaz is the oldest and the most kindly of Job's three friends, yet underneath his words is the iron hand of condemnation.

Job 4:1–8; 5:1–18

Then Eliphaz the Temanite answered:

"If one ventures a word with you, will you be offended?
   Yet who can keep from speaking?
Behold, you have instructed many,
   and you have strengthened the weak hands.
Your words have upheld him who was stumbling,
   and you have made firm the feeble knees.
But now it has come to you, and you are impatient;
   it touches you and you are dismayed.
Is not your fear of God your confidence,
   and the integrity of your ways your hope?

"Think now, who that was innocent ever perished?
   Or where were the upright cut off?
As I have seen, those who plow iniquity
   and sow trouble reap the same.

"Call now; is there any one who will answer you?
To which of the holy ones will you turn?
Surely vexation kills the fool,
   and jealousy slays the simple.
I have seen the fool taking root,
   but suddenly I cursed his dwelling.

His sons are far from safety,
　　they are crushed in the gate,
　　and there is no one to deliver them.
His harvest the hungry eat,
　　and he takes it even out of thorns;
　　and the thirsty pant after his wealth.
For affliction does not come from the dust.
　　nor does trouble sprout from the ground;
but man is born to trouble
　　as the sparks fly upward.

"As for me, I would seek God,
　　and to God would I commit my cause;
who does great things and unsearchable,
　　marvelous things without number:
he gives rain upon the earth
　　and sends waters upon the fields;
he sets on high those who are lowly,
　　and those who mourn are lifted to safety.
He frustrates the devices of the crafty,
　　so that their hands achieve no success.
He takes the wise in their own craftiness;
　　and the schemes of the wily are brought to a quick end.
They meet with darkness in the daytime,
　　and grope at noonday as in the night.
But he saves the fatherless from their mouth,
　　the needy from the hand of the mighty.
So the poor have hope,
　　and injustice shuts her mouth.

"Behold, happy is the man whom God reproves;
　　therefore despise not the chastening of the Almighty.
For he wounds, but he binds up;
　　he smites, but his hands heal."

Job's First Answer to Eliphaz

The implied condemnation awakens Job, first to resentment and then to loneliness. He has a right to expect sympathy from his friends. He turns to God and pleads for release. Why does God torture helpless man?

Job 6:1-4, 8-13, 24-27; 7:16-21

Then Job answered:

"O that my vexation were weighed,
    and all my calamity laid in the balances!
For then it would be heavier than the sand of the sea;
    therefore my words have been rash.
For the arrows of the Almighty are in me;
    my spirit drinks their poison;
    the terrors of God are arrayed against me.

O that I might have my request,
    and that God would grant my desire;
that it would please God to crush me,
    that he would let loose his hand and cut me off!
This would be my consolation;
    I would even exult in pain unsparing;
    for I have not denied the words of the Holy One.
What is my strength, that I should wait?
    And what is my end, that I should be patient?
Is my strength the strength of stones,
    or is my flesh bronze?
In truth I have no help in me,
    and any resource is driven from me.

Teach me, and I will be silent;
    make me understand how I have erred.
How forceful are honest words!
    But what does reproof from you reprove?
Do you think that you can reprove words,
    when the speech of a despairing man is wind?
You would even cast lots over the fatherless,
    and bargain over your friend.
I loathe my life; I would not live for ever.
    Let me alone, for my days are a breath.
What is man, that thou dost make so much of him,
    and that thou dost set thy mind upon him,
dost visit him every morning,
    and test him every moment?
How long wilt thou not look away from me,
    not let me alone till I swallow my spittle?
If I sin, what do I do to thee, thou watcher of men?
    Why hast thou made me thy mark?

Why have I become a burden to thee?
Why dost thou not pardon my transgression
and take away my iniquity?
For now I shall lie in the earth;
thou wilt seek me, but I shall not be."

Bildad's First Reply

Bildad is shocked that Job would imply the possibility of God's injustice. He says plainly that Job is being punished for his sins.

Job 8:1–4, 13–15, 20–22

Then Bildad the Shuhite answered:

"How long will you say these things,
and the words of your mouth be a great wind?
Does God pervert justice?
Or does the Almighty pervert the right?
If your children have sinned against him,
he has delivered them into the power of their transgression.

"Such are the paths of all who forget God;
the hope of the godless man shall perish.
His confidence breaks in sunder,
and his trust is a spider's web.
He leans against his house, but it does not stand;
he lays hold of it, but it does not endure.

"Behold, God will not reject a blameless man,
nor take the hand of evildoers.
He will yet fill your mouth with laughter,
and your lips with shouting.
Those who hate you will be clothed with shame,
and the tent of the wicked will be no more."

Job's First Answer to Bildad

Job begins with a sneer. He raises the question: Is it Godlike to create me simply to torture me?

Job 9:1–3, 14–21; 10:18–22

Then Job answered:

"Truly I know that it is so:
But how can a man be just before God?

If one wished to contend with him,
　　one could not answer him once in a thousand times.
How then can I answer him,
　　choosing my words with him?
Though I am innocent, I cannot answer him;
　　I must appeal for mercy to my accuser.
If I summoned him and he answered me,
　　I would not believe that he was listening to my voice.
For he crushes me with a tempest,
　　and multiplies my wounds without cause;
he will not let me get my breath,
　　but fills me with bitterness.
If it is a contest of strength, behold him!
　　If it is a matter of justice, who can summon him?
Though I am innocent, my own mouth would condemn me;
　　though I am blameless, he would prove me perverse.
I am blameless; I regard not myself;
　　I loathe my life.

"Why didst thou bring me forth from the womb?
　　Would that I had died before any eye had seen me,
and were as though I had not been,
　　carried from the womb to the grave.
Are not the days of my life few?
　　Let me alone, that I may find a little comfort
before I go whence I shall not return
　　to the land of gloom and deep darkness.
the land of gloom and chaos
　　where light is as darkness."

Zophar's First Speech

Zophar is hard and unsympathetic. He implies that if God were
to show Job his real guilt, he would see that he was suffering less
than he deserved.

Job 11:1–6, 13–15

Then Zophar the Naamathite answered:

"Should a multitude of words go unanswered,
　　and a man full of talk be vindicated?
Should your babble silence men,
　　and when you mock, shall no one shame you?
For you say, 'My doctrine is pure,

and I am clean in God's eyes.'
But oh, that God would speak,
    and open his lips to you,
and that he would tell you the secrets of wisdom!
    For he is manifold in understanding.
Know then that God exacts of you less than your guilt deserves.

"If you set your heart aright,
    you will stretch out your hands toward him.
If iniquity is in your hand, put it far away,
    and let not wickedness dwell in your tents.
Surely then you will lift up your face without blemish;
    you will be secure, and will not fear."

Job's First Answer to Zophar

Job answers with sarcasm: They all wish God would reveal his
sins. Why should they try to defend God?

Job 12:1–5; 13:1–6; 14:15–17

Then Job answered:

"No doubt you are the people,
    and wisdom will die with you.
But I have understanding as well as you;
    I am not inferior to you.
    Who does not know such things as these?
I am a laughingstock to my friends;
    I, who called upon God and he answered me,
    a just and blameless man, am a laughingstock.
In the thought of one who is at ease there is contempt for
        misfortune;
    it is ready for those whose feet slip.

"Lo, my eye has seen all this,
    my ear has heard and understood it.
What you know, I also know;
    I am not inferior to you.
But I would speak to the Almighty.
    and I desire to argue my case with God.
As for you, you whitewash with lies;
    worthless physicians are you all.
Oh that you would keep silent,
    and it would be your wisdom!

Hear now my reasoning,
    and listen to the pleading of my lips.
Thou wouldest call, and I would answer thee;
    thou wouldest long for the work of thy hands.
For then thou wouldest number my steps,
    thou wouldest not keep watch over my sin;
my transgression would be sealed up in a bag,
    and thou wouldest cover over my iniquity."

The first cycle closes. The friends have asserted God's justice. Job has denied that any justice has been shown; there is only power. The friends must conclude that Job is a great sinner, but they will not abandon their efforts to convert him. The second cycle begins.

Eliphaz's Second Speech
Job has dared treat his three friends' wisdom with contempt. Everyone knows that the wicked are punished.

Job 15:1–6, 20–22

Then Eliphaz the Temanite answered:

"Should a wise man answer with windy knowledge,
    and fill himself with the east wind?
Should he argue in unprofitable talk,
    or in words with which he can do no good?
But you are doing away with the fear of God,
    and hindering meditation before God.
For your iniquity teaches your mouth,
    and you choose the tongue of the crafty.
Your own mouth condemns you, and not I;
    your own lips testify against you.
The wicked man writhes in pain all his days,
    through all the years that are laid up for the ruthless.
Terrifying sounds are in his ears;
    in prosperity the destroyer will come upon him.
He does not believe that he will return out of darkness,
    and he is destined for the sword."

Job's Second Answer to Eliphaz
Job appeals for sympathy. His mood turns to despair, but he refuses to lose confidence in ultimate divine justice.

Job 16:1–11; 17:6–16

Then Job answered:

"I have heard many such things;
    miserable comforters are you all.
Shall windy words have an end?
    Or what provokes you that you answer?
I also could speak as you do,
    if you were in my place;
I could join words together against you,
    and shake my head at you.
I could strengthen you with my mouth,
    and the solace of my lips would assuage your pain.

"If I speak, my pain is not assuaged,
    and if I forbear, how much of it leaves me?
Surely now God has worn me out;
    he has made desolate all my company.
And he has shriveled me up,
    which is a witness against me;
and my leanness has risen up against me,
    it testifies to my face.
He has torn me in his wrath, and hated me;
    he has gnashed his teeth at me;
    my adversary sharpens his eyes against me.
Men have gaped at me with their mouth,
    they have struck me insolently upon the cheek,
    they mass themselves together against me.
God gives me up to the ungodly,
    and casts me into the hands of the wicked.

"He has made me a byword of the peoples,
    and I am one before whom men spit.
My eye has grown dim from grief,
    and all my members are like a shadow.
Upright men are appalled at this,
    and the innocent stirs himself up against the godless.
Yet the righteous holds to his way,
    and he that has clean hands grows stronger and stronger.
But you, come on again, all of you,
    and I shall not find a wise man among you.
My days are past, my plans are broken off,
    the desires of my heart.
They make night into day;
    'The light,' they say, 'is near to the darkness.'

If I look for Sheol as my house,
    if I spread my couch in darkness,
if I say to the pit, 'You are my father,'
    and to the worm, 'My mother,' or 'My sister,'
where then is my hope?
    Who will see my hope?
Will it go down to the bars of Sheol?
    Shall we descend together into the dust?''

Bildad's Second Reply

Bildad is more harsh than in his first speech. The wicked live
and die in misery. He reflects upon Job's disasters.

Job 18:1–12

Then Bildad the Shuhite answered:

"How long will you hunt for words?
    Consider, and then we will speak.
Why are we counted as cattle?
    Why are we stupid in your sight?
You who tear yourself in your anger,
    shall the earth be forsaken for you,
    or the rock be removed out of its place?

"Yea, the light of the wicked is put out,
    and the flame of his fire does not shine.
The light is dark in his tent,
    and his lamp above him is put out.
His strong steps are shortened
    and his own schemes throw him down
For he is cast into a net by his own feet,
    and he walks on a pitfall.
A trap seizes him by the heel,
    a snare lays hold of him.
A rope is hid for him in the ground,
    a trap for him in the path.
Terrors frighten him on every side,
    and chase him at his heels.
His strength is hunger-bitten,
    and calamity is ready for his stumbling.''

Job's Second Answer to Bildad

Job replies with hot indignation, then turns to his sad condition. It has come from God. There is no help.

Job 19:1–12, 23–27

Then Job answered:

"How long will you torment me,
    and break me in pieces with words?
These ten times you have cast reproach upon me;
    are you not ashamed to wrong me?
And even if it be true that I have erred
    my error remains with myself.
If indeed you magnify yourselves against me,
    and make my humiliation an argument against me,
know then that God has put me in the wrong,
    and closed his net about me.
Behold, I cry out, 'Violence!' but I am not answered;
    I call aloud, but there is no justice.
He has walled up my way, so that I cannot pass,
    and he has set darkness upon my paths.
He has stripped from me my glory,
    and taken the crown from my head.
He breaks me down on every side, and I am gone,
    and my hope has he pulled up like a tree.
He has kindled his wrath against me,
    and counts me as his adversary.
His troops come on together;
    they have cast up siegeworks against me,
    and encamp round about my tent.

"Oh that my words were written!
    Oh that they were inscribed in a book!
Oh that with an iron pen and lead
    they were graven in the rock for ever!
For I know that my redeemer lives,
    and at last he will stand upon the earth;
and after my skin has been thus destroyed,
    then from my flesh I shall see God,
whom I shall see on my side,
    and my eyes shall behold, and not another.
My heart faints within me!"

Zophar's Second Reply

Zophar tries to draw a picture, like Bildad, of the wicked man, and it is a picture of Job.

Job 20:1–8

Then Zophar the Naamthite answered:

"Therefore my thoughts answer me,
  because of my haste within me.
I hear censure which insults me,
  and out of my understanding a spirit answers me.
Do you not know this from of old,
  since man was placed upon earth,
that the exulting of the wicked is short,
  and the joy of the godless but for a moment?
Though his height mount up to the heavens,
  and his head reach to the clouds,
he will perish for ever like his own dung;
  those who have seen him will say, 'Where is he?'
He will fly away like a dream, and not be found;
  he will be chased away like a vision of the night."

Job's Second Answer to Zophar

Job flatly denies Zophar's contention. The wicked, he suggests, do live and die in peace. They have no more suffering than the righteous.

Job 21:1–9, 17–26, 29–34

Then Job answered:

"Listen carefully to my words,
  and let this be your consolation.
Bear with me, and I will speak,
  and after I have spoken, mock on.
As for me, is my complaint against man?
  Why should I not be impatient?
Look at me, and be appalled,
  and lay your hand upon your mouth.
When I think of it I am dismayed,
  and shuddering seizes my flesh.
Why do the wicked live,
  reach old age, and grow mighty in power?

Their children are established in their presence,
    and their offspring before their eyes.
Their houses are safe from fear,
    and no rod of God is upon them.

"How often is it that the lamp of the wicked is put out?
    That their calamity comes upon them?
    That God distributes pains in his anger?
That they are like straw before the wind,
    and like chaff that the storm carries away?
You say, 'God stores up their iniquity for their sons.'
    Let him recompense it to themselves, that they may know it.
Let their own eyes see their destruction,
    and let them drink of the wrath of the Almighty.
For what do they care for their houses after them,
    when the number of their months is cut off?
Will any teach God knowledge,
    seeing that he judges those that are on high?
One dies in full prosperity,
    being wholly at ease and secure,
his body full of fat
    and the marrow of his bones moist.
Another dies in bitterness of soul,
    never having tasted of good.
They lie down alike in the dust,
    and the worms cover them.
Have you not asked those who travel the roads,
    and do you not accept their testimony
that the wicked man is spared in the day of calamity,
    that he is rescued in the day of wrath?
Who declares his way to his face,
    and who requites him for what he has done?
When he is borne to the grave,
    watch is kept over his tomb.
The clods of the valley are sweet to him;
    all men follow after him,
    and those who go before him are innumerable.
How then will you comfort me with empty nothings?
    There is nothing left of your answers but falsehood."

The second cycle closes. The friends have tried to show that the wicked always suffer. God's view and man's view have both been presented.
The third cycle begins.

Eliphaz's Third Reply

As before, Eliphaz begins. He charges Job with the sins of opression, which are especially easy for the rich and powerful men of the East.

Job 22:1–11, 27–30

Then Eliphaz the Temanite answered:

"Can a man be profitable to God?
  Surely he who is wise is profitable to himself.
Is it any pleasure to the Almighty if you are righteous,
  or is it gain to him if you make your ways blameless?
Is it for your fear of him that he reproves you,
  and enters into judgment with you?
Is not your wickedness great?
  There is no end to your iniquities.
For you have exacted pledges of your brothers for nothing,
  and stripped the naked of their clothing.
You have given no water to the weary to drink,
  and you have withheld bread from the hungry.
The man with power possessed the land,
  and the favored man dwelt in it.
You have sent widows away empty,
  and the arms of the fatherless were crushed.
Therefore snares are round about you,
  and sudden terror overwhelms you;
your light is darkened, so that you cannot see,
  and a flood of water covers you.
You will make your prayer to him, and he will hear you;
  and you will pay your vows.
You will decide on a matter, and it will be established for you,
  and light will shine on your ways.
For God abases the proud,
  but he saves the lowly.
He delivers the innocent man;
  you will be delivered through the cleanness of your hands."

Job Refuses To Answer Eliphaz

Job does not answer Eliphaz, but continues the statement to himself of the puzzle of the universe. He is no longer confident and sees little hope for his predicament. He cannot find God. The wicked prosper. Talk about justice seems useless.

Job 23:1–17

Then Job answered:

"Today also my complaint is bitter,
    his hand is heavy in spite of my groaning.
Oh, that I knew where I might find him,
    that I might come even to his seat!
I would lay my case before him
    and fill my mouth with arguments.
I would learn what he would answer me,
    and understand what he would say to me.
Would he contend with me in the greatness of his power?
    No; he would give heed to me.
There an upright man could reason with him,
    and I should be acquitted for ever by my judge.

"Behold, I go forward, but he is not there;
    and backward, but I cannot perceive him;
on the left hand I seek him, but I cannot behold him;
    I turn to the right hand, but I cannot see him.
But he knows the way that I take;
    when he has tried me, I shall come forth as gold.
My foot has held fast to his steps;
    I have kept his way and have not turned aside.
I have not departed from the commandment of his lips;
    I have treasured in my bosom the words of his mouth.
But he is unchangeable and who can turn him?
    What he desires, that he does.
For he will complete what he appoints for me;
    and many such things are in his mind.
Therefore I am terrified at his presence;
    when I consider, I am in dread of him.
God has made my heart faint;
    the Almighty has terrified me;
for I am hemmed in by darkness,
    and thick darkness covers my face."

Bildad Replies a Third Time

Bildad is amazed at the arrogance of Job. How can any man claim to be righteous before God?

Job 25:1–6

Then Bildad the Shuhite answered:

"Dominion and fear are with God;
    he makes peace in his high heaven.
Is there any number to his armies?
    Upon whom does his light not arise?
How then can man be righteous before God?
    How can he who is born of woman be clean?
Behold, even the moon is not bright
    and the stars are not clean in his sight;
how much less man, who is a maggot,
    and the son of man, who is a worm!"

Job Reflects on the Power of God

Job again does not answer his friend, but, rather, reflects.

Job 26:1–14; 27:1–6; 28:12–24; 29:1–5, 21–25;
        30:1–8; 31:1–40

Then Job answered:

"How you have helped him who has no power!
    How you have saved the arm that has no strength!
How you have counseled him who has no wisdom,
    and plentifully declared sound knowledge!
With whose help have you uttered words,
    and whose spirit has come forth from you?
The shades below tremble,
    the waters and their inhabitants.
Sheol is naked before God,
    and Abaddon has no covering.
He stretches out the north over the void,
    and hangs the earth upon nothing.
He binds up the waters in his thick clouds,
    and the cloud is not rent under them.
He covers the face of the moon,
    and spreads over it his cloud.
He has described a circle upon the face of the waters
    at the boundary between light and darkness.
The pillars of heaven tremble,
    and are astounded at his rebuke.

By his power he stilled the sea;
    by his understanding he smote Rahab.
By his wind the heavens were made fair;
    his hand pierced the fleeing serpent.
Lo, these are but the outskirts of his ways;
    and how small a whisper do we hear of him!
    But the thunder of his power who can understand?''

And Job again took up his discourse, and said:

"As God lives, who has taken away my right,
    and the Almighty, who has made my soul bitter;
as long as my breath is in me,
    and the spirit of God is in my nostrils;
my lips will not speak falsehood,
    and my tongue will not utter deceit.
Far be it from me to say that you are right;
    till I die I will not put away my integrity from me.
I hold fast my righteousness, and will not let it go:
    my heart does not reproach me for any of my days.

"But where shall wisdom be found?
    And where is the place of understanding?
Man does not know the way to it,
    and it is not found in the land of the living.
The deep says, 'It is not in me,'
    and the sea says, 'It is not with me.'
It cannot be gotten for gold,
    and silver cannot be weighed as its price.
It cannot be valued in the gold of Ophir,
    in precious onyx or sapphire.
God and glass cannot equal it,
    nor can it be exchanged for jewels of fine gold.
No mention shall be made of coral or of crystal;
    the price of wisdom is above pearls.
The topaz of Ethiopia cannot compare with it,
    nor can it be valued in pure gold.

"Whence then comes wisdom?
    And where is the place of understanding?
It is hid from the eyes of all living,
    and concealed from the birds of the air.

Abaddon and Death say,
    'We have heard a rumor of it with our ears.'

"God understands the way to it,
    and he knows its place.
For he looks to the ends of the earth,
    and sees everything under the heavens."

And Job again took up his discourse, and said:

"Oh, that I were as in the months of old,
    as in the days when God watched over me;
when his lamp shone upon my head,
    and by his light I walked through darkness;
as I was in my autumn days,
    when the friendship of God was upon my tent;
when the Almighty was yet with me,
    when my children were about me;

"Men listened to me, and waited,
    and kept silence for my counsel.
After I spoke they did not speak again,
    and my word dropped upon them.
They waited for me as for the rain;
    and they opened their mouths as for the spring rain.
I smiled on them when they had no confidence;
    and the light of my countenance they did not cast down.
I chose their way, and sat as chief,
    and I dwelt like a king among his troops,
    like one who comforts mourners.

"But now they make sport of me,
    men who are younger than I,
whose fathers I would have disdained
    to set with the dogs of my flock.
What could I gain from the strength of their hands,
    men whose vigor is gone?
Through want and hard hunger
    they gnaw the dry and desolate ground;
they pick mallow and the leaves of bushes,
    and to warm themselves the roots of the broom.
They are driven out from among men;

they shout after them as after a thief.
In the gullies of the torrents they must dwell,
 in holes of the earth and of the rocks.
Among the bushes they bray;
 under the nettles they huddle together.
A senseless, a disreputable brood,
 they have been whipped out of the land.

"I have made a covenant with my eyes;
 how then could I look upon a virgin?
What would be my portion from God above,
 and my heritage from the Almighty on high?
Does not calamity befall the unrighteous,
 and disaster the workers of iniquity?
Does not he see my ways,
 and number all my steps?

"If I have walked with falsehood,
 and my foot hastened to deceit;
(Let me be weighed in a just balance,
 and let God know my integrity!)
if my step has turned aside from the way,
 and my heart has gone after my eyes,
 and if any spot has cleaved to my hands;
then let me sow, and another eat;
 and let what grows for me be rooted out.

"If my heart has been enticed to a woman,
 and I have lain in wait at my neighbor's door;
then let my wife grind for another,
 and let others bow down upon her.
For that would be a heinous crime;
 that would be an iniquity to be punished by the judges;
for that would be a fire which consumes unto Abaddon,
 and it would burn to the root all my increase.

"If I have rejected the cause of my manservant or
 my maidservant,
 when they brought a complaint against me;
what then shall I do when God rises up?
 When he makes inquiry, what shall I answer him?
Did not he who made me in the womb make him?
 And did not one fashion us in the womb?

"If I have withheld anything that the poor desired,

or have caused the eyes of the widow to fail,
or have eaten my morsel alone,
    and the fatherless has not eaten of it
(for from his youth I reared him as a father,
    and from his mother's womb I guided him);
if I have seen any one perish for lack of clothing,
    or a poor man without covering;
if his loins have not blessed me,
    and if he was not warmed with the fleece of my sheep;
if I have raised my hand against the fatherless,
    because I saw help in the gate;
then let my shoulder blade fall from my shoulder,
    and let my arm be broken from its socket.
For I was in terror of calamity from God,
    and I could not have faced his majesty.

"If I have made gold my trust,
    or called fine gold my confidence;
if I have rejoiced because my wealth was great,
    or because my hand had gotten much;
if I have looked at the sun when it shone,
    or the moon moving in splendor,
and my heart has been secretly enticed,
    and my mouth has kissed my hand;
this also would be an iniquity to be punished by the judges,
    for I should have been false to God above.

"If I have rejoiced at the ruin of him that hated me,
    or exulted when evil overtook him
(I have not let my mouth sin by
    asking for his life with a curse);
if the men of my tent have not said,
    'Who is there that has not been filled with his meat?'
(the sojourner has not lodged in the street;
    I have opened my doors to the wayfarer);
if I have concealed my transgressions from men,
    by hiding my iniquity in my bosom,
because I stood in great fear of the multitude,
    and the contempt of families terrified me,
    so that I kept silence, and did not go out of doors—
Oh, that I had one to hear me!
    (Here is my signature! let the Almighty answer me!)
    Oh, that I had the indictment written by my adversary!

Surely I would carry it on my shoulder;
    I would bind it on me as a crown;
I would give him an account of all my steps;
    like a prince I would approach him.

"If my land has cried out against me,
    and its furrows have wept together;
if I have eaten its yield without payment,
    and caused the death of its owners;
let thorns grow instead of wheat,
    and foul weeds instead of barley."

The cycle of argument is over. The friends still maintain that Job has sinned; Job still asserts his innocence. They have appealed to God for judgment; so has he. The debate has not been resolved.

Elihu's Criticism

Unexpectedly a new character arrives, Elihu, a young man, conceited and wordy, but he has the redeeming quality of earnestness. Job has asked for a mediator between himself and God; Elihu is that mediator. Job complains that God doesn't hear him. Righteousness, he says, does not profit.

Job 32:1–10; 33:8–14; 35:1–8; 36:5–12; 37:14–24

So these three men ceased to answer Job, because he was righteous in his own eyes. Then Elihu the son of Barachel the Buzite, of the family of Ram, became angry. He was angry at Job because he justified himself rather than God; he was angry also at Job's three friends because they had found no answer, although they had declared Job to be in the wrong. Now Elihu had waited to speak to Job because they were older than he. And when Elihu saw that there was no answer in the mouth of these three men, he became angry.

And Elihu the son of Barachel the Buzite answered:

"I am young in years,
    and you are aged;
therefore I was timid and afraid
    to declare my opinion to you.
I said, 'Let days speak,
    and many years teach wisdom.'

But it is the spirit in a man,
    the breath of the Almighty, that makes him understand.
It is not the old that are wise,
    nor the aged that understand what is right.
Therefore I say, 'Listen to me;
    let me also declare my opinion.'

"Surely, you have spoken in my hearing,
    and I have heard the sound of your words.
You say, 'I am clean, without transgression;
    I am pure, and there is no iniquity in me.
Behold, he finds occasions against me,
    he counts me as his enemy;
he puts my feet in the stocks,
    and watches all my paths.'

"Behold, in this you are not right. I will answer you.
    God is greater than man.
Why do you contend against him,
    saying, 'He will answer none of my words'?
For God speaks in one way,
    and in two, though man does not perceive it."

And Elihu said:

"Do you think this to be just?
    Do you say, 'It is my right before God,'
that you ask, 'What advantage have I?
    How am I better off than if I had sinned?'
I will answer you
    and your friends with you.
Look at the heavens, and see;
    and behold the clouds, which are higher than you.
If you have sinned, what do you accomplish against him?
    And if your transgressions are multiplied, what do you do to
        him?
If you are righteous, what do you give to him;
    or what does he receive from your hand?
Your wickedness concerns a man like yourself,
    and your righteousness a son of man.
"Behold, God is mighty, and does not despise any;
    he is mighty in strength of understanding.
He does not keep the wicked alive,
    but gives the afflicted their right.

He does not withdraw his eyes from the righteous,
　　but with kings upon the throne
　　he sets them for ever, and they are exalted.
And if they are bound in fetters
　　and caught in the cords of affliction,
then he declares to them their work
　　and their transgressions, that they are behaving arrogantly.
He opens their ears to instruction,
　　and commands that they return from iniquity.
If they hearken and serve him,
　　they complete their days in prosperity,
　　and their years in pleasantness.
But if they do not hearken, they perish by the sword,
　　and die without knowledge.

"Hear this, O Job;
　　stop and consider the wondrous works of God.
Do you know how God lays his command upon them,
　　and causes the lightning of his cloud to shine?
Do you know the balancings of the clouds,
　　the wondrous works of him who is perfect in knowledge,
you whose garments are hot
　　when the earth is still because of the south wind?
Can you, like him, spread out the skies,
　　hard as a molten mirror?
Teach us what we shall say to him;
　　we cannot draw up our case because of darkness.
Shall it be told him that I would speak?
　　Did a man ever wish that he would be swallowed up?

"And now men cannot look on the light
　　when it is bright in the skies,
　　when the wind has passed and cleared them.
Out of the north comes golden splendor;
　　God is clothed with terrible majesty.
The Almighty—we cannot find him;
　　he is great in power and justice,
　　and abundant righteousness he will not violate.
Therefore men fear him;
　　he does not regard any who are wise in their own conceit."

God Speaks

The speeches of Jehovah form the culmination of the book. God
does not discuss the problem over which Job has agonized, his

torturing sufferings. Rather God speaks of His divine power in nature. Job must turn all things to its solution. Since Job cannot understand nature, how can he expect to understand human life? The world does not provide an intellectual solution to the problem of suffering, but, rather, one must seek the wisdom of God.

Job 38:1–41; 39:1–30; 40:1–9

Then the Lord answered Job out of the whirlwind:

"Who is this that darkens counsel by words without
      knowledge?
Gird up your loins like a man,
    I will question you, and you shall declare to me.

"Where were you when I laid the foundation of the earth?
    Tell me, if you have understanding.
Who determined its measurements—surely you know!
    Or who stretched the line upon it?
On what were its bases sunk,
    or who laid its cornerstone,
when the morning stars sang together,
    and all the sons of God shouted for joy?

"Or who shut in the sea with doors,
    when it burst forth from the womb;
when I made clouds its garment,
    and thick darkness its swaddling band,
and prescribed bounds for it,
    and set bars and doors,
and said, 'Thus far shall you come, and no farther,
    and here shall your proud waves be stayed'?

"Have you commanded the morning since your days began,
    and caused the dawn to know its place,
that it might take hold of the skirts of the earth,
    and the wicked be shaken out of it?
It is changed like clay under the seal,
    and it is dyed like a garment.
From the wicked their light is withheld,
    and their uplifted arm is broken.

"Have you entered into the springs of the sea,
    or walked in the recesses of the deep?

Have the gates of death been revealed to you,
    or have you seen the gates of deep darkness?
Have you comprehended the expanse of the earth?
    Declare, if you know all this.

"Where is the way to the dwelling of light,
    and where is the place of darkness,
that you may take it to its territory
    and that you may discern the paths to its home?
You know, for you were born then,
    and the number of your days is great!

"Have you entered the storehouses of the snow,
    or have you seen the storehouses of the hail,
which I have reserved for the time of trouble,
    for the day of battle and war?
What is the way to the place where the light is distributed,
    or where the east wind is scattered upon the earth?

"Who has cleft a channel for the torrents of rain
    and a way for the thunderbolt,
to bring rain on a land where no man is,
    on the desert in which there is no man;
to satisfy the waste and desolate land,
    and to make the ground put forth grass?

"Has the rain a father,
    or who has begotten the drops of dew?
From whose womb did the ice come forth,
    and who has given birth to the hoarfrost of heaven?
The waters become hard like stone,
    and the face of the deep is frozen.

"Can you bind the chains of the Pleiades,
    or loose the cords of Orion?
Can you lead forth the Mazzaroth in their season,
    or can you guide the Bear with its children?
Do you know the ordinances of the heavens?
    Can you establish their rule on the earth?

"Can you lift up your voice to the clouds,
    that a flood of waters may cover you?
Can you send forth lightnings, that they may go
    and say to you, 'Here we are'?

Who has put wisdom in the clouds,
   or given understanding to the mists?
Who can number the clouds by wisdom?
   Or who can tilt the waterskins of the heavens,
when the dust runs into a mass
   and the clods cleave fast together?

"Can you hunt the prey for the lion,
   or satisfy the appetite of the young lions,
when they crouch in their dens,
   or lie in wait in their covert?
Who provides for the raven its prey,
   when its young ones cry to God,
   and wander about for lack of food?

"Do you know when the mountain goats bring forth?
   Do you observe the calving of the hinds?
Can you number the months that they fulfil,
   and do you know the time when they bring forth,
   when they crouch, bring forth their offspring,
   and are delivered of their young?
Their young ones become strong, they grow up in the open;
   they go forth, and do not return to them.

"Who has let the wild ass go free?
   Who has loosed the bonds of the swift ass,
to whom I have given the steppe for his home,
   and the salt land for his dwelling place?
He scorns the tumult of the city;
   he hears not the shouts of the driver.
He ranges the mountains as his pasture,
   and he searches after every green thing.

"Is the wild ox willing to serve you?
   Will he spend the night at your crib?
Can you bind him in the furrow with ropes,
   or will he harrow the valleys after you?
Will you depend on him because his strength is great,
   and will you leave to him your labor?
Do you have faith in him that he will return,
   and bring your grain to your threshing floor?
"The wings of the ostrich wave proudly;
   but are they the pinions and plumage of love?

For she leaves her eggs to the earth,
    and lets them be warmed on the ground,
forgetting that a foot may crush them,
    and that the wild beast may trample them.
She deals cruelly with her young, as if they were not hers;
    though her labor be in vain, yet she has no fear;
because God has made her forget wisdom,
    and given her no share in understanding.
When she rouses herself to flee,
    she laughs at the horse and his rider.

"Do you give the horse his might?
    Do you clothe his neck with strength?
Do you make him leap like the locust?
    His majestic snorting is terrible.
He paws in the valley, and exults in his strength;
    he goes out to meet the weapons.
He laughs at fear, and is not dismayed;
    he does not turn back from the sword.
Upon him rattle the quiver,
    the flashing spear and the javelin.
With fierceness and rage he swallows the ground;
    he cannot stand still at the sound of the trumpet.
When the trumpet sounds, he says 'Aha!'
    He smells the battle from afar,
    the thunder of the captains, and the shouting.

"Is it by your wisdom that the hawk soars,
    and spreads his wings toward the south?
Is it at your command that the eagle mounts up
    and makes his nest on high?
On rock he dwells and makes his home
    in fastness of the rocky crag.
Thence he spies out the prey;
    his eyes behold it afar off.
His young ones suck up blood;
    and where the slain are, there is he."

And the Lord said to Job:

"Shall a faultfinder contend with the Almighty?
    He who argues with God, let him answer it."

Then Job answered the Lord:

"Behold, I am of small account; what shall I answer thee?
    I lay my hand on my mouth.
I have spoken once, and I will not answer;
    twice, but I will proceed no further."

Then the Lord answered Job out of the whirlwind:

"Gird up your loins like a man;
    I will question you, and you declare to me.
Will you even put me in the wrong?
    Will you condemn me that you may be justified?
Have you an arm like God,
    and can you thunder with a voice like his?"

EPILOGUE

The final portion of the book tells of the restoration of Job's prosperity; it condemns his friends for their behavior and justifies Job.

Job 42:1–17

Then Job answered the Lord:

"I know that thou canst do all things,
    and that no purpose of thine can be thwarted.
'Who is this that hides counsel without knowledge?'
Therefore I have uttered what I did not understand,
    things too wonderful for me, which I did not know.
'Hear, and I will speak;
    I will question you, and you declare to me.'
I had heard of thee by the hearing of the ear,
    but now my eye sees thee;
therefore I despise myself,
    and repent in dust and ashes."

After the Lord had spoken these words to Job, the Lord said to Eliphaz the Temanite: "My wrath is kindled against you and against your two friends; for you have not spoken of me what is right, as my servant Job has. Now therefore take seven bulls and seven rams, and go to my servant Job, and offer up for yourselves a burnt offering; and my servant Job shall pray for you, for I will accept his prayer not to deal with you according to your folly; for you have not spoken of me what is right, as my servant Job has." So Eliphaz the Temanite and Bildad the Shuhite and Zophar the Naamathite went and did what the Lord had told them; and the Lord accepted Job's prayer.

And the Lord restored the fortunes of Job, when he had prayed for his friends; and the Lord gave Job twice as much as he had before. Then came to him all his brothers and sisters and all who had known him before, and ate bread with him in his house; and they showed him sympathy and comforted him for all the evil that the Lord had brought upon him; and each of them gave him a piece of money and a ring of gold. And the Lord blessed the latter days of Job more than his beginning; and he had fourteen thousand sheep, six thousand camels, a thousand yoke of oxen, and a thousand she-asses. He had also seven sons and three daughters. And he called the name of the first Jemimah; and the name of the second Keziah; and the name of the third Kerenhappuch. And in all the land there were no women so fair as Job's daughters; and their father gave them inheritance among their brothers. And after this Job lived a hundred and forty years, and saw his sons, and his sons' sons, four generations. And Job died, an old man, and full of days.

Prophetic
Literature

*T*HE TERM PROPHECY means much more than "prediction" or "foretelling." Prophecy essentially means "forth-pouring" or "out-pouring" of discourse. It is the channel of an immediate divine message. The prophet, thus, was an interpreter of God. Written prophecy is distinctive from other writings in both its spirit and subject.

Prophecy rested on the belief that man may do deeds and speak words under the direct inspiration of God. The prophet was the one who received the word of his God and spoke it to his fellows.

The prophet voiced a strong national consciousness as the Hebrews were passing from a disorganized collection of tribes to a unified nation. To the prophet, patriotism and national religion were the same.

Prophets did not generally write their prophecy; they lived it. It was conveyed in action, and its presentation in literature is the narrative of that action. They had realized to the full the moral implications of being their brothers' keeper. They sought to denounce evil doing, foretell disaster, and predict final redemption. They sought to relay the message with imagination and to illustrate their meaning by parable, allegory, and picturesque imagery.

PROPHETIC DISCOURSE

Prophetic discourse is the simplest form of prophecy. It is the counterpart of the modern sermon: a divine message. The text, in this case a source of information or authority, and the recommendatory matter are fused together without distinction by the merging of the divine message with exhortations. In most prophetic discourses there is no clear structural plan; but, rather, writings contain warnings, descriptions, reflections, and appeals.

THE TEN COMMANDMENTS

Exodus 19:7–25; 20:1–26

So Moses came and called the elders of the people, and set before them all these words which the Lord had commanded him. And all the people answered together and said, "All that the Lord has spoken we will do." And Moses reported the words of the people to the Lord. And the Lord said to Moses, "Lo, I am coming to you in a thick cloud, that the people may hear when I speak with you, and may also believe you for ever."

Then Moses told the words of the people to the Lord. And the Lord said to Moses, "Go to the people and consecrate them today and tomorrow, and let them wash their garments, and be ready by the third day; for on the third day the Lord will come down upon Mount Sinai in the sight of all the people. And you shall set bounds for the people round about, saying, 'Take heed that you do not go up into the mountain or touch the border of it; whoever touches the mountain shall be put to death; no hand shall touch him, but he shall be stoned or shot; whether beast or man, he shall not live.' When the trumpet sounds a long blast, they shall come up to the mountain." So Moses went down from the mountain to the people, and consecrated the people; and they washed their garments. And he said to the people, "Be ready by the third day; do not go near a woman."

On the morning of the third day there were thunders and lightnings, and a thick cloud upon the mountain, and a very loud trumpet blast, so that all the people who were in the camp trembled. Then Moses brought the people out of the camp to meet God; and they took their stand at the foot of the mountain. And Mount Sinai was wrapped in smoke, because the Lord descended upon it in fire; and the smoke of it went up like the smoke of a kiln, and the whole mountain quaked greatly. And as the sound of the trumpet grew louder and louder, Moses spoke, and God answered him in thunder. And the Lord came down upon Mount Sinai, to the top of the mountain; and the Lord called Moses to the top of the mountain, and Moses went up. And the Lord said to Moses, "Go down and warn the people, lest they break through to the Lord to gaze and many of them perish. And also let the priests who come near to the Lord consecrate themselves, lest the Lord break out upon them." And Moses said to the Lord, "The people cannot come up to Mount Sinai; for thou thyself didst charge us, saying, 'Set bounds about the mountain, and consecrate it.' " And the Lord said to him, "Go down, and come up bringing Aaron with you; but do not let the priests and the people break through to come up to the Lord, lest he break out against them." So Moses went down to the people and told them.

And God spoke all these words, saying,

"I am the Lord your God, who brought you out of the land of Egypt, out of the house of bondage.

"You shall have no other gods before me.

"You shall not make for yourself a graven image, or any likeness of anything that is in heaven above, or that is in the earth beneath, or that is in the water under the earth; you shall not bow down to them or serve them; for I the Lord your God am a jealous God, visiting the iniquity of the fathers upon the children to the third and the fourth generation of those who hate me, but showing steadfast love to thousands of those who love me and keep my commandments.

"You shall not take the name of the Lord your God in vain; for the Lord will not hold him guiltless who takes his name in vain.

"Remember the sabbath day, to keep it holy. Six days you shall labor, and do all your work; but the seventh day is a sabbath to the Lord your God; in it you shall not do any work, you, or your son, or your daughter, your manservant, or your maidservant, or your cattle, or the sojourner who is within your gates; for in six days the Lord made heaven and earth, the sea, and all that is in them, and rested the seventh day; therefore the Lord blessed the sabbath day and hallowed it.

"Honor your father and your mother, that your days may be long in the land which the Lord your God gives you.

"You shall not kill.

"You shall not commit adultery.

"You shall not steal.

"You shall not bear false witness against your neighbor.

"You shall not covet your neighbor's house; you shall not covet your neighbor's wife, or his manservant, or his maidservant, or his ox, or his ass, or anything that is your neighbor's."

Now when all the people perceived the thunderings and the lightnings and the sound of the trumpet and the mountain smoking, the people were afraid and trembled; and they stood afar off, and said to Moses, "You speak to us, and we will hear; but let not God speak to us, lest we die." And Moses said to the people, "Do not fear; for God has come to prove you, and that the fear of him may be before your eyes, that you may not sin."

And the people stood afar off, while Moses drew near to the thick darkness where God was. And the Lord said to Moses, "Thus you shall say to the people of Israel: 'You have seen for yourselves that I have talked with you from heaven. You shall not make gods of silver to be with me, nor shall you make for yourselves gods of gold. An altar of earth you shall make for me and sacrifice on it your burnt offerings and your peace offerings, your sheep and your oxen; in every place where I cause my name to be remembered I will come to you and bless you. And if you make me an altar of stone, you shall not build it of hewn stones; for if you wield your tool upon it you profane it. And you shall not go up by steps to my altar, that your nakedness be not exposed on it.'

GOD WILL NOT FORGET

Isaiah 8:16-22; 9:1–21; 10:1–27

Bind up the testimony, seal the teaching among my disciples. I will wait for the Lord, who is hiding his face from the house of Jacob, and I will hope in him. Behold, I and the children whom the Lord has given me are signs and portents in Israel from the Lord of hosts, who dwells on Mount Zion. And when they say to you, "Consult the mediums and the wizards who chirp and mutter," should not a people consult their God? Should they consult the dead on behalf of the living? To the teaching and to the testimony! Surely for this word which they speak there is no dawn. They will pass through the land, greatly distressed and hungry; and when they are hungry, they will be enraged and will curse their king and their God, and turn their faces upward; and they will look to the earth, but behold, distress and darkness, the gloom of anguish; and they will be thrust into thick darkness.

But there will be no gloom for her that was in anguish. In the former time he brought into contempt the land of Zebulun and the land of Naphtali, but in the latter time he will make glorious the way of the sea, the land beyond the Jordan, Galilee of the nations.

The people who walked in darkness
    have seen a great light;
those who dwelt in a land of deep darkness,
    on them has light shined.
Thou hast multiplied the nation,
    thou hast increased its joy;
they rejoice before thee

as with joy at the harvest,
   as men rejoice when they divide the spoil.
For the yoke of his burden,
   and the staff for his shoulder,
   the rod of his oppressor,
   thou hast broken as on the day of Midian.
For every boot of the tramping warrior in battle tumult
   and every garment rolled in blood
   will be burned as fuel for the fire.
For to us a child is born,
   to us a son is given;
and the government will be upon his shoulder,
   and his name will be called
"Wonderful Counselor, Mighty God,
   Everlasting Father, Prince of Peace."
Of the increase of his government and of peace
   there will be no end,
upon the throne of David, and over his kingdom,
   to establish it, and to uphold it
with justice and with righteousness
   from this time forth and for evermore.
The zeal of the Lord of hosts will do this.

The Lord has sent a word against Jacob,
   and it will light upon Israel;
and all the people will know,
   Ephraim and the inhabitants of Samaria,
   who say in pride and in arrogance of heart:
"The bricks have fallen,
   but we will build with dressed stones;
the sycamores have been cut down,
   but we will put cedars in their place."
So the Lord raises adversaries against them,
   and stirs up their enemies.
The Syrians on the east and the Philistines on the west
   devour Israel with open mouth.
For all this his anger is not turned away
   and his hand is stretched out still.

The people did not turn to him who smote them,
   nor seek the Lord of hosts.
So the Lord cut off from Israel head and tail,
   palm branch and reed in one day—

the elder and honored man is the head,
  and the prophet who teaches lies is the tail;
for those who lead this people lead them astray,
  and those who are led by them are swallowed up.
Therefore the Lord does not rejoice over their young men,
  and has no compassion on their fatherless and widows;
for every one is godless and an evildoer,
  and every mouth speaks folly.
For all this his anger is not turned away
  and his hand is stretched out still.

For wickedness burns like a fire,
  it consumes briers and thorns;
it kindles the thickets of the forest,
  and they roll upward in a column of smoke.
Through the wrath of the Lord of hosts
  the land is burned,
and the people are like fuel for the fire;
  no man spares his brother.
They snatch on the right, but are still hungry,
  and they devour on the left, but are not satisfied;
each devours his neighbor's flesh,
Manasseh Ephraim, and Ephraim Manasseh,
  and together they are against Judah.
For all this his anger is not turned away
  and his hand is stretched out still.

Woe to those who decree iniquitous decrees,
  and the writers who keep writing oppression,
to turn aside the needy from justice
  and to rob the poor of my people of their right,
that widows may be their spoil,
  and that they may make the fatherless their prey!
What will you do on the day of punishment,
  in the storm which will come from afar?
To whom will you flee for help,
  and where will you leave your wealth?
Nothing remains but to crouch among the prisoners
  or fall among the slain.
For all this his anger is not turned away
  and his hand is stretched out still.
Ah, Assyria, the rod of my anger,
  the staff of my fury!

Against a godless nation I send him,
    and against the people of my wrath I command him,
to take spoil and seize plunder,
    and to tread them down like the mire of the streets.
But he does not so intend,
    and his mind does not so think;
but it is in his mind to destroy,
    and to cut off nations not a few;
for he says:
"Are not my commanders all kings?
Is not Calno like Carchemish?
    Is not Hamath like Arpad?
    Is not Samaria like Damascus?
As my hand has reached to the kingdoms of the idols
    whose graven images were greater than those of Jerusalem
        and Samaria,
shall I not do to Jerusalem and her idols
    as I have done to Samaria and her images?"

When the Lord has finished all his work on Mount Zion and on Jerusalem he will punish the arrogant boasting of the king of Assyria and his haughty pride. For he says:

"By the strength of my hand I have done it,
    and by my wisdom, for I have understanding;
I have removed the boundaries of peoples,
    and have plundered their treasures;
    like a bull I have brought down those who sat on thrones.
My hand has found like a nest
    the wealth of the peoples;
and as men gather eggs that have been forsaken
    so I have gathered all the earth;
and there was none that moved a wing,
    or opened the mouth, or chirped."

Shall the axe vaunt itself over him who hews with it,
    or the saw magnify itself against him who wields it?
As if a rod should wield him who lifts it,
    or as if a staff should lift him who is not wood!
Therefore the Lord, the Lord of hosts,
    will send wasting sickness among his stout warriors,
and under his glory a burning will be kindled,
    like the burning of fire.

The light of Israel will become a fire,
    and his Holy One a flame;
and it will burn and devour
    his thorns and briers in one day.
The glory of his forest and his fruitful land
    the Lord will destroy, both soul and body,
    and it will be as when a sick man wastes away.
The remnant of the trees of his forest will be so few
    that a child can write them down.

In that day the remnant of Israel and the survivors of the house
of Jacob will no more lean upon him that smote them, but will
lean upon the Lord, the Holy One of Israel, in truth. A remnant will
return, the remnant of Jacob, to the mighty God. For though your
people Israel be as the sand of the sea, only a remnant of them
will return. Destruction is decreed, overflowing with righteousness. For the Lord, the Lord of hosts, will make a full end, as
decreed, in the midst of all the earth.

Therefore thus says the Lord, the Lord of hosts: "O my people,
who dwell in Zion, be not afraid of the Assyrians when they smite
with the rod and lift up their staff against you as the Egyptians
did. For in a very little while my indignation will come to an end,
and my anger will be directed to their destruction. And the Lord
of hosts will wield against them a scourge, as when he smote
Midian at the rock of Oreb; and his rod will be over the sea, and
he will lift it as he did in Egypt. And in that day his burden will
depart from your shoulder, and his yoke will be destroyed from
your neck."

SYMBOLIC PROPHECY

Symbolic prophecy differs from prophetic discourse in that the
text is represented by a symbol, sometimes a commonplace object
such as a pot and sometimes by a supernatural occurrence. No matter which method is used, the text is clearly separated from the
rest of the material and presented in a symbolic manner.

EMBLEM PROPHECY

Emblem prophecy is the simplest type of symbolic prophecy. It
is a sermon in verse where the text is illustrated by some physical
object with which the reader or listener is familiar. For example,
God's plan in *Jeremiah* is likened to a potter working on a clay
vessel. Just as the potter works and reworks the clay to form the

vessel, so God works and reworks the nation of Israel. Very often in emblem prophecy an actual object is held up by the speaker to drive home the message. For a relatively unsophisticated people, this method of discourse was and is extremely effective.

JEREMIAH'S WAISTCLOTH

Jeremiah 13:1–11

Thus said the Lord to me, "Go and buy a linen waistcloth, and put it on your loins, and do not dip it in water." So I bought a waistcloth according to the word of the Lord, and put it on my loins. And the word of the Lord came to me a second time, "Take the waistcloth which you have bought, which is upon your loins, and arise, go to the Euphrates, and hide it there in a cleft of the rock." So I went, and hid it by the Euphrates, as the Lord commanded me. And after many days the Lord said to me, "Arise, go to the Euphrates, and take from there the waistcloth which I commanded you to hide there." Then I went to the Euphrates, and dug, and I took the waistcloth from the place where I had hidden it. And behold, the waistcloth was spoiled, it was good for nothing.

Then the word of the Lord came to me: "Thus says the Lord: Even so will I spoil the pride of Judah and the great pride of Jerusalem. This evil people, who refuse to hear my words, who stubbornly follow their own heart and have gone after other gods to serve them and worship them, shall be like this waistcloth, which is good for nothing. For as the waistcloth clings to the loins of a man, so I made the whole house of Israel and the whole house of Judah cling to me, says the Lord, that they might be for me a people, a name, a praise, and a glory, but they would not listen."

THE POTTER'S VESSEL

Jeremiah 18:1–10

The word that came to Jeremiah from the Lord: "Arise, and go down to the potter's house, and there I will let you hear my words." So I went down to the potter's house, and there he was working at his wheel. And the vessel he was making of clay was spoiled in the potter's hand, and he reworked it into another vessel, as it seemed good to the potter to do.

Then the word of the Lord came to me: "O house of Israel, can I not do with you as this potter has done? says the Lord. Behold, like the clay in the potter's hand, so are you in my hand, O house of Israel. If at any time I declare concerning a nation or a kingdom, that I will pluck up and break down and destroy it, and if that nation, concerning which I have spoken, turns from its evil, I will repent of the evil that I intended to do to it. And if at any time I declare concerning a nation or a kingdom that I will build and plant it, and if it does evil in my sight, not listening to my voice, then I will repent of the good which I had intended to do to it."

THE BROKEN BOTTLE

Jeremiah 19:1-3, 10-13

Thus said the Lord, "Go, buy a potter's earthen flask, and take some of the elders of the people and some of the senior priests, and go out to the valley of the son of Hinnom at the entry of the Potsherd Gate, and proclaim there the words that I tell you. You shall say, 'Hear the word of the Lord, O kings of Judah and inhabitants of Jerusalem. Thus says the Lord of hosts, the God of Israel, Behold, I am bringing such evil upon this place that the ears of every one who hears of it will tingle.

"Then you shall break the flask in the sight of the men who go with you, and shall say to them, 'Thus says the Lord of hosts: So will I break this people and this city, as one breaks a potter's vessel, so that it can never be mended. Men shall bury in Topheth because there will be no place else to bury. Thus will I do to this place, says the Lord, and to its inhabitants, making this city like Topheth. The houses of Jerusalem and the houses of the kings of Judah—all the houses upon whose roofs incense has been burned to all the host of heaven, and drink offerings have been poured out to other gods—shall be defiled like the place of Topheth.' "

THE TWO BASKETS OF FIGS

Jeremiah 24:1-10

After Nebuchadnezzar king of Babylon had taken into exile from Jerusalem Jeconiah the son of Jehoiakim, king of Judah, together with the princes of Judah, the craftsmen, and the smiths, and had brought them to Babylon, the Lord showed me this vision: Behold, two baskets of figs placed before the temple of the Lord. One basket had very good figs, like first-ripe figs, but the other basket had very bad figs, so bad that they could not be eaten. And the Lord said to me, "What do you see, Jeremiah?" I said, "Figs, the good figs very good, and the bad figs very bad, so bad that they cannot be eaten."

Then the word of the Lord came to me: "Thus says the Lord, the God of Israel: Like these good figs, so I will regard as good the exiles from Judah, whom I have sent away from this place to the land of the Chaldeans. I will set my eyes upon them for good, and I will bring them back to this land. I will build them up, and not tear them down; I will plant them, and not uproot them. I will give them a heart to know that I am the Lord; and they shall be my people and I will be their God, for they shall return to me with their whole heart.

"But thus says the Lord: Like the bad figs which are so bad they cannot be eaten, so will I treat Zedekiah the king of Judah, his princes, the remnant of Jerusalem who remain in this land, and those who dwell in the land of Egypt. I will make them a horror to all the kingdoms of the earth, to be a reproach, a byword, a taunt, and a curse in all the places where I shall drive them. And I will send sword, famine, and pestilence upon them, until they shall be utterly destroyed from the land which I gave to them and their fathers."

THE PIECE OF TILE

Ezekiel 4:1–17; 5:1–4

(The sermon is acted out, then preached.)

"And you, O son of man, take a brick and lay it before you, and portray upon it a city, even Jerusalem; and put siegeworks against it, and build a siege wall against it, and cast up a mound against it; set camps also against it, and plant battering rams against it round about. And take an iron plate, and place it as an iron wall between you and the city; and set your face toward it, and let it be in a state of seige, and press the seige against it. This is a sign for the house of Israel.

"Then lie upon your left side, and I will lay the punishment of the house of Israel upon you; for the number of the days that you lie upon it, you shall bear their punishment. For I assign to you a number of days, three hundred and ninety days, equal to the number of the years of their punishment; so long shall you bear the punishment of the house of Israel. And when you have completed these, you shall lie down a second time, but on your right side, and bear the punishment of the house of Judah; forty days I assign you, a day for each year. And you shall set your face toward the siege of Jerusalem, with your arm bared; and you shall prophesy against the city. And behold, I will put cords upon you, so that you cannot turn from one side to the other, till you have completed the days of your siege.

"And you, take wheat and barley, beans and lentils, millet and spelt, and put them into a single vessel, and make bread of them. During the number of days that you lie upon your side, three hundred and ninety days, you shall eat it. And the food which you eat shall be by weight, twenty shekels a day; once a day you shall eat it. And water you shall drink by measure, the sixth part of a hin; once a day you shall drink. And you shall eat it as a barley cake, baking it in their sight on human dung." And the Lord said, "Thus shall the people of Israel eat their bread unclean, among the nations whither I will drive them." Then I said, "Ah Lord God! behold, I have never defiled myself; from my youth up till now I have never eaten what died of itself or was torn by beasts, nor has foul flesh come into my mouth." Then he said to me, "See, I will let you have cow's dung instead of human dung, on which you may prepare your bread." Moreover he said to me, "Son of man, behold, I will break the staff of bread in Jerusalem; they shall eat bread by weight and with fearfulness; and they shall drink water by measure and in dismay. I will do this that they may lack bread and water, and look at one another in dismay, and waste away under their punishment.

"And you, O son of man, take a sharp sword; use it as a barber's razor and pass it over your head and your beard; then take balances for weighing, and divide the hair. A third part you shall burn in the fire in the midst of the city, when the days of the siege are completed; and a third part you shall take and strike with the sword round about the city; and a third part you shall scatter to the wind, and I will unsheathe the sword after them. And you shall take from these a small number, and bind them in the skirts of your robe. And of these again you shall take some, and cast them into the fire, and burn them in the fire; from there a fire will come forth into all the house of Israel."

THE HEALING WATERS OF THE TEMPLE

Ezekiel 47:1–12

Then he brought me back to the door of the temple; and behold, water was issuing from below the threshold of the temple toward the east (for the temple faced east); and the water was flowing down from below the south end of the threshold of the temple, south of the altar. Then he brought me out by way of the north gate, and led me round on the outside to the outer gate, that faces toward the east; and the water was coming out on the south side.

Going on eastward with a line in his hand, the man measured a thousand cubits, and then led me through the water; and it was ankle-deep. Again he measured a thousand, and led me through the water; and it was knee-deep. Again he measured a thousand, and led me through the water; and it was up to the loins. Again he measured a thousand, and it was a river that I could not pass through, for the water had risen; it was deep enough to swim in, a river that could not be passed through. And he said to me, "Son of man, have you seen this?"

Then he led me back along the bank of the river. As I went back, I saw upon the bank of the river very many trees on the one side and on the other. And he said to me, "This water flows toward the eastern region and goes down into the Arabah; and when it enters the stagnant waters of the sea, the water will become fresh. And wherever the river goes every living creature which swarms will live, and there will be very many fish; for this water goes there, that the waters of the sea may become fresh; so everything will live where the river goes. Fishermen will stand beside the sea; from Engedi to Eneglaim it will be a place for the spreading of nets; its fish will be of very many kinds, like the fish of the Great Sea. But its swamps and marshes will not become fresh; they are to be left for salt. And on the banks, on both sides of the river, there will grow all kinds of trees for food. Their leaves will not wither nor their fruit fail, but they will bear fresh fruit every month, because the water for them flows from the sanctuary. Their fruit will be for food and their leaves for healing."

EZEKIEL'S SONG OF THE SWORD

Ezekiel 21:1–32

The word of the Lord came to me: "Son of man, set your face toward Jerusalem and preach against the sanctuaries; prophesy against the land of Israel and say to the land of Israel, Thus says the Lord: Behold, I am against you, and will draw forth my sword out of its sheath, and will cut off from you both righteous and wicked. Because I will cut off from you both righteous and wicked, therefore my sword shall go out of its sheath against all flesh from south to north; and all flesh shall know that I the Lord have drawn my sword out of its sheath; it shall not be sheathed again. Sigh therefore, son of man; sigh with breaking heart and bitter grief before their eyes. And when they say to you, 'Why do you sigh?' you shall say, 'Because of the tidings. When it comes, every heart will melt and all hands will be feeble, every spirit will faint and all knees will be weak as water. Behold, it comes and it will be fulfilled,' " says the Lord God.

And the word of the Lord came to me: "Son of man, prophesy and say, Thus says the Lord, Say:

A sword, a sword is sharpened
and also polished,
sharpened for slaughter,
polished to flash like lightning!

Or do we make mirth? You have despised the rod, my son, with everything of wood. So the sword is given to be polished, that it may be handled; it is sharpened and polished to be given into the hand of the slayer. Cry and wail, son of man, for it is against my people; it is against all the princes of Israel; they are delivered over to the sword with my people. Smite therefore upon your thigh. For it will not be a testing—what could it do if you despise the rod?" says the Lord God.

"Prophesy therefore, son of man; clap your hands and let the sword come down twice, yea thrice, the sword for those to be slain; it is the sword for the great slaughter, which encompasses them, that their hearts may melt, and many fall at all their gates. I have given the glittering sword; ah! it is made like lightning, it is polished for slaughter. Cut sharply to right and left where your edge is directed. I also will clap my hands, and I will satisfy my fury; I the Lord have spoken."

The word of the Lord came to me again: "Son of man, mark two ways for the sword of the king of Babylon to come; both of them shall come forth from the same land. And make a signpost, make it at the head of the way to a city; mark a way for the sword to come to Rabbah of the Ammonites and to Judah and to Jerusalem the fortified. For the king of Babylon stands at the parting of the way, at the head of the two ways, to use divination; he shakes the arrows, he consults the teraphim, he looks at the liver. Into his right hand comes the lot for Jerusalem, to open the mouth with a cry, to lift up the voice with shouting, to set battering rams against the gates to cast up mounds, to build seige towers. But to them it will seem like a false divination; they have sworn solemn oaths; but he brings their guilt to remembrance, that they may be captured.

"Therefore thus says the Lord God: Because you have made your guilt to be remembered, in that your transgressions are uncovered, so that in all your doings your sins appear—because you have come to remembrance, you shall be taken in them. And you, O unhallowed wicked one, prince of Israel, whose day has come, the time of your final punishment, thus says the Lord God: Remove the turban, and take off the crown; things shall not remain as they are; exalt that which is low, and abase that which is high. A ruin, ruin, ruin I will make it; there shall not be even a trace of it until he comes whose right it is; and to him I will give it.

"And you, son of man, prophesy, and say, Thus says the Lord God concerning the Ammonites, and concerning their reproach; say, A sword, a sword is drawn for the slaughter, it is polished to glitter and to flash like lightning—while they see for you false visions, while they divine lies for you—to be laid on the necks of the unhallowed wicked, whose day has come, the time of their final punishment. Return it to its sheath. In the place where you were created, in the land of your origin, I will judge you. And I will pour out my indignation upon you; I will blow upon you with the fire of my wrath; and I will deliver you into the hands of brutal men, skilful to destroy. You shall be fuel for the fire; your blood shall be in the midst of the land; you shall be no more remembered; for I the Lord have spoken."

VISION PROPHECY

Vision prophecy at times is hardly distinguishable from emblem prophecy. The texts are merely presented in supernatural vision rather than as being seen by the ordinary eyesight. For example, God, rather than instructing his prophet to observe the potter making vessels and thereby understanding His will, now presents in a vision to Ezekiel a valley of dry bones to symbolize that without God the nation of Israel is nothing.

THE VISION OF THE VALLEY OF DRY BONES
Ezekiel 37:1–14

The hand of the Lord was upon me, and he brought me out by the Spirit of the Lord, and set me down in the midst of the valley; it was full of bones. And he led me round among them; and behold, there were very many upon the valley; and lo, they were very dry. And he said to me, "Son of man, can these bones live?" And I answered, "O Lord God, thou knowest." Again he said to me, "Prophesy to these bones, and say to them, O dry bones, hear the word of the Lord. Thus says the Lord God to these bones: Behold, I will cause breath to enter you, and you shall live. And I will lay sinews upon you, and will cause flesh to come upon you, and cover you with skin, and put breath in you, and you shall live; and you shall know that I am the Lord."

So I prophesied as I was commanded; and as I prophesied, there was a noise, and behold, a rattling; and the bones came together, bone to its bone. And as I looked, there were sinews on them, and flesh had come upon them, and skin had covered them; but there was no breath in them. Then he said to me, "Prophesy to the breath, prophesy, son of man, and say to the breath, Thus says the Lord God: Come from the four winds, O breath, and breathe upon these slain, that they may live." So I prophesied as he commanded me, and the breath came into them, and they lived, and stood upon their feet, an exceedingly great host.

Then he said to me, "Son of man, these bones are the whole house of Israel. Behold, they say, 'Our bones are dried up, and our hope is lost; we are clean cut off.' Therefore prophesy, and say to them, Thus says the Lord God: Behold, I will open your graves, and raise you from your graves, O my people; and I will bring you home into the land of Israel. And you shall know that I am the Lord, when I open your graves, and raise you from your graves, O my people. And I will put my Spirit within you, and you shall live, and I will place you in your own land; then you shall know that I, the Lord, have spoken, and I have done it, says the Lord."

INTERPRETATION OF THE HANDWRITING ON THE WALL

Daniel 5:1–31

King Belshazzar made a great feast for a thousand of his lords, and drank wine in front of the thousand.

Belshazzar, when he tasted the wine, commanded that the vessels of gold and of silver which Nebuchadnezzar his father had taken out of the temple in Jerusalem be brought, that the king and his lords, his wives, and his concubines might drink from them. Then they brought in the golden and silver vessels which had been taken out of the temple, the house of God in Jerusalem; and the king and his lords, his wives, and his concubines drank from them. They drank wine, and praised the gods of gold and silver, bronze, iron, wood, and stone.

Immediately the fingers of a man's hand appeared and wrote on the plaster of the wall of the king's palace, opposite the lampstand; and the king saw the hand as it wrote. Then the king's color changed, and his thoughts alarmed him; his limbs gave way and his knees knocked together. The king cried aloud to bring in the enchanters, the Chaldeans, and the astrologers. The king said to the wise men of Babylon, "Whoever reads this writing, and shows me its interpretation, shall be clothed with purple, and have a chain of gold about his neck, and shall be the third ruler in the kingdom." Then all the king's wise men came in, but they could not read the writing or make known to the king the interpretation. Then King Belshazzar was greatly alarmed, and his color changed; and his lords were perplexed.

The queen, because of the words of the king and his lords, came into the banqueting hall; and the queen said, "O king, live for ever! Let not your thoughts alarm you or your color change. There is in your kingdom a man in whom is the spirit of the holy gods. In the days of your father light and understanding and wisdom, like the wisdom of the gods, were found in him, and King Nebuchadnezzar, your father, made him chief of the magicians, enchanters, Chaldeans, and astrologers, because an excellent spirit, knowledge, and understanding to interpret dreams, explain riddles, and solve problems were found in this Daniel, whom the king named Belteshazzar. Now let Daniel be called, and he will show the interpretation."

Then Daniel was brought in before the king. The king said to Daniel, "You are that Daniel, one of the exiles of Judah, whom the king my father brought from Judah. I have heard of you that the spirit of the holy gods is in you, and that light and understanding and excellent wisdom are found in you. Now the wise men, the enchanters, have been brought in before me to read this writing and make known to me its interpretation; but they could not show the interpretation of the matter. But I have heard that you can give interpretations and solve problems. Now if you can read the writing and make known to me its interpretation, you shall be clothed with purple, and have a chain of gold about your neck, and shall be the third ruler in the kingdom."

Then Daniel answered before the king, "Let your gifts be for yourself, and give your rewards to another; nevertheless I will read the writing to the king and make known to him the interpretation. O king, the Most High God gave Nebuchadnezzar your father kingship and greatness and glory and majesty; and because of the greatness that he gave him, all peoples, nations, and languages trembled and feared before him; whom he would he slew, and whom he would he kept alive; whom he would he raised up, and whom he would he put down. But when his heart was lifted up and his spirit was hardened so that he dealt proudly, he was deposed from his kingly throne, and his glory was taken from him; he was driven from among men, and his mind was made like that of a beast, and his dwelling was with the wild asses; he was fed grass like an ox; and his body was wet with the dew of heaven, until he knew that the Most High God rules the kingdom of men, and sets over it whom he will. And you his son, Belshazzar, have not humbled your heart, though you knew all this, but you have lifted up yourself against the Lord of heaven; and the vessels of his house have been brought in before you, and you and your lords, your wives, and your concubines have drunk wine from them; and you have praised the gods of silver and gold, of bronze, iron, wood, and stone, which do not see or hear or know, but the God in whose hand is your breath, and whose are all your ways, you have not honored.

"Then from his presence the hand was sent, and this writing was inscribed. And this is the writing that was inscribed, MENE, MENE, TEKEL, AND PARSIN. This is the interpretation of the matter: MENE, God has numbered the days of your kingdom and brought it to an end; TEKEL, you have been weighed in the balances and found wanting; PERES, your kingdom is divided and given to the Medes and Persians."

Then Belshazzar commanded, and Daniel was clothed with purple, a chain of gold was put about his neck, and proclamation was made concerning him, that he should be the third ruler in the kingdom.

That very night Belshazzar the Chaldean king was slain. And Darius the Mede received the kingdom, being about sixty-two years old.

THE FIERY FURNACE EPISODE
Daniel 3:8–30

Therefore at that time certain Chaldeans came forward and maliciously accused the Jews. They said to King Nebuchadnezzar, "O king, live for ever! You, O king, have made a decree, that every man who hears the sound of the horn, pipe, lyre, trigon, harp, bagpipe, and every kind of music, shall fall down and worship the golden image; and whoever does not fall down and worship shall be cast into a burning fiery furnace. There are certain Jews whom you have appointed over the affairs of the province of Babylon: Shadrach, Meshach, and Abednego. These men, O king, pay no heed to you; they do not serve your gods or worship the golden image which you have set up."

Then Nebuchadnezzar in furious rage commanded that Shadrach, Meshach, and Abednego be brought. Then they brought these men before the king. Nebuchadnezzar said to them, "Is it true, O Shadrach, Meshach, and Abednego, that you do not serve my gods or worship the golden image which I have set up? Now if you are ready when you hear the sound of the horn, pipe, lyre, trigon, harp, bagpipe, and every kind of music, to fall down and worship the image which I have made, well and good; but if you do not worship, you shall immediately be cast into a burning fiery furnace; and who is the god that will deliver you out of my hands?"

Shadrach, Meshach, and Abednego answered the king, "O Nebuchadnezzar, we have no need to answer you in this matter. If it be so, our God whom we serve is able to deliver us from the burning fiery furnace; and he will deliver us out of your hand, O king. But if not, be it known to you, O king, that we will not serve your gods or worship the golden image which you have set up."

Then Nebuchadnezzar was full of fury, and the expression of his face was changed against Shadrach, Meshach, and Abednego. He ordered the furnace heated seven times more than it was wont to be heated. And be ordered certain mighty men of his army to bind Shadrach, Meshach, and Abednego, and to cast them into the burning fiery furnace. Then these men were bound in their mantles, their tunics, their hats, and their other garments, and they were cast into the burning fiery furnace. Because the king's order was strict and the furnace very hot, the flame of the fire slew those men who took up Shadrach, Meshach, and Abednego. And these three men, Shadrach, Meshach, and Abednego, fell bound into the burning fiery furnace.

Then King Nebuchadnezzar was astonished and rose up in haste. He said to his counselors, "Did we not cast three men bound into the fire?" They answered the king, "True, O king." He answered, "But I see four men loose, walking in the midst of the fire, and they are not hurt; and the appearance of the fourth is like a son of the gods."

Then Nebuchadnezzar came near to the door of the burning fiery furnace and said, "Shadrach, Meshach, and Abednego, servants of the Most High God, come forth, and come here!" Then Shadrach, Meshach, and Abednego came out from the fire. And the satraps, the prefects, the governors, and the king's counselors gathered together and saw that the fire had not had any power over the bodies of those men; the hair of their heads was not singed, their mantles were not harmed, and no smell of fire had come upon them. Nebuchadnezzar said, "Blessed be the

God of Shadrach, Meshach, and Abednego, who has sent his angel and delivered his servants, who trusted in him, and set at nought the king's command, and yielded up their bodies rather than serve and worship any god except their own God. Therefore I make a decree: Any people, nation, or language that speaks anything against the God of Shadrach, Meshach, and Abednego shall be torn limb from limb, and their houses laid in ruins; for there is no other god who is able to deliver in this way." Then the king promoted Shadrach, Meshach, and Abednego in the province of Babylon.

PROPHETIC PARABLE

The prophetic parable is a sermon with a symbolic text, but this time the emblem is narrated instead of being visibly presented. For example, in the parable of the vineyard, the vineyard is *described,* not actually presented.

PARABLE OF THE VINEYARD
Isaiah 5:1–10

Let me sing for my beloved
a love song concerning his vineyard:
My beloved had a vineyard
    on a very fertile hill.
He digged it and cleared it of stones,
    and planted it with choice vines;
he built a watchtower in the midst of it,
    and hewed out a wine vat in it;
and he looked for it to yield grapes,
    but it yielded wild grapes.

And now, O inhabitants of Jerusalem
    and men of Judah,
judge, I pray you, between me
    and my vineyard.
What more was there to do for my vineyard,
    that I have not done in it?
When I looked for it to yield grapes,
    why did it yield wild grapes?

And now I will tell you
    what I will do to my vineyard

I will remove its hedge,
    and it shall be devoured;
I will break down its wall,
    and it shall be trampled down.
I will make it a waste;
    it shall not be pruned or hoed,
    and briers and thorns shall grow up;
I will also command the clouds
    that they rain no rain upon it.

For the vineyard of the Lord of hosts
    is the house of Israel,
and the men of Judah
    are his pleasant planting;
and he looked for justice,
    but behold, bloodshed;
for righteousness,
    but behold, a cry!

Woe to those who join house to house,
    who add field to field,
until there is no more room,
    and you are made to dwell alone
    in the midst of the land.
The Lord of hosts has sworn in my hearing:
"Surely many houses shall be desolate,
    large and beautiful houses, without inhabitant.
For ten acres of vineyard shall yield but one bath,
    and a homer of seed shall yield but an ephah."

VINE UNPROFITABLE FOR USE
Ezekiel 15:1–8

And the word of the Lord came to me: "Son of man, how does the wood of the vine surpass any wood, the vine branch which is among the trees of the forest? Is wood taken from it to make anything? Do men take a peg from it to hang any vessel on? Lo, it is given to the fire for fuel; when the fire has consumed both ends of it, and the middle of it is charred, is it useful for anything? Behold, when it was whole, it was used for nothing; how much less, when the fire has consumed it and it is charred, can it ever be used for anything! Therefore thus says the Lord God: Like the wood of the vine among the trees of the forest, which I have given to the fire for fuel, so will I give up the inhabitants of Jerusalem. And I will set my face against them; though they escape from the fire, the fire shall yet consume them; and you will know that I am the Lord, when I set my face against them. And I will make the land desolate, because they have acted faithlessly, says the Lord God."

PROPHETIC INTERCOURSE

Prophetic intercourse is two-directional as opposed to discourse which suggests a one-directional message. The prophet has intercourse with God or with inquirers or with the world in general. The message of God is revealed through the discourse. It is somewhat doubtful that these discourses were meant for publication.

DANIEL'S EXPERIENCE IN THE LION'S DEN

Daniel 6:1–28

It pleased Darius to set over the kingdom a hundred and twenty satraps, to be throughout the whole kingdom; and over them three presidents, of whom Daniel was one, to whom these satraps should give account, so that the king might suffer no loss. Then this Daniel became distinguished above all the other presidents and satraps, because an excellent spirit was in him; and the king planned to set him over the whole kingdom. Then the presidents and the satraps sought to find a ground for complaint against Daniel with regard to the kingdom; but they could find no ground for complaint or any fault, because he was faithful, and no error or fault was found in him. Then these men said, "We shall not find any ground for complaint against this Daniel unless we find it in connection with the law of his God."

Then these presidents and satraps came by agreement to the king and said to him, "O King Darius, live for ever! All the presidents of the kingdom, the prefects and the satraps, the counselors and the governors are agreed that the king should establish an ordinance and enforce an interdict, that whoever makes petition to any god or man for thirty days, except to you, O king, shall be cast into the den of lions. Now, O king, establish the interdict and sign the document, so that it cannot be changed, according to the law of the Medes and the Persians, which cannot be revoked." Therefore King Darius signed the document and interdict.

When Daniel knew that the document had been signed, he went to his house where he had windows in his upper chamber open toward Jerusalem; and he got down upon his knees three times a day and prayed and gave thanks before his God, as he had done previously. Then these men came by agreement and found Daniel making petition and supplication before his God. Then they came near and said before the king, concerning the interdict, "O king! Did you not sign an interdict, that any man who makes petition to any god or man within thirty days except to you, O king, shall be cast into the den of lions?" The king answered, "The thing stands fast, according to the law of the Medes and Persians, which cannot be revoked." Then they answered before the king, "That Daniel, who is one of the exiles from Judah, pays no heed to you, O king, or the interdict you have signed, but makes his petition three times a day."

Then the king, when he heard these words, was much distressed, and set his mind to deliver Daniel; and he labored till the sun went down to rescue him. Then these men came by agreement to the king, and said to the king, "Know, O king, that it is a law of the Medes and Persians that no interdict or ordinance which the king establishes can be changed."

Then the king commanded, and Daniel was brought and cast into the den of lions. The king said to Daniel, "May your God, whom you serve continually, deliver you!" And a stone was brought and laid upon the mouth of the den, and the king sealed it with his own signet and with the signet of his lords, that nothing might be changed concerning Daniel. Then the king went to his palace, and spent the night fasting; no diversions were brought to him, and sleep fled from him.

Then, at break of day, the king arose and went in haste to the den of lions. When he came near to the den where Daniel was, he cried out in a tone of anguish and said to Daniel, "O Daniel, servant of the living God, has your God, whom you serve continually, been able to deliver you from the lions?" Then Daniel said to the king, "O king, live for ever! My God sent his angel and shut the lions' mouths, and they have not hurt me, because I was found blameless before him; and also before you, O king, I have done no wrong." Then the king was exceedingly glad, and commanded that Daniel be taken up out of the den. So Daniel was taken up out of the den, and no kind of hurt was found upon him, because he had trusted in his God. And the king commanded, and those men who had accused Daniel were brought and cast into the den of lions—they, their children, and their wives; and before they reached the bottom of the den the lions overpowered them and broke all their bones in pieces.

Then King Darius wrote to all the peoples, nations, and languages that dwell in all the earth: "Peace be multiplied to you. I make a decree, that in all my royal dominion men tremble and fear before the God of Daniel,

for he is the living God,
    enduring for ever;
his kingdom shall never be destroyed,
    and his dominion shall be to the end.
He delivers and rescues,
    he works signs and wonders
    in heaven and on earth,
he who has saved Daniel
    from the power of the lions."

So this Daniel prospered during the reign of Darius and the reign of Cyrus the Persian.

THE BOOK OF MALACHI

The book of Malachi is a dialectic. It is not an actual interview between the prophet and God, but the discourse takes the form of a reply to imaginary objections or interruptions.

Malachi

The oracle of the word of the Lord to Israel by Malachi.

"I have loved you," says the Lord. But you say, "How hast thou loved us?" "Is not Esau Jacob's brother?" says the Lord. "Yet I have loved Jacob but I have hated Esau; I have laid waste his hill country and left his heritage to jackals of the desert." If Edom says, "We are shattered but we will rebuild the ruins," the Lord of hosts says, "They may build, but I will tear down, till they are called the wicked country, the people with whom the Lord is angry for ever." Your own eyes shall see this, and you shall say, "Great is the Lord, beyond the border of Israel!"

"A son honors his father, and a servant his master. If then I am a father, where is my honor? and if I am a master, where is my fear? says the Lord of hosts to you, O priests, who despise my name. You say, 'How have we despised thy name?' By offering polluted food upon my altar. And you say, 'How have we polluted it?' By thinking that the Lord's table may be despised. When you offer blind animals in sacrifice, is that no evil? And when you offer those that are lame or sick, is that no evil? Present that to your governor; will he be pleased with you or show you favor? says the Lord of hosts. And now entreat the favor of God, that he may be gracious to us. With such a gift from your hand, will he show favor to any of you? says the Lord of hosts. Oh, that there were one among you who would shut the doors, that you might not kindle fire upon my altar in vain! I have no pleasure in you, says the Lord of hosts, and I will not accept an offering from your hand. For from the rising of the sun to its setting my name is great among the nations, and in every place incense is offered to my name, and a pure offering; for my name is great among the nations, says the Lord of hosts. But you profane it when you say that the Lord's table is polluted, and the food for it may be despised. 'What a weariness this is,' you say, and you sniff at me, says the Lord of hosts. You bring what has been taken by violence or is lame or sick, and this you bring as your offering! Shall I accept that from your hand? says the Lord. Cursed be the cheat who has a male in his flock, and vows it, and yet sacrifices to the Lord what is blemished; for I am a great King, says the Lord of hosts, and my name is feared among the nations.

"And now, O priests, this command is for you. If you will not listen, if you will not lay it to heart to give glory to my name, says the Lord of hosts, then I will send the curse upon you and I will curse your blessings; indeed I have already cursed them, because you do not lay it to heart. Behold, I will rebuke your off-spring, and spread dung upon your faces, the dung of your offerings, and I will put you out of my presence. So shall you know that I have sent this command to you, that my covenant with Levi may hold, says the Lord of hosts. My covenant with him was a covenant of life and peace, and I gave them to him, that he might fear; and he feared me, he stood in awe of my name. True instruction was in his mouth, and no wrong was found on his lips. He walked with me in peace and uprightness, and he turned many from iniquity. For the lips of a priest should guard knowledge, and men should seek instruction from his mouth, for he is the messenger of the Lord of hosts. But you have turned aside from the way; you have caused many to stumble by your instruction; you have corrupted the covenant of Levi, says the Lord of hosts, and so I make you despised and abased before all the people, inasmuch as you have not kept my ways but have shown partiality in your instruction."

Have we not all one father? Has not one God created us? Why then are we faithless to one another, profaning the covenant of our fathers? Judah has been faithless, and abomination has been committed in Israel and in Jerusalem; for Judah has profaned the sanctuary of the Lord, which he loves, and has married the daughter of a foreign god. May the Lord cut off from the tents of Jacob, for the man who does this, any to witness or answer, or to bring an offering to the Lord of hosts!

And this again you do. You cover the Lord's altar with tears, the weeping and groaning because he no longer regards the offering or accepts it with favor at your hand. You ask, "Why does he not?" Because the Lord was witness to the covenant between you and the wife of your youth, to whom you have been faithless, though she is your companion and your wife by covenant. Has not the one God made and sustained for us the spirit of life? And what does he desire? Godly offspring. So take heed to yourselves, and let none be faithless to the wife of his youth. "For I hate divorce, says the Lord the God of Israel, and covering one's garment with violence, says the Lord of hosts. So take heed to yourselves and do not be faithless."

You have wearied the Lord with your words. Yet you say, "How have we wearied him?" By saying, "Every one who does evil is good in the sight of the Lord, and he delights in them," Or by asking, "Where is the God of justice?"

"Behold, I send my messenger to prepare the way before me, and the Lord whom you seek will suddenly come to his temple; the messenger of the covenant in whom you delight, behold, he is coming, says the Lord of hosts. But who can endure the day of his coming, and who can stand when he appears?

"For he is like a refiner's fire and like fullers' soap; he will sit as a refiner and purifier of silver, and he will purify the sons of Levi and refine them like gold and silver, till they present right offerings to the Lord. Then the offering of Judah and Jerusalem will be pleasing to the Lord as in the days of old and as in former years.

"Then I will draw near to you for judgment; I will be a swift witness against the sorcerers, against the adulterers, against those who swear falsely, against those who oppress the hireling in his wages, the widow and the orphan, against those who thrust aside the sojourner, and do not fear me, says the Lord of hosts.

"For I the Lord do not change; therefore you, O sons of Jacob, are not consumed. From the days of your fathers you have turned aside from my statutes and have not kept them. Return to me, and I will return to you, says the Lord of hosts. But you say, 'How shall we return?' Will man rob God? Yet you are robbing me. But you say, 'How are we robbing thee?' In your tithes and offerings. You are cursed with a curse, for you are robbing me; the whole nation of you. Bring the full tithes into the storehouse, that there may be food in my house; and thereby put me to the test, says the Lord of hosts, if I will not open the windows of heaven for you and pour down for you an overflowing blessing. I will rebuke the devourer for you, so that it will not destroy the fruits of your soil; and your vine in the field shall not fail to bear, says the Lord of hosts. Then all nations will call you blessed, for you will be a land of delight, says the Lord of hosts.

"Your words have been stout against me, says the Lord. Yet you say, 'How have we spoken against thee?' You have said, 'It is vain to serve God. What is the good of our keeping his charge or of walking as in mourning before the Lord of hosts? Henceforth we deem the arrogant blessed; evildoers not only prosper but when they put God to the test they escape.' "

Then those who feared the Lord spoke with one another; the Lord heeded and heard them, and a book of remembrance was written before him of those who feared the Lord and thought on his name. "They shall be mine, says the Lord of hosts, my special possession on the day when I act, and I will spare them as a man spares his son who serves him. Then once more you shall distinguish between the righteous and the wicked, between one who serves God and one who does not serve him.

"For behold, the day comes, burning like an oven, when all the arrogant and all evildoers will be stubble; the day that comes shall burn them up, says the Lord of hosts, so that it will leave them neither root nor branch. But for you who fear my name the sun of righteousness shall rise, with healing in its wings. You shall go forth leaping like calves from the stall. And you shall tread down the wicked, for they will be ashes under the soles of your feet, on the day when I act, says the Lord of hosts.

"Remember the law of my servant Moses, the statutes and ordinances that I commanded him at Horeb for all Israel.

"Behold, I will send you Elijah the prophet before the great and terrible day of the Lord comes. And he will turn the hearts of fathers to their children and the hearts of children to their fathers, lest I come and smite the land with a curse."

DRAMATIC PROPHECY

In dramatic prophecy a scene is presented entirely by dialogue without any description or comment from the prophet, except so far as he may be a party to the scene. Often the voice of God is heard in tones of comfort. The book of Micah is the most interesting of dramatic prophecies, especially Chapters 6 and 7.

Micah 6:1–16; 7:1–20

Hear what the Lord says:

Arise, plead your case before the mountains,
and let the hills hear your voice.

Hear, you mountains, the controversy of the Lord,
  and you enduring foundations of the earth;
for the Lord has a controversy with his people,
  and he will contend with Israel.

"O my people, what have I done to you?
  In what have I wearied you? Answer me!
For I brought you up from the land of Egypt,
  and redeemed you from the house of bondage;
and I sent before you Moses,
  Aaron, and Miriam.
O my people, remember what Balak king of Moab devised,
  and what Balaam the son of Beor answered him,
and what happened from Shittim to Gilgal,
  that you may know the saving acts of the Lord."

"With what shall I come before the Lord,
  and bow myself before God on high?
Shall I come before him with burnt offerings,
  with calves a year old?
Will the Lord be pleased with thousands of rams,
  with ten thousands of rivers of oil?
Shall I give my first-born for my transgression,
  the fruit of my body for the sin of my soul?"
He has showed you, O man, what is good;
  and what does the Lord require of you
but to do justice, and to love kindness,
  and to walk humbly with your God?

The voice of the Lord cries to the city—
  and it is sound wisdom to fear thy name:
"Hear, O tribe and assembly of the city!
  Can I forget the treasures of wickedness in the house of the
    wicked,
  and the scant measure that is accursed?
Shall I acquit the man with wicked scales
  and with a bag of deceitful weights?
Your rich men are full of violence;
  your inhabitants speak lies,
  and their tongue is deceitful in their mouth.
Therefore I have begun to smite you,
  making you desolate because of your sins.
You shall eat, but not be satisfied,
  and there shall be hunger in your inward parts;

you shall put away, but not save,
    and what you save I will give to the sword.
You shall sow, but not reap;
    you shall tread olives, but not anoint yourselves with oil;
    you shall tread grapes, but not drink wine.
For you have kept the statutes of Omri,
    and all the works of the house of Ahab;
    and you have walked in their counsels;
that I may make you a desolation, and your inhabitants a
        hissing;
    so you shall bear the scorn of the peoples."

Woe is me! For I have become
    as when the summer fruit has been gathered,
    as when the vintage has been gleaned:
there is no cluster to eat,
    no first-ripe fig which my soul desires.
The godly man has perished from the earth,
    and there is none upright among men;
they all lie in wait for blood,
    and each hunts his brother with a net.
Their hands are upon what is evil, to do it diligently;
    the prince and the judge ask for a bribe,
and the great man utters the evil desire of his soul;
    thus they weave it together.
The best of them is like a brier,
    the most upright of them a thorn hedge.
The day of their watchmen, of their punishment, has come;
    now their confusion is at hand.
Put no trust in a neighbor,
    have no confidence in a friend;
guard the doors of your mouth
    from her who lies in your bosom;
for the son treats the father with contempt,
    the daughter rises up against her mother,
the daughter-in-law against her mother-in-law;
    a man's enemies are the men of his own house.
But as for me, I will look to the Lord,
    I will wait for the God of my salvation;
    my God will hear me.

Rejoice not over me, O my enemy;
    when I fall, I shall rise;

when I sit in darkness,
    the Lord will be a light to me.
I will bear the indignation of the Lord
    because I have sinned against him,
until he pleads my cause
    and executes judgment for me.
He will bring me forth to the light;
    I shall behold his deliverance.
Then my enemy will see,
    and shame will cover her who said to me,
    "Where is the Lord your God?"
My eyes will gloat over her;
    now she will be trodden down
    like the mire of the streets.
A day for the building of your walls!
    In that day the boundary shall be far extended.
In that day they will come to you,
    from Assyria to Egypt,
and from Egypt to the River,
    from sea to sea and from mountain to mountain.
But earth will be desolate
    because of its inhabitants,
    for the fruit of their doings.

Shepherd thy people will thy staff,
    the flock of thy inheritance,
who dwell alone in a forest
    in the midst of a garden land;
let them feed in Bashan and Gilead
    as in the days of old.

As in the days when you came out of the land of Egypt
    I will show them marvelous things.

The nations shall see and be ashamed
    of all their might;
they lay their hands on their mouths;
    their ears shall be deaf;
they shall lick the dust like a serpent,
    like the crawling things of the earth;
they shall come trembling out of their strongholds,
    they shall turn in dread to the Lord our God,
    and they shall fear because of thee.

Who is a God like thee, pardoning iniquity
    and passing over transgression
    for the remnant of his inheritance?
He does not retain his anger for ever
    because he delights in steadfast love.
He will again have compassion upon us,
    he will tread our iniquities under foot.
Thou wilt cast all our sins
    into the depths of the sea.
Thou wilt show faithfulness to Jacob
    and steadfast love to Abraham,
as thou hast sworn to our fathers
    from the days of old.

THE DIVINE YEARNING

Hosea 11:1–11

When Israel was a child, I loved him,
    and out of Egypt I called my son.
The more I called them,
    the more they went from me;
they kept sacrificing to the Baals,
    and burning incense to idols.

Yet it was I who taught Ephraim to walk,
    I took them up in my arms;
    but they did not know that I healed them.
I led them with cords of compassion,
    with the bands of love,
and I became to them as one
    who eases the yoke on their jaws,
    and I bent down to them and fed them.

They shall return to the land of Egypt,
    and Assyria shall be their king,
    because they have refused to return to me.
The sword shall rage against their cities,
    consume the bars of their gates,
    and devour them in their fortresses.
My people are bent on turning away from me;
    so they are appointed to the yoke,
    and none shall remove it.

How can I give you up, O Ephraim!
How can I hand you over, O Israel!
How can I make you like Admah!
How can I treat you like Zeboiim!
My heart recoils within me,
my compassion grows warm and tender.
I will not execute my fierce anger,
I will not again destroy Ephraim;
for I am God and not man,
the Holy One in your midst,
and I will not come to destroy.

They shall go after the Lord,
he will roar like a lion;
yea, he will roar,
and his sons shall come trembling from the west;
they shall come trembling like birds from Egypt,
and like doves from the land of Assyria;
and I will return them to their homes, says the Lord.

THE DOOM SONG

Prophets exercised great influence in foreign policy, as well as in domestic questions. Questions of the temporary policy and the perpetual policy of Israel as a nation in upholding the worship of the true God amidst nations of adolaters were the chief concerns of many prophets. Doom songs are prophetic utterances directed against some particular city, nation, or country. Doom songs are the pourings from "the cup of the Lord's fury" against particular kingdoms.

THE DOOM OF TYRE

Ezekiel 26:1-8; 27:1-9; 28:1-8

In the eleventh year, on the first day of the month, the word of the Lord came to me: "Son of man, because Tyre said concerning Jerusalem, 'Aha, the gate of the peoples is broken, it has swung open to me; I shall be replenished, now that she is laid waste,' therefore thus says the Lord God: Behold, I am against you, O Tyre, and will bring up many nations against you, as the sea brings up its waves. They shall destroy the walls of Tyre, and break down her towers; and I will scrape her soil from her, and make her a bare rock. She shall be in the midst of the sea a place for the spreading of nets; for I have spoken, says the Lord God; and she shall become a spoil to the nations; and her daughters on the mainland shall be slain by the sword. Then they will know that I am the Lord.

"For thus says the Lord God: Behold, I will bring upon Tyre from the north Nebuchadnezzar king of Babylon, king of kings, with horses and chariots, and with horsemen and a host of many soldiers. He will slay with the sword your daughters on the mainland; he will set up a siege wall against you, and throw up a mound against you, and raise a roof of shields against you.

The word of the Lord came to me: "Now you, son of man, raise a lamentation over Tyre, and say to Tyre, who dwells at the entrance to the sea, merchant of the peoples on many coastlands, thus says the Lord God:

"O Tyre, you have said,
  'I am perfect in beauty.'
Your borders are in the heart of the seas;
  your builders made perfect your beauty.
They made all your planks
  of fir trees from Senir;
they took a cedar from Lebanon
  to make a mast for you.
Of oaks of Bashan
  they made your oars;
they made your deck of pines
  from the coasts of Cyprus,
  inlaid with ivory.
Of fine embroidered linen from Egypt
  was your sail,
  serving as your ensign;
blue and purple from the coasts of Elishah
  was your awning.
The inhabitants of Sidon and Arvad
  were your rowers;
skilled men of Zemer were in you,
  they were your pilots.
The elders of Gebal and her skilled men were in you,
  caulking your seams;
all the ships of the sea with their mariners were in you,
  to barter for your wares."

The word of the Lord came to me: "Son of man, say to the prince of Tyre, Thus says the Lord God:

"Because your heart is proud,
   and you have said, 'I am a god,
I sit in the seat of the gods,
   in the heart of the seas,'
yet you are but a man, and no god,
   though you consider yourself as wise as a god—
you are indeed wiser than Daniel;
   no secret is hidden from you;
by your wisdom and your understanding
   you have gotten wealth for yourself,
and have gathered gold and silver
   into your treasuries;
by your great wisdom in trade
   you have increased your wealth,
   and your heart has become proud in your wealth—
therefore thus says the Lord God:
"Because you consider yourself
   as wise as a god,
therefore, behold, I will bring strangers upon you,
   the most terrible of the nations;
and they shall draw their swords against the beauty of
         your wisdom
   and defile your splendor.
They shall thrust you down into the Pit,
   and you shall die the death of the slain
   in the heart of the seas."

JONAH'S SONG TO NINEVEH

The entire book of Jonah is an attempt
by God to persuade a nation to turn to him.
Jonah manages to complicate matters.

Jonah

Now the word of the Lord came to Jonah the son of Amittai, saying, "Arise, go to Nineveh, that great city, and cry against it; for their wickedness has come up before me." But Jonah rose to flee to Tarshish from the presence of the Lord. He went down to

Joppa and found a ship going to Tarshish; so he paid the fare, and went on board, to go with them to Tarshish, away from the presence of the Lord.

But the Lord hurled a great wind upon the sea, and there was a mighty tempest on the sea, so that the ship threatened to break up. Then the mariners were afraid, and each cried to his god; and they threw the wares that were in the ship into the sea, to lighten it for them. But Jonah had gone down into the inner part of the ship and had lain down, and was fast asleep. So the captain came and said to him, "What do you mean, you sleeper? Arise, call upon your god! Perhaps the god will give a thought to us, that we do not perish."

And they said to one another, "Come, let us cast lots, that we may know on whose account this evil has come upon us." So they cast lots, and the lot fell upon Jonah. Then they said to him, "Tell us on whose account this evil has come upon us. What is your occupation? And whence do you come? What is your country? And of what people are you?" And he said to them, "I am a Hebrew; and I fear the Lord, the God of heaven, who made the sea and the dry land." Then the men were exceedingly afraid, and said to him, "What is this that you have done!" For the men knew that he was fleeing from the presence of the Lord, because he had told them.

Then they said to him, "What shall we do to you, that the sea may quiet down for us?" For the sea grew more and more tempestuous. He said to them, "Take me up and throw me into the sea; then the sea will quiet down for you; for I know it is because of me that this great tempest has come upon you." Nevertheless the men rowed hard to bring the ship back to land, but they could not, for the sea grew more and more tempestuous against them. Therefore they cried to the Lord, "We beseech thee, O Lord, let us not perish for this man's life, and lay not on us innocent blood; for thou, O Lord, hast done as it pleased thee." So they took up Jonah and threw him into the sea; and the sea ceased from its raging. Then the men feared the Lord exceedingly, and they offered a sacrifice to the Lord and made vows.

And the Lord appointed a great fish to swallow up Jonah; and Jonah was in the belly of the fish three days and three nights.

Then Jonah prayed to the Lord his God from the belly of the fish, saying,

"I called to the Lord, out of my distress,
    and he answered me;

out of the belly of Sheol I cried,
   and thou didst hear my voice.
For thou didst cast me into the deep,
   into the heart of the seas,
   and the flood was round about me;
all thy waves and thy billows
   passed over me.
Then I said, 'I am cast out
   from thy presence;
how shall I again look
   upon thy holy temple?'
The waters closed in over me,
   the deep was round about me;
weeds were wrapped about my head
   at the roots of the mountains.
I went down to the land
   whose bars closed upon me for ever;
yet thou didst bring up my life from the Pit,
   O Lord my God.
When my soul fainted within me,
   I remembered the Lord;
and my prayer came to thee,
   into thy holy temple.
Those who pay regard to vain idols
   forsake their true loyalty.
But I with the voice of thanksgiving
   will sacrifice to thee;
what I have vowed I will pay.
   Deliverance belongs to the Lord!"

And the Lord spoke to the fish, and it vomited out Jonah upon the dry land.

Then the word of the Lord came to Jonah the second time, saying, "Arise, go to Nineveh, that great city, and proclaim to it the message that I tell you." So Jonah arose and went to Nineveh, according to the word of the Lord. Now Nineveh was an exceedingly great city, three days' journey in breadth. Jonah began to go into the city, going a day's journey. And he cried, "Yet forty days, and Nineveh shall be overthrown!" And the people of Nineveh believed God; they proclaimed a fast, and put on sackcloth, from the greatest of them to the least of them.

Then tidings reached the king of Nineveh, and he arose from his throne, removed his robe, and covered himself with sackcloth, and sat in ashes. And he made proclamation and published through Nineveh, "By the decree of the king and his nobles: Let neither man nor beast, herd nor flock, taste anything; let them not feed, or drink water, but let man and beast be covered with sack-cloth, and let them cry mightily to God; yea, let every one turn from his evil way and from the violence which is in his hands. Who knows, God may yet repent and turn from his fierce anger, so that we perish not?"

When God saw what they did, how they turned from their evil way, God repented of the evil which he had said he would do to them; and he did not do it.

But it displeased Jonah exceedingly, and he was angry. And he prayed to the Lord and said, "I pray thee, Lord, is not this what I said when I was yet in my country? That is why I made haste to flee to Tarshish; for I knew that thou art a gracious God and merci-ful, slow to anger, and abounding in steadfast love, and repentest of evil. Therefore now, O Lord, take my life from me, I beseech thee, for it is better for me to die than to live." And the Lord said, "Do you do well to be angry?" Then Jonah went out of the city and sat to the east of the city, and made a booth for himself there. He sat under it in the shade, till he should see what would become of the city.

And the Lord God appointed a plant, and made it come up over Jonah, that it might be a shade over his head, to save him from his discomfort. So Jonah was exceedingly glad because of the plant. But when dawn came up the next day, God appointed a worm which attacked the plant, so that it withered. When the sun rose, God appointed a sultry east wind, and the sun beat upon the head of Jonah so that he was faint; and he asked that he might die, and said, "It is better for me to die than to live." But God said to Jonah, "Do you do well to be angry for the plant?" And he said, "I do well to be angry, angry enough to die." And the Lord said, "You pity the plant, for which you did not labor, nor did you make it grow, which came into being in a night, and perished in a night. And should not I pity Nineveh, that great city, in which there are more than a hundred and twenty thousand persons who do not know their right hand from their left, and also much cattle?"

ELIJAH'S SONG TO AHAB

1 Kings 18:1–46; 19:1–8

After many days the word of the Lord came to Elijah, in the third year, saying, "Go, show yourself to Ahab; and I will send rain upon the earth." So Elijah went to show himself to Ahab. Now the famine was severe in Samaria. And Ahab called Obadiah, who was over the household. (Now Obadiah revered the Lord greatly; and when Jezebel cut off the prophets of the Lord, Obadiah took a hundred prophets and hid them by fifties in a cave, and fed them with bread and water.) And Ahab said to Obadiah, "Go through the land to all the springs of water and to all the valleys; perhaps we may find grass and save the horses and mules alive, and not lose some of the animals." So they divided the land between them to pass through it; Ahab went in one direction by himself, and Obadiah went in another direction by himself.

And as Obadiah was on the way, behold, Elijah met him; and Obadiah recognized him, and fell on his face, and said, "Is it you, my lord Elijah?" And he answered him, "It is I. Go, tell your lord, 'Behold, Elijah is here.' " And he said, "Wherein have I sinned, that you would give your servant into the hand of Ahab, to kill me? As the Lord your God lives, there is no nation or kingdom whither my lord has not sent to seek you; and when they would say, 'He is not here,' he would take an oath of the kingdom or nation, that they had not found you. And now you say, 'Go, tell your lord, "Behold, Elijah is here." ' And as soon as I have gone from you, the spirit of the Lord will carry you whither I know not; and so, when I come and tell Ahab and he cannot find you, he will kill me, although I your servant have revered the Lord from my youth. Has it not been told my lord what I did when Jezebel killed the prophets of the Lord, how I hid a hundred men of the Lord's prophets by fifties in a cave, and fed them with bread and water? And now you say, 'Go, tell your lord, "Behold, Elijah is here" '; and he will kill me." And Elijah said, "As the Lord of hosts lives, before whom I stand, I will surely show myself to him today." So Obadiah went to meet Ahab, and told him; and Ahab went to meet Elijah.

When Ahab saw Elijah, Ahab said to him, "Is it you, you troubler of Israel?" And he answered, "I have not troubled Israel; but you have, and your father's house, because you have forsaken the commandments of the Lord and followed the Baals. Now therefore send and gather all Israel to me at Mount Carmel, and the four hundred and fifty prophets of Baal and the four hundred prophets of Asherah, who eat at Jezebel's table."

So Ahab sent to all the people of Israel, and gathered the prophets together at Mount Carmel. And Elijah came near to all the people, and said, "How long will you go limping with two different opinions? If the Lord is God, follow him; but if Baal, then follow him." And the people did not answer him a word. Then

Elijah said to the people, "I, even I only, am left a prophet of the Lord; but Baal's prophets are four hundred and fifty men. Let two bulls be given to us; and let them choose one bull for themselves, and cut it in pieces and lay it on the wood, but put no fire to it; and I will prepare the other bull and lay it on the wood, and put no fire to it. And you call on the name of your god and I will call on the name of the Lord; and the God who answers by fire, he is God." And all the people answered, "It is well spoken." Then Elijah said to the prophets of Baal, "Choose for yourselves one bull and prepare it first, for you are many; and call on the name of your god, but put no fire to it." And they took the bull which was given them, and they prepared it, and called on the name of Baal from morning until noon, saying, "O Baal, answer us!" But there was no voice, and no one answered. And they limped about the altar which they had made. And at noon Elijah mocked them, saying, "Cry aloud, for he is a god; either he is musing, or he has gone aside, or he is on a journey, or perhaps he is asleep and must be awakened." And they cried aloud, and cut themselves after their custom with swords and lances, until the blood gushed out upon them. And as midday passed, they raved on until the time of the offering of the oblation, but there was no voice; no one answered, no one heeded.

Then Elijah said to all the people, "Come near to me"; and all the people came near to him. And he repaired the altar of the Lord that had been thrown down; Elijah took twelve stones, according to the number of the tribes of the sons of Jacob, to whom the word of the Lord came, saying, "Israel shall be your name"; and with the stones he built an altar in the name of the Lord. And he made a trench about the altar, as great as would contain two measures of seed. And he put the wood in order, and cut the bull in pieces and laid it on the wood. And he said, "Fill four jars with water, and pour it on the burnt offering, and on the wood." And he said, "Do it a second time"; and they did it a second time. And he said, "Do it a third time"; and they did it a third time. And the water ran round about the altar, and filled the trench also with water.

And at the time of the offering of the oblation, Elijah the prophet came near and said, "O Lord, God of Abraham, Isaac, and Israel, let it be known this day that thou art God in Israel, and that I am thy servant, and that I have done all these things at thy word. Answer me, O Lord, answer me, that this people may know that thou, O Lord, art God, and that thou hast turned their hearts back." Then the fire of the Lord fell, and consumed the burnt offering, and the wood, and the stones, and the dust, and licked up the water that was in the trench. And when all the people saw it, they fell on their faces; and they said, "The Lord, he is God; the Lord, he is God." And Elijah said to them, "Seize the prophets of Baal; let not one of them escape." And they seized them; and Elijah brought them down to the brook Kishon, and killed them there.

And Elijah said to Ahab, "Go up, eat and drink; for there is a sound of the rushing of rain." So Ahab went up to eat and to drink. And Elijah went up to the top of Carmel; and he bowed himself down upon the earth, and put his face between his knees. And he said to his servant, "Go up now, look toward the sea." And he went up and looked, and said, "There is nothing." And he said, "Go again seven times." And at the seventh time he said, "Behold, a little cloud like a man's hand is rising out of the sea." And he said, "Go up, say to Ahab, 'Prepare your chariot and go down, lest the rain stop you.'" And in a little while the heavens grew black with clouds and wind, and there was a great rain. And Ahab rode and went to Jezreel. And the hand of the Lord was on Elijah; and he girded up his loins and ran before Ahab to the entrance of Jezreel.

Ahab told Jezebel all that Elijah had done, and how he had slain all the prophets with the sword. Then Jezebel sent a messenger to Elijah, saying, "So may the gods do to me and more also, if I do not make your life as the life of one of them by this time tomorrow." Then he was afraid, and he arose and went for his life, and came to Beer-sheba, which belongs to Judah, and left his servant there.

But he himself went a day's journey into the wilderness, and came and sat down under a broom tree; and he asked that he might die, saying, "It is enough; now, O Lord, take away my life; for I am no better than my fathers." And he lay down and slept under a broom tree; and behold, an angel touched him, and said to him, "Arise and eat." And he looked, and behold, there was at his head a cake baked on hot stones and a jar of water. And he ate and drank, and lay down again. And the angel of the Lord came again a second time, and touched him, and said, "Arise and eat, else the journey will be too great for you." And he arose, and ate and drank, and went in the strength of that food forty days and forty nights to Horeb the mount of God.

THE RHAPSODY

Prophets at times wished to display the incidents themselves before our imagination. This demonstrated the working of events as a part of God's judgment. Such dramatic compositions borrow from all literary departments and blend them together into the most highly wrought and spiritual of literary forms. The simplest rhapsodies present a problem of current history in dramatic dialogue, present attempts at the solution in mingled recitations or the doom song, and then present the solution in the full splendor of a lyric ode. Similar fusions take place in music, as in the Oratorio and the Cantata.

THE RHAPSODY OF THE CHALDEANS

The Chaldeans were a cruel, godless, mighty nation and were to be God's instrument of judgment. The question arises: Is not the Chaldean nation worse than the Hebrew nation against whom they would be used?

The Book of Habakkuk

PROPHET:

> O Lord, how long shall I cry for help,
>   and thou wilt not hear?
> Or cry to thee "Violence!"
>   and thou wilt not save?
> Why dost thou make me see wrongs
>   and look upon trouble?
> Destruction and violence are before me;
>   strife and contention arise.
> So the law is slacked
>   and justice never goes forth.
> For the wicked surround the righteous,
>   so justice goes forth perverted.

GOD:

> Look among the nations, and see;
>   wonder and be astounded.
> For I am doing a work in your days
>   that you would not believe if told.
> For lo, I am rousing the Chaldeans,
>   that bitter and hasty nation,
> who march through the breadth of the earth,
>   to seize habitations not their own.
> Dread and terrible are they;
>   their justice and dignity proceed from themselves.
> Their horses are swifter than leopards,
>   more fierce than the evening wolves;
>   their horsemen press proudly on.

Yea, their horsemen come from afar;
    they fly like an eagle swift to devour.
They all come for violence;
    terror of them goes before them.
    They gather captives like sand.
At kings they scoff,
    and of rulers they make sport.
They laugh at every fortress,
    for they heap up earth and take it.
Then they sweep by like the wind and go on,
    guilty men, whose own might is their god!

PROPHET:
Art thou not from everlasting,
    O Lord my God, my Holy One?
    We shall not die.
O Lord, thou hast ordained them as a judgment;
    and thou, O Rock, hast established them for chastisement.
Thou who art of purer eyes than to behold evil
    and canst not look on wrong,
why dost thou look on faithless men,
    and art silent when the wicked swallows up
    the man more righteous than he?
For thou makest men like the fish of the sea,
    like crawling things that have no ruler.
He brings all of them up with a hook,
    he drags them out with his net,
he gathers them in his seine;
    so he rejoices and exults.
Therefore he sacrifices to his net
    and burns incense to his seine;
for by them he lives in luxury,
    and his food is rich.
Is he then to keep on emptying his net,
    and mercilessly slaying nations forever?

The paradox is now opened—the solution will now be sought. The prophet retires to his watchtower to await God's answer; the answer comes in imagery (four woes).

Soliloquy by the Prophet

I will take my stand to watch,
    and station myself on the tower,

and look forth to see what he will say to me,
    and what I will answer concerning my complaint.
And the Lord answered me:
"Write the vision;
    make it plain upon tablets,
    so he may run who reads it.
For still the vision awaits its time;
    it hastens to the end—it will not lie.
If it seem slow, wait for it;
    it will surely come, it will not delay.
Behold, he whose soul is not upright in him shall fail,
    but the righteous shall live by his faith.
Moreover, wine is treacherous;
    the arrogant man shall not abide.
His greed is as wide as Sheol;
    like death he has never enough.
He gathers for himself all nations,
    and collects as his own all peoples."

Shall not all these take up their taunt
against him, in scoffing derision of him, and say,
"Woe to him who heaps up what is not his own—
    for how long?—
    and loads himself with pledges!"
Will not your debtors suddenly arise,
    and those awake who will make you tremble?
    Then you will be booty for them.
Because you have plundered many nations,
    all the remnant of the peoples shall plunder you,
for the blood of men and violence to the earth,
    to cities and all who dwell therein.

Woe to him who gets evil gain for his house,
    to set his nest on high,
    to be safe from the reach of harm!
You have devised shame to your house
    by cutting off many peoples;
    you have forfeited your life.
For the stone will cry out from the wall,
    and the beam from the woodwork respond.

Woe to him who builds a town with blood,
    and founds a city on iniquity!

Behold, is it not from the Lord of hosts
    that peoples labor only for fire,
    and nations weary themselves for nought?
For the earth will be filled
    with the knowledge of the glory of the Lord,
    as the waters cover the sea.

Woe to him who makes his neighbors drink
    of the cup of his wrath, and makes them drunk,
    to gaze on their shame!
You will be sated with contempt instead of glory.
    Drink, yourself, and stagger!
The cup in the Lord's right hand
    will come around to you,
    and shame will come upon your glory!
The violence done to Lebanon will overwhelm you;
    the destruction of the beasts will terrify you,
for the blood of men and violence to the earth,
    to cities and all who dwell therein.

What profit is an idol
    when its maker has shaped it,
    a metal image, a teacher of lies?
For the workman trusts in his own creation
    when he makes dumb idols!
Woe to him who says to a wooden thing, Awake;
    to a dumb stone, Arise!
    Can this give revelation?
Behold, it is overlaid with gold and silver,
    and there is no breath at all in it.

But the Lord is in his holy temple;
    let all the earth keep silence before him.

The third section is a Biblical ode. Intervention is to be immediate, not in the future.

PRELUDE BY THE PROPHET:
    A prayer of Habakkuk the prophet, according to Shigionoth.
    O Lord, I have heard the report of thee,
        and thy work, O Lord, do I fear.
    In the midst of the years renew it;

in the midst of the years make it known;
in wrath remember mercy.

VISION OF THE PROPHET:
God came from Teman,
and the Holy One from Mount Paran.
His glory covered the heavens,
and the earth was full of his praise.

Selah

His brightness was like the light,
rays flashed from his hand;
and there he veiled his power.
Before him went pestilence,
and plague followed close behind.
He stood and measured the earth;
he looked and shook the nations;
then the eternal mountains were scattered,
the everlasting hills sank low.
His ways were as of old.
I saw the tents of Cushan in affliction;
the curtains of the land of Midian did tremble.

QUESTION BY THE PROPHET:
Was thy wrath against the rivers, O Lord?
Was thy anger against the rivers,
or thy indignation against the sea,
when thou didst ride upon thy horses,
upon thy chariot of victory?
Thou didst strip the sheath from thy bow,
and put the arrows to the string.

Selah

Thou didst cleave the earth with rivers.
The mountains saw thee, and writhed;
the raging waters swept on;
the deep gave forth its voice,
it lifted its hands on high.
The sun and moon stood still in their habitation
at the light of thine arrows as they sped,
at the flash of thy glittering spear.
Thou didst bestride the earth in fury,
thou didst trample the nations in anger.
Thou wentest forth for the salvation of thy people,
for the salvation of thy anointed.

Thou didst crush the head of the wicked,
  laying him bare from thigh to neck.

                                                    Selah

Thou didst pierce with thy shafts the head of his warriors,
  who came like a whirlwind to scatter me,
    rejoicing as if to devour the poor in secret.
Thou didst trample the sea with thy horses,
  the surging of mighty waters.

POSTLUDE BY THE PROPHET:
  I hear, and my body trembles,
    my lips quiver at the sound;
  rottenness enters into my bones,
    my steps totter beneath me.
  I will quietly wait for the day of trouble
    to come upon people who invade us.

Though the fig tree do not blossom,
  nor fruit be on the vines,
the produce of the olive fail
  and the fields yield no food,
the flock be cut off from the fold
  and there be no herd in the stalls,
yet I will rejoice in the Lord,
  I will joy in the God of my salvation.
God, the Lord, is my strength;
  he makes my feet like hinds' feet,
  he makes me tread upon my high places.

To the choirmaster: with stringed instruments.

RHAPSODY OF ZION REDEEMED

The last twenty-seven chapters of the book of Isaiah form a single composition. The unity in the whole work is sometimes questioned because there is no sign of a logical plan; however, reasoning abounds. The rhapsody goes forward from an immediate deliverance, on to the final judgment of the nations, and on to the restoration of the remnant in a Messianic kingdom.

There are several divisions to the rhapsody. But the divisions are not seven stages of advance. Rather, they are seven independent "visions," side by side and partly successive, each complete in itself and drawing from all parts of the national history.

Prelude

Isaiah 40:1–31; 41:1–10; 42:1–17; 43:8–21; 44:1–7, 9–23;
45:9–13, 18–21; 48:12–19; 49:1–7, 14–18; 50:4–11; 51:1–3;
52:3–10; 53:1–12; 54:1–8; 55:1–13; 56:1–5; 57:14–21;
58:1–9; 59:1–8, 15–21; 60:1–7, 19–22; 61:1–4, 8–11; 62:1–9;
63:1–19; 64:1–2, 8–12; 65:1–7, 13–25; 66:1–4, 10–23

The voice of God is heard commanding the prophet to speak comfort to Jerusalem. Her iniquity is pardoned.

Comfort, comfort my people, says your God.
Speak tenderly to Jerusalem,
    and cry to her
that her warfare is ended,
    that her iniquity is pardoned,
that she has received from the Lord's hand
    double for all her sins.

A voice cries:
"In the wilderness prepare the way of the Lord,
    make straight in the desert a highway for our God.
Every valley shall be lifted up,
    and every mountain and hill be made low;
the uneven ground shall become level,
    and the rough places a plain.
And the glory of the Lord shall be revealed,
    and all flesh shall see it together,
    for the mouth of the Lord has spoken."

A voice says, "Cry!"
    And I said, "What shall I cry?"
All flesh is grass,
    and all its beauty is like the flower of the field.
The grass withers, the flower fades,
    when the breath of the Lord blows upon it;
    surely the people is grass.
The grass withers, the flower fades;
    but the word of our God will stand for ever.

Get you up to a high mountain,
    O Zion, herald of good tidings;

lift up your voice with strength,
    O Jerusalem, herald of good tidings,
    lift it up, fear not;
say to the cities of Judah,
    "Behold your God!"

Behold, the Lord God comes with might,
    and his arm rules for him;
behold, his reward is with him,
    and his recompense before him.
He will feed his flock like a shepherd,
    he will gather the lambs in his arms,
he will carry them in his bosom,
    and gently lead those that are with young.

Vision 1

Vision 1 is an introduction, in the form of meditation, about the supremacy of Jehovah.

Who has measured the waters in the hollow of his hand
    and marked off the heavens with a span,
enclosed the dust of the earth in a measure
    and weighed the mountains in scales
    and the hills in a balance?
Who has directed the Spirit of the Lord,
    or as his counselor has instructed him?
Whom did he consult for his enlightenment,
    and who taught him the path of justice,
and taught him knowledge,
    and showed him the way of understanding?
Behold, the nations are like a drop from a bucket,
    and are accounted as the dust on the scales;
    behold, he takes up the isles like fine dust.
Lebanon would not suffice for fuel,
    nor are its beasts enough for a burnt offering.
All the nations are as nothing before him,
    they are accounted by him as less than nothing and
        emptiness.

To whom then will you liken God,
    or what likeness compare with him?
The idol! a workman casts it,
    and a goldsmith overlays it with gold,
    and casts for it silver chains.

He who is impoverished chooses for an offering
    wood that will not rot;
he seeks out a skilful craftsman
    to set up an image that will not move.

Have you not known? Have you not heard?
    Has it not been told you from the beginning?
    Have you not understood from the foundations of the earth?
It is he who sits above the circle of the earth,
    and its inhabitants are like grasshoppers;
who stretches out the heavens like a curtain,
    and spreads them like a tent to dwell in;
who brings princes to nought,
    and makes the rulers of the earth as nothing.

Scarcely are they planted, scarcely sown,
    scarcely has their stem taken root in the earth,
when he blows upon them, and they wither,
    and the tempest carries them off like stubble.

To whom then will you compare me,
    that I should be like him? says the Holy One.
Lift up your eyes on high and see:
    who created these?
He who brings out their host by number,
    calling them all by name;
by the greatness of his might,
    and because he is strong in power
    not one is missing.

Why do you say, O Jacob,
    and speak, O Israel,
"My way is hid from the Lord,
    and my right is disregarded by my God"?
Have you not known? Have you not heard?
The Lord is the everlasting God,
    the Creator of the ends of the earth.
He does not faint or grow weary,
    his understanding is unsearchable.
He gives power to the faint,
    and to him who has no might he increases strength.
Even youths shall faint and be weary,
    and young men shall fall exhausted;

but they who wait for the Lord shall renew their strength;
    they shall mount up with wings like eagles,
they shall run and not be weary,
    they shall walk and not faint.

The nations are summoned to the bar of God to hear his will.

Listen to me in silence, O coastlands;
    let the peoples renew their strength;
let them approach, then let them speak;
    let us together draw near for judgment.

Who stirred up one from the east
    whom victory meets at every step?
He gives up nations before him,
    so that he tramples kings under foot;
he makes them like dust with his sword,
    like driven stubble with his bow.
He pursues them and passes on safely,
    by paths his feet have not trod.
Who has performed and done this,
    calling the generations from the beginning?
I, the Lord, the first,
    and with the last; I am He.

The coastlands have seen and are afraid,
    the ends of the earth tremble;
    they drawn near and come.
Every one helps his neighbor,
    and says to his brother, "Take courage!"
The craftsman encourages the goldsmith,
    and he who smooths with the hammer him who strikes
        the anvil,
saying of the soldering, "It is good";
    and they fasten it with nails so that it cannot be moved.

But you, Israel, my servant,
    Jacob, whom I have chosen,
    the offspring of Abraham, my friend;
you whom I took from the ends of the earth,
    and called from its farthest corners,
saying to you, "You are my servant,
    I have chosen you and not cast you off";

fear not, for I am with you,
  be not dismayed, for I am your God;
I will strengthen you, I will help you,
  I will uphold you with my victorious right hand.

Israel is proclaimed to the nations as God's servant, who is to bring forth judgment to the Gentiles.

Behold my servant, whom I uphold,
  my chosen, in whom my soul delights;
I have put my Spirit upon him,
  he will bring forth justice to the nations.
He will not cry or lift up his voice,
  or make it heard in the street;
a bruised reed he will not break,
  and a dimly burning wick he will not quench;
  he will faithfully bring forth justice.
He will not fail or be discouraged
  till he has established justice in the earth;
  and the coastlands wait for his law.

Thus says God, the Lord,
  who created the heavens and stretched them out,
  who spread forth the earth and what comes from it,
who gives breath to the people upon it
  and spirit to those who walk in it:
"I am the Lord, I have called you in righteousness,
  I have taken you by the hand and kept you;
I have given you as a covenant to the people,
  a light to the nations,
  to open the eyes that are blind,
to bring out the prisoners from the dungeon,
  from the prison those who sit in darkness.
I am the Lord, that is my name;
  my glory I give to no other,
  nor my praise to graven images.
Behold, the former things have come to pass,
  and new things I now declare;
before they spring forth
  I tell you of them."

Sing to the Lord a new song,
  his praise from the end of the earth!

Let the sea roar and all that fills it,
    the coastlands and their inhabitants.
Let the desert and its cities lift up their voice,
    the villages that Kedar inhabits;
let the inhabitants of Sela sing for joy,
    let them shout from the top of the mountains.
Let them give glory to the Lord,
    and declare his praise in the coastlands.
The Lord goes forth like a mighty man,
    like a man of war he stirs up his fury;
he cries out, he shouts aloud,
    he shows himself mighty against his foes.

For a long time I have held my peace,
    I have kept still and restrained myself;
now I will cry out like a woman in travail,
    I will gasp and pant.
I will lay waste mountains and hills,
    and dry up all their herbage;
I will turn the rivers into islands,
    and dry up the pools.
And I will lead the blind
    in a way that they know not,
in paths that they have not known
    I will guide them.
I will turn the darkness before them into light,
    the rough places into level ground.
These are the things I will do,
    and I will not forsake them.
They shall be turned back and utterly put to shame,
    who trust in graven images,
who say to molten images,
    "You are our gods."

The assembly of nations are challenged to bring witnesses to
show counsel from of old. They are silent. Israel is to be witness.

Bring forth the people who are blind, yet have eyes,
    who are deaf, yet have ears!
Let all the nations gather together,
    and let the peoples assemble.

Who among them can declare this,
    and show us the former things?
Let them bring their witnesses to justify them,
    and let them hear and say, It is true.
"You are my witnesses," says the Lord,
    "and my servant whom I have chosen,
that you may know and believe me
    and understand that I am He.
Before me no god was formed,
    nor shall there be any after me.
I, I am the Lord,
    and besides me there is no savior.
I declared and saved and proclaimed,
    when there was no strange god among you;
    and you are my witnesses," says the Lord.
"I am God, and also henceforth I am He,
    there is none who can deliver from my hand;
    I work and who can hinder it?"

Thus says the Lord,
    your Redeemer, the Holy One of Israel:
"For your sake I will send to Babylon
    and break down all the bars,
    and the shouting of the Chaldeans will be turned to
        lamentations.
I am the Lord, your Holy One,
    the Creator of Israel, your King."
Thus says the Lord,
    who makes a way in the sea,
    a path in the mighty waters,
who brings forth chariot and horse,
    army and warrior;
they lie down, they cannot rise,
    they are extinguished, quenched like a wick:
"Remember not the former things,
    nor consider the things of old.
Behold, I am doing a new thing;
    now it springs forth, do you not perceive it?
I will make a way in the wilderness and rivers in the desert.
The wild beasts will honor me,
    the jackals and the ostriches;
for I give water in the wilderness,
    rivers in the desert,

> to give drink to my chosen people,
>> the people whom I formed for myself
>> that they might declare my praise."

God asserts his Godhead, and pours out scorn on the gods of the nations.

> "But now hear, O Jacob my servant,
>> Israel whom I have chosen!
> Thus says the Lord who made you,
>> who formed you from the womb and will help you:
> Fear not, O Jacob my servant,
>> Jeshurun whom I have chosen.
> For I will pour water on the thirsty land,
>> and streams on the dry ground;
> I will pour my Spirit upon your descendants,
>> and my blessing on your offspring.
> They shall spring up like grass amid waters,
>> like willows by flowing streams.
> This one will say, 'I am the Lord's,'
>> another will call himself by the name of Jacob,
> and another will write on his hand, 'The Lord's,'
>> and surname himself by the name of Israel."

> Thus says the Lord, the King of Israel
>> and his Redeemer, the Lord of hosts:
> "I am the first and I am the last;
>> besides me there is no god.
> Who is like me? Let him proclaim it,
>> let him declare and set it forth before me.
> Who has announced from of old the things to come?
>> Let them tell us what is yet to be."

The fashioners of graven images are plunged into confusion: the work they do cannot witness for them to save them from shame.

All who make idols are nothing, and the things they delight in do not profit; their witnesses neither see nor know, that they may be put to shame. Who fashions a god or casts an image, that is profitable for nothing? Behold, all his fellows shall be put to shame, and the craftsmen are but men; let them all assemble, let them stand forth, they shall be terrified, they shall be put to shame together.

The ironsmith fashions it and works it over the coals; he shapes it with hammers, and forges it with his strong arm; he becomes hungry and his strength fails, he drinks no water and is faint. The carpenter stretches a line, he marks it out with a pencil; he fashions it with planes, and marks it with a compass; he shapes it into the figure of a man, with the beauty of a man, to dwell in a house. He cuts down cedars; or he chooses a holm tree or an oak and lets it grow strong among the trees of the forest; he plants a cedar and the rain nourishes it. Then it becomes fuel for a man; he takes a part of it and warms himself, he kindles a fire and bakes bread; also he makes a god and worships it, he makes it a graven image and falls down before it. Half of it he burns in the fire; over the half he eats flesh, he roasts meat and is satisfied; also he warms himself and says, "Aha, I am warm, I have seen the fire!" And the rest of it he makes into a god, his idol; and falls down to it and worships it; he prays to it and says, "Deliver me, for thou art my god!"

They know not, nor do they discern; for he has shut their eyes, so that they cannot see, and their minds, so that they cannot understand. No one considers, nor is there knowledge or discernment to say, "Half of it I burned in the fire, I also baked bread on its coals, I roasted flesh and have eaten; and shall I make the residue of it an abomination? Shall I fall down before a block of wood?" He feeds on ashes; a deluded mind has led him astray, and he cannot deliver himself or say, "Is there not a lie in my right hand?"

Remember these things, O Jacob,
    and Israel, for you are my servant;
I formed you, you are my servant;
    O Israel, you will not be forgotten by me.
I have swept away your transgressions like a cloud,
    and your sins like mist;
return to me, for I have redeemed you.

Sing, O heavens, for the Lord has done it;
    shout, O depths of the earth;
break forth into singing, O mountains,
    O forest, and every tree in it!
For the Lord has redeemed Jacob,
    and will be glorified in Israel.

"Woe to him who strives with his Maker,
    an earthen vessel with the potter!
Does the clay say to him who fashions it, 'What are you
            making'?
    or 'Your work has no handles'?

Woe to him who says to a father, 'What are you begetting?'
    or to a woman, 'With what are you in travail?' "
Thus says the Lord,
    the Holy One of Israel, and his Maker:
"Will you question me about my children,
    or command me concerning the work of my hands?
I made the earth,
    and created man upon it;
it was my hands that stretched out the heavens,
    and I commanded all their host.
I have aroused him in righteousness,
    and I will make straight all his ways;
he shall build my city
    and set my exiles free,
not for price or reward,"
    says the Lord of hosts.

For thus says the Lord,
who created the heavens
    (he is God!),
who formed the earth and made it
    (he established it;
he did not create it a chaos,
    he formed it to be inhabited!):
"I am the Lord, and there is no other.
I did not speak in secret,
    in a land of darkness;
I did not say to the offspring of Jacob,
    'Seek me in chaos.'
I the Lord speak the truth,
    I declare what is right.

"Assemble yourselves and come,
    draw near together,
    you survivors of the nations!
They have no knowledge
    who carry about their wooden idols,
and keep on praying to a god
    that cannot save.
Declare and present your case;
    let them take counsel together!
Who told this long ago?

Who declared it of old?
Was it not I, the Lord?
    And there is no other god besides me,
a righteous God and a Savior;
    there is none besides me."

Israel too falls under the rebuke, because God's name is used but not in truth nor in righteousness.

"Hearken to me, O Jacob,
    and Israel, whom I called!
I am He, I am the first,
    and I am the last.
My hand laid the foundation of the earth,
    and my right hand spread out the heavens;
when I call to them,
    they stand forth together.

"Assemble, all of you, and hear!
    Who among them has declared these things?
The Lord loves him;
    he shall perform his purpose on Babylon,
    and his arms shall be against the Chaldeans.
I, even I, have spoken and called him,
    I have brought him, and he will prosper in his way.
Draw near to me, hear this:
    from the beginning I have not spoken in secret,
    from the time it came to be I have been there."
And now the Lord God has sent me and his Spirit.

Thus, says the Lord,
    your Redeemer, the Holy One of Israel:
"I am the Lord your God,
    who teaches you to profit,
    who leads you in the way you should go.
O that you had hearkened to my commandments!
    Then your peace would have been like a river,
    and your righteousness like the waves of the sea;
your offspring would have been like the sand,
    and your descendants like its grains;
their name would never be cut off
    or destroyed from before me."

Vision 2

Israel is commissioned as God's servant.

Listen to me, O coastlands,
    and hearken, you peoples from afar.
The Lord called me from the womb,
    from the body of my mother he named my name.
He made my mouth like a sharp sword,
    in the shadow of his hand he hid me;
he made me a polished arrow,
    in his quiver he hid me away.

And he said to me, "You are my servant,
    Israel, in whom I will be glorified."
But I said, "I have labored in vain,
    I have spent my strength for nothing and vanity;
yet surely my right is with the Lord,
    and my recompense with my God."

And now the Lord says,
    who formed me from the womb to be his servant,
to bring Jacob back to him,
    and that Israel might be gathered to him,
for I am honored in the eyes of the Lord,
    and my God has become my strength—
he says:
"It is too light a thing that you should be my servant
    to raise up the tribes of Jacob
    and to restore the preserved of Israel;
I will give you as a light to the nations,
    that my salvation may reach to the end of the earth."

Thus says the Lord,
    the Redeemer of Israel and his Holy One,
to one deeply despised, abhorred by the nations,
    the servant of rulers:
"Kings shall see and arise;
    princes, and they shall prostrate themselves;
because of the Lord, who is faithful,
    the Holy One of Israel, who has chosen you."

But Zion said, "The Lord has forsaken me,
    my Lord has forgotten me."

"Can a woman forget her sucking child,
    that she should have no compassion on the son of her
        womb?"
Even these may forget,
    yet I will not forget you.
Behold, I have graven you on the palms of my hands;
    your walls are continually before me.
Your builders outstrip your destroyers,
    and those who laid you waste go forth from you.
Lift up your eyes round about and see;
    they all gather, they come to you.
As I live, says the Lord,
    you shall put them all on as an ornament,
    you shall bind them on as a bride does.

Israel is given the tongue of the learned in order to sustain "him
that is weary."

The Lord God has given me
    the tongue of those who are taught,
that I may know how to sustain with a word
    him that is weary.
Morning by morning he wakens,
    he wakens my ear
    to hear as those who are taught.
The Lord God has opened my ear,
    and I was not rebellious,
    I turned not backward.
I gave my back to the smiters,
    and my cheeks to those who pulled out the beard;
I hid not my face
    from shame and spitting.

For the Lord God helps me;
    therefore I have not been confounded;
therefore I have set my face like a flint,
    and I know that I shall not be put to shame;
    he who vindicates me is near.
Who will contend with me?
    Let us stand up together.
Who is my adversary?
    Let him come near to me.

Behold, the Lord God helps me;
    who will declare me guilty?
Behold, all of them will wear out like a garment;
    the moth will eat them up.

Who among you fears the Lord
    and obeys the voice of his servant,
who walks in darkness
    and has no light,
yet trusts in the name of the Lord
    and relies upon his God?
Behold, all you who kindle a fire,
    who set brands alight!
Walk by the light of your fire,
    and by the brands which you have kindled!
This shall you have from my hand:
    you shall lie down in torment.

Vision 3

God cries to his people to seek him, to look to their past and take comfort.

"Hearken to me, you who pursue deliverance,
    you who seek the Lord;
look to the rock from which you were hewn,
    and to the quarry from which you were digged.
Look to Abraham your father
    and to Sarah who bore you;
for when he was but one I called him,
    and I blessed him and made him many.
For the Lord will comfort Zion;
    he will comfort all her waste places,
and will make her wilderness like Eden,
    her desert like the garden of the Lord;
joy and gladness will be found in her,
    thanksgiving and the voice of song."

For thus says the Lord: "You were sold for nothing, and you shall be redeemed without money. For thus says the Lord God: My people went down at the first into Egypt to sojourn there, and the Assyrian oppressed them for nothing. Now therefore what have I here, says the Lord, seeing that my people are taken away for nothing? Their rulers wail, says the Lord, and continually all the day my name is despised. Therefore my people shall know my name;

therefore in that day they shall know that it is I who speak; here
am I."

> How beautiful upon the mountains
>   are the feet of him who brings good tidings,
> who publishes peace, who brings good tidings of good,
>   who publishes salvation,
>   who says to Zion, "Your God reigns."
> Hark, your watchmen lift up their voice,
>   together they sing for joy;
> for eye to eye they see
>   the return of the Lord to Zion.
> Break forth together into singing,
>   you waste places of Jerusalem;
> for the Lord has comforted his people,
>   he has redeemed Jerusalem.
> The Lord has bared his holy arm
>   before the eyes of all the nations;
> and all the ends of the earth shall see
>   the salvation of our God.

Vision 4

This is the central vision. It presents Israel as prosperous and
highly exalted to the astonishment of other nations.

> Who has believed what we have heard?
>   And to whom has the arm of the Lord been revealed?
> For he grew up before him like a young plant,
>   and like a root out of dry ground;
> he had no form or comeliness that we should look at him,
>   and no beauty that we should desire him.
> He was despised and rejected by men;
>   a man of sorrows, and acquainted with grief;
> and as one from whom men hide their faces
>   he was despised, and we esteemed him not.
>
> Surely he has borne our griefs
>   and carried our sorrows;
> yet we esteemed him stricken,
>   smitten by God, and afflicted.
> But he was wounded for our transgressions,
>   he was bruised for our iniquities;
> upon him was the chastisement that made us whole,
>   and with his stripes we are healed.

All we like sheep have gone astray;
    we have turned every one to his own way:
and the Lord has laid on him
    the iniquity of us all.

He was oppressed, and he was afflicted,
    yet he opened not his mouth;
like a lamb that is led to the slaughter,
    and like a sheep that before its shearers is dumb,
    so he opened not his mouth.
By oppression and judgment he was taken away;
    and as for his generation, who considered
that he was cut off out of the land of the living,
    stricken for the transgression of my people?
And they made his grave with the wicked
    and with a rich man in his death,
although he had done no violence,
    and there was no deceit in his mouth.

Yet it was the will of the Lord to bruise him;
    he has put him to grief;
when he makes himself an offering for sin,
    he shall see his offspring, he shall prolong his days;
the will of the Lord shall prosper in his hand;
    he shall see the fruit of the travail of his soul and be
        satisfied;
by his knowledge shall the righteous one, my servant,
    make many to be accounted righteous;
    and he shall bear their iniquities.
Therefore I will divide him a portion with the great,
    and he shall divide the spoil with the strong;
because he poured out his soul to death,
    and was numbered with the transgressors;
yet he bore the sin of many,
    and made intercession for the transgressors.

Vision 5

This vision is a series of Songs of Zion in her exaltation and calls the other nations to join in the covenant.

"Sing, O barren one, who did not bear;
    break forth into singing and cry aloud,
    you who have not been in travail!

For the children of the desolate one will be more
    than the children of her that is married, says the Lord.
Enlarge the place of your tent,
    and let the curtains of your habitations be stretched out;
hold not back, lengthen your cords
    and strengthen your stakes.
For you will spread abroad to the right and to the left,
    and your descendants will possess the nations
    and will people the desolate cities.
Fear not, for you will not be ashamed;
    be not confounded, for you will not be put to shame;
for you will forget the shame of your youth,
    and the reproach of your widowhood you will remember no
        more.
For your Maker is your husband,
    the Lord of hosts is his name;
and the Holy One of Israel is your Redeemer,
    the God of the whole earth he is called.
For the Lord has called you
    like a wife forsaken and grieved in spirit,
like a wife of youth when she is cast off,
    says your God.
For a brief moment I forsook you,
    but with great compassion I will gather you.
In overflowing wrath for a moment
    I hid my face from you,
but with everlasting love I will have compassion on you,
    says the Lord, your Redeemer.

"Ho, every one who thirsts,
    come to the waters;
and he who has no money,
    come, buy and eat!
Come, buy wine and milk
    without money and without price.
Why do you spend your money for that which is not bread,
    and your labor for that which does not satisfy?
Hearken diligently to me, and eat what is good,
    and delight yourselves in fatness.
Incline your ear, and come to me;
    hear, that your soul may live;
and I will make with you an everlasting covenant,
    my steadfast, sure love for David.

Behold, I made him a witness to the peoples,
    a leader and commander for the peoples.
Behold, you shall call nations that you know not,
    and nations that knew you not shall run to you,
because of the Lord your God, and of the Holy One of Israel,
    for he has glorified you.

"Seek the Lord while he may be found,
    call upon him while he is near;
let the wicked forsake his way,
    and the unrighteous man his thoughts;
let him return to the Lord, that he may have mercy on him,
    and to our God, for he will abundantly pardon.
For my thoughts are not your thoughts,
    neither are your ways my ways, says the Lord.
For as the heavens are higher than the earth,
    so are my ways higher than your ways
    and my thoughts than your thoughts.

"For as the rain and the snow come down from heaven,
    and return not thither but water the earth,
making it bring forth and sprout,
    giving seed to the sower and bread to the eater,
so shall my word be that goes forth from my mouth;
    it shall not return to me empty,
but it shall accomplish that which I purpose,
    and prosper in the thing for which I sent it.

"For you shall go out in joy,
    and be led forth in peace;
the mountains and the hills before you
    shall break forth into singing,
    and all the trees of the field shall clap their hands.
Instead of the thorn shall come up the cypress;
    instead of the brier shall come up the myrtle;
and it shall be to the Lord for a memorial,
    for an everlasting sign which shall not be cut off."

Vision 6

This vision presents the work of redemption exercised upon Zion. Before the final judgment of the nations, a purified nation is presented.

Thus says the Lord:
"Keep justice, and do righteousness,
for soon my salvation will come,
    and my deliverance be revealed.
Blessed is the man who does this,
    and the son of man who holds it fast,
who keeps the sabbath, not profaning it,
    and keeps his hand from doing any evil."

Let not the foreigner who has joined himself to the Lord say,
    "The Lord will surely separate me from his people";
and let not the eunuch say,
    "Behold, I am a dry tree."
For thus says the Lord:
"To the eunuchs who keep my sabbaths,
    who choose the things that please me
    and hold fast my covenant,
I will give in my house and within my walls
    a monument and a name
    better than sons and daughters;
I will give them an everlasting name
    which shall not be cut off."

And it shall be said,
"Build up, build up, prepare the way,
    remove every obstruction from my people's way."
For thus says the high and lofty One
    who inhabits eternity, whose name is Holy:
"I dwell in the high and holy place,
    and also with him who is of a contrite and humble spirit,
to revive the spirit of the humble,
    and to revive the heart of the contrite.
For I will not contend for ever,
    nor will I always be angry;
for from me proceeds the spirit,
    and I have made the breath of life.
Because of the iniquity of his covetousness I was angry,
    I smote him, I hid my face and was angry;
    but he went on backsliding in the way of his own heart.
I have seen his ways, but I will heal him;
    I will lead him and requite him with comfort,
    creating for his mourners the fruit of the lips.

Peace, peace, to the far and to the near, says the Lord;
 and I will heal him.
But the wicked are like the tossing sea;
 for it cannot rest,
 and its waters toss up mire and dirt.
There is no peace, says my God, for the wicked."

Israel attempts to follow God's righteous ordinances, but they
wonder if God sees their attempts.

"Cry aloud, spare not,
 lift up your voice like a trumpet;
declare to my people their transgression,
 to the house of Jacob their sins.
Yet they seek me daily,
 and delight to know my ways,
as if they were a nation that did righteousness
 and did not forsake the ordinance of their God;
they ask of me righteous judgments,
 they delight to draw near to God.
'Why have we fasted, and thou seest it not?
 Why have we humbled ourselves, and thou takest no
   knowledge of it?'
Behold, in the day of your fast you seek your own pleasure,
 and oppress all your workers.
Behold, you fast only to quarrel and to fight
 and to hit with wicked fist.
Fasting like yours this day
 will not make your voice to be heard on high.
Is such the fast that I choose,
 a day for a man to humble himself?
Is it to bow down his head like a rush,
 and to spread sackcloth and ashes under him?
Will you call this a fast,
 and a day acceptable to the Lord?

"Is not this the fast that I choose:
 to loose the bonds of wickedness,
 to undo the thongs of the yoke,
to let the oppressed go free,
 and to break every yoke?

Is it not to share your bread with the hungry,
    and bring the homeless poor into your house;
when you see the naked, to cover him,
    and not to hide yourself from your own flesh?
Then shall your light break forth like the dawn,
    and your healing shall spring up speedily;
your righteousness shall go before you,
    the glory of the Lord shall be your rear guard.
Then you shall call, and the Lord will answer;
    you shall cry, and he will say, Here I am."

Israel arouses itself to repentance and judgment is turned.

Behold, the Lord's hand is not shortened, that it cannot save,
    or his ear dull, that it cannot hear;
but your iniquities have made a separation
    between you and your God,
and your sins have hid his face from you
    so that he does not hear.
For your hands are defiled with blood
    and your fingers with iniquity;
your lips have spoken lies,
    your tongue mutters wickedness.
No one enters suit justly,
    no one goes to law honestly;
they rely on empty pleas, they speak lies,
    they conceive mischief and bring forth iniquity.
They hatch adders' eggs,
    they weave the spider's web;
he who eats their eggs dies,
    and from one which is crushed a viper is hatched.
Their webs will not serve as clothing;
    men will not cover themselves with what they make.
Their works are works of iniquity,
    and deeds of violence are in their hands.
Their feet run to evil,
    and they make haste to shed innocent blood;
their thoughts are thoughts of iniquity,
    desolation and destruction are in their highways.
The way of peace they know not,
    and there is no justice in their paths;
they have made their roads crooked,
    no one who goes in them knows peace.

The Lord saw it, and it displeased him
    that there was no justice.
He saw that there was no man,
    and wondered that there was no one to intervene;
then his own arm brought him victory,
    and his righteousness upheld him.
He put on righteousness as a breastplate,
    and a helmet of salvation upon his head;
he put on garments of vengeance for clothing,
    and wrapped himself in fury as a mantle.
According to their deeds, so will he repay,
    wrath to his adversaries, requital to his enemies;
    to the coastlands he will render requital.
So they shall fear the name of the Lord from the west,
    and his glory from the rising of the sun;
for he will come like a rushing stream,
    which the wind of the Lord drives.
And he will come to Zion as Redeemer,
    to those in Jacob who turn from transgression, says the Lord.

"And as for me, this is my covenant with them, says the Lord: my spirit which is upon you, and my words which I have put in your mouth, shall not depart out of your mouth, or out of the mouth of your children, or out of the mouth of your children's children, says the Lord, from this time forth and for evermore."

Israel pleads for the Redeemer to come.

Arise, shine; for your light has come,
    and the glory of the Lord has risen upon you.
For behold, darkness shall cover the earth,
    and thick darkness the peoples;
but the Lord will arise upon you,
    and his glory will be seen upon you.
And nations shall come to your light,
    and kings to the brightness of your rising.

Lift up your eyes round about, and see;
    they all gather together, they come to you;
your sons shall come from far,
    and your daughters shall be carried in the arms.
Then you shall see and be radiant,
    your heart shall thrill and rejoice;

because the abundance of the sea shall be turned to you,
    the wealth of the nations shall come to you.
A multitude of camels shall cover you,
    the young camels of Midian and Ephah;
    all those from Sheba shall come.
They shall bring gold and frankincense,
    and shall proclaim the praise of the Lord.
All the flocks of Kedar shall be gathered to you,
    the rams of Nebaioth shall minister to you;
they shall come up with acceptance on my altar,
    and I will glorify my glorious house.

The sun shall be no more
    your light by day,
nor for brightness shall the moon
    give light to you by night;
but the Lord will be your everlasting light,
    and your God will be your glory.
Your sun shall no more go down,
    nor your moon withdraw itself;
for the Lord will be your everlasting light,
    and your days of mourning shall be ended.
Your people shall all be righteous;
    they shall possess the land for ever,
the shoot of my planting, the work of my hands,
    that I might be glorified.
The least one shall become a clan,
    and the smallest one a mighty nation;
I am the Lord;
    in its time I will hasten it.

The Redeemer comes and meditates upon his glorious task.

The Spirit of the Lord God is upon me,
    because the Lord has anointed me
to bring good tidings to the afflicted,
    he has sent me to bind up the brokenhearted,
to proclaim liberty to the captives,
    and the opening of the prison to those who are bound;
to proclaim the year of the Lord's favor,
    and the day of vengeance of our God;
    to comfort all who mourn;
to grant to those who mourn in Zion—
    to give them a garland instead of ashes,

the oil of gladness instead of mourning,
    the mantle of praise instead of a faint spirit;
that they may be called oaks of righteousness,
    the planting of the Lord, that he may be glorified.
They shall build up the ancient ruins,
    they shall raise up the former devastations;
they shall repair the ruined cities,
    the devastations of many generations.

For I the Lord love justice,
    I hate robbery and wrong;
I will faithfully give them their recompense,
    and I will make an everlasting covenant with them.
Their descendants shall be known among the nations,
    and their offspring in the midst of the peoples;
all who see them shall acknowledge them,
    that they are a people whom the Lord has blessed.

I will greatly rejoice in the Lord,
    my soul shall exult in my God;
for he has clothed me with the garments of salvation,
    he has covered me with the robe of righteousness
as a bridegroom decks himself with a garland,
    and as a bride adorns herself with her jewels.
For as the earth brings forth its shoots,
    and as a garden causes what is sown in it to spring up,
so the Lord God will cause righteousness and praise
    to spring forth before all the nations.

The Redeemer for Zion's sake will know no peace until her righteousness shines before all kings.

For Zion's sake I will not keep silent,
    and for Jerusalem's sake I will not rest,
until her vindication goes forth as brightness,
    and her salvation as a burning torch.
The nations shall see your vindication,
    and all the kings your glory;
and you shall be called by a new name
    which the mouth of the Lord will give.
You shall be a crown of beauty in the hand of the Lord,
    and a royal diadem in the hand of your God.
You shall no more be termed Forsaken,
    and your land shall no more be termed Desolate;

but you shall be called My delight is in her,
     and your land Married;
for the Lord delights in you,
     and your land shall be married.
For as a young man marries a virgin,
     so shall your sons marry you,
and as the bridegroom rejoices over the bride,
     so shall your God rejoice over you.

Upon your walls, O Jerusalem,
     I have set watchmen;
all the day and all the night
     they shall never be silent.
You who put the Lord in remembrance,
     take no rest,
and give him no rest
     until he establishes Jerusalem
     and makes it a praise in the earth.
The Lord has sworn by his right hand
     and by his mighty arm:
"I will not again give your grain
     to be food for your enemies,
and foreigners shall not drink your wine
     for which you have labored;
but those who garner it shall eat it and praise the Lord,
and those who gather it shall drink it
     in the courts of my sanctuary."

Vision 7
The seventh vision brings the final judgment.

Who is this that comes from Edom,
     in crimsoned garments from Bozrah,
he that is glorious in his apparel,
     marching in the greatness of his strength?

"It is I, announcing vindication,
     mighty to save."

Why is thy apparel red,
     and thy garments like his that treads in the wine press?

"I have trodden the wine press alone,
     and from the peoples no one was with me;

I trod them in my anger
and trampled them in my wrath;
their lifeblood is sprinkled upon my garments,
and I have stained all my raiment.
For the day of vengeance was in my heart,
and my year of redemption has come.
I looked, but there was no one to help;
I was appalled, but there was no one to uphold;
so my own arm brought me victory,
and my wrath upheld me.
I trod down the peoples in my anger,
I made them drunk in my wrath,
and I poured out their lifeblood on the earth."

Israel speaks and gathers the whole national history into a song of thanksgiving, confession, and supplication for judgment.

I will recount the steadfast love of the Lord,
and the praises of the Lord,
according to all that the Lord has granted us,
and the great goodness to the house of Israel
which he has granted them according to his mercy,
according to the abundance of his steadfast love.
For he said, Surely they are my people,
sons who will not deal falsely;
and he became their Savior.
In all their affliction he was afflicted,
and the angel of his presence saved them;
in his love and in his pity he redeemed them;
he lifted them up and carried them all the days of old.

But they rebelled
and grieved his holy Spirit;
therefore he turned to be their enemy,
and himself fought against them.
Then he remembered the days of old,
of Moses his servant.
Where is he who brought up out of the sea
the shepherds of his flock?
Where is he who put in the midst of them
his holy Spirit,
who caused his glorious arm

to go at the right hand of Moses,
who divided the waters before them
    to make for himself an everlasting name,
    who led them through the depths?
Like a horse in the desert,
    they did not stumble.
Like cattle that go down into the valley,
    the Spirit of the Lord gave them rest.
So thou didst lead thy people,
    to make for thyself a glorious name.

Look down from heaven and see,
    from thy holy and glorious habitation.
Where are thy zeal and thy might?
    The yearning of thy heart and thy compassion
    are withheld from me.
For thou art our Father,
    though Abraham does not know us
    and Israel does not acknowledge us;
thou, O Lord, art our Father,
    our Redeemer from of old is thy name.
O Lord, why dost thou make us err from thy ways
    and harden our heart, so that we fear thee not?
Return for the sake of thy servants,
    the tribes of thy heritage.
Thy holy people possessed thy sanctuary a little while;
    our adversaries have trodden it down.
We have become like those over whom thou hast never ruled,
    like those who are not called by thy name.

O that thou wouldst rend the heavens and come down
    that the mountains might quake at thy presence—
as when fire kindles brushwood
    and the fire causes water to boil—
to make thy name known to thy adversaries,
    and that the nations might tremble at thy presence!

Yet, O Lord, thou art our Father;
    we are the clay, and thou art our potter;
    we are all the work of thy hand.
Be not exceedingly angry, O Lord,
    and remember not iniquity for ever.
    Behold, consider, we are all thy people.

Thy holy cities have become a wilderness
    Zion has become a wilderness,
    Jerusalem a desolation.
Our holy and beautiful house,
    where our fathers praised thee,
has been burned by fire,
    and all our pleasant places have become ruins.
Wilt thou restrain thyself at these things, O Lord?
    Wilt thou keep silent, and afflict us sorely?

The response came in the judgment that finally separates between the holy and the evil.

I was ready to be sought by those who did not ask for me;
    I was ready to be found by those who did not seek me.
I said, "Here am I, here am I,"
    to a nation that did not call on my name.
I spread out my hands all the day
    to a rebellious people,
who walk in a way that is not good,
    following their own devices;
a people who provoke me
    to my face continually,
sacrificing in gardens
    and burning incense upon bricks;
who sit in tombs,
    and spend the night in secret places;
who eat swine's flesh,
    and broth of abominable things is in their vessels;
who say, "Keep to yourself,
    do not come near me, for I am set apart from you."
These are a smoke in my nostrils,
    a fire that burns all the day.
Behold, it is written before me:
    "I will not keep silent, but I will repay,
yea, I will repay into their bosom
    their iniquities and their fathers' iniquities together,
                                                    says the Lord;
because they burned incense upon the mountains
    and reviled me upon the hills,
I will measure into their bosom
    payment for their former doings."

Therefore thus says the Lord God:
"Behold, my servants shall eat,
   but you shall be hungry;
behold, my servants shall drink,
   but you shall be thirsty;
behold, my servants shall rejoice,
   but you shall be put to shame;
behold, my servants shall sing for gladness of heart,
   but you shall cry out for pain of heart,
   and shall wail for anguish of spirit.
You shall leave your name to my chosen for a curse,
   and the Lord God will slay you;
   but his servants he will call by a different name.
So that he who blesses himself in the land
   shall bless himself by the God of truth,
and he who takes an oath in the land
   shall swear by the God of truth;
because the former troubles are forgotten
   and hid from my eyes.

"For behold, I create new heavens
   and a new earth;
and the former things shall not be remembered
   or come into mind.
But be glad and rejoice for ever
   in that which I create;
for behold, I create Jerusalem a rejoicing,
   and her people a joy.
I will rejoice in Jerusalem,
   and be glad in my people;
no more shall be heard in it the sound of weeping
   and the cry of distress.
No more shall there be in it
   an infant that lives but a few days,
   or an old man who does not fill out his days,
for the child shall die a hundred years old,
   and the sinner a hundred years old shall be accursed.
They shall build houses and inhabit them;
   they shall plant vineyards and eat their fruit.

They shall not build and another inhabit;
   they shall not plant and another eat;

for like the days of a tree shall the days of my people be,
    and my chosen shall long enjoy the work of their hands.
They shall not labor in vain,
    or bear children for calamity;
for they shall be the offspring of the blessed of the Lord,
    and their children with them.
Before they call I will answer,
    while they are yet speaking I will hear.
The wolf and the lamb shall feed together,
    the lion shall eat straw like the ox;
    and dust shall be the serpent's food.
They shall not hurt or destroy
    in all my holy mountain,

                          says the Lord."

God punishes the wicked; Israel has peace.

Thus says the Lord:
    "Heaven is my throne
    and the earth is my footstool;
what is the house which you would build for me,
    and what is the place of my rest?
All these things my hand has made,
    and so all these things are mine,

                          says the Lord.
But this is the man to whom I will look,
    he that is humble and contrite in spirit,
    and trembles at my word.

"He who slaughters an ox is like him who kills a man;
    he who sacrifices a lamb, like him who breaks a dog's neck;
he who presents a cereal offering, like him who offers swine's
        blood;
    he who makes a memorial offering of frankincense, like him
        who blesses an idol.
These have chosen their own ways,
    and their soul delights in their abominations;
I also will choose affliction for them,
    and bring their fears upon them;
because, when I called, no one answered,
    when I spoke they did not listen;
but they did what was evil in my eyes,
    and chose that in which I did not delight."

"Rejoice with Jerusalem, and be glad for her,
    all you who love her;
rejoice with her in joy,
    all you who mourn over her;
that you may suck and be satisfied
    with her consoling breasts;
that you may drink deeply with delight
    from the abundance of her glory."

For thus says the Lord:
"Behold, I will extend prosperity to her like a river,
    and the wealth of the nations like an overflowing stream;
and you shall suck, you shall be carried upon her hip,
    and dandled upon her knees.
As one whom his mother comforts,
    so I will comfort you;
    you shall be comforted in Jerusalem.
You shall see, and your heart shall rejoice;
    your bones shall flourish like the grass;
and it shall be known that the hand of the Lord is with his
            servants,
    and his indignation is against his enemies.

"For behold, the Lord will come in fire,
    and his chariots like the stormwind,
to render his anger in fury,
    and his rebuke with flames of fire.
For by fire will the Lord execute judgment,
    and by his sword, upon all flesh;
    and those slain by the Lord shall be many.

"Those who sanctify and purify themselves to go into the gardens, following one in the midst, eating swine's flesh and the abomination and mice, shall come to an end together, says the Lord.
"For I know their works and their thoughts, and I am coming to gather all nations and tongues; and they shall come and shall see my glory, and I will set a sign among them. And from them I will send survivors to the nations, to Tarshish, Put, and Lud, who draw the bow, to Tubal and Javan, to the coastlands afar off, that have not heard my fame or seen my glory; and they shall declare my glory among the nations. And they shall bring all your brethren from all the nations as an offering to the Lord, upon horses, and in

chariots, and in litters, and upon mules, and upon dromedaries, to my holy mountain Jerusalem, says the Lord, just as the Israelites bring their cereal offering in a clean vessel to the house of the Lord. And some of them also I will take for priests and for Levites, says the Lord.

"For as the new heavens and the new earth
　　which I will make
shall remain before me, says the Lord;
　　so shall your descendants and your name remain.
From new moon to new moon,
　　and from sabbath to sabbath,
all flesh shall come to worship before me,
says the Lord."

Questions
for
Discussion

EPIC STORIES / PAGE 2

1. Is there significance in the order of creative acts in "The Beginnings"? Notice that the style is vivid, direct, and majestic. Six out of seven paragraphs end in the same refrain: "And there was evening and there was morning, one day." What is the significance of the absence of subordinate conjunctions but the large number of coordinate? What is the one special truth from the passage?

2. Explain in "The Temptations of Adam and Eve" the passage, "They were naked and not ashamed." What was the real sin of Adam and Eve? What plan did God have for the redemption of His creation?

3. What was the real conflict that led to the first murder in the "Cain and Abel" story? What was God's reaction? How may one explain the marked difference in the nature of the two brothers?

4. From "The Flood" story what do you judge to have been the moral condition of the world in Noah's day? What was the purpose of the project? Explain the experiments with the birds.

5. In the story "Joshua Halts the Sun" why was it necessary for God to intervene?

6. In what ways did "Gideon's 300" use psychological warfare? Why did God wish only a few soldiers?

407

EPIC CYCLES / PAGE 21

1. In the "Abraham" cycle what characteristics of the epic quality do you find? What was Abraham's role in the history of mankind? What elements in the story suggest objectivity of presentation?
2. In what ways was the "Isaac" cycle a test? Why was the sacrifice of Isaac likened to Christ? How was the wooing of Rebekah both romantic and realistic?
3. Using the "Jacob" cycle compare the concepts of birthright and inheritance to today's concepts. In what ways may one justify the stolen blessing on the basis of end results?
4. From the cycle of "Samuel" propose the advantages of apprenticeships. Why was Samuel's lengthy apprenticeship necessary?
5. Compare the qualities of leadership exhibited in the "Saul" cycle to the modern leaders. Is there evidence that Saul continued to revere God? What led to his unacceptability?
6. In what ways was "David" uniquely trained for leadership? How did warfare differ in style from modern times? The Bible presents objective accounts of characters giving both good and bad qualities. How does the David cycle illustrate this objective approach?
7. From the "Absalom" cycle trace the effects of sin. What were Absalom's innovations to appeal to the masses? What devices did the author use to hold the interest of the reader and to create suspense?
8. Prior to reading the "Solomon" cycle, read Job 18 and explain the Hebrew idea of wisdom. Of what sort of wisdom did Solomon desire? The story of the choice of mothers exemplified which of the following: knowledge, wisdom, intelligence, understanding, discretion? How?

EPIC HISTORY / PAGE 79

1. From the history of "Joseph" what do you conclude about the nature of family life in this period? The nature of political organization? The social and economic standards? How does the term *Pharoah* compare with the terms *Caesar, Kaiser, czar*? Is the story told objectively or subjectively?
2. What were the two levels of education "Moses" received? Many of the plaques were aimed directly at the gods of Egypt and were designed to give convincing proof of the superiority of the God of Israel over the pagan gods of Egypt. In what ways

were these gods worshipped by the Egyptians? In what way was Passover like the American Independence Day? In what ways was the Passover a historical picture of Christ? Compare the teachings of Jesus in Matthew 5:17–48 to the commandments God gave to Moses.

3. In what way was "Ruth" a picture of domestic life in a time of anarchy and trouble? Was the interest chiefly in plot or character? Compare the story with Joseph and his brethren in this respect. The book of Ruth is considered by many to be the perfect example of the idyllic short story. What elements do you find to support this?

SPECIAL HISTORY / PAGE 120

1. How was "John the Baptizer" related to Elijah? What similarities were there between the births of John and Jesus? Angels made frequent announcements. Compare the announcements to Zacharias, to Mary, to Joseph, and to the shepherds.

2. In the "Birth of Jesus" story why was the connection with the lineage of David so important? What supernatural elements surround the birth?

3. In the "Boyhood Visit to the Temple" how does one explain Jesus' extraordinary knowledge? Explain the theologians' amazement. Why was Jesus' absence in the caravan unnoticed?

4. The "Preaching of John the Baptist" was a unique ministry. How was his life in solitude an advantage? Explain the tremendous success of his message to repent. Why did John so swiftly pass off the scene?

5. What did the "Temptation of Jesus" story reveal about the person of the devil? What was the nature of the three temptations?

6. In the "Call for Discipleship" what common elements are to be found in the various calls of Jesus for disciples? From what social strata were the disciples selected?

7. Explain why it may be said that Jesus' entire ministry was an illustration of the "Sermon on the Mount." Compare the form of the Sermon to the proverbs in the Old Testament. The Sermon unfolds in two separate themes: Jesus' relationship to the Law and the inner motives of religious life. Find examples to illustrate both.

8. What kind of preferred treatment does the "Test of Discipleship" story indicate that the prospective disciples expected?

9. How does the story of the "Five Thousand Fed" illustrate Jesus'

love of order? What were the desires of the people when they realized the extent of the miracle?

10. After "Jesus Walks on Water" how does he explain Peter's sinking? What in Peter's character made him attempt to walk on water?

11. Explain the "Discourse on Humility" in the light that the disciples were fresh from the Transfiguration. Was the incident ever repeated? Explain the significance of Jesus' answer.

12. From "Peter's Confession" explain the concept of the diety of of Jesus. What was the "rock" on which Jesus was to build his church?

13. In the "Rich Man and Lazarus" story explain the terms Paradise and Hades. Characterize these places. How would the beliefs in the reality of heaven and hell alter behavior on earth, as suggested in the story? What were the implications of this teaching?

14. In what ways was the "Rich Young Ruler" a model young man? What was the real reason for his hesitation? The needle's eye was a small gate for foot passengers located near a large city gate. A camel, by kneeling and with great difficulty, could pass through it. What might be other possible interpretations of the needle's eye?

15. Compare the "Raising of Lazarus" with Jesus' two other raisings, Jairus' daughter in Mark 5:21–43 and Nain's son in Luke 7:11–17. What were the differences in circumstances? What impression did the miracle have on the people and the rulers in Jerusalem?

16. Describe the manner of Jesus' acceptance in Jerusalem at the time of his "Triumphal Entry into Jerusalem." What expectations did Jesus have of the entry into Jerusalem? What factors of the entry reenforced the Messianic predictions?

17. In the "Betrayal of Judas" why was an open arrest unfeasible? If Jesus knew the heart of Judas, why did Jesus select Judas as one of the Twelve? Explain Judas' suicide.

18. Trace the events leading up to the "Crucifixion of Jesus." What elements of the trials defy justice? What supernatural elements surrounded the crucifixion?

19. From "Peter's Denial" account for the change in Peter since Jesus' arrest. What effect did Jesus' look have on Peter?

20. What proofs were offered of the "Resurrection of Jesus"? Name the appearances of Jesus. What was the importance of the resurrection to Christianity?

21. In "Jesus Convinces Thomas" what significance did the special appearance to Thomas have?

22. What was the purpose of Jesus' "Resurrection Ministry"? How did the death, resurrection, and ascension contrast with the expectations of the disciples? What prediction was made at the ascension scene?

23. As "Saul Persecutes the Church" what charges are brought against Stephen? What evidences were there that Saul had planned a general persecution? Discuss the rampage of the church.

24. In the "Conversion of Saul" distinguish between a vision and a dream. What were the effects of the incident?

25. In the story "Paul and Barnabus Called Gods" account for the change in the attitudes of the people of Lystra toward Paul and Barnabus, calling them gods at first and then stoning them.

26. What led to the placement of "Paul and Silas in Jail"? What attitudes of Paul and Silas led to the jailer's conversion? Why were the city officials of Philippi anxious to remove the apostles?

27. "Paul in Athens" confronts a number of philosophies. Name some of the famous Greek philosophers of Athens and the primary themes of their teachings.

28. Outline his ministry as "Paul Summarizes His Ministry to King Agrippa." What was Agrippa's reaction to Paul's oratory?

29. Account for the relative freedom and treatment of "Paul in Rome."

LYRIC POETRY / PAGE 156

1. Characterize "The Song." How does anthropomorphic nature promote the common themes of songs? Find illustrations that suggest the sympathetic interest of nature in man.

2. Distinguish between the song and "The Ode." Which characteristics of the ode contribute to the formality of this poetic form?

3. Characterize "The Elegy." What occasions give rise to the mourning in the illustrative poems?

4. Why is "Meditation Poetry" an integral part of religious life? What kind of themes are celebrated in this poetic form?

5. What distinguishes "Dramatic Lyrics"? What elements in the poems are dramatic?

6. Characterize "Ritual Lyrics." How were ritual lyrics used in church history? In modern churches?

7. How is "Lyric Idyl" related to dramatic lyrics? How does it differ from dramatic lyrics? How does the impersonal reciting

chorus affect the poems? Has the expressions of affection changed much with the passing of time?

EPISTOLARY LITERATURE / PAGE 220

1. What is the nature of epistolary literature?
2. First Corinthians 13 is one of the best loved chapters in the Bible. Why is love the ultimate force in the universe? What characteristics of love are examined? The resurrection of Jesus from the dead is a constant refrain in the New Testament. Why, according to 1 Corinthians 15, is the resurrection so important?
3. In Galations 6 what are the spiritual laws? How did Paul prove that he was a genuine apostle of Jesus?
4. In Philippians 2 how is Christ an example of humility? What was the end result of Christ's humility and suffering?
5. The theme of 1 Thessalonians 4 is recurrent in the New Testament. What is the nature of the coming? What is meant by those who have "fallen asleep"?
6. Second Timothy is the triumphant cry of a dying conqueror. What claims does Paul make of his association with Christ? What prediction does Paul make about the church in chapter 3. Chapter 4 reveals much about the personal life of Paul. What can be assumed from this chapter?
7. Why in Titus does Paul exhort the believers to be faithful? What is the power of a beautiful life? What is the "blessed hope" of believers?
8. Characterize Philemon. Why does Paul appeal to Philemon in Onesimus' behalf? What comparison does Paul make between Onesimus and himself?
9. In Romans 12 of what does Paul warn the church leaders? What are the heavenly qualities to be found in believers?
10. Hebrews 11 is sometimes called the "hymn of faith." How did the listed heroes exhibit faith?
11. In James 2 Paul advises believers to respect others. How may this be practiced? How does Paul justify the apparent conflict between faith and works?
12. Revelation 1 reveals Christ in heaven. Compare the Christ on earth to the Christ of heaven. In Revelation 22 what final affirmations are made? What is the final invitation of the Bible?
13. In Colossians 3 what is the error in Paul's warning? According to verse 16 what are the main means of promoting in the Christian life? Ephesians 6 discusses spiritual warfare. Who are the

protagonists and the antagonists? What are the weapons? Defenses?

14. In 1 Peter 4 what, according to Paul, are the advantages of trials and persecution?

15. Jude is concerned with false teachers in the church. How may they be identified? Who is their leader? What should be done about them? In 2 Peter 3, Peter clarifies the delay in the coming of Christ in order that the churches may not be dissuaded by apostates. What is his reasoning concerning this delay?

16. According to 2 John 2 how may a man be considered a righteous and a good man?

ORATORY / PAGE 243

1. What advantage does oratory (spoken rhetoric) have over the written page?

2. Deuteronomy is largely a collection of loosely connected essays. What promises did God make to Israel specifically and mankind in general? How did man fail God? What was man's responsibility toward God?

3. In "Elijah's Address on Mount Carmel", what elements of faith were illustrated in the story? How did Elijah settle the issue with the false prophets?

4. In order to insure "The True Worship of God," what did Isaiah denounce vigorously? What was the solution suggested?

5. What did "Amos' Speech at Bethel" announce? What had Israel done to incur God's displeasure? What was the message conveyed through the imagery?

6. "Hosea's Speech to Israel" was a personal illustration. He had married an unchaste woman. How did this symbolic act illustrate the current condition and future disposition of Israel?

7. What in "Peter's Address at Pentecost" introduced the beginning of a great and notable era? What was the central point of the speech? What evidences of God's power surround the speech?

8. What mistakes led to "Paul's Address at Lystra"? What was the appeal of his speech? What was the effect of the speech?

9. In what ways was Paul's reception in Athens his poorest? How did Paul use the beliefs of the Athenians to his advantage? What was the result?

10. What circumstances brought "Paul before Agrippa"? What is the one issue, noted in the speech, that apparently led to Paul's arrest? How did Agrippa react to Paul's defense?

FORMAL SPEECHES / PAGE 244

1. Is the Sermon really a sermon? To what Bible form is it closest? What are the predominant themes? What does the sermon teach on the following subjects:
   a. Christ and the Law, b. divorce, c. externalism in religion, d. prayer, e. riches, f. anxiety, g. judgment of others, h. false teachers, i. philosophy

FABLES, ALLEGORIES, AND PARABLES / PAGE 261

1. Characterize the fable.
2. The theme of "Jothan's Fable" was the eternal struggle for power. How did the fable illustrate this struggle?
3. In the fable about "The Members and the Body," what truths did Paul wish to illustrate about believers? What were the advantages of the Body? The Members?
4. Characterize allegory.
5. In the allegory "The Good Shepherd" what was the significance of the teaching that Jesus was the Shepherd of mankind?
6. What was Jesus' warning to the disciples in "The Vine"?
7. The miracle of "Water Turned to Wine" occurred during a festive occasion. What did Jesus wish to illustrate in the miracle?
8. "Isaiah's Vineyard" was God's nation Israel. What was Isaiah's message in the allegory? How did Jesus' allegory of "The Vine" echo and expand this parable?
9. Characterize the parable. How was the parable a more suitable form for Jesus?
10. Who was symbolized as "Tares among the Wheat"? What was to occur at the separation?
11. If the "Grain and the Mustard Seed" and the "Leaven" parables symbolized the kingdom of Christ, what was the significance of the teaching to believers? To the world?
12. The "Hidden Treasure" and the "Pearl" parables referred to Christ himself. What is the teaching about his relation to the human soul?
13. What did the "Dragnet" represent in Christ's teaching about the attitude of the world toward His Gospel? What was the projection about the end of the world?
14. What did the parable of the "Marriage Feast" teach about

God's own elect nation? What was the warning to the new-comers?

15. The parable of "The Sower" is about God's Word. What was the effect of the Word upon the various hearers? How was the parable a prophecy?

16. Who was symbolized as "The Sheepfold"? What were the implications about Christ himself? Why would this parable be cherished among Christians?

17. The compassion of Jesus is boundless, even if his followers stumble and stumble and stumble. How did the three parables "Lost Sheep," "Lost Coin," and "Prodigal Son" illustrate his compassion? This is further illustrated in Luke 7:36–50 in the story of the Sinful Woman and in John 8:1–11 in the story of the Adultrous Woman.

18. The parable of "The Rich Man and Lazarus" characterized "Abraham's bosom," one of the names of Paradise. What were the implications of the parable related to the standards of the world, rulers, and the church? How did Jesus contrast heaven and hell?

19. The parable of "The Pounds" illustrated the same general truth as "The Talents" in Matthew 25:14–30, accountability. What should be the disposition of the wise man? In what areas must he be wise?

20. What did the parable of "The Garment and the Bottle" suggest about exhibiting holiness?

21. What did the parable "Laborers in the Vineyard" teach about one's expectation in heaven? In what other ways in the Bible were heavenly standards and earthly standards different?

22. The parable of "The Fig Tree" predicted the return of Christ as King. How does the fig tree illustrate the timing of his return? How precise is the timing?

WISDOM LITERATURE / PAGE 275

1. What were the primary considerations of the wisdom writers? Their purposes? What were the subjects of wisdom writers?

2. How does "The Riddle" qualify to be classified as wisdom literature? In what way was Samson unfair in his riddle? How did the treachery backfire?

3. Explain the formation of "The Unit Proverb." Trace the development of the unit proverb in its changes to form the epigram, sonnet, maxim, and essay. How is the Bible essay unique?

4. Account for the true greatness of "The Book of Job." How is the theme of the book considered universal? Explain the person and activities of the devil. What was Job's estimate of the sincerity of his friends? How did Job, his friends, and God judge the suffering? Which questions are left unanswered at the end of the story? Why did Job repent?

PROPHETIC DISCOURSE / PAGE 329

1. Characterize prophetic discourse.
2. How did Moses receive delivery of the Ten Commandments? What was to be the total effect of the Commandments? It is suggested that four of the Ten Commandments have to do with the Hebrew attitude toward God; six with their attitude toward their fellow man. Categorize them. It is also suggested that Jesus condensed the Ten Commandments into just two. Examine the prospect.
3. What new information about the Messiah is revealed in Isaiah 9? Additional glances are revealed in Isaiah 2:2–4; 4:2–6; 7:14; and chapters 11 and 12.

SYMBOLIC PROPHECY / PAGE 336

1. How does symbolic prophecy differ from prophetic discourse?
2. Of what is "The Woman and the Child" a sign? What suggestions about the Messiah appear in the prophecy?
3. How did the change in the appearance of "The Girdle" symbolize the Hebrew nation?
4. How did "The Potter's Vessel" illustrate God's power to alter the destiny of a nation? What is the result of Jeremiah's appeal?
5. What did "The Broken Bottle" demonstration illustrate? What was the impression among the observers?
6. How did Jeremiah symbolize two groups of people in his use of "The Two Baskets of Figs"?
7. Why was "The Scroll" important? What did the sinking of the scroll symbolize?
8. What did Ezekiel's "Piece of Tile" represent?
9. How did "The Baggage and the Hole in the Wall" symbolize Jerusalem's doom?
10. What did Ezekiel's song of "The Sword" predict?
11. If the meat taken out of the boiling pot represented captives, what did "The Rusty Pot" represent?
12. Identify "The Two Sticks."

VISION PROPHECY / PAGE 343

1. What is the center of vision prophecy?
2. What is the nature of "Isaiah's call"? What predictions were made?
3. In what form did God choose to appear in "Ezekiel's Vision"? What characteristics of God were revealed?
4. Point out Ezekiel's symbolic action in "The Siege."
5. Ezekiel chapter 37 was one of the most significant prophecies in the Old Testament, in that it predicted the national resurrection of scattered Israel, their return to their own land, and the leadership of an everlasting king called "David." How did Ezekiel reveal these truths?
6. What comforting truth did Ezekiel reveal in the "Vision of the Restored Community"? How would the interpretation differ if the Temple were viewed figuratively rather than literally?
7. What visionary experience did Daniel's three friends have to enable them to meet "The Fiery Furnace Episode"? What was King Nebuchadnezzar's reaction?
8. What was Daniel's "Interpretation of the Handwriting on the Wall"? On what other occasion had Daniel been the means of interpretation for a Babylonian king?
9. The "Call of Amos" was connected to his plumb-line assignment. What was the purpose of Amos' vision about the plumb-line?
10. "Zachariah's Seven-fold Vision" was both review and preview. What were the references to Israel's past and to her future? How did God express his affection for his people?
11. Point out the visionary aspects of "The Call of Saul" of Tarsus in the New Testament. What were the effects of Saul's vision on his fellow-travelers and himself?
12. What was the significance of "Peter's Vision at Joppa"? Why was the vision necessary?
13. How did John the Apostle describe "The New Jerusalem"? How did the vision of the new world compare to the present world?

PROPHETIC PARABLE / PAGE 348

1. How does the prophetic parable differ from vision prophecy? How does the prophetic parable compare to a fable?
2. What elements in the "Parable of the Vineyard" suggested a sort of funeral dirge? God's vineyard was his nation. What was predicted for the nation? Explain how Jesus' parable of the vine-

yard in Matthew 21:33-45 is an expansion of this parable. Which sins were denounced by Isaiah?

PROPHETIC INTERCOURSE / PAGE 350

1. Distinguish between d   intercourse.
2. How did "Daniel's Lions Den Experience" illustrate prophetic intercourse? How was his personal devotion to God tested?

DRAMATIC PROPHECY / PAGE 355

1. What dramatic elements are present in this form?
2. Why was Israel's destruction prophesied? What elements of hope were provided? Who is Zion? What is Zion's kingdom to be like?

THE DOOM SONG / PAGE 360

1. Characterize the doom song.
2. Trace the progress in the "Doom of Tyre and Sidon." How is Tyre pictured under the imagery of a majestic ship in Ezekiel 27?
3. How was "Elijah's Song to Ahab" a venture in faith? After all Elijah's victories, how can his discouragement and wish to die be explained?
4. "Jonah's Song to Nineveh" was a sad song. Why did he resist God's instructions? How did God convince Jonah? It is suggested that the story of Jonah is a historical picture of the Messiah's resurrection and mission to all nations. In what ways may this be true? Why is Jonah disappointed at the repentance of Nineveh? What does he wish to befall him?

THE RHAPSODY / PAGE 368

1. Characterize rhapsody.
2. What was Habakkuk's complaint to God in his "Rhapsody of the Chaldeans"? How could one justify God's actions? How was Habakkuk partly relieved? What did Habakkuk's prayer reveal about his attitude?
3. Describe the destruction in Joel's "Rhapsody of the Locust Plague." What was the result of their cry to God? What was Joel's new message? How may the second half of Joel be a picture of the Christian age? What is the judgment to which the prophet refers?